The Principal Navigations, Voyages, Traffiques Discoveries of the English Nation — Volume 09; Asia, Part II

Richard Hakluyt

Alpha Editions

This edition published in 2024

ISBN 9789362513359

Design and Setting By
Alpha Editions
www.alphaedis.com
Email - info@alphaedis.com

As per information held with us this book is in Public Domain.
This book is a reproduction of an important historical work.
Alpha Editions uses the best technology to reproduce historical work
in the same manner it was first published to preserve its original nature.
Any marks or number seen are left intentionally to preserve.

Contents

VOL. IX	- 1 -
ASIA. PART II.	- 2 -
OF THE ENGLISH NATION IN ASIA.	- 3 -
CAPVT. 38.	- 3 -
CAPVT. 39.	- 10 -
CAPVT. 40.	- 12 -
END OF PART II.	- 24 -
MANDEVILLE'S VOYAGES.	- 24 -
PART III.	- 25 -
CAPVT. 41.	- 26 -
CAPVT 42.	- 29 -
CAPVT. 43.	- 31 -
CAPVT. 44.	- 33 -
CAPVT. 45.	- 35 -
CAPVT. 46.	- 39 -
CAPVT. 47.	- 50 -
CAPVT. 48.	- 52 -
CAPVT. 49.	- 61 -
CAPVT. 50.	- 67 -
END OF MANDEVILLE'S VOYAGES.	- 74 -
BABYLON:	- 244 -
BALSARA:	- 244 -
ORMVZ:	- 246 -
GOA.	- 249 -

COCHIN. - 251 -

MALACCA. - 252 -

VOL. IX

ASIA. PART II.

Nauigations, Voyages, Traffiques, and Discoueries

OF THE ENGLISH NATION IN ASIA.

CAPVT. 38.

De territorio Cathay, et moribus Tartarorum.

Totum Imperium Imperatoris Grand Can distinctum est in 12. magnas prouincias, iuxta numerum duodecim filiorum primi Genitoris Can, quarum quælibet in se continet circiter 6. millia ciuitatum, præter villas non numeratas quæ sunt Velut ábsque numero. Habent et singulæ prouinciæ regem principalem, hoc est 12. reges prouinciales, et horum quisque sub se reges Insularum plurimos, alij 50. alij centum, alij plures, qui omnes et singuli subiectissimè obediunt Grand Can Imperatori. Harum prouinciarum maior, et nobilior dícitur Cathay, qui consistit in Asia profunda. Tres enim sunt Asiæ, scilicet quæ profunda dicitur, et Asia dicta maior quæ nobis est satis propinquior et tertia minor intra quam est Ephesus beati Ioannis Euangelistæ sepultura, de qua habes in præcedentibus. Audistis statum magnatum et nobilium esse permagnificum, et gloriosum, sed sciatis longè secus esse apud communes et priuatos homines tam in ciuitatibus quam in forensibus totius Tartariae. In prouincijs autem Cathay habetur tantum de mercimonijs specierum, et de operibus sericosis; quòd multis facilius acquirere esset praetiosum indumentam, quàm camisium de lino. Vnde et quicunque sunt alicuius honestatis non carent desuper precioso vestimento.

Omnes tam viri quam faemina similibus in forma vestibus inducuntur, videlicet valdè latis, et breuibus vsque ad genua cum apertura in lateribus quam firmant (dum volunt) ansis quibusdam, nam vtérque sexus est brachijs seu femoralibus plenè tectus. Nunquam vtuntur toga aut collobio, sed nec caputio vndè nec per aspectum indumentorum potest haberi differentia inter virum et mulierem innuptam. Sed nupta (vt supra dictum est) gestat per aliquod tegumentum in capite formam pedes viri.

Nubit illic vir quotquot placet mulieribus, vt nonnulli habeant decem vel duodecim vxores aut plures. Nam quísque maritus iungitur licentèr cuilibet mulieri, exceptis matre, et amita, sorore, et filia. Sicut viri equitant, tendunt, et currunt per patriam pro negotijs sic et mulieres, quoniam et ipse operantur omnia ferè artificia mechanica sicut pannos et quicquid efficiter de panno, corio, sericoque, minantque carrucas, et vehicula, sed viri fabricant de ferro et de omni metallo, lapidibus atque ligno, nec vir nec mulier nobilis aut degener comedit vltra semel in die communiter. Multa nutriunt pecora sed nullos porcos, parum comeditur ibi de pane exceptis magnatibus et diuitibus, sed carnes edunt pecorum, bestiarum, et bestiolarum vtpote boum, ouium, caprarum, equorum, asinorum, canum, cattorum, murium, et rattorum, ius carnium sorbentes, et omnis generis lac bibentes.

Nobiles autem bibunt lac equarum, seu lamentorum, pro nobilissimo potu et pauperes aquam bullitam cum modico mellis, quia nec vinum ibi habetur, nec ceruisia conficitur: et multi ac plurimi fontes consulunt in sua siti, per villas, et rura. Domus, et habitacula rotundae sunt formae, compositae et contextae paruis lignis, et flexilibus virgulis, ad modum cauearum quas nos facimus pro auiculis, habentes rotundam in culmine aperturam praestantem duo beneficia habitationi, quoniam et ignis quem in medio domus constituunt, fumum emittit, et pro aspiciendo lumen immittit. Intrinsecus sunt parietes vndíque de filtro, sed et tectum filtreum est: has domus, dum locum habitandi mutare volunt, vel dum indiuitina expeditione procedunt, ducunt secum in plaustris quasi tentoria.

Multas superuacuas obseruant ceremonias, quia respiciunt in vanitates et insanias falsas: solem et lunam praecipuè adorant, eisque frequentèr genua curuant, et ad nouilunium, quicquid est magni estimant inchoandum.

Nullus omnino vtitur calcaribus in equitando, sed cogunt equum flagello scorpione, reputantes peccatum non leue si quis ad hoc flagellum appodiat, aut iumentum percuteret suo freno, pleráque similia, quæ parum aut nihil nocent, ponderant vt grauia, sicut imponere cultellum in igne, os osse confringere, lac seu aliud potabile in terram effundere, nec non et huiusmodi multa.

[Sidenote: Mingere intra dominum peccatum capitale.] Sed super hæc, tenent pro grauiori admisso mingere intra domum quæ inhabitatur, et qui de tanto crimine proclamaretur assuetus, mitteretur ad mortem. Et de singulis necesse est vt confiteatur peccator Flamini suæ legis, et soluat summam pecuniarum delicti. Et si peccatum deturpationis habitaculi venerit in publicum, oportebit reconciliari domum per sacerdotem, priusquam vllus audebit intrare. Insuper et peccatorem necesse erit pertransire ignem, semel, bis, dut ter iuxta iudicium Flaminis, quatenus per ignis acrimoniam purgetur à tanti inquinatione peccati.

Neminem hominum prohibent inter se habitare, sed indifferentèr receptant, Iudæos, Christiános, Saracenos, et homines cuiuscúnque nationis, vel legis, dicentes se satis putare suum ritum non ita securum ad salutem, nisi quandóque; traherentur ad ritum magis salutarem, quem tamen determinate nunc ignorant, imò multi de nobilibus sunt iam in Christianitate baptizati.

Attamen qui illorum sunt curiales Imperatoris non vellent in palatio publicari.

Poenè oblitus eram, quod nunc hic dico notandum, quia dum ab extra Imperium, quis veniens nuntius aut legatus cupit tradere proprijs manibus literas Imperatori [Marginal note: Seu Gubernatorum.], vel deponere coram illo mandata, non permittitur, donec prius in puris transeat liueas ad venum ad minus regurn pro sui purgatione, ne quid forsitan afferat cuius visu, vel odoratu seu tactu rex possit grauari.

[Sidenote: Arma Tartarorum.] Porrò Tartari in præcincto expeditionis habent singuli duos arcus, cum magna pluralitate teloram: Nam omnes sunt sagittarij ad manum et cum rigida et longa lancea. Nobilis autem in equis preciosè phaleratis ferunt gladios, ver spatas breues et latas, scindentes pro vno latere, et in capitibus galeas, de corio cocto, non altas, sed ad capitis formara depressas.

Quicúnque de suis fugerit de prælio, ipso facto conseriptus est, vt siquando inuentus fuerit occidatur. Si Castrum vel ciuitas obsessa se illis reddere voluerit, nullam acceptant conditionem nisi cum morte omnium inimicorum, vel si quis homo singularis se dederit victum nihilominus ábsque vlla miseratione occidunt, detruncantes illi protinus aures, quas postea coquentes, et in aceto (dum habuerint) ponentes mittunt inuicem ad conuiuia pro extremo ferculo: [Sidenote: Tartari retro sagittantes.] dumque ipsi in bellis arte fugam simulant, periculosum est eos insequi, quoniam iaciunt sagittas à tergo, quibus equos et homines occidere norunt. Et quando in prima acie comparant ad bellandum, mirabilitèr sese constringunt, vt media pars numeri eoram vix credatur.

Generalitèr noueritis, omnes Tartaros habere paruos oculos, et modicam vel raram barbam: in proprijs locis raro inter se litigant, contendunt, aut pugnant, timentes legum pergraues emendas. Et inuenitur ibi rarius vespilio, latro, fur, homicida, iniurians, adulter, aut fornicarius, quia tales criminatores inuestigatione sollicita requiruntur, et sine redemptione aliqua perimuntur.

Dum quis decumbit infirmus figitur lancea iuxta illum in terra, et cum appropinquauerit morti, nullus remanet iuxta ipsum, cum verò mortuus esse scitur, confestim in campis, et cum lancea sepelitur.

The English Version.

And zee schulle undirstonde, that the empire of this gret Chane is devyded in 12 provynces; and every provynce hathe mo than 2000 cytees; and of townes with outen nombre. This contree is fulle gret. For it hathe 12 pryncypalle kynges, in 12 provynces. And every of tho kynges han many kynges undre hem; and alle thei ben obeyssant to the gret Chane. And his lond and his lordschipe durethe so ferre that a man may not gon from on hed to another, nouther be see ne lond, the space of 7 zeer. And thorghe the desertes of his lordschipe, there as men may fynde no townes, there ben innes ordeyned be every iorneye, to resceyve bothe man and hors; in the whiche thei schalle fynde plentee of vytaylle, and of alle thing, that hem nedethe, for to go be the contree.

And there is a marveylouse custom in that contree, (but is profitable) that zif ony contrarious thing, that scholde ben preiudice or grevance to the Emperour, in ony kynde, anon the Emperour hathe tydynges there of and fulle knowleche in a day, thoughe it be 3 or 4 iorneys fro him or more. For his ambassedours taken here dromedaries or hire hors, and thei priken in alle that evere thei may toward on of the innes: and whan thei comen there, anon thei blowen an horne; and anon thei of the in knowen wel y now that there ben tydynges to warnen the Emperour of sum rebellyoun azenst him. And thanne anon thei maken other men redy, in alle haste that thei may, to beren lettres, and pryken in alle that evere thei may, tille thei come to the other innes with here lettres: and thanne thei maken fressche men redy, to pryke forthe with the lettres, toward the Emperour; whille that the laste bryngere reste him, and bayte his dromedarie or his hors. And so fro in to in, tille it come to the Emperour. And thus anon hathe he hasty tydynges of ony thing, that berethe charge, be his corrours, that rennen so hastyly, thorghe out alle the contree. And also whan the Emperour sendethe his corrours hastyly, thorghe out his lond, everyche of hem hathe a large thong fulle of smale belles; and whan thei neyghen nere to the innes of other corroures, that ben also ordeyned be the iorneyes, thei ryngen here belles, and anon the other corrours maken hem redy, and rennen here weye unto another in: and thus rennethe on to other, fulle spedyly and swyftly, till the Emperours entent be served, in alle haste. And theise currours ben clept chydydo, aftre here langage, that is to seye, a messagere.

Also whan the Emperour gothe from o contree to another, as I have told you here before, and he passe thorghe cytees and townes, every man makethe a fuyr before his dore, and puttethe there inne poudre of gode gommes, that ben swete smellynge, for to make gode savour to the Emperour. And alle the peple knelethe doun azenst him, and don him gret reverence. And there where religyouse Cristene men dwellen, as thei don in many cytees in thei lond, thei gon before him with processioun with cros and holy watre; and thei seyngen, *Veni Creator, spiritus*, with an highe voys, and gon towardes him. And whan he herethe hem, he commaundethe to his lordes to ryde besyde him, that the religiouse men may come to him. And whan thei ben nyghe him, with the cros, thanne he dothe a down his galaothe, that syt upon his hede, in manere of a chapelet, that is made of gold and preciouse stone and grete perles. And it is so ryche, that, men preysen it to the value of a roialme, in that contre. And than he knelethe to the cros. And than the prelate of the religiouse men seythe before him certeyn orisouns, and zevethe him a blessynge with the cros: and he enclynethe to the blessynge fulle devoutly. And thanne the prelate zevethe him sum maner frute, to the nombre of 9, in a platere of sylver, with peres or apples or other manere frute. And he takethe on; and than men zeven to the othere lordes, that ben aboute him. For the custom is suche, that no straungere schalle come before him, but zif he zeve hym sum manere thing, aftre the olde lawe, that seythe, *Nemo accedat in conspectu meo vacuus*. And thanne the Emperour seythe to the religious men, that thei withdrawe hem azen, that thei ne be hurt ne harmed of the gret multytude of hors that comen behynde him. And also in the same maner don the religious men, that dwellen there, to the Emperesses, that passen by hem, and to his eldest sone; and to every of hem, thei presenten frute.

And zee schulle undirstonde, that the people, that he hathe so many hostes offe, abouten hym and aboute his wyfes and his sone, thei dwelle not contynuelle with him: but alle weys, whan him lykethe, thei ben sent fore; and aftre whan thei han don, thei retournen to hire owne housholdes; saf only thei that ben dwellynge with hym in houshold, for to serven him and his wyfes and his sones, for to governen his houshold. And alle be it, that the othere ben departed fro him, aftre that thei han perfourmed hire servyse, zit there abydethe contynuelly with him in court, 50000 men at horse, and 200000 men a fote; with outen mynstrelles, and tho that kepen wylde bestes and dyverse briddes, of the whiche I have tolde zou the nombre before.

Undre the firmament, is not so gret a lord, ne so myghty, ne so riche, as the gret Chane: nought Prestre Johan, that is Emperour of the highe Ynde, ne the Sowdan of Babylone, ne the Emperour of Persye. Alle theise ne ben not in comparisoun to the grete Chane; nouther of myght, ne of noblesse, ne of ryaltee, ne of richesse: for in alle theise, he passethe alle erthely princes. Wherfore it is gret harm, that he belevethe not feithfully in God. And natheles he wil gladly here speke of God; and he suffrethe wel, that Cristene men duelle in his lordschipe, and that men of his feythe ben made Cristene men, zif thei wile, thorghe out alle his contree. For he defendethe no man to holde no lawe, other than him lykethe.

In that contree, sum man hathe an 100 wyfes, summe 60, mo, somme lesse. And thei taken the nexte of hire kyn, to hire wyfes, saf only, that thei out taken hire modres, hire doughtres, and hire sustres on the fadir syde, of another womman, thei may wel take; and hire bretheres wyfes also aftre here dethe; and here step modres also in the same wyse.

Of the Lawe and customs of the Tartarienes, duellynge in Chatay; and how that men don, whan the Emperour schal dye, and how he schal be chosen.

[Sidenote: Cap. XXIII.] The folk of that contree usen alle longe clothes, with outen furroures. And thei ben clothed with precious clothes of Tartarye; and of clothes of gold. And here clothes ben slytt at the syde; and thei ben festned with laces of silk. And thei clothen hem also with pylches, and the hyde with outen. And thei usen nouther cappe ne hood. And in the same maner as the men gon, the wommen gon; so that no man may unethe knowe the men fro the wommen, saf only tho wommen, that ben maryed, that beren the tokne upon hire hedes of a mannes foot, in signe that thei ben undre mannes fote and undre subieccioun of man. And here wyfes ne dwelle not to gydere but every of hem be hire self. And the husbonde may ligge with whom of hem, that him lykethe. Everyche hathe his hous, bothe man and womman. And here houses ben made rounde of staves; and it hathe a rounde wyndowe aboven, that zevethe hem light, and also that servethe for delyverance of smoke. And the helynge of here houses, and the wowes and the dores ben alle of wode.

And whan thei gon to werre, thei leiden hire houses with hem, upon chariottes; as men don tentes or pavyllouns. And thei maken hire fuyr, in the myddes of hire houses. And thei han gret multytude of alle maner of bestes, saf only of swyn: for thei bryngen non forthe. And thei beleeven wel, o God, that made and formede alle thinges. And natheles zit han thei ydoles of gold and sylver, and of tree, and of clothe. And to tho ydoles, thei offren alle weys hyre first mylk of hire bestes, and also of hire metes, and of hire drynkes, before thei eten. And thei offren often tymes hors and bestes. And the clepen the God of Kynde, Yroga. And hire Emperour also, what name that evere behave, thei putten evermore therto Chane. And whan I was there, hire Emperour had to name Thiaut; so that he was clept Thiaut Chane. And his eldeste sone was clept Tossue. And whanne he schalle ben emperour, he schalle ben clept Tossue Chane. And at that tyme, the Emperour hadde 12 sones, with outen him; that were named, Cuncy, Ordii, Chahaday, Buryn, Negu, Nocab, Cadu, Siban, Cuten, Balacy, Babylan and Garegan, And of his 3 wyfes, the firste and the pryncypalle, that was Prestre Johnes doughtre, hadde to name Serioche Chan; and the tother Borak Chan; and the tother Karanke Chan.

The folk of that contree begynnen alle hire thinges in the newe mone: and thei worschipen moche the mone and the sonne, and often tyme knelen azenst hem. And alle the folk of the contree ryden comounly with outen spores: but thei beren alle weys a lytille whippe in hire hondes, for to chacen with hire hors. And thei had gret conscience, and holden it for a gret synne, to casten a knyf in the fuyr, and for to drawe flessche out of a pot with a knyf, and for to smyte an hors with the handille of a whippe, or to smyte an hors with a brydille, or to breke o bon with another, or for to caste mylk or ony lykour, that men may drynke, upon the erthe, or for to take and sle lytil children. And the moste synne, that ony man may do, is to pissen in hire houses, that thei dwellen in. And who so that may be founden with that synne, sykerly thei slen hym. And of everyche of theise synnes, it behovethe hem to ben schryven of hire prestes, and to paye gret somme of silver for hire penance. And it behovethe also, that the place, that men han pissed in, be halewed azen; and elles dar no man entren there inne. And whan thei han payed hire penance, men maken hem passen thorghe a fuyr or thorghe 2, for to clensen hem of hire synnes. And also whan ony messangere comethe and bryngethe lettres or ony present to the Emperour, it behovethe him, that he with the thing that he bryngethe, passe thorghe 2 brennynge fuyres, for to purgen hem, that he brynge no poysoun ne venym, ne no wykked thing, that myght be grevance to the lord. And also, zif ony man or womman be taken in avowtery or fornycacyoun, anon thei sleen him. Men of that contree ben alle gode archeres, and schooten right welle, bothe men and women, als wel on hors bak, prykynge, as on fote, rennynge. And the wommen maken alle thinges and alle maner mysteres and craftes; as of clothes, botes and other thinges; and thei dryven cartes, plowes and waynes and chariottes; and thei maken houses and alle maner of mysteres, out taken bowes and arwes and armures, that men maken. And alle the wommen weren breech, as wel as men. Alle the folk of that contree ben fulle obeyssant to hire sovereynes; ne thei fighten not ne chiden not, on with another. And there ben nouther thefes ne robboures in that contree; and every man worschipethe othere: but no man there dothe no reverence to no straungeres, but zif thei ben grete princes. And thei eten houndes, lyounes, lyberdes, mares and foles, asses, rattes and mees, and alle maner of bestes, grete and smale; saf only swyn, and bestes that weren defended by the olde lawe. And thei eaten alle the bestes, with outen and with inne, with outen castynge awey of ony thing, saf only the filthe. And thei eten but litille bred, but zif it be in courtes of grete lordes. And thei have not, in many places, nouther pesen ne benes, ne non other potages, but the brothe of the flessche. For littile ete thei ony thing, but flessche and the brothe. And whan thei han eten, thei wypen hire hondes upon hire skirtes: for thei use non naperye, ne towaylles, but zif it be before grete lordes: but the common peple hathe none. And whan thei han eten, thei putten hire dissches unwasschen in to the pot or cawdroun, with remenant of the flessche and of the brothe, till thei wole eten azen. And the ryche men drynken mylk of mares or of camaylles or of asses or of other bestes. And thei wil ben lightly dronken of mylk, or of another drynk, that is made of hony and of watre soden to gidre. For in that contree is nouther wyn ne ale. Thei lyven fulle wrecched liche; and thei eten but ones in the day, and that but lyttle, nouther in courtes ne in other places. And in soothe, o man allone in this contree wil ete more in a day, than on of hem will ete in 3 dayes. And zif ony straunge messagre come there to a lord, men maken him to ete but ones a day, and that fulle litille.

And whan thei werren, thei werren fulle wisely, and alle weys don here besynes, to destroyen hire enemyes. Every man there berethe 2 bowes or 3, and of arwes gret plentee, and a gret ax. And the gentyles han schorte speres and large, and fulle trenchant on that o syde: and thei han plates and helmes, made of quyrboylle; and hire hors covertoures of the same. And who so fleethe fro the bataylle, thei sle him. And whan thei holden ony sege abouten castelle or toun, that is walled and defensable, thei behoten to hem that ben with inne, to don alle the profite and gode, that it is marveylle to here: and thei graunten also to hem that ben with inne, alle that thei wille asken hem. And aftre that thei ben zolden, anon thei sleen hem alle, and kutten of hire eres, and sowcen hem in vynegre, and there of thei maken gret servyse for lordes. Alle here lust and alle here ymaginacioun, is for to putten alle londes undre hire subieccioun. And thei seyn, that thei knowen wel be hire prophecyes, that thei schulle ben overcomen by archieres, and be strengthe of hem: but they knowe not of what nacioun, ne of what lawe thei schulle ben offe, that schulle overcomen hem. And therfore thei suffren, that folk of alle lawes may peysibely duellen amonges hem.

Also whan thei wille make hire ydoles, or an ymage of ony of hire frendes, for to have remembrance of hym, thei maken alle weys the ymage alle naked, with outen any maner of clothinge. For thei seyn, that in gode love scholde be no coverynge, that man scholde not love for the faire clothinge, ne for the riche aray, but only for the body, suche as God hathe made it, and for the gode vertues that the body is endowed with of nature; but only for fair clothinge, that is not of kyndely nature.

And zee schulle undirstonde, that it is gret drede for to pursue the Tartarines, zif thei fleen in bataylle. For in fleynge, thei schooten behynden hem, and sleen bothe men and hors. And whan thei wil fighte, thei wille schokken hem to gidre in a plomp; that zif there be 20000 men, men schalle not wenen, that there be scant 10000. And thei cone wel wynnen lond of straungeres, but thei cone not kepen it. For thei han grettre lust to lye in tentes with outen, than for to lye in castelle or in townes. And thei preysen no thing the wytt of other naciouns. And amonges hem, oyle of olyve is fulle dere: for thei holden it for fulle noble medicyne. And alle the Tartarienes han smale eyen and litille of berd, and not thikke hered, but schiere. And thei ben false and traytoures: and thei lasten noghte that thei behoten. Thei ben fulle harde folk, and moche peyne and wo mow suffren and disese, more than ony other folk: for thei ben taughte therto in hire owne contree, of Zouthe: and therfore thei spenden, as who seythe, right nought.

And whan ony man schalle dye, men setter a spere besyde him: and whan he drawethe towardes the dethe, every man fleethe out of the hous, tille he be ded; and aftre that, thei buryen him in the feldes.

CAPVT. 39.

De sepultura Imperatoris Grand Can, et creatione successoris.

Imperator Grand Can postquam eius cognita fuerit defunctio defertur mox à paucis viris in parco palatij, ad præuisum locum vbi debeat sepeliri. Et nudato prius toto illo loco à graminibus cum cespite figitur ibi tentorium, in quo velut in solio regali de ligno corpus defuncti residens collocatur, paraturque mensa plena coram eo cibarijs præciosis, et potu de lacte iumentorum. Instabulatur ibi et equa cum suo pullo, sed et ipse albus, nobilitèr phaleratus, et onustatus certo pondere auri et argenti. Et est totum Tentorij pauimentum de mundo stramine stratum.

Tuncque effodiunt in circuitu fossam latam valdè, et profundam vt totum tentorium cum omnibus contentis descendat in illam. Eoque facto ita equalitèr terram planificantes adoperiunt graminibus, vt in omni tempore locus sepulturæ non valeat apparere. Et quoniam ignorantiæ nubilo turpiter excæcati putant in alio seculo homines delectationibus frui, dicunt quòd tentorium erit ei pro hospitio, cibi ad edendum, lac ad potandum, equus ad equitandum, aurum et argentum ad respiciendum, sed et equa lac sempèr præstabit, et pullos equinos successiue generabit.

Post has itaque Imperatoris defuncti miseras exequias, nullus omnino audebit de ipso loqui coram vxoribus et filijs, et propinquis, sed nec nominare, quia per hoc putarent derogari paci, et quieti illius, qua non dubitant eum dominari, in maiori satis gloria Paradisi quam hic stetit.

Igitur Imperatore Grand Can sepulto obliuioni tradito, conueniunt quàm citò nobiles de septem tribubus prouinciæ Cathay, et cui Imperium ex propinquitate competit, dicunt sic.

> Ecce volumus, ordinamus, atque precamur, vt sis noster Dominus et Imperator.

Qui respondet

> Si vultis me super vos, sicut et iuris mei est, imperare, oportebit vos fore mihi obedientes tam ad mortem quàm ad vitam.

Et respondentes dicunt.

Nos faciemus quicquid præceperitis.

Túncque Imperator addit hæc verba: Ergo scitote, quod ex nunc verbum meum acutum et scindens erit vt meus ensis: [Sidenote: i. cathedra.] Pergit quóque sessum in suo Philtro nigro super pauimentum in conspectu throni expanso, et cum ipso Philtro eleuatur ab omnibus, et infertur Imperij solio, ac coronatur diademate præcedentis Imperatoris.

De inde singuli principes, et singuæ ciuitates, oppida, et villæ per vniuersum imperium mittunt ei munera iocalia, vasa, pannos, equos, elephantes, aurum, argentum, et lapides preciosos, quorum, qualium, et quantorum vix vel in numero haberi potest aestimatio.

CAPVT. 40.

De multis regionibus Imperio Tartariae subiectis.

Breuitèr et nunc intendo cursum describere aliquarum magnarum regionum et
Insularum Imperij Tartariæ. Et primò illas quæ descendunt à prouincia Cathay per septentrionalem plagam, vsque ad fines Christianitatis Prussiae, et Russiae.

Ergò prouincia Cathay descendens in sui oriente à regno Tharsis iungitur ab occidente regno Turquescen, in quo et sunt plurimae ciuitates, quarum formosior dicitur Octopar. Ipsum autem Turquescen regnum iungitur ad occidentem sui regno, seu Imperio. Persiae, et ad septentrionem regno Corasinae, quod spaciosum este valde, habens versus orientem sui vltra centum diaetas deserti: hoc regnum est multis bonis abundans, et appellatur eius melior ciuitas etiam Corasine.

Isti quoque regno iungitur in occidente versus partes nostras regnum Commanorum, quod et similiter longum est, et latum, sed in paucis sui locis inhabitatum: Nam in quibusdam est frigus nimium, in alijs nimius calor, et in nonnullis nimia muscarum multitudo.

De istis Commanis venit olim fugata quædam pluralitas populi vsque in terram Ægypti quae ibidem succreta nunc ita inualuit, vt suppressis indigenis videatur regnare: Nam et de seipsis constituerunt hunc, qui modo est Soldanus, Melech Mandibron. Per Commanorum regnum decurrit Grandis fluuius Echil, qui omni hyemali tempore in magna spissitudine gelatur; in superiori quoque parte huius regni inter duo freta Caspiæ, et Oceani, mons sublimis est valde Chocas. Nota quod à nostris partibus non possit vsque in Indiam superiorem duci magnus exercitus per terras, nisi per tres tantummodo transitus, quorum iste est vnus, qui tamen non valet transiri nisi tempore glaciei, et hic appellatus est Lodekonc.

Alter per Turquescen, et per Persiam, tamen ibi sunt deserta plurium dietarum, in quibus nisi esset exercitus bene prouisus, posset perire.

Tertius ad primos fines regni Commanorum, transfretando tamen mare vsque in regnum Abchaz: principalis ciuitas Commanorum dicitur Sarach.

Ab hoc regno versus partes nostras inuenitur regio Laiton quae est vltima paganismi, iungitur iste finis terræ Christianitatitis regno Prussiæ, et Russiæ.

Post potestatem Imperij Tartariæ descendendo à prouincia Cathay in Australem plagam venitur versus Persiam, Syriam, et Greciam. Versus terram Christianorum possum aliqualiter in summa (quantum conuenit huic scripto) connotare. Dixi supra iam prouinciam Cathay iungi regno Turquescen ad occidentem, et illud quòque iungi regno seu Imperio Persiæ. Ad quod sciendum, quamuis rex Persiæ habet etiam ab olim nomen Imperatoris; quia (cum tenet aliquas terras sui Imperij ab Imperatore Tartarorum) necesse est vt in tanto subiectus sit illi.

Sunt autem in Persia duæ regiones: vna altæ Persiæ, quæ à regno Turquescen descendens, iungitur ad occidentem sui fluuis Pyson. In ista habentur renominatæ ciuitates, quarum meliores duæ dicuntur Bocura et Seonargant, quam aliqui appellant Samarkand. Et altera Regio bassæ Persiæ, descendens à flumine Pyson, qui ad sui occidentem iungiter regno Mediæ et terræ minoris Armeniæ, et ad Aquilonem mari Caspio, et ad Austrum terræ minoris Indiæ.

In hac bassa Persia tres principaliores ciuitates sunt Aessabor, Saphaon, Sarmasaule. In terra autem maioris Armeniæ quondam habebantur quatuor regna quæ nunc dicuntur subesse Imperio Persarum, habétque famam terræ nobilis, et ad occidentem sui iungitur Regno Turciæ.

Hec Armenia multas valdè bonas continet ciuitates, quarum famosior est Taurisa. Regnum Mediæ quod subest Regi Persarum quamuis non latum est, tamen longum est, et ad occidentem sui regno Chaldeæ coniunctum. In Media meliores duæ ciuitates sunt, Seras, et Keremen.

[Sidenote: Georgia. Abchas, aliàs Alchaz.] Hinc ad occidentem sui, iuncta est regio Georgiæ, quæ modo constat diuisa in duo regna: Nam pars superior, quæ iungitur Mediæ, reseruauit sibi nomen Georgiæ, sed inferior pars dicitur regnum Abchaz. Ambo hæc regna, et regis eorum, sunt de fide Christiana, et homines ita deuoti vt ad minus semel in hebdomada communicent sacramentis, iuxta ritum Græcorum confectis. Et quidem regnum Georgiæ subiacet imperio Grand Can: sed Abchaz nunquam ab ipso Imperatore Tartariæ, neque Persarum, neque Medorum domino subdi potuit, eo quòd munitum est aquis et rupibus et alijs prouisionibus contra impugnationes hostiles.

[Sidenote: In parte regni Georgiæ sunt tenebrae.] Iuxta hoc regnum Abchaz habetur vnum minum et mirabile, nam magnus est territorij locus dictus Hamson, et continens in circuitu spacium viæ quatuor diætarum: videter semper opertus tenebris densis vt nemo audeat illic intrare profundè, quoniam si qui presumpserint, non sunt visi reuerti. Attamen fatentur vicini sub illis se tenebris audisse nonnunquam clamores hominum, hinnitus, mugitus, rugitus, et boatus pecudum, et bestiarum, sed et cantus gallorum, vt per hæc et alia signa constet ibi habitare gentes: nam et fluuius decurrens monstrat signa sæpè certissima in suo exitu: ignoratur tamen si tenebræ per totum territorium sint eiusdem densitatis, an forte sint in circuitu per aliquod spacium, et intrinsecus plus luminosum.

Dicuntur autem tenebræ istæ olim per diuinum miraculum aduenisse. Saboere enim Imperatore Persarum, circa annum Gratiæ ducentessimum quinquagessimum in persecutione Christianorum tendente cum pleno exercitu per hunc locum, et Christianis tyrannidem eius fugientibus, contigit ex improuiso eos ità arctari, vt se effugere desperarent, quapropter statim ad orationis refugium omnes se sternentes clamauerunt ad Christum auxiliatorem suum: Et deus, qui pro puro corde Christianos ad se orantes semper exaudit, expleuit illic literam vaticinij Isaiæ: quia ecce tenebræ operient terram et caligo populos, monstrans per tenebram terrenam, quam eis superduxit, quas passuri essent inimici nominis Christi tenebras infernales, indicansque per temporalem vitam, quam sibi fidelibus conseruauit, eam quam possessuri sunt viri Christiani vitam perpetuam, et coelestem.

Itaque hoc regnum Abchaz ad occidentem sui iungitur regno Turciæ, quod in longo et lato valdè extensum multas continet prouincias scilicet Iconiæ, Cappadociæ, Sauræ, Brike, Besicon, Patan, et Gennoch; hij omnes Turci, cum tota Syria et Arabia vsque ad Galliziam Hispaniæ, subsunt Imperatori Babyloniæ Soldano, et sunt in singulis prouinciis et regionibus ciuitates magnæ, ac multæ nimis. Consequentèr huic regno Turciæ ad Occidentem sui in ciuitate Cathasa [Marginal note: Vel Sathata.] iungitur per mare Greciæ superior pars potestatis Imperatoris Constantinopolitani, et quasi ad Aquilonem contiguatur regno Syriæ: cuius vna prouincia est terra promissionis, prout hoc satis dictum est suprà. Sunt et aliæ terre, et Insulæ, et patriæ latæ, et spatiosæ, continentes in se multa regna, et reges, et gentes diuersas, de quibus nunc per singula pertractare non est consilij.

Ad supradictam Chaldæam iungitur Mesopotamia, et minor Armenia, et velut ad Austrum eius Æthiopia, Mauritania, Lybia alta et bassa, et Nubia. [Sidenote: Extensio Imperij Grand Can.] Excepto ergò duntaxat districtu Imperij Persiæ, et potestate Soldani, omnes sæpè pertractatæ terræ, regiones, regna et Insulæ descendendo tam par Aquilonem, quam ad Austrum à prouincia Cathay, vsque ad Christianitatem sunt de Imperio Tartariæ Grand Can. [Sidenote: Distantia à Roma ad Cathayam per Institores.] Et notandum de spacio distantiæ, quod institores de Roma, vel Venetia festinantes tam per terras, quàm per mare, expendunt de tempore 11. menses, et quandoque duodecim, priusquam in Cathay valeant peruenire.

Hijs itaque visis describam saltem aliquas à prouincia Cathay in orientem terras Imperij Tartarorum. [Sidenote: Cadilla Regio orientalior Cathay. Angli nostri hanc bestiolam nuper viderunt in Persia.] Illic habetur regio Cadilla spaciosa multum, simul et speciosa: crescunt namque in ea fructus ad quantitatem magnorum Cawardorum, in quibus inuenitur vna bestiola, in carne et sanguine ad formam agnelli absque lana, et manducatur totus fructus cum bestiola. Sunt et alij plures diuersi fructus, quorum penes nos non est respectus nec vsus. Nam et sunt ibi nonnullæ speciales vites ferentes botros incredibiliter magnos, quorum vnum vix virilis vir valet in hasta portare.

Et deinde in meridiem per aliquas diætas, potest perueniri ad primas Caspiæ alpes, quæ descendendo descendunt vsque ad Amazoniam, insulam mulierum, de qua tractatum est. Inter has Alpes retinetur maxima multitudo Iudæorum decem tribum Israel, per Dei voluntatem ita inclusa, vt in copiosa numerositate non possint à nostra parte exire, quamuis aliqui pauci nonnunquam sunt visi transisse. Haberent autem competentem exitum circa insulam Amazoniæ, sed illum diligenter regina obseruat.

[Sidenote: Racchariæ Regnum vel Boghariæ.] Porrò de regione Cadilla in orientem venitur ad regnum Backariae, in qua mali et multum crudeles habitant homines, nec est securum itinerare per illam, quòd ad modicam occasionem (si Deus non conseruaret) occiderent viatorem et manducarent. [Sidenote: Arbor Lanifera.] Illic sunt arbores ferentes lanam velut ouium, ex qua texunt pannos ad vestimenta. Hypocentauri sunt ibi pro media superiori parte in forma humana, et pro inferiori figura equorum, seu taurorum, venantes in terris, et piscantes in aquis quod comedunt, et super omnia carnes hominum, quos capere possunt. [Sidenote: Gryphones, de quibus Paulus Venetæ] Nec non et gryphi illic apparent pro media posteriori parte in forma leonis, pro anteriori in forma aquilæ. Sed sciatis, corpus magni gryphi maius esse octo leonibus de partibus istis. Nam postquam equum, bouem vel hominem, etiam asinum occiderit, leuat et asportat pleno volatu: tanquam cornua bouis aut vaccae sunt illi vngulæ, de quibus etiam fieri solent ciphi ad bibendum, qui plurimùm reputantur preciosi. Fiunt quóque de pennis alarum eius arcus rigidi, et fortes ad iaciendum missilia et sagittas. Ad istius regni Baccariae extremitates in Orientum finitur terra potestatis Grand Can: Et iungitur ei terra potestatis magni Imperatoris Indiæ, qui semper vocatur Præsbyter Ioannes. Notandum, quoties per prouincias totius Imperij Grand Can, quicquam accidit, quod Imperatorem non oportet latere, confestim mittuntur per reges aut barones nuncij in dromedarijs aut equis, qui celerrimè festinant ad certa hospitia, ad hoc ipsum, velut ábsque numero per imperium instituta: Isque nuncius hospitio appropinquans, et cornu resonans, dum auditor paratur minicius alter, qui de manu suscipiens literas, per recentem dromedarium festinat ad aliud hospitium, et sic in breui tempore perferuntur rumores ad curia aures. [Sidenote: Cursores, Chidibo Tartaricè dicti.] Similique modo nuncij pedites permutantur de hospitio in hospitium, vt citiùs percipiatur negocium huius nuncij: appellantur sua lingua Chidibo.

[Sidenote: Charita Mandeuilli.] Ergò per præmissa satis elucet magnam esse nobilitatem, potestatem, reuerentiam, et dominationem Imperatoris Tartariæ Grand Can de Cathay, et quòd nullus ab ista parte Imperator nec Persiæ, nec Babylonia, nec Greciæ, sed nec Romæ est illi comparandus. Vndè et multum miserandum est, quia ipse cùm toto Imperio nec est fide Catholica illustratus, nec salutari lauachro regeneratus: et hoc oremus vt in breui eueniat, per Iesum Christum Dominum nostrum.

Explicit pars secunda huius opens.

The English Version.

And whan the emperour dyethe, men setten him in a chayere in myddes the place of his tent: and men setten a table before him clene, covered with a clothe, and there upon flesche and dyverse vyaundes, and a cuppe fulle of mares mylk: And men putten a mare besyde him, with hire fole, and an hors saddled and brydeled; and thei leyn upon the hors gold and silver gret quantytee: and thei putten abouten him gret plentee of stree: and than men maken a gret pytt and a large; and with the tent and alle theise other thinges, then putten him in erthe. And thei seyn, that whan he schalle come in to another world, he schalle not ben with outen an hows, ne with owten hors, ne with outen gold and sylver: and the mare schalle zeven him mylk, and bryngen him forthe mo hors, tille he be wel stored in the tother world. For thei trowen, that aftre hire dethe, thei schulle be etynge and drynkynge in that other world, and solacynge hem with hire wifes, as thei diden here. And aftre tyme, that the emperour is thus entered, no man schalle be so hardy to speke of him before his frendes, And zit natheles somtyme fallethe of manye, that thei maken hem to ben entered prevylly be nyghte, in wylde places, and putten azen the grasse over the pytt for to growe: or elle men coveren the pytt with gravelle and sond, that no man schalle perceyve where, ne knowe where the pytt is, to that entent, that never aftre, non of his frendes schulle han mynde ne rememberance of him. And thanne thei seyn, that he is ravissht in to another world where he is a grettre lord, than he was here. And thanne aftre the dethe of the emperour, the 7 lynages assemblen hem to gidere, and chesen his eldest sone, or the nexte aftre him, of his blood: and thus thei seye to him; wee wolen and wee preyen and ordeynen, that zee ben oure lord and oure emperour. And thanne he answerethe, zif yee wile, that I regne over zou, as lord, do eyeryche of zou, that I schalle commanden him, outher to abyde or to go; and whom soever that I commaunde to ben slayn, that anon he be slayn. And thei answeren alle with o voys, what so evere zee commanden, it schalle be don. Thanne seythe the emperour, now undirstondethe wel, that my woord from hens forthe, is scharp and bytynge as a swerd. After men setten him upon a blak stede, and so men bryngen him to a cheyere fulle richely arrayed, and there thei crownen hym. And thanne alle the cytees and gode townes senden hym ryche presentes; so that at that iourneye, he schalle have more than 60 chariottes charged with gold and sylver, with outen jewelles of gold and precyouse stones, that lordes zeven hym, that ben withouten estymacioun: and with outen hors and clothes of gold and of Camakaas and Tartarynes, that ben with outen nombre.

Of the Roialme of Thurse and the Londes and Kyngdomes towardes the Septentrionale parties, in comynge down from the Lond of Cathay.

This lond of Cathay is in Asye the depe. And aftre, on this half, is Asyetthe more. The kyngdom of Cathay marchethe toward the west, unto the kyngdom of Tharse; the whiche was on of the kinges, that cam to presente our Lord in Betheleem. And thei that ben of the lynage of that kyng, arn somme Cristene. In Tharse, thei eten no flessche, ne thei drynken no wyn. And on this half, towardes the west, is the kyngdom of Turquesten, that strecchethe him toward the west, to the kyngdom of Persie; and toward the Septrentionalle, to the kyngdom of Chorasme. In the contre of Turquesten, ben but fewe gode cytees: but the beste cytee of that lond highte Octorar. There ben grete pastures; but fewe Coornes; and therfore, for the most partie, thei ben alle herdemen: and thei lyzn in tentes, and thei drynken a maner ale, made of hony.

And aftre, on this half, is the kyngdom of Chorasme, that is a gode lond and a plentevous, with outen wyn. And it hathe a desert toward the est, that lastethe more than an 100 iourneyes. And the beste cytee of that contree is clept Chorasme. And of that cytee, berethe the contree his name. The folk of that contree ben hardy werryoures. And on this half is the kyngdom of Comanye, where of the Comayns that dwelleden in Grece, somtyme weren chaced out. This is on of the grettest kyngdomes of the world: but it is not alle enhabyted. For at on of the parties, there is so gret cold, that no man may dwelle there: and in another partie, there is so grete hete, that no man may endure it. And also there ben so many flyes, that no man may knowe on what syde he may turne him. In that contree is but lytille arberye, ne trees that beren frute, ne othere. Thei lyzn in tentes. And thei brenen the dong of bestes for defaute of wode.

This kyngdom descendeth on this half toward us, and toward Pruysse, and toward Rossye. And thorghe that contree rennethe the ryvere of Ethille, that is on of the grettest ryveres of the world. And it fresethe so strongly alle zeres, that many tymes men han foughten upon the Ise with grete hostes, bothe parties on fote, and hire hors voyded for the tyme: and what on hors and on fote, mo than 200000 persones on every syde. And betweene that ryvere and the grete see ocean, that thei clepen the see maure, lyzn alle theise Roialmes. And toward the hede benethe in that Roialme, is the mount Chotaz, that is the hiest mount of the world: and it is betwene the see Maure and the see Caspy. There is fulle streyt and dangerous passage, for to go toward Ynde. And therfore Kyng Alysandre leet make there a strong cytee, that men clepen Alizandre, for to kepe the contree, that no man scholde passe with outen his leve. And now men clepen that cytee, the Zate of Helle. And the princypalle cytee of Comenye is clept Sarak, that is on of the 3 weyes for to go in to Ynde: but be the weye, ne may not passe no gret multytude of peple, but zif it be in wyntre. And that passage men clepen the Derbent. The tother weye is for to go fro the citee of Turquesten, be Persie: and be that weye, ben manye iourneyes be desert. And the thridde weye is that comethe fro Comanye, and than to go be the grete see and be the kyngdom of Abchaz.

And zee schulle undirstonde, that alle theise kyngdomes and alle theise londes aboveseyd, unto Pruysse and to Rossye, ben alle obeyssant to the grete Chane of Cathay; and many othere contrees, that marchen to other costes. Wherfore his powere and his lordschipe is fulle gret, and fulle myghty.

Of the Emperour of Persye, and of the lond of darknesse and of other Kyngdomes, that belongen to the grete Chane of Cathay, and other Londes of his, unto the See of Greece.

[Sidenote: Cap. XXV.] Now sithe I have devysed zou the londes and the kyngdoms toward the parties septentrionales, in comynge down from the lond of Cathay, unto the londes of the Cristene, towardes Pruysse and Rossye; now schalle I devyse zou of other londes and kyngdomes, comynge doun be other costes, toward the right syde, unto the see of Grece, toward the lond of Cristene men: and therfore that, aftre Ynde and aftre Cathay, the Emperour of Persie is the gretteste lord. Therfore I schalle telle zou of the kyngdom of Persie. First, where he hathe 2 kyngdomes; the firste kyngdom begynnethe toward the est, toward the kyngdom of Turquesten, and it strecchethe toward the west, unto the ryvere of Phison, that is on of the 4 ryveres, that comen out of paradys. And on another syde, it strecchethe toward the septemtrion, unto the see of Caspye: and also toward the southe, unto the desert of Ynde. And this contree is gode and pleyn and fulle of peple. And there ben manye gode cytees. But the 2 princypalle cytees ben theise, Boyturra and Seornergant, that sum men clepen Sormagant. The tother kyngdom of Persie strecchethe toward the ryvere of Phison, and the parties of the west, unto the kyngdom of Mede: and fro the grete Armenye, and toward the septemtrion, to the see of Caspie; and toward the southe, to the land of Ynde. That is also a gode lond and a plentefous; and it hath 3 grete princypalle cytees, Messabor, Caphon and Sarmassane.

And thanne aftre is Armenye, in the which weren wont to ben 4 kyngdomes: that is a noble contree, and fulle of godes. And it begyinnethe at Persie, and strecchethe toward the west in lengthe, unto Turkye. And in largenesse, it durethe to the cytee of Alizandre, that now is clept the Zate of Helle, that I spak offe beforn, undre the kyngdom of Mede. In this Armenye ben fulle manye gode cytees: but Tanrizo is most of name.

Aftre this, is the kyngdom of Mede, that is fulle long: but it is not fulle large, that begynnethe toward the est, to the land of Persie, and to Ynde the lesse. And it strecchethe toward the west, toward the kyngdom of Caldee, and toward the septemtrion, descendynge toward the litille Armenye. In that kyngdom of Medee, ther ben many grere hilles, and litille of pleyn erthe. There duellen Sarazines, and another maner of folk, that men clepen Cordynes. The beste 2 cytees of that kyngdom, ben Sarras and Karemen.

Aftre that, is the kyngdom of George, that begynnethe toward the est; to the gret mountayne, that is clept Abzor; where that duellen many dyverse folk of dyverse naciouns. And men clepen the contree Alamo. This kyngdom strecchethe him towardes Turkye, and toward the grete see: and toward the south, it marchethe to the grete Armenye. And there ben 2 kyngomes in that contree; that on is the kyngdom of Georgie, and that other is the kyngdom of Abcaz. And alle weys in that contree ben 2 kynges, and thei ben bothe Cristene: but the Kyng of Georgie is in subieccioun to the grete Chane. And the King of Abcaz hathe the more strong contree: and he alle weyes vigerously defendethe his contree; azenst alle tho that assaylen him; so that no man may make him in subieccioun to no man. In that kyngdom of Abcaz is a gret marvaylle. For a provynce of the contree, that hathe wel in circuyt 3 iorneyes, that men clepen Hanyson, is alle covered with derknesse, with outen ony brightnesse or light; so that no man may see ne here, ne no man dar entren in to hem. And natheles, thei of the contree seyn, that som tyme men heren voys of folk, and hors nyzenge, and cokkes crowynge. And men witen wel, that men duellen there: but thei knowe not what men. And thei seyn, that the derknesse befelle be myracle of God. For a cursed Emperour of Persie, that highte Saures, pursuede alle Cristene men, to destroye hem, and to compelle hem to make sacrifise to his ydoles; and rood with grete host, in alle that ever he myghte, for to confounde the Cristene men. And thanne in that contree, dwellen manye gode Cristene men, the whiche that laften hire godes, and wolde han fled in to Grece: and whan they weren in a playn, that highte Megon, anon this cursed emperour mett with hem, with his hoost, for to have slayn hem, and hewen hem to peces. And anon the Cristene men kneleden to the grounde, and made hire preyeres to God to sokoure hem. And anon a gret thikke clowde cam, and covered the emperour and alle his hoost: and so thei enduren in that manere, that thei ne mowe not gon out, on no syde; and so schulle thei ever more abyden in derknesse, tille the day of dome, be the myracle of God. And thanne the Cristene men wenten, where hem lykede best, at hire own plesance, with outen lettynge of ony creature; and hire enemyes enclosed and confounded in derknesse, with outen ony strok. Wherfore we may wel seye, with David, *A Domino factum est istud; et est mirable in oculis nostris*. And that was a gret myracle, that God made for hem. Wherfore methinkethe, that Cristene men scholden ben more devoute, to serven oure Lord God, than ony other men of ony other secte. For with outen ony drede, ne were cursednesse and synne of Cristene men, thei scholden be lordes of alle the world. For the banere of Jesu Crist is alle weys displayed, and redy on alle sydes, to the help of his trewe lovynge servauntes: in so moche, that o gode Cristene man, in gode beleeve, scholde overcomen and out chacen a 1000 cursed mysbeleevynge men: as David seyth in the Psautere, *Quoniam persequebatur unus mille, et duo fugarent decem milia*. Et, *Cadent a latere tuo mille, et decem milia a dextris tuis*. And how that it myghte ben, that on scholde chacen a 1000, David himself seythe, folewynge, *Quia manus Domini fecit hæc omnia*. And oure Lord himself seythe, be the prophetes mouth, *Si in viis meis ambulaveritis, super tribulantes vos misissem manum meam*. So that wee may seen apertely, that zif wee wil be gode men, non enemye ne may not enduren azenst us. Also zee schulle undirstonde, that out of that lond of derknesse, gothe out a gret ryvere, that schewethe wel, that there ben folk dwellynge, be many redy tokenes: but no man dar not entre in to it.

And wytethe well, that in the kyngdoms of Georgie, of Abchaz and of the litile Armenye, ben gode Cristene men and devoute. For thei schryven hem and howsele hem evermore ones or twyes in the woke. And there ben many of hem, that howsele hem every day: and so do wee not on this half; alle be it that Seynt Poul commandethe it, seyenge, *Omnibus diebus dominicis ad communicandum hortor*. Thei kepen that commandement: but wee ne kepen it not.

Also aftre, on this half, is Turkye, that marchethe to the gret Armenye. And there ben many provynces, as Capadoche, Saure, Brique, Quesiton, Pytan and Gemethe. And in everyche of theise ben many gode cytees. This Turkye strecchethe unto the cytee of Sachala, that sittethe upon the see of Grece; and so it marchethe to Syrie. Syrie is a gret contree and a gode, as I have told zou before. And also it hathe, aboven toward Ynde, the kyngdom of Caldee, that strecchethe fro the mountaynes of Calde, toward the est, unto the cytee of Nynyvee, that sittethe upon the ryvere of Tygre: and in largenesse, it begynnethe toward the northe, to the cytee of Maraga; and it strecchethe toward the southe, unto the see occean. In Caldee is a pleyn contree, and fewe hilles and few ryveres.

Aftre is the kyngdom of Mesopotayme, that begynnethe toward the est, to the flom of Tygre, unto a cytee that is clept Moselle: and it strecchethe toward the west, to the flom of Eufrate, unto a cytee that is clept Roianz: and in lengthe it gothe to the mount of Armenye, unto the desert of Ynde the lesse. This is a gode contree and a pleyn; but it hathe fewe ryveres. It hathe but 2 mountaynes in that contree: of the whiche, on highte Symar, and that other Lyson. And this lond marchethe to the kyngdom of Caldee.

Zit there is, toward the parties meridionales, many contrees and many regyouns; as the lond of Ethiope, that marchethe, toward the est, to the grete desertes; toward the west, to the kyngdom of Nubye; toward the southe, to the kyngdom of Moretane; and toward the north to the Rede See. Aftre is Moretane, that durethe fro the mountaynes of Ethiope, unto Lybie the hize. And that contree lyzth a long fro the see ocean, toward the southe; and toward the northe, it marchethe to Nubye, and to the highe Lybye. (Theise men of Nubye ben Cristene.) And it marchethe fro the londes aboveseyd to the desertes of Egypt. And that is the Egypt, that I have spoken of before. And aftre is Libye the hye, and Lybye the lowe, that descendethe down lowe, toward the grete see of Spayne. In the whiche contree ben many kyngdomes and many dyverse folk. Now I have devysed zou many contrees, on this half the kyngdom of Cathay: of the whiche, many ben obeyssant to the grete Chane.

Of the Contrees and Yles, that ben bezonde the Lond of Cathay; and of the Frutes there; and of 22 Kynges enclosed within the Mountaynes.

[Sidenote: Cap. XXVI.]

Now schalle I seye zou sewyngly of contrees and yles, that ben bezonde the contrees that I have spoken of. Wherfore I seye zou, in passynge be the lond of Cathaye, toward the highe Ynde, and toward Bacharye, men passen be a kyngdom, that men clepen Caldilhe; that is a fulle fair contree. And there growethe a maner of fruyt, as thoughe it weren gowrdes: and whan thei ben rype, men kutten hem a to, and men fynden with inne a lytylle best, in flessche, in bon and blode, as though it were a lytylle lomb, with outen wolle. And men eten bothe the frut and the best: and that is a gret marveylle. Of that frute I have eten; alle thoughe it were wondirfulle: but that I knowe wel, that God is marveyllous in his werkes. And natheles I told hem, of als gret a marveylle to hem, that is amonges us: and that was of the Bernakes. For I tolde hem, that in oure contree weren trees, that beren a fruyt, that becomen briddes fleeynge: and tho that fellen in the water, lyven; and thei that fallen on the erthe, dyen anon: and thei ben right gode to mannes mete. And here of had thei als gret marvaylle, that summe of hem trowed, it were an impossible thing to be. [Footnote: The Barnacle-bearing trees are said to have grown in Ireland.] In that contree ben longe apples of gode savour; where of ben mo than 100 in a clustre, and als manye in another; and thei han gret longe leves and large, of 2 fote long or more. And in that contree, and in other contrees there abouten, growen many trees, that beren clowe gylofres and notemuges, and grete notes of Ynde and of canelle and of many other spices. And there ben vynes, that beren so grete grapes, that a strong man scholde have y now to done, for to bere o clustre with alle the grapes. In that same regioun ben the mountaynes of Caspye, that men clepen Uber in the contree. Betwene the mountaynes, the Jewes of 10 lynages ben enclosed, that men clepen Gothe and Magothe: and thei mowe not gon out on no syde. There weren enclosed 22 kynges with hire peple, that duelleden betwene the mountaynes of Sythye. There Kyng Alisandre chacede hem betwene tho mountaynes; and there he thoughte for to enclose hem thorghe werk of his men. But whan he saughe, that he myghte not don it, ne bryng it to an ende, he preyed to God of Nature, that he wolde parforme that that he had begonne. And alle were it so, that he was a Payneme and not worthi to ben herd, zit God of his grace closed the mountaynes to gydre: so that thei dwellen there, alle faste y lokked and enclosed with highe mountaynes alle aboute, saf only on o syde; and on that syde is the see of Caspye. Now may sum men asken, Sithe that the see is on that o syde, wherfore go thei not out on the see syde, for to go where that hem lykethe? But to this question, I schal answere, That see of Caspye gothe out be londe, undre the mountaynes, and rennethe be the desert at o syde of the contree; and aftre it strecchethe unto the endes of Persie. And alle thoughe it be clept a see, it is no see, ne it touchethe to non other see; but it is a lake, the grettest of the world. And thoughe thei wolden putten hem in to that see, thei ne wysten never, where that thei scholde arryven. And also thei conen no langage, but only hire owne, that no man knowethe but thei: and therfore mowe thei not gon out. And also zee schulle undirstond, that the Jewes han no propre lond of hire owne for to dwellen inne, in alle the world, but only that lond betwene the mountaynes. And zit thei zelden tribute for that lond to the Queen of Amazoine, the whiche makethe hem to ben kept in cloos fulle diligently, that thei schalle not gon out on no syde, but be the cost of hire lond. For hire lond marchethe to tho mountaynes. And often it hathe befallen, that summe of the Jewes han gon up the mountaynes, and avaled down to the valeyes: but gret nombre of folk ne may not do so. For the mountaynes ben so hye and so streghte up, that thei moste abyde there, maugre hire myghte. For thei mowe not gon out, but be a littille issue, that was made be strengthe of men; and it lastethe wel a 4 gret myle. And aftre, is there zit a lond alle desert, where men may fynde no watre, ne for dyggynge, ne for non other thing. Wherfore men may not dwellen in that place: so it is fulle of dragounes, of serpentes and of other venymous bestes, that no man dar not passe, but zif it be strong wyntre. And that streyt passage, men clepen in that contree, Clyron. And that is the passage, that the Queen of Amazoine makethe to ben kept. And thoghe it happene, sum of hem, be fortune, to gon out; thei conen no maner of langage but Ebrow: so that thei can not speke to the peple. And zit natheles, men seyn, thei schalle gon out in the tyme of Antecrist, and that thei schulle maken gret slaughtre of Cristene men. And therfore alle the Jewes, that dwellen in alle londes, lernen alle weys to speken Ebrew, in hope that whan the other Jewes schulle gon out, that thei may undirstonden hire speche, and to leden hem in to Cristendom, for to destroye the Cristene peple. For the Jewes seyn, that they knowen wel, be hire Prophecyes, that thei of Caspye schulle been undre hire subieccioun, als longe as they had ben in subieccioun of hem. And zif that zee wil wyte, how that thei schulle fynden hire Weye, aftre that I have herd seye, I schalle telle zou. In the time of Antecrist, a fox schalle make there his trayne, and mynen an hole, where Kyng Alisandre leet make the Zates: and so longe he schalle mynen and perce the erthe, till that he schalle passe thorghe, towardes that folk. And whan thei seen the fox thei schulle have gret marveylle of him, be cause that thei saughe never suche a best. For of alle other bestes, thei han enclosed amonges hem, saf only the fox. And thanne thei schullen chacen him and pursuen him so streyte, tille that he come to the same place, that he cam fro. And thanne thei schullen dyggen and mynen so strongly, tille that thei fynden the zates, that Kyng Alisandre leet make of grete stones and passynge huge, wel symented and made stronge for the maystrie. And tho zates thei schulle breken, and so gon out, be fyndynge of that issue.

Fro that lond, gon men toward the lond of Bacharie, where ben fulle cruelle. In that lond ben trees, that beren wolle, as thoghe it were of scheep; where of men maken clothes, and alle thing that may ben made of wolle. In that contree ben many Ipotaynes, that dwellen somtyme in the watre, and somtyme on the lond: and thei ben half man and half hors, as I have seyd before: and thei eten men, whan thei may take hem. And there ben ryveres of watres, that ben fulle byttere, three sythes more than is the watir of the see. In that contree ben many Griffounes, more plentee than in ony other contree. Sum men seyn, that thei han the body upward, as an eagle, and benethe as a Lyoun: and treuly thei seyn sothe, that thei ben of that schapp. But o griffoun hathe the body more gret and is more strong thanne 8 lyouns, of suche lyouns as ben o this half; and more gret and strongere, than an 100 egles, suche as we han amonges us. For o griffoun there will bere, fleynge to his neste, a gret hors, or 2 oxen zoked to gidere, as thei gon at the plowghe. For he hathe his talouns so longe and so large and grete, upon his feet, as thoughe thei weren hornes of grete oxen or of bugles or of Kyzn; so that men maken cuppes of hem, to drynken of: and of hire ribbes and of the pennes and of hire wenges, men maken bowes fulle stronge, to schote with arwes and quarelle. From thens gon men, be many iourneyes, thorghe the lond of Prestre John, the grete Emperour of Ynde. And men clepen his Roialme, the Yle of Pentexoire,

END OF PART II.

MANDEVILLE'S VOYAGES.

PART III.

Tertia pars.

CAPVT. 41.

De magnificentia Imperatoris Indiæ et preciositate Palatij.

[Sidenote: Seu Pentoxoria Ciuitas Nyse] Cum in præcedentibus Imperator Indiæ dictus sit magnus, restat de illius magnificentia aliquid poni hoc loco: cuius vtique gloria, nobilitas, et potestas, dici non habetur minor, est tamen in aliquibus satis maior, quia omne æquale non est idem cum illo cui æquatur: itáque à finibus regni Bachariæ supradicti vbi contiguatur Imperio Indiæ, eundo per multas diætas intratur in Pentoxyriæ quod est magnæ latitudinis, et abundantiæ in multis bonis: huius nominatior ciuitas, dicitur Nyse, et in ea habet Imperator palatium Imperiale, in quo residet dum sibi placet. Imperator iste semper vocitatus est Præsbyter Ioannes, cuius nominis causam audieram quandoque non veram: sed in illis partibus accepi rationem indubitatam, quam breuiter hîc enarro. [Sidenote: Narratio de rebus gestis Ogeri Ducis Daniæ.] Circa annum ab incarnatione Domini octingentesimum, dux Ogerus de Danemarchia, cum quindecim cognationis suæ baronibus, et armatis viginti milibus transiuit mare Greciæ, et fauente sibi Deo conquisiuit Christianitati per multa prælia pené omnes terras, regiones, et insulas, quas esse de potestate Grand Can prædixi, nec non et omnes, quæ sunt de potestate Imperij huius Imperatoris Indiæ. Eratque inter Barones vnus denominatus Ioannes filius Goudebucf, regis Frisonum: qui dictus Ioannes Deo deuotus fuit, et dum licuit Ecclesiarum limina iniuit, vnde et barones ei dabant quasi per iocum Præsbyter Ioannes vocabulum. [Sidenote: Vndè Presbyter Ioannis sit dictus. 4000. Insulæ.] Dum ergo Ogerus dictas regiones expugnatas diuideret in hijs quindecim suis cognatis, et quemlibet eorum in suo loco constitueret regem, quatenus Christiana religio in illa orbis superficie semper stabilis permaneret, tradidit isti Præsbytero Ioanni superiorem Indiam, cum 4000. insulis, regionibus, et ipsum præfecit Imperatorem super reliquos cognatos, vt ei certa tributa impenderent, et in omnibus obedirent, átque ex tunc omnes successores Indiæ sunt vocati Præsbyter Ioannes et vsque in hodiernum tempus boni manserunt Christiani, et religionis æmulatores. Interim cum causa matrimoniorum aut procurationis filiorum dispersa est primi Imperij integritas, et multæ de insulis conuersæ vel potius peruersæ retrocesserunt ad vetustum squalorem paganismi primi. Nota. Recedens à Cambalu versus orientem post 50. dietas ad terram Præsbyteri Ioannes, principalis ciuitas terræ vocatur Cosan, satis parua sicut Vincentia: habet etiam sub se multas alias ciuitates. Ex pacto semper habet in vxorem vnam de filiabus Grand Can.

Per multas peruenitur ad prouinciam Casan, quæ est secunda melior de mundo, vbi subtilior est, habet dietas 50. longior, 60. et est vna de duodecim partibus Imperij Grand Can. Odericus. Vide infra capitulo 49. de Cassan, et de Epulone. Deinde venitur in Thebeth prouinciam, quæ India est confinis. Itaque Rex et Imperator iste tenet spatiosissimum Imperium plenum valdè multis Regionibus et Insulis amplis, diuisum inter quatuor flumina magna de Paradiso terrestri descendentia, Pyson, Gyon, Tygrim, et Euphratem. Nam vltra fines orientales eius Imperij, et terrestram Paradisum, nullus hominum habitat vel domitatur.

Præterea imperat multis alijs regionibus et insulis quæ distinguntur per brachia maris Oceani, et in quibus singulis continetur grandis numerositas ciuitatum ac villarum, et multitudo innumera populorum præ abundantia, et præciositate omnium terrenorum bonorum.

Imperium Indiæ habetur famosum per vniuersum orbem. Sed et famosius haberetur si mercatores mundi communitèr possint et auderent adire sicut Cathay, Nostratibus enim perrarus est illic accessus, tam præ longinquitate, quàm præ marinis periculis. Nam exceptis alijs sunt ibi quamplures Adamantini colles, ad oram maris, et intra mare, qui sua virtute attrahunt sibi naues ferrum continentes. Quoniam et mihi nauiganti monstrabatur per nautas à remotis quasi paruula Insula in mari, quam asserebant totalitèr ab antiquis temporibus paulatim ibi cumulatam de nauibus per Adamantes retentis.

[Sidenote: Latitudo Imperij Præsbyteri Ioannis est 4. mensium iter.] Estimatur autem latitudo huius Imperij per dietas quatuor mensium, sed longitudini non datur estimatio, eo quòd tenditur vsque Paradisum vbi nullus accedit.

Distinctum est Imperium per duodecim prouincias, quibus totidem præsunt reges principales seu prouinciales, et quorum singuli habent sub se Reges, Duces, Marchiones, et Barones, praestantes atque reddentes Praesbytero Ioanni promptam obedientiam, et certa tributa. Saepius et communitèr tenet Sedem Imperator in palatio vrbis Imperialis Suse. Hoc autem Palatium tale et tantum est, vt per me non credatur debite estimandum. Istud tamen dico audentèr in summa, quòd grandius, nobilius, preciosius, et placidius est, in auro, gemmis, structuris, et schemate supra descripto palatio Grand Can in Caydo.

Et ex speciali sciatis, istius palatij principales portas esse de Sardonico, vndique in ebore circumcluso: sed et transuersæ lineæ sunt omnes Eburneæ, aularum et cubiculorum fenestræ christallinæ. Mensarum quaedam Smaragdinæ, aliquæ Haematistinæ, caeterorumque lapidum preciosorum per aurum sibimet coniunctorum. Et nonnullæ in toto aureæ vel gemmunculis disseminatæ, et vnaquaeque de mensis cum stabilimento proprij generis. De throni quoque preciositate, quia meæ demonstrationis excellit modum, solummodo dico, singulos ascensionis gradus esse singulorum lapidum preciosorum: Primum onychis, secundum christallai, tertium iaspidis, quartum haematisti, quintum sardij, sextum cornelij. Et septimus qui est sub sedentis Imperatoris pedibus, ipse est, chrysolitus, omnes circumfusi, et inclusoria arte formati, auro splendida relucentes. Sed et ambo throni reclinatoria ex smaragdis auro combinatis, eoque distincto nobilissimis granis, et gemmis: cuncti pilarij in camera Regis dormitoria consistunt de auro fuluo, disseminati baccis, et quampluribus carbunculorum rubetis, totum de nocte habitaculum illustrantibus.

Et nihilominus in ea christallina lampas plena balsamo pistico sed ardens et lucens, tam pro augendo lumine, quàm pro corrigendo aere, tamen etiam pro ministrando optimo odore.

Forma lecti Imperatoris compacta est de puris et nobilissimis Saphyris, conclusi vtique aureis vel eburneis ligaturis, vt virtute lapidum capiat suauem somnum, motusque carnis inhonesti stimuli, in eo refrenentur. Nunquam enim iungitur mulieri nisi soli coniugi propriæ, sed nec illi nisi quatuor quindenis anni videlicet in capite hyemis, veris, æstatis, et autumni causa sobolis generandæ.

Vtque breuitèr transeam de multa huius palatij nobilitate, mirabile hoc solummodò praemissis super addo. Quia circa medium illius in summo apice turris maioris, duo sunt nodi seu pomella de decoctissimi auri metallo miræ magnitudinis, et serenæ resplendentiæ, et in ipsis formati duo carbunculi grandes, et lati, sua virtute tenebras effugantes, et velut splendorem plenilunij nocturno tempore mentientes.

The English Version.

Of the Ryalle estate of Prestre John; and of a riche man, that made a marveyllous Castelle, and cleped it Paradys; and of his Sotyltee.

[Sidenote: Chap. XXVII.] This Emperour Prestre John holt fulle gret lond, and hathe many fulle noble cytees and gode townes in his royalme, and many grete dyvene yles ond large. For alle the contree of Ynde is devysed in yles, for the grete flodes, that comen from Paradys, that departen alle the lond in many parties. And also in the see, he hathe fulle manye yles. And the beste cytee in the yle of Pentexoire is Nyse, that is a fulle ryalle cytee and a noble, and fulle riche. This Prestre John hathe undre him many kynges and many yles and many dyverse folk of dyverse condiciouns. And this lond is fulle gode and ryche; but not so riche as is the lond of the grete Chane. For the marchauntes come not thidre so comounly, for to bye marchandises, as thei don in the lond of the gret Chane: for it is to fer to travaylle to. And on that other partie, in the yle of Cathay, men fynden alle maner thing, that is nede to man; clothes of gold, of silk, and spycerie. And therfore, alle be it that men han grettre chep in the yle of Prestre John, natheles men dreden the longe wey and the grete periles in the see, in tho parties. For in many places of the see ben grete roches of stones of the adamant, that of his propre nature drawethe iren to him. And therfore there passen no schippes, that han outher bondes or nayles of iren with in hem: and zif there do, anon the roches of the adamantes drawen hem to hem, that never thei may go thens. I my self have seen o ferrom in that see, as thoughe it hadde ben a gret yle fulle of trees and buscaylle, fulle of thornes and breres, gret plentee. And the schipmen tolde us, that alle that was of schippes, that weren drawen thidre be the adamauntes, for the iren that was in hem. And of the rotenesse and other thing that was with in the schippes, grewen suche buscaylle and thornes and breres and grene grasse and suche maner of thing; and of the mastes and the seylle zerdes; it semed a gret wode or a grove. And suche roches ben in many places there abouten. And therfore dur not the marchauntes passen there, but zif thei knowen wel the passages, or elle that thei han gode lodes men. And also thei dreden the longe weye: and therfore thei gon to Cathay; for it is more nyghe: and zit is not so nyghe, but that men moste ben travayllynge be see and lond, 11 monethes or 12, from Gene or from Venyse, or he come to Cathay. And zit is the lond of Prestre John more ferr, be many dredfulle iourneyes. And the marchauntes passen be the kyngdom of Persie, and gon to a cytee that is clept Hermes: for Hermes the philosophre founded it. And aftre that, thei passen an arm of the see, and thanne thei gon to another cytee that is clept Golbache: and there thei fynden marchandises, and of popengayes, as gret plentee as men fynden here of gees. And zif thei will passen ferthere, thei may gon sykerly i now. In that contree is but lytylle whete or berley: and therfore thei eten ryzs and hony and mylk and chese and frute.

This Emperour Prestre John takethe alle weys to his wif, the doughtre of the grete Chane: and the gret Chane also in the same wise, the doughtre of Prestre John. For theise 2 ben the grettest lordes undir the firmament.

In the lond of Prestre John, ben manye dyverse thinges and many precious stones, so gret and so large, that men maken of hem vesselle: as plateres, dissches and cuppes. And many other marveylles ben there; that it were to cumbrous and to long to putten it in scripture of bokes.

CAPVT 42.

De frequentia palatij et comitatu Imperatoris.

Seruiunt et praestò sunt iugitèr Domino Imperatori septem reges, qui in capite singulorum mensium, alijs septem regibus pro illis palatium ingredientibus recedunt ad propria, donec reuoluatur eis tempus statutum. Hij curam habent de gubernatione administrationum in aula maiori per subiectos eis 72. duces, et 300. et 63. comites seu barones, quorum vnusquisque optimè nouit et diligentèr intendit proprio ministerio.

Nam isti sunt Imperatoris Cubicularij, isti Camerarij, isti scindunt Regi morsellos: alij de apponendis curam gerunt ferculis et deponendis, deafferendis, deasportandis, alij pincernæ, Archimandritæ, ostiarij, et sic de singulis.

Nec non absque iam dictis, manducant omni die in aula coràm Imperatore, duodecim Archiepiscopi, 220. Episcopi, quibus etiam alij totidem certis temporibus succedunt per vices. Verumtamen ad quotidianas expensas vsque praemissas, veniunt de Curia 300. millia personarum, sed non ampliùs: sed sicut praedixi de Curia praecedentis Imperatoris sic nullus hic, cuiuscunque sit status, aut sexus, comedit vltrà semel in die, et hoc ipsum sobriè satis: quoniam prout æstimare possum, expensæ duodecim hominum de nostris communitèr compensarent triginta hominum in partibus illis.

Dum Ioannem Presbyterum contingit procedere cum exercitu in plena exhibitione, non deferuntur vexilla, sed tredecim cruces magnæ altitudinis et grossitudinis, de auro distincto pretiosissimis petris, in honorem Christi et suorum Apostolorum duodecim. Hæ vectantur in singulis curribus, et singularum ad hoc maximis curribus cum custodia cuiuscunque crucis, decem mille equitum, et centum mille peditum, nec tamen hic numerus auget vel minuit principalem exercitum Paganorum.

Tempore pacis per terras proprias de palatio ad palatium, aut de regno ad regnum, dum tendere ei placet, comitatur vtique magna multitudine hominum antè et retrò, et ex vtroque laterum.

Tùncque portantur coràm eo tria valdè notabilia, quæ tam illi quàm omnibus ea dignè notantibus esse possunt salutaria. Praecedit enim eum in spatio circiter octodecim passuum discus onustus velut omni genere pretiosorum vasorum auri et argenti, gemmarum, et inæstimabilis artificij. Illumque discum subsequitur propinquiùs Imperatori ad spatium centum passuum, alia crux lignea nullo penitùs auro, nulloue colore aut preciositate artificialis operis adornata.

Dehinc ad sex passuum succedit ibidem propinquans Imperatori discus aureus terra nigerrima plenus. Sunt enim prædicti comitatus in custodiam et honorem personæ Imperatoris, discus vassorum in ostensionem diuitiarum, et maiestatis Imperialis. Crux in recordatione passionis et mortis, quam in cruce ligni simplice Christus passus est pro nobis. Et terra nigra in memoriam diræ mortis, qua caro ipsius Imperatoris, quæ terra est, in terram ibit corruptionis.

The English Version.

But of the princypalle yles and of his estate and of his lawe, I schalle telle zou som partye. This Emperour Prestre John is Cristene; and a gret partie of his contree also; but zit thei have not alle the articles of oure feythe, as wee have. Thei beleven wel in the Fadre, in the Sone and in the Holy Gost: and thei ben fulle devoute, and righte trewe on to another. And thei sette not be no barettes, ne by cawteles, ne of no disceytes. And he hathe undre him 72 provynces; and in every provynce is a kyng. And theise kynges han kynges undre hem; and alle ben tributaries to Prestre John.

CAPVT. 43.

De quibusdam miris per regiones Indiæ.

Licèt plurima mira habeantur in terra Imperij Presbyteri Ioannis, ne materia operis nimiùm proteletur, multa tego silentio: et solùm de quibusdam in principalibus Insulis narro. [Sidenote: Magnum mare arenosum] Ergò in primis dico vidisse me magnum mare arenosum, quod de solùm minuta arena sine vlla aqua cum lapillorum granellis currit, et fluit per altas eleuationes, et depressiones ad similitudinem maris aquæ, nec vnquam quiescit: et quòd ipse non cesso stupere, inueniuntur pisces ad littus proiecti, qui cum sint alterius formæ et speciei, quàm de nostro mari, videntur tamen gustui in edendo delicatiores. [Sidenote: In orientali India vsque hodie venti anniuersarij arenis ostia fluminum suffocant.] Nullo tamen humano ingenio videtur hoc mare transuadari, aut nauigari, aut illo piscari, sed nec propter sui longitudinem, et plura impedimenta de propè circuiri.

Item ab hoc latere maris per tres dietas habentur magnæ montium alpes, inter quas venit quasi oriens de Paradiso fluuius decurrentibus petris, nihil penitùs habens aquæ, in quibus æstimandæ sunt plurimum magnarum esse virtutum, quamuis de singulis humanæ scientiæ constare non potest.

Hîc petrarum fluuius currit ad intercisum tempus, quasi in tribus septimanæ diebus, per spatium deserti Indiæ plurium dietarum, velut fluuius, quousque tandem se perdat in mare arenosum praedictum, atque ex tunc ipsi lapides penitùs non comparent. Tempore autem sui cursus nullus appropinquare praesumit, præ strepitu eius et motu: sed tempore quietis aditur sine periculo vitæ.

In Orientem versus fluuij originem ad ingressum deserti magni inter quosdam de montibus, cernitur grandis terræ planicies tanquam spatiosi campi totalitèr arenosi, in quo videntur ad Solis ortum exurgere de arena, et secundùm eleuationem Solis excrescere quaedam virgulta, atque in feruore meridiei producere fructum. Ac de illo in Solis decliuo fructus cum arbustulis paulatim minui, et in occasu penitùs deperire, vnde et nullus hominum audet illorum vti fructibus, ne sit quid fantasticum et nociuum.

In huius deserti interioribus, vidi homines in toto syluestres, qui etsi in superioribus formam praetendere videantur humanam, descendunt in subterioribus ad formam bestiæ alicuius.

Horum quidam frontes gerunt cornibus asperatas, grinientes vt feræ vel apri: alij nonnulla vti videntur loquela, quam nemo rationalium nonit, et quibusdam signis concepta depromunt. Et est illic pluralitas syluestrium canum, qui dicuntur papiones, quibus postquam edomiti, et ad venandum instructi fuerint, valent capi multæ bestiæ per desertum. [Sidenote: Papagalli.] Est et copiositas papingonum auium viridium in colore quas appellant phicake, et quarum diuersa sunt genera, nobiliores habent latas in rostro linguas, et in vtroque pede digitos duos. Et quaedam ex istis naturaliter loquuntur verba aut prouerbia, seu salutationes, in patriæ idiomate, vt euidenter salutes, concedant, et reddant viatoribus, et nonnunquam debitum iter errantibus per desertum ostendant. Minus autem nobiles non loquuntur ex natura, sed si latas habent linguas, et non sunt vltrà duorum annorum ætatis, possunt per assiduitatem instrui ad loquelam.

Aliæ nec loquuntur, nec eradiuntur, sed solùm clamitant pro voce milui, et nisi tres digitos habent in pede.

Nota: in quarta orientali Deus dedit fratribus minoribus magnam gratiam, vnde in magna Tartaria ita expellunt ab obsessis daemones, sicut de domo canes: vnde quandoque per decem dietas ad eos adducuntur daemoniaci alligati, et statim fratribus praecipientibus in nomine Iesu Christi, exeunt, et liberati baptizantur, et comburunt idola, et plures credunt, et quandoque exeunt idola de igne, et fratres proijciunt aquam benedictam, et clamat daemon, Vide, de meo habitaculo expellor propter fratres minores. Ita multi credunt, et baptizantur. Odericus.

[Sidenote Melescorde Regio. Vel regionis.] Item nota: dum recederem de terra Praesbyteri Ioannis versos occidentem, applicui ad contratam vnam, quæ dicitur Melescorde, quæ pulchra est, et multùm fertilis: inter montes duos huius contratæ fecerat quidam murum circundantem montem, et in eo fontes nobilissimos, et omne detectabile. Et hunc locum dicebant paradisum, sicut hic ferè continetur. Ideò Odericus, qui posteà narrat de valle infausta in hoc se terminat.

[Sidenote: Mischorach.] Ad supradictum Indiæ regnum Pentexoriæ satis propè, et lata est et longa Insula, Mischorach, bonis copiosè referta, de qua vnum scribo praeteritum mirum.

Ante paucos hos annos, villanus ditissimus, sibi valdè preciosum construxerat palatium, quasi pro Paradiso terrestri, circundatum, munitum fortalitijs, ac repletum omnibus corporalibus delicijs.

Illic areæ, turres, cameræ, cubicula, cum alijs ædificijs, in multo numero, et gloria permagnifica, ac historiarum picturis, inter quas, nonnunquam prodigioso artificio bestiæ et bestiolæ, aues et auiculæ discurrebant, volitibant, et per pugnas, garritus, collusiones, mentiebantur viuere.

[Sidenote: Ditissimi villani paradisus fictitius.] Illic prata, et pometa, et seruatoria circà deliciosi collis congestum, distincta velut omni genere florum, arborum, et herbarum, cum multis fontibus et riuulis, quorum perspicuitas, et fluxus in glaris suauem et auditui præstabant refectionem, et super aliquos fuerunt exceptioris artificij, circumstructi auro, et argento, et gemmis, et tres principales fontes emittentes ad palatium Domini per occultas conductas, riuulos vini, lactis, et mellis.

Copiosus quoque numerus formosorum puerorum, et puellarum, ætatis inter decem et sex decem annos, indutorum torquibus, et cycladibus exauratis, exercentium inter iocos cantus et spectacula, ac seruientium suo Domino prope nutum. Audiebantur ex turrium custodibus, nec non videbantur dulcisonæ, symphoniæ, generum diuersorum, vt certissimè putares, non hominum, sed Angelorum: et in istis, ac similibus, deliciebatur iste villanus.

Sed et aurum liuido nil iuuat, imò nocet: quia enim hic inuidiæ et otij facibus super ingenuitatem mentis omnium generaliter nobilium principum verebatur in corde: (ingenuitas enim, et rusticitas nunquam cohabitant in cordis vno domicilio) Composuerat ista sibi in hunc finem, vt per se singulos aduocaret aliquos vasallos corpore robustos, menteque audaces, atque ad omnem proteruiam benè procliues: et cuilibet pro placitis muneribus commisit vt illum seu illum principem seu Baronem, quem dicebat sibi aduersarium, clàm per insidias vel impetum, occideret, promittens quenquam post factum ad se recepturum perpetuò in hunc locum: sed et velut vaticinans pseudo prædicauit, si quem illorum pro his flagitijs contigeret corporaliter tradi morti, nihilominùs animam eius in hunc amoenum Paridisum recipi, et viuere in æeternum.

[Sidenote: Mandeuillus oculatus testis.] Per hunc igitur modum nonnulis nobilibus occisis, et interfectis, tandem nudabatur eius nequitia tanta, et congregati regionis Barones miserum occiderunt, eius opera destruentes. Ipse ego inibi ductus vidi fontium loca, et multa rei vestigia.

CAPVT. 44.

De loco et dispositione vallis infaustæ.

Huius ad insulæ extremitates non procul à fluuio Pyson, habetur locus mirabilis pariter et terribilis, vltrà omne mundanum, penè et procul: de euentibus, ac laboribus infinitis, quæ mihi meísque in tempore itinerationis acciderunt hucusque subticui, cùm iam vnum de maioribus ecce narro.

Est illic in alpibus vallis infausta, quatuor fermè leucarum: longitudo vallis, quasi ad quatuor milliaria Lombardica, appellata vallis incantationis, seu periculosa, seu propiùs daemoniosa: intrà quam diebus ac noctibus resonant boatus et tumultus tonitruorum, tempestatum, clamorum, et stridorum, diuersique generis sonituum terribilium, quos illic exercet multitudo spirituum malignorum.

Propè ad vallis medium sub vna rupium, apparet omni tempore visibiliter integrum ac maximum caput daemonis vsque ad humeros tantùm, cuius speciem præ horrore nullus pleno intuitu humanus audet diu oculus sustinere: nam respicientes contrà aspicit truculentèr, agitans oculos minacitèr, tanquam ex palpebris eiecturus (quæ et scintillant) flammas in altum. Totumque caput sese rotat ad minas, et variat terribilitèr modum et continentiam sub repentè diuersis maneriebus. Exitque de illo per totum ignis obscuratus fumo, et foetor, tantus, quòd per magnum spatium viæ pessimam vallem infectat.

Ingredi autem volentibus, apparet semper ad introitum vallis, magna copia auri, argenti, vasorum, vestium, et rerum pretiosarum, quas proculdubio ibi daemones confingunt, quibus et ab olim multi insipientium hominum concupiscentia tracti intrarunt, et vsque nunc intrant pro colligendo thesauro: sed de Infidelibus paucissimi reuertuntur, imò nec de Christianis, qui auaritiæ causa ingrediuntur: per vallis autem semitam, quæ inter montes et monticulos, tortuosa et aspera est, gradientes vident, et audiunt, daemoniacos spiritus multos volutantes, et imaginibus corporum visibilium, serpentum, volucrum, vlularum, lamiarum, et huiusmodi specierum horribilium dentibus minitantes, vngulas erigentes, incognitos sibilos spirantes propè super capita ad aures transgredientium. Sempérque minuitur lumen aeris, donec ventum fuerit ad terribilissimum locum capitis antedicti.

Si quis autem sinceræ fidei Christianus per contritionem veram et confessionem, se posuerit in statu saluationis, munitus corporis Christi mysterijs, ac signo crucis, cum intentione ibidem agendi poenitentiam de admissis, et cauendi de admittendis, putatur posse hanc transire vallem securus quidem à morte, non tamen liber à laboribus, horroribus, et tormentis, et exire, de omnibus culpis praeteritis corruptis, ac de futuris magis solito cautus, sicut scriptum est, territi purgabuntur.

Nota aliud mirabile magnum. Vidi cùm irem per vnam vallem positam iuxta flumen quod egreditur de paradiso, vidi in ea multa corpora mortuorum, in qua etiam audiui multa genera Musicorum, qui ibi mirabilitèr pulsabant: tantus erat ibi tinnitus Musicorum, quòd incussit mihi timorem horribilem.

Est autem longitudo illius vallis quasi ad quatuor milliaria Lombardica, in qua si vnus Infidelis intrat, nunquam egreditur, sed sine mora moritur: Et licet sciui, quòd intrantes moriuntur, tamen acceptaui intrare, vt viderem quid ibi esset. Dum intrassem tot humana cadauera ibi vidi, quod nisi quis videret, credere non posset.

In hac valle, ab vno eius latere, vidi faciem hominis valdè horribilem, qui tantum horrorem mihi incussit, quòd putaui me spiritum exhalare, propter quod saepè repetij verbum vitæ, scilicet, verbum Caro factum est.

Ad illam faciem non audebam accedere, nisi ad distantiam octo passuum: posteà iui ad caput vallis, et ascendi super montem arenosum, in quo vndique circumspiciens, nihil videbam, nisi instrumenta musicalia, quæ audiebam fortitèr pulsare. Cùm fuissem in capite montis, reperi multum argentum congregatum ibi in similitudinem squamarum piscium, vnde posui in gremio, sed quod de ipso non curabam, dimisi illud, et sic illaesus transiui Deo concedente.

Sarraceni cùm hoc scirent, reuerebantur me esse baptizatum, et sanctum: mortuos nunc in valle dicebant, homines infernales.

Odericus ad literam hic terminat suum librum: non fuit tot perpessus in valle, sicut ego. Anno Domini 1331. Ianuarij nono, migrauit ad Christum, in conuentu Minorum: cuius vitam statim in fine, et vsque nunc claris miraculis diuina prouidentia approbat, et commendat, prout continebatur in quaterno, à quo concordantias hic superseminaui.

CAPVT. 45.

De periculo et tormentis in valle eadem.

Itaque dico vobis, cùm sodalibus, qui simul eramus, quatuordecim diuersarum nationum ante ingressum huius tanti periculi peruenissemus, nos tractatu longo, et deliberatione acuta consiliabamur, vtrùmnam ingredi deberemus, et quidam affirmabant, alii verò negabant. Erant autem in numero duo deuoti fratres, de religione beati Francisci, natione Lombardi, qui videbantur pro seipsis non multum curare ingressum, nisi quia noluerunt nos animare ad ingressum, dicentes, si qui nostrum per confessionem, et Eucharistiæ susceptionem se ibidem praemunirent, ingrederentur cum illis: quo, ab omnibus mediante debita prouisione, quam ipsi fratres penes se gerebant peracto, parauimus mentes nostras cum pedibus ad intrandum.

Sed ecce quinque de nobis, duo Graeci et tres Hispani, semetipsos ab alijs segregantes, visi sunt alium requirere introitum nos praecedere cupientes, et certè nos illos exinde non vidimus, et quid eis acciderit an periculum subierint, velne ignoramus.

Nos autem nouem per vallem processimus in silentio, et cum cordis ea deuotione, quam quisque sibi potuerit obtinere: et ecce in breui transacto spatio apparuerunt cumuli massarum auri et argenti, et preciosorum copia vasorum. Sed dico vobis pro parte mea, quia nihil horum tetigi, reputans id fallaciam dæmonum confinxisse ad mittendum concupiscentiam in cor nostram, imò sine intermissione conabar cor meum custodire ad deuotionem inceptam.

Procedentibus igitur nobis lux coeli minuebator paulatim et augebatur horror, quoniam propè nos vndique etiam sub pedibus nostris apparebant iacere cadauera mortuorum hominum penitùs defuncta: alia adhuc spirantia, et nonulla semiuiua, super quæ dum nos aliquando calcare contingeret, conquerebantur, ac dolorosè submurmurabant.

Et licèt non certum id habebam, æstimaui hoc fieri in parte vel in toto fictione dæmonum, reputans in breui tempore tantam multitudinem hominum spontaneè vallem intrasse, et si à longo tempore in ea perijssent putrefactos fuisse.

Ergò in initio nostri processus quasi propè leucam inuenitur iter sub pedibus satis promptum, sed lumine tanquam ad medium nobis sufficiente, via torquebatur nimis, et asperabatur: et ecce figuræ dæmonum, circum et suprà in aere se ferentium, ad imagines horribilium luporum, leonum, laruarum, megerarum, iuxtà cuiuscunque genus vlulantium, rugentium, stridentium, gannientium, hiantes ore, intentantes dentibus, rostris, ac vnguibus, nos terrere, mordere, discerpere, deglutire.

Quapropter pro breui interdum soluto silentio nos inuicèm hortabamur, ne quis pro pusillanimitate terrori cederet, et tanto deficeret in agone. Hoc igitur modo per secundam leucam expirante nobis vsque ad tenebras lumine, quousque quis vix vmbram proximi agnoscere possit, præter prædicta in aere tormenta, incurrebant nobis ad tibias, et pedes pluralitas quasi porcorum, vrsorum, et caprarum grinnientium, et impellentium nos ad lapsum, quod vel ad tertium, vel quartum, aut sextum passum solatenus cadebamus in palmas, seu genua, vel prosternebamur in faciem, aut supini.

Ac superuenere præter hoc ventorum turbines, fulgurum coruscationes, tonitruorum boatus, drandium casus et exundatio pluuiarum, quantas et quales nunquam accepimus in hoc mundo, quibus iactabamur, ruebamus, quassabamur, et periclitati fuimus extrà narrandum.

Interdum quoque sensimus tanquam graues baculorum ictus, per humeros, dorsa, latera, et ad renes, alij quidem grauiores, alij vt puta secundum demeritum vniuscuiusque. Et certè dum per tanta tormenta, quasi exhaustis totis viribus, iam propè medium locum vallis erat ventum, accidit repentè, sub vnico instanti temporis, quibusdam nostrum expalmatio ita dura, vt omnes pariter collisi, et prostrati iaceremus in extasi per vnam vul duas forsitan horas.

Et isto defectu vidit quilibet suo modo spiritualem visionem supermirabilem, et excedentem omne dictum, et scriptum.

Ego verò de visione mea nihil ausus sum scribere, vel loqui, quia et fratres singuli inhibuerunt, nisi de his, quæ corporalitèr intuebamur, et passi sumus.

Grauissimum singuli sustinuimus ictum per corporis loca diuersa, vnus in facie, alius in pectore, ad costas, in dorso, vel ad humerum, et mansit cuique signum percussuræ nigerrimum, ad formam virilis manus humanæ:

[Sidenote: Mirabilis ictus.] Ictum autem meum in colli ceruice tali ac tanta passione, vt putabam caput abscissum de corpore auolare: et hinc ad octodecimum annum mansit mihi in prima magnitudine signum: sed et vsque nunc variato colore locus ille demonstrat penissimè cicatricem, donec cum cadauere tota mutabitur in sepulchro: porrò vbi nos ab extasi in his tenebris separauimus singuli per diuinam gratiam respirando, loquendo, palpando, erigendo nos ipsos mutua humanitate, vt potuimus, recollegimus, et cohortabamur, cùm subitò nobis apparuit sub tenebroso lumine, vel potiùs fumosa caligine, locus ille spatiosus mediæ vallis, continens antedictum horribile caput daemonis, plenus foetore inaestimabili, et iugi occupatus exercitatione innumerorum spirituum malignorum.

Hunc ergo locum ineptum cùm vitare vellemus in toto nequiuimus extremitatem eius, quocunque girantes, nullus nostrorum perfecto aspectu audebat respicere quæ gerebantur ibidem, quia inuadens tremor statuebat horripilationem extrahebat, sudorem, et pudorem omnes extinguere videbantur. Nec tamen potuit esse consilium de reuertendo, ne propter immutatum propositum confestim à daemonibus strangularemur.

Transiuimus, Dei gratia nobis opitulante, sed non sine maximo horroris, foetorisque tormento: rursumque ex tunc procedentes nos apprehendebat tenebrosa, validaque tempestas, ventorum, coruscationum, tonitruum, grandinum, et pluuiarum, cuius, quassatione collabebamur in facies, et in dorso dextrorsum, et sinistrorsum, interuoluente ad tibias, sicut priùs multitudine grinnientium bestiarum, nec dubito scribere quoque ampliùs, quàm 500. vicibus per hanc vallem quisque nostrum sternebatur ad terram.

Post verò exactam tertiam leucam, coepit nobis augeri lux aeris, ex quo animosiores effecti, in vno tranquilliori loco nos parùm pausantes, gratias Deo palmis extensis in caelum, reddidimus immensas, et praecipuè quod nullus deesset de nouenario numero sociorum.

Nihilominùs tamen spiritus in aere nobis minari non cessabant, pretendentes in derisionem sua pudenda simul, et foeda virilia et posteriora.

Pro certo ergò habeatis de his quæ vidi, et sensi, nullam possum vobis tradere æquipollentiam verborum, cùm quia grauissima erant, tum quia, singulis ne mihi deuotionem minueret non attendebam, tum etiam, quod præ horrore, labore, et dolore multa memoriæ non commendabam.

Per quartam autem leucam (ductrice gratia) leuiùs transeuntes, sustinuimus tamen sub pedibus hominum cadauera mortuorum, propè vallis exitum rerum tentamina preciosarum.

Nunc itaque obsecro magno cordis effectu, haec legentes et audientes ego, qui in illa hora quid erga me agebat misericordissimi Dei pietas ignorabam, vt velitis pro me, simul et mecum ex mentis intimo collaudare ipsum Dominum, qui tunc de potestate tenebrarum illarum eripuit me indignum, et prout confido, à delictis iuuentutis me purgauit, quatenùs de posteà commissis, et committendis, mihi propitiùs fore dignetur, cùm iam senior sim effectus. Quoniam etsi ex tunc proposui mores corrigere, ex nunc statuo in melius emendare, per filium eius Iesum Christum Dominum nostrum.

Ad hoc, addo breuitèr, quòd non auderem hortari quenquam, me consulentem, vt spontaneè ingrederetur hanc vallem infaustam, quamuis ego curiosus intraui. Venientes posthac ad proximas habitationes, necesse fuit nobis intendere ad recreandum corpora cibarijs, et balneis, et ad medendum vulneribus, et quassaturis, donec per aliquod tempus vnusquisque acciperet deliberationem super suo futuro.

CAPVT. 46.

De quibusdam alijs admirandis per Indorum insulas.

[Sidenote: Gigantes Anthropophagi.] Vt modò procedam in tractatu. Sciatis ad paucas inde dietas grandem insulam haberi gigantum, ad straturam altitudinis viginti quinque pedum nostrorum, de quibus ipse vidi nonnullos, sed extrà terram eorum, et audiuimus esse intrinsecùs quosdam triginta pedum, et vltrà: hi operiuntur non vestibus, sed bestiarum pellibus vtcunque sibi appensis, comedentes animalium carnes crudas, et lac pro potu sorbentes, atque appetentes super omnem esum carnes humanas.

Istorum non curaui intrare insulam: nam et audiui quòd ad maris littus solent insidiari nauigantibus, nauesque submergere, nisi interdum redimantur tribus aut quatuor per sortem hominibus sibi datis.

[Sidenote: Letiferi aspectus mulierum.] Versus Austrum hinc in mari Oceano, habetur inter alias insulas vna, vbi crudelibus quibusdam mulieribus nascitur in oculis lapis rarus, et malus, quæ si per iram respexerint hominem, more Basilisci interficiunt solo visu.

Et vltrà hanc insulam alia maior et populosior, vbi cùm multi sint vsus nobis insueti, vnum describo.

[Sidenote: Insula vbi virgines vitiantur antequam nubant.] Dum desponsauerit vir puellam, virginem, mandat hominem incompositum, velut ribaldum, qui sua idonea claue per expertos super hoc diligentèr considerata, si reputatur idonea reseret et vestiget sub nocte vnica virginalem conclauem, pro mercede sibi tradita competenti. Et si postera nocte accedens sponsus ita non inuenerit, poterit, et consueuit hominem impetere ad mortis iudicium indeclinabile. Cumque huius moris discere voluissem causam, accepi responsum, pro certis temporibus apud eos, virgines habuisse in matricibus paruos serpentes, quibus nocebantur primi ad illas intrantes.

Ideoque et viri, que pro mercede tantum subeunt periculum, vocant sua loquela cadibrum, est, stultos desperatos.

Ex hac, apparet Insula in qua inter alios vsus, peruersæ sunt matres contra naturam et scripturam, cum pepererent contristantur, et dum proles moritur iocundantur, iactantes in magno igne cum conuiuio et exultatione, dumque maritus ante vxorem decidit, patebit vxoris plena dilectio, si cum corpore mariti, quod rogo traditur se iactat cremandum, vt quia in isto seculo steterunt amoris vinculo colligati, non sint alio separati.

Nec tamen intelligunt illud seculum, nisi quod sibi confingunt terrestrem Paradisum. Purum aut minorem annis, trahet mater secum si placet, sed ætatis puer perfectæ, eliget pro proprio placito viuere superstes, aut mori iuxta parentes.

Hic etiam non succedunt Reges per generationem sed per electionem, vt assumatur non nobilior, aut fortior, sed morigeratior, et iustior, 50 ad minus annorum, nullam habens sobolem aut vxorem, seruaturque illic iusticiæ rigor in plena censura, in omnibus et contra omnes, etiamsi forefecerit ipse Rex, qui nec eximitur a traditis legibus pro concupiscentia vel contemptione quarumlibet personarum.

Veruntamen Rex si peccauerit non occiditur ob reuerentiam, sed quòd sub poena mortis, publicè inhibetur, ne quispiam in Regione ei verbo vel vllo facto communicet, et quoniam sui loco alter rex constituitur, necesse est illi breui vita degere vel perpetuò exulare. Constat post ipsam, et alia Insula, multis bonis locuples, et hominibus populosa, de qua recolo scribendum, quod nulla occasione comedunt tria genera carnium, gallinarum, leporam, et aucarum, quas etsi nutriant in copijs, vtuntur duntaxat pellibus aut plumis.

Caeterarum vero bestiarum et animalium licitè vescuntur carnibus pro victu, et lacte pro potu. Ibi quisque vir licitè potest coniungi cuique mulieri; quantumcunque propinquet, exceptis progenitoribus, patre matre. Nam cohabitatio, et commixtio omnium virorum ad singulas mulieres apparet ibi communis, vnde mater natum paruulum suum, adicit pro sui placito cuicunque viro, qui circa generationis tempus secumn dormierit, nec valet vllus virorum esse certus de proprio generato, quem modum exlegem arbitror et turpem.

Sicut ergò praefatus sum, multa mira videntur per Regiones Indorum, mira quidem nobis, sed illis assueta, quibus si nostra recitarentur assueta, audirent pro miris. Nam et dum quibusdam dixi aucas viuas apud nos nasci in arboribus, admirati sunt satis. In multis locis seminatur singulis annis sementum de Cothon, quod nos dicimus lanam arboream, exurgunt ei modica arbusta, vel potius arbustula de quibus talis lana habetur: est arbor Iuniperus, de cuius ligno desiccato, si carbones viuos sub proprijs cineribus tenueris diligenter opertos, igniti seruabuntur ad annum.

Est et genus Nucum incredibilis magnitudinis ad quantitatem magni capitis: et bestia vocata, oraflans, vel serfans, corpore in nostrorum aldtudine caballorum, et collo in 20 longitudine cubitorum ad prospiciendum vltra domos et muros, quorum posteriora apparent vt hinniculi siue lerni.

Genus est etiam Camelionum ad formam hynnulorum, qui semper patulo tendunt ore, vel nil manducantes. Viuunt de aere, quæ etiam ad suum libitum videntur sibi variare colorem, exceptis (vt dicitur) albo vel rubeo.

Maximi quóque serpentes, inuicem qualitate, et genere differentes atque colore.

Aliqui cristam in capite gerunt, quidam more hominum ad duos pedes erecti incedunt, et nonnulli qui dicuntur Reguli, venenum per ora distillare non cessant, nec non quam plures cocodrilli, de quibus aliquid in praecedentibus retuli; [Sidenote: Apri ingentes. Leones albi. Louheraus.] et apri in nostrorum magnitudine boum, spinosi ericij, in quantitate porcorum, leones albi in altitudine dextrariorum. Louheraus, seu Edouches per Indiam habentur, quod ferarum genus satis est maius nostris communibus equis, geren in fronte tetri capitis tria longa cornua, ad formam pugionis, ex vtraque parte scindentia, vt eis nonnunquam interficiant Elephantes.

Aliæ quoque bestiæ crudeles vt vrsi cum capitibus ferè aprorum et habentes pedes senos, qui finduntur latis vngulis bis acutis, et cum caudis leonum siue pardorum.

Et quod vix credetur, mures pro quantitate, 10, aut 12. nostrorum et vespertiliones ad modum coruorum.

Sed et aucæ in triplo maiores nostris, plumis indutæ rubris, nisi quod in pectore et collo apparet nigredo.

Et breuiter tam ibi quàm alibi, habentur pisces, bestiæ, volucres, aut vermes diuersorum generum, aut specierum, de quibus hoc loco, vel inutilis, vel prolixa posset fieri narratio, quod nec illis qui nunquam propria exierunt, credibilis videretur.

The English Version.

And he hathe in his lordschipes many grete marveyles. For in his contree, is the see that men clepen the Gravely See, that is alle gravelle and sond, with outen ony drope of watre: and it ebbethe and flowethe in grete wawes, as other sees don: and it is never stille ne in pes, in no maner cesoun. And no man may passe that see be navye, be no maner of craft: and therfore may no man knowe, what lond is bezond that see. And alle be it that it have no watre, zit men fynden there in and on the bankes, fulle gode fissche of other maner of kynde and schappe, thanne men fynden in ony other see; and thei ben of right goode tast, and delycious to mannes mete.

And a 3 iourneys long fro that see, ben gret mountaynes; out of the whiche gothe out a gret flood, that comethe out of paradys: and it is fulle of precious stones, with outen ony drope of water: and it rennethe thorghe the desert, on that o syde; so that it makethe the see gravely: and it berethe in to that see, and there it endethe. And that flomme rennethe also, 3 dayes in the woke, and bryngethe with him grete stones, and the roches also therewith, and that gret plentee. And anon as thei ben entred in to the gravely see, thei ben seyn no more; but lost for evere more. And in tho 3 dayes, that that ryvere rennethe, no man dar entren in to it: but in the other dayes, men dar entren wel y now. Also bezonde that flomme, more upward to the desertes, is a gret pleyn alle gravelly betwene the mountaynes: and in that playn, every day at the sonne risynge, begynnen to growe smale trees; and thei growen til mydday, berynge frute: but no man dar taken of that frute; for it is a thing of fayrye. And aftre mydday, thei discrecen and entren azen in to the Erthe, so that at the goynge doun of the Sonne, thei apperen no more; and so thei don every day; and that is a gret marvaille.

In that desert ben many wylde men, that ben hidouse to loken on: for thei ben horned; and thei speken nought, but thei gronten, as pygges. And there is also gret plentee of wylde Houndes. And there ben manye popegayes, that thei clepen psitakes in hire langage: and thei speken of hire propre nature, and salven men that gon thorghe the desertes, and speken to hem als appertely, as thoughe it were a man. And thei that speken wel, han a large tonge, and han 5 toos upon a Fote. And there ben also of other manere, that han but 3 toos upon a fote; and thei speken not, or but litille: for thei cone not but cryen.

This Emperour Prestre John, whan he gothe in to battaylle, azenst ony other Lord, he hathe no baneres born before him: but he hathe 3 crosses of gold, fyn, grete and hye, fulle of precious stones: and every of the crosses ben sett in a chariot, fulle richely arrayed. And for to kepen every cros, ben ordeyned 10000 men at Armes, and mo than 100000 men on Fote, in maner as men wolde kepe a Stondard in oure Contrees, whan that wee ben in lond of werre. And this nombre of folk is with outen the pryncipalle Hoost, and with outen Wenges ordeynd for the bataylle. And he hathe no werre, but ridethe with a pryvy meynee, thanne he hathe bore before him but o cross of tree, with outen peynte peynture, and with outen gold or silver or precious stones; in remembrance, that Jesus suffred dethe upon a cros of tree. And he hathe born before him also a plater of gold fulle of erthe, in tokene that his noblesse and his myghte and his flessche schalle turnen to erthe. And he hathe born before him also a vesselle of silver, fulle of noble jewelles of gold fulle riche, and of precious stones, in tokene of his lordschipe and of his noblesse and of his myght. He duellethe comounly in the cytee of Suse; and there is his principalle palays, that is so riche and so noble, that no man wil trowe it by estymacioun, but he had seen it. And aboven the chief tour of the palays, ben 2 rounde pomeles of gold; and in everyche of hem ben 2 carboncles grete and large, that schynen fulle brighte upon the nyght. And the principalle zates of his palays ben of precious ston, that men clepen sardoyne: and the bordure and the barres ben of ivorye: and the wyndowes of the halles and chambres ben of cristalle: and the tables where on men eten, somme ben of emeraudes, summe of amatyst and summe of gold, fulle of precious stones; and the pileres, that beren up the tables, ben of the same precious stones. And the degrees to gon up to his throne, where he sittethe at the mete, on is of oniche, another is of cristalle, and another of jaspre grene, another of amatyst, another of sardyne, another of corneline, and the sevene that he settethe on his feet, is of crisolyte. And alle theise degrees ben bordured with fyn gold, with the tother precious stones, sett with grete perles oryent. And the sydes of the sege of his throne ben of emeraudes, and bordured with gold fulle nobely, and dubbed with other precious stones and grete perles. And alle the pileres in his chambre, ben of fyne gold with precious stones, and with many carboncles, that zeven gret lyght upon the nyght to alle peple. And alle be it that the charboncle zeve lyght right y now, natheles at alle tymes brennethe a vesselle of cristalle fulle of bawme, for to zeven gode smelle, and odour to the emperour, and to voyden awey alle wykkede eyres and corrupciouns. And the forme of his bedd is of fyne saphires bended with gold, for to make him slepen wel, and to refreynen him from lecherye. For he wille not lyze with his wyfes, but 4 sithes in the zeer, aftre the four cesouns: and that is only for to engendre children. He hathe also a fulle fayr palays and a noble, at the cytee of Nyse, where that he dwellethe, whan him best lykethe; but the ayr is not so attempree, as it is at the cytee of Suse. And zee schulle undirstonde, that in alle his contree, ne in the contrees there alle aboute, men eten noghte but ones in the day, as men don in the court of the grete Chane. And so thei eten every day in his court, mo than 30000 persones, with outen goeres and comeres. But the 30000 persones of his contree, ne of the contree of the grete Chane, ne spenden noghte so moche gode, as don 12000 of oure contree. This Emperour Prestre John hathe evere more 7 kynges with him, to serve him: and thei departen hire service be certeyn monethes. And with theise kynges serven alle weys 72 dukes and 360 erles. And alle the dayes of the zeer, there eten in his houshold and in his court, 12 erchebysshoppes and 20 bisshoppes. And the patriark of Seynt Thomas is there, as is the Pope here. And the erchebisshoppes and the bisshoppes and the abboties in that contree, ben alle kynges. And everyche of theise grete lordes knowen wel y now the attendance of hire servyse. This on is mayster of his houshold, another is his chamberleyn, another servethe him of a dissche, another of the cuppe, another is styward, another is mareschalle, another is prynce of his armes: and thus is he fulle nobely and ryally served. And his lond durethe in verry brede 4 moneths iorneyes, and in lengthe out of measure; that is to seyn, alle the yles undir erthe, that wee supposen to ben undir us.

Besyde the yle of Pentexoire, that is the lond of Prestre John, is a gret yle long and brode, that men clepen Milsterak; and it is in the lordschipe of Prestre John. In that yle is gret plentee of godes. There was dwellynge somtyme a ryche man, and it is not longe sithen, and men clept him

Gatholonabes; and he was fulle of cauteles and of sotylle disceytes; and he hadde a fulle fair castelle, and a strong, in a mountayne, so strong and so noble, that no man cowde devise a fairere ne a strangere. And he had let muren alle the mountayne aboute with a strong walle and a fair. And with inne tho walles he had the fairest gardyn, that ony man myghte beholde; and therein were trees berynge alle maner of frutes, that ony man cowde devyse; and there in were also alle maner vertuous herbes of gode smelle, and alle other herbes also, that beren faire floures. And he had also in that gardyn, many faire welles; and beside tho welles, he had lete make faire halles and faire chambres, depeynted alle with gold and azure. And there weren in that place many a dyverse thinges and many dyverse stories: and of bestes and of bryddes, that songen fulle delectabely; and meveden be craft, that it semede that thei weren quyke. And he had also in his gardyn alle maner of foules and of bestes that ony man myghte thenke on, for to have pley or desport to beholde hem. And he had also in that place, the faireste zonge Damyseles, that myghte ben founde undir the age of 15 zere, and the faireste zonge striplynges, that men myghte gete of that same age: and alle thei weren clothed in clothes of gold fully richely: and he seyde, that tho weren aungeles. And he had also let make 3 welles, faire and noble, and alle envyround with ston of jaspre, of cristalle, pyapred with gold, and sett with precious stones and grete orient perles. And he had made a conduyt undir erthe, so that the 3 weles, at his list, on scholde renne milk, another wyn, and another hony. And that place he clept paradys. And whan that ony gode knyghte, that was hardy and noble, cam to see this rialtee, he wolde lede him into his paradys, and schewen him theise wondirfulle thinges, to his desport, and the marveyllous and delicious song of dyverse briddes, and the faire damyseles, and the faire welles of mylk, wyn and hony, plentevous rennynge. And he wolde let make dyyerse Instrumentes of Musick to sownen in an highe Tour, so merily that it was joye for to here; and no man scholde see the craft thereof: and tho, he seyde, weren aungeles of God, and that place was paradys, that God had behighte to his frendes, seyenge, *Dabo vobis terram fluentem lacte et mel.* And thanne wolde he maken hem to drynken of certeyn drynk, where of anon thei scholden be dronken. And thanne wolde hem thinken gretter delyt, than thei hadden before. And than wolde he seye to hem, that zif thei wolde dyen for him and for his love, that aftir hire dethe, thei scholde come to his paradys; and thei scholde ben of the age of the damyseles, and thei scholde pleyen with hem, and zit ben maydenes. And aftir thai, zit scholde he putten hem in a fayrere paradys, where that thei schold see God of Nature visibely, in His majestee and in His blisse. And than wolde He schewe hem His entent, and seye hem, that zif thei wolde go sle suche a Lord, or suche a man, that was his enemye, or contrarious to his list, that thei scholde not dred to done it, and for to be slayn therefore hemself: for aftir hire dethe, he wold putten hem into another paradys, that was an 100 fold fairer than ony of the tothere; and there schode thei dwellen with the most fairest damyselles that myghte be, and play with hem ever more. And thus wenten many dyverse lusty bacheleres for to sle grete lords, in dyverse countrees, that weren his enemyes, and maden hem self to ben slayn, in hope to have that paradys. And thus often tyme, he was revenged of his enemyes, be his sotylle disceytes and false cauteles. And whan the worthi men of the contree hadden perceyved this sotylle falshod of this Gatholonabes, thei assembled hem with force, and assayleden his castelle, and slowen him, and destroyden alle the faire places, and alle the nobletees of that paradys. The place of the welles and of the walles and of many other thinges, ben zit apertly sene: but the richesse is voyded clene. And it is not longe gon, sithe that place was destroyed.

Of the Develes Hede in the Valeye perilous; and of the Customs of folk in dyverse Yles, that ben abouten, in the Lordschipe of Prestre John.

[Sidenote: Chap. XXVIII.] Besyde that Yle of Mistorak, upon the left syde, nyghe to the ryvere of Phison, is a marveylous thing. There is a vale betwene the mountaynes, that durethe nyghe a 4 myle: and summen clepen it the Vale Enchaunted; some clepen it the Vale of Develes, and some clepen it the Vale Perilous. In that vale, heren men often tyme grete tempestes and thondres and grete murmures and noyses, alle dayes and nyghtes: and gret noyse, as it were sown of tabours and of nakeres and trompes, as thoughe it were of a gret feste; This ale is alle fulle of develes, and hathe ben alle weyes. And men seyn there, that it is on of the entrees of helle. In that vale is gret plentee of gold and sylver: wherefore many mysbelevynge men, and manye Christene men also, gon in often tyme, for to have of the thresoure, that there is: but fewe comen azen; and namely of the mys belevynge men, ne of the Cristene men nouther: for thei ben anon strangled of develes. And in mydde place of that vale, undir a roche, is an hed and the visage of a devyl bodyliche, fulle horrible and dreadfulle to see, and it schewethe not but the hed, to the schuldres. But there is no man in the world so hardy, Cristene man ne other, but that he wolde ben a drad for to beholde it: and that it wolde semen him to dye for drede; so is it hidous for to beholde. For he beholdethe even man so scharply, with dreadfulle eyen, that ben evere more mevynge and sparklynge, as fuyr, and chaungethe and sterethe so often in dyverse manere, with so horrible countenance, that no man dar not neighen towardes him. And fro him comethe out smoke and stynk and fuyr, and so moche abhomynacioun, that unethe no man may there endure. But the gode Cristene men, that ben stable in the feythe, entren welle withouten perile. For thei wil first schryven hem, and marken hem with the tokene of the Holy Cros; so that the fendes ne han no power over hem. But alle be it that thei ben with outen perile, zit natheles ne ben thei not with outen drede, whan that thei seen the develes visibely and bodyly alle aboute hem, that maken fully dyverse assautes and manaces in eyr and in erthe, and agasten hem with strokes of thondre blastes and of tempestes. And the most drede is, that God wole taken vengeance thanne, of that men han mys don azen his wille. And zee schulle undirstonde, that whan my fellows and I weren in that vale, wee weren in gret thought, whether that wee dursten putten oure bodyes in aventure, to gon in or non, in the proteccioun of God. And somme of oure fellowes accordeden to enter, and somme noght. So there weren with us 2 worthi men, Frere Menoures, that weren of Lombardye, that seyden, that zif ony man wolde entren, thei wolde gon in with us. And when thei hadden seyd so, upon the gracyous trust of God and of hem, wee leet synge masse, and made every man to ben schryven and houseld: and thanne wee entreden 14 personnes; but at oure goynge out, wee weren but 9. And so we wisten nevere, whether that oure fellowes weren lost, or elle turned azen for drede: but wee ne saughe hem never after: and tho weren 2 men of Grece and 3 of Spayne. And oure other fellows, that wolden not gon in with us, thei wenten by another coste, to ben before us, and so thei were. And thus wee passeden that perilous vale, and founden thereinne gold and sylver and precious stones and riche jewelles gret plentee, both here and there, as us semed: but whether that it was, as us semede, I wot nere: for I touched none, because that the develes ben so subtyle to make a thing to seme otherwise than it is, for to disceyve mankynde; and therfore I towched none; and also because that I wolde not ben put out of my devocioun: for I was more devout thanne, than evere I was before or after, and alle for the drede of fendes, that I saughe in dyverse figures; and also for the gret multytude of dede bodyes, that I saughe there liggynge be the weye, be alle the vale, as thoughe there had ben a bataylle betwene 2 kynges and the myghtyest of the contree, and that the gretter partye had ben discomfyted and slayn. And I trowe, that unethe scholde ony contree have so moche peple with in him, as lay slayn in that vale, as us thoughte; the whiche was an hidouse sight to seen. And I merveylled moche, that there weren so manye, and the bodyes all hole, with outen rotynge. But I trowe, that fendes made hem semen to ben so hole, with outen rotynge. But that myghte not ben to myn avys, that so manye scholde have entred so newely, ne so manye newely slayn, with outen stynkynge and rotynge. And manye of hem were in habite of Cristene men: but I trowe wel, that it weren of suche, that wenten in for covetyse of the thresoure, that was there, and hadden over moche feblenesse in feithe; so that hire hertes ne myghte not enduren in the beleve for drede. And therfore weren wee the more devout a gret del: and zit wee weren cast doun and beten down many tymes to the hard erthe, be wyndes and thondres and tempestes: but evere more God of His grace halp us: and so we passed that perilous vale, with outen perile and with outen encombrance. Thanked be alle myghty Godd.

Aftre this, bezonde the vale, is a gret yle, where the folk ben grete geauntes of 28 fote longe or of 30 fote longe; and thei han no clothinge, but of skynnes of bestes, that thei hangen upon hem: and thei eten no breed, but alle raw flesche: and thei drynken mylk of bestes; for thei han plentee of alle bestaylle. And thei have none houses, to lyen inne. And thei eten more gladly mannes flessche, thanne ony other flesche. In to that yle dar no man gladly entren: and zif thei seen a schipp and men there inne, anon thei entren in to the see, for to take hem.

And men seyden us, that in an yle bezonde that, weren geantes of grettere stature: summe of 45 fote, or 50 fote long, and as some men seyn, summe of 50 cubytes long: but I saghe none of tho; for I hadde no lust to go to tho parties, because that no man comethe nouther in to that yle ne in to the other, but zif he be devoured anon. And among tho geauntes ben scheep, als grete as oxen here; and thei beren gret wolle and roughe. Of the scheep I have seyn many tymes. And men han seyn many tymes tho geauntes taken men in the see out of hire schippes, and broughte hem to lond, 2 in on hond and 2 in another, etynge hem goynge, alle rawe and alle quyk.

Another yle is there toward the northe, in the see occean, where that ben fulle cruele and ful evele wommen of nature; and thei han precious stones in hire eyen: and thei ben of that kynde, that zif thei beholden ony man with wratthe, thei slen him anon with the beholdynge, as dothe the basilisk.

Another yle is there, fulle fair and gode and gret, and fulle of peple, where the custom is suche, that the firste nyght that thei ben maryed, thei maken another man to lye be hire wifes, for to have hire maydenhode: and therfore thei taken gret huyre and gret thank. And ther ben certeyn men in every town, that serven of non other thing; and thei clepen hem Cadeberiz, that is to seyne, the foles of Wanhope. For thei of the contree holden it so gret a thing and so perilous, for to haven the maydenhode of a woman, that hem semethe that thei that haven first the maydenhode, puttethe him in aventure of his lif. And zif the husbonde fynde his wif mayden, that other next nyghte, aftre that she scholde have ben leyn by of the man, that is assigned therefore, perauntes for dronkenesse or for some other cause, the husbonde schalle pleyne upon him, that he hathe not don his deveer, in suche cruelle wise, as thoughe he wolde have him slayn therfore. But after the firste nyght, that they ben leyn by, thei kepen hem so streytely, that thei ben not so hardy to speke with no man. And I asked hem the cause, whi that thei helden suche custom: and thei seyden me, that of old tyme, men hadden ben dede for deflourynge of maydenes, that hadden serpentes in hire bodyes, that stongen men upon hire zerdes, that thei dyeden anon: and therfore thei helden that custom, to make other men, ordeyn'd therefore, to lye be hire wyfes, for drede of dethe, and to assaye the passage be another, rather than for to putte hem in that aventure.

Aftre that, is another yle, where that wommen maken gret sorwe, whan hire children ben y born: and whan thei dyen, thei maken gret feste and gret joye and revelle, and thanne thei casten hem into a gret fuyr brennynge. And tho that loven wel hire husbondes, zif hire husbondes ben dede, thei casten hem also in the fuyr, with hire children, and brennen hem. And thei seyn, that the fuyr schalle clensen hem of alle filthes and of alle vices, and thei schulle gon pured and clene in to another world, to hire husbondes, and thei schulle leden hire children with hem. And the cause whi that they wepen, when hire children ben born, is this, for whan thei comen in to this world, thei comen to labour, sorwe and hevynesse: and whi thei maken ioye and gladnesse at hire dyenge, is be cause that, as thei seyn, thanne thei gon to Paradys, where the ryveres rennen mylk and hony, where that men seen hem in ioye and in habundance of godes, with outen sorwe and labour. In that yle men maken hire kyng evere more be eleccioun: and thei ne chese him nought for no noblesse ne for no ricchesse, but suche an on as is of gode maneres and of gode condiciouns, and therewith alle rightfulle; and also that he be of gret age, and that he have no children. In that yle men ben fulle rightfulle, and thei don rightfulle iuggementes in every cause, bothe of riche and pore, smale and grete, aftre the quantytee of the trespas, that is mys don. And the kyng may nought deme no man to dethe, with outen assent of his barouns and other wyse men of conseille, and that alle the court accorde therto. And zif the kyng him self do ony homycydie or ony cryme, as to sle a man, or ony suche cas, he schalle dye therefore; but he schalle not be slayn, as another man, but men schulle defende in peyne of dethe, that no man be so hardy to make him companye, ne to speke with hym, ne that no man zeve him ne selle him ne serve him nouther of mete ne drynk: and so schalle he dye in myschef. Thei spare no man that hath trespaced, nouther for love ne for favour ne for ricchesse ne for noblesse, but that he schalle have aftre that he hathe don.

Bezonde that yle, is another yle, where is gret multytude of folk; and thei wole not for nothing eten flesche of hares, ne of hennes, ne of gees: and zit thei bryngen forthe y now, for to seen hem and to beholden hem only. But thei eten Flesche of alle other bestes, and drynken mylk. In that contre, thei taken hire doughtres and hire sustres to here wyfes, and hire other kynneswomen. And zif there ben 10 or 12 men or mo dwellynge in an hows, the wif of eyeryche of hem schalle ben comoun to hem alle, that duellen in that hows; so that every man may liggen with whom he wole of hem, on o nyght. And zif sche have ony child, sche may zeve it to what man sche list, that hathe companyed with hire; so that no man knoweth there, whether the child be his or anotheres. And zif ony man seye to hem, that thei norrischen other mennes children, thei answeren, that so don other men hires. In that contre and be all Ynde, ben gret plentee of cokodrilles, that is the maner of a longe serpent, as I haye seyd before. And in the nyght, thei dwellen in the watir, and on the day, upon the lond, in roches and caves. And thei ete no mete in all the wynter: but thei lyzn as in a drem, as don the serpentes. Theise serpentes slen men, and thei eten hem wepynge: and whan thei eten, thei meven the over Jowe, and noughte the nether Jowe; and thei have no Tonge. In that contree, and in many other bezonde that, and also in manye on this half, men putten in werke the sede of cotoun: and thei sowen it every zeer, and than growthe it in smale trees, that beren cotoun. And so don men every zeer; so that there is plentee of cotoun, at alle tymes. Item, in this yle and in many other, there is a manner of wode, hard and strong: who so coverethe the coles of that wode undir the assches there offe, the coles wil duellen and abyden alle quyk, a zere or more. And that tre hathe many leves, as the gynypre hathe. And there ben also many trees, that of nature thei wole never brenne ne rote in no manere. And there ben note trees, that beren notes, als grete as a mannes hed. There also ben many bestes, that ben clept orafles. [Footnote: Giraffes.] In Arabye, thei ben clept gerfauntz; that is a best pomelee or apotted; that is but a litylle more highe, than is a stede; but he hathe the necke a 20 cubytes long: and his croup and his tayl is as of an hert: and he may loken over a gret highe Hous. And there ben also in that contree manye camles, that is a lytille best as a goot, that is wylde and he lyvethe be the eyr, and etethe nought ne drynkethe nought at no tyme. And he chaungethe his colour often tyme: for men seen him often scithes, now in o colour and now in another colour: and he may chaunge him in to alle maner of coloures that him list, saf only in to red and white. There ben also in that contree passynge grete serpentes, sume of 120 Fote long, and thei ben of dyverse coloures, as rayed, rede, grene and zalowe, blewe and blake, and alle spekelede. And there ben othere, that han crestes upon hire hedes: and thei gon upon hire feet upright: and thei ben wel a 4 fadme gret or more: and thei duellen alle weye in roches or in mountaynes: and thei han alle wey the throte open, of whens thei droppen venym alle weys. And there ben also wylde swyn of many coloures, als gret as ben oxen in oure contree, and thei ben alle spotted, as ben zonge fownes. And there ben also urchounes, als gret as wylde swyn here. Wee clepen hem poriz de spyne. And ther ben lyouns alle whyte gret and myghty. And ther ben also of other bestes, als grete and more gretter than is a destrere: and men clepen hem loerancz: and sum men clepen hem odenthos: and thei han a blak hed and 3 longe hornes trenchant in the front, scharpe as a sword; and the body is sclender. And he is a fulle felonous best: and he chacethe and sleethe the olifaunt. There ben also manye other bestes, fullye wykked and cruelle, that ben not mocheles more than a bere; and thei han the hed lyche a bore; and thei han 6 feet: and on every foote 2 large clawes trenchant: and the body is lyche a bere, and the tayl as a lyoun. And there ben also myse, als gret as houndes; and zalowe myse, als grete as ravenes. And ther ben gees alle rede, thre sithes more gret than oure here: and thei han the hed, the necke and the brest alle black. And many other dyverse bestes ben in tho contrees, and elle where there abouten: and manye dyverse briddes also; of the whiche, it were to longe for to telle zou: and therefore I passe over at this tyme.

CAPVT. 47.

De Bracmannorum et aliorum Insulis.

Bracmannorum Insula quasi ad medium Imperij consistit Praesbyteri Ioannis. Hic licet Christiani non sunt, viuunt tamen naturali optimo more. Rudes enim et incomparati, simplices, et inscij omnis artis apparent. Non cupidi, superbi, inuidi, iracundi, gulosi, aut luxuriosi nec iurant, fraudant, aut mentiuntur. Laborant corpora, sed intendunt animo implere quo ad valent naturale mandatum, hoc facias alijs quod tibi vis fieri: credentes et adorantes omnium creatorum Deum, et sperantes ab ipso simpliciter Paradisum.

Sobrij quoque sunt, quapropter et longo tempore viuunt: et si quis ab eorum moribus degenerat, proscribitur perpetuò sine mora, omnibus nulla posita differentia personarum, vnde et in iusto Dei iudicio, quòd naturalem exercere iustitiam contendunt, Elementa eis naturaliter obsequuntur, et rarò eos tangit tempestas, aut fames, pestilentia aut gladius.

[Sidenote: Flumen Chene.] Magna riparia dicta Chene currit per Insulam, ministrans piscium et aquarum copiam: Istos olim Alexander rex Grecorum debellare cupiens, misit eis literas comminationis, cui inter caetera notabilia remandauerunt, nihil se habere curiosi, quod Rex tantus deberet concupiscere, nihilque ita se timere perdituros sicut pacem bonam, quam hactenus habuerunt inconcussam: sicque diuino nutu est actum vt Rex truculentus ad alia se verteret, atque in breui postmodùm caderet, quia dissipat Dominus eos, qui bella volunt, et istis manet pax multa diligentibus eam.

[Sidenote: Pytan.] Pytan Insula breuis continet paucos et breues habitatores, Pygmaeis modico longiores, qui decoris vultibus nullo vnquam cibo vescentes, specialis pomi quod secum portant sustentantur odore, quo si carerent ad parum, color in vultu marcesceret, et die tertia vita periret.

Discretio et rationabilitas ijs adest modica, nec enim habent laborare nisi pro vestitu, quem sibi circa arbusta colligunt: Et conficit vnusquisque pro 12 annis vitæ suæ.

Vltra hanc Insulam siluestres, et fortes habentur homines, sed bestiales, vestiti per totum corpus proprijs capillis et pilis, exceptis palmis, et faciebus, qui videntur penitus gubernatione et politia carere: venantur carnes per siluas, et discurrunt piscantes in aquis, omnia cruda vorantes.

[Sidenote: Fluius Briemer.] Huius ad terræ metas manat fluuius Briemer latitudinis duarum leucarum, et semis, quem nos transire nequiuimus, nec ausi fuimus. Quoniam illo transmisso instant deserta 15, aut plurium diætatum inhabitata nunc temporis (prout audieramus) diuersis et nobis ignotis generibus bestiarum, serpentum, draconum, gryphium, aspidum, dypsarum, et colubrorum in multitudine tanta, vt centum millia armatorum simul pertingere vsquè ad arbores, quæ ibi dicuntur solis et lunæ, vix possent. Attamen suo tempore Alexander magnus scribitur pertigisse, et quaedam ab arboribus fictitia succepisse responsa.

[Sidenote: Balsamum indicum.] Circa has arbores excolitur Balsamum, cuius liquoris comparatio nusquam scitur contineri sub coelo. Nam ibidem homines, de istarum arborum fructibus et Balsamo vtentes dicuntur illorum virtute quadringentis aut pluribus annis viuere.

Peruenit autem et Dux Danus Ogerus, ac manducauit de illis, vnde et nonnulli præ sensus stoliditate vel fidei leuitate putant ipsum adhuc alibi viuere in terris. Ego autem quia tantum pro dilatanda Christianitate laborauit arbitror magis, eum regnare cum Christo in coelis.

[Sidenote: Taprobana Insula, et eius descriptio.] Versus Orientales partes Indorum consistit magna regio Taprobane exuberans optimis terrenorum bonorum, in quam nauigio intrauimus in octo vel circa diaetis per aquam satis tenuem, haud profundam. Ibi, sicut et in alijs multis Insulis, rex non nascitur sed eligitur per partes terræ: et est haec vna de quindecim nominatis Regionibus conquisitionis Ogeri. Ista, cum modicum declinet à circulo terræ sub Æquatore, patitur in anno duas æstates, et duas hyemes, si tamen hyems aliqua dici debeat, et non magis æstas, quia nullus hic dies anni caret fructu, flore, germine.

Habitatores sunt discreti, et honesti, vnde et mercatores de remotis partibus libenter cum ijs communicant: et sparsim per regionem habitant plurimi diuites Christiani.

[Sidenote: Orilla. Argita.] Hijs iunguntur duæ insulæ (quas nos vocamus, Orilla, et Argita), quanquam illa lingua aliter nominentur. In quarum prima sunt multæ mineriæ auri, in secunda argenti, et propter quandam crassitudinem aeris continuam, perpauca apparent sydera, praeter vnum quod dicunt Canopum, quod æstimo planetam Veneris. [Sidenote: Hunc locum notat Gerardus Mercator in sua charta generali.] Et quod mirum est valdè de omni lunatione ijs apparet nisi 2. quarta. Cuius rei probabilis ratio effugit etiam Astronomos valdè peritos. Atque per has Insulas quoddam rubrum mare à mari Oceano segregatur.

Itaque in Orilla in locis multis effoditur, colligitur, et conflatur optimum auri metallum, per viros, mulieres, et paruulos in hoc instructos, sed et in nonnullis ibi montibus monstrantur congregationes bestiolarum in quantitate nostrorum catulorum, in formicarum forma ac natura totali: qui pro suis viribus effodiunt, purificant, et colligunt cum intenta occupatione auri minutias, eas reponentes, et repositas retrahentes de cauernis et specubus in cauernas et specus. Et in conseruando sum diligentes et acres, vt nemo audeat de facili propinquare, nisi quod interdum ab illis pausantibus; seu ab æstu se occultantibus, aliqui non sine periculo in dromedarijs et veredarijs rapiunt, vel furantur.

Solet etiam ab eis obtineri, quòd excogitato ingenio super equam quæ nuper foetum ediderit, imponentes homines duas de ligno cistulas, seu cophinos nouos, vacuos, et apertos à lateribus dependentes propè terram: hanc famelicam dimittunt vt se pascat ad herbas in montem: Quam formicæ videntes solam salientes et iocantes, colludunt ad eam et ad eius confines pro nouitate: et quoniam eis est naturale, vt circa se omne vacuum implere conentur comportant certatim aurum suum in vasculis suis mundis. Cumque homines a remotis tempus obseruauerint, emittunt pellum equæ vt videat matrem, cuius aspectu iam diu stetit priuatus, ad cuius hinnitum protinus equa reuertitur onusta de auro. Hijs ergò et similibus modis homines aurum diripiunt à formicis.

CAPVT. 48.

Aliquid de loco Paradisi terrestris per auditum.

A Finibus Imperij Indiæ recta linea in orientem nihil est habitatum vel habitabile, propter rupium, et montium altitudinem, et asperitatem, et propter aeris inter Alpes diuersitatem: nam in multis locis, licet quandoque aer sit serenus, nunc fit spissus nunc fumosus, vel venenosus, et frequenter die medio tenebrosus. Durantque aut potius aggrauescunt huiusmodi difficultates, vsque ad illum amænissimum Paradisi locum, quem protoplausti per inobedientiam sibi et posteris perdidisse noscuntur, quod spacium si metiri posset, est multarum vtique diætarum. Quia iam non vlterius processi, nec procedere quiui, pauca duntaxat de illo loco referam verisimilia, quæ didici per auditum.

[Sidenote: Descriptio Paradisi.] Paradisus terrestris dicitur locus spaciosus ad amplitudinem quasi quinque Insularum nostrarum, Angliæ, Normanniæ, Hiberniæ, Scotiæ, et Noruegiæ, aut forsan satis plurium. Cuius situs est pertingens in altitudine ad aeris supremam superficiem, eò quod illic terra vel terræ orbis sit multum spissior quàm alibi per modum excentricum à vero centro mundi, nec valet hoc deinde ab aliquo experto refelli, scriptura veritatis clamante, quòd ibi sit fons irrigans vniuersam superficiem terrae: aquae enim est natura semper fluere ad Ima.

Exeunt autem ab illo fonte versus nostri partes hemispherij, hoc est nobis de illo loco in occidentem quatuor flumina, Pyson, Gyon, Tygris, et Euphrates, ab ista dimidia parte terrae circa Æquatoris circulum terrae influentes, quapropter et merito credendum videtur, exire de eodem fonte et alia quatuor flumina irrigantia terram oppositam, quae est circa alteram dimidiam partem circuli Æquatoris, quamuis nos eorum fluminum loca, virtutes, et nomina ignoramus, quòd homines habitant ab alia parte Æquinoctij.

[Sidenote: Gentes ad austrum Aequatoris.] Hoc tamen volo sciri pro vero et audiui, illic terræ faciem inhabitatam in maxima multitudine ciuitatum, vrbium, et regionum, quoniam et eorum institores Indiam frequentant, et nunciant sibi inuicem gentes et principes per literas, ac alijs modis destinare sunt visi.

[Sidenote: Ganges fluuius.] Vnus nostrorum fluuiorum Pyson currit per Indiam, et per eius deserta quandoque sub terra, sed saepiùs supra, qui et Ganges illic appellatus est, ab illo vltimo Paganitatis rege, quem Dux Ogerus deuictum cùm baptizari renueret in ipso flumine proiectum submersit.

Ad littus huius reperiuntur multi lapides praeciositatis immensæ et metalli grani carissimi, nec non et auri mineriæ, multumque descendit in eo natans lignum Aloes ex Paradiso, quod rebus miræ virtutis inserit Salomon in Canticis.

Hinc secundus fluuius Gyon, currit per Aethiopiam, vnde dum venit in Ægyptum, accipit nomen Nilus. Tertius Tygris veniens per Assyriam influit maiorem Armeniam et Persiam: tandemque fluuij singuli per loca singula se iactant in mare per quod defluunt vsque ad Nador, id est, ad oppositum diametrum paradisi: Ideoque merito æstimantur omnes vniuerso orbe aquæ dulces originem capere, à supradicto paradisi fonte, quamuis secundum distantiam maiorem vel minorem, et secundum naturas rerum per quas meant diuersos habere inueniuntur sapores, atque virtutes.

Porrò ipsum Paradisi locum audiui à tribus plagis, orientali, meridionali, et septentrionali, inaccessibilem tam hominibus quàm bestijs, eo quòd apparet ripis perpendiculariter abscissa, tanquam inestimabilis altitudinis. Et ab occidente id est nostra parte tanquam super omnium humanorum intuitum rogus ardens, qui in scripturis rumphea flammea appellator, vt nulli creaturæ terrenæ ascensus in eum credatur nisi quibusdam volatilibus, prout decreuit iusti iudicij Deus.

Ambulantibus enim illuc siue repentibus hominibus obstarent tenebræ imo rupes, aer infestus, bestiæ, serpentes, frigus, et camua. Nauigare autem contra ictum fluminis nitentes impediret intrinsecus recursus, ac impetuosus et quandoque subterraneus aquæ cursus descendentis cum vehementia ab euectissimo, vt dictum est, loco, qui suo quoque strepitu, per petras atque strictos aliosque diuersos cadens gurgites, efficeret surdos, et aeris mutatio caecos, vnde et multi tam nobiles quàm ignobiles, fatua sese audacia in isto ponentes periculo perierunt, alijs excoecatis, alijs absurdatis, et nonnullis in ipso accessu subitanea morte peremptis. Ex quo nimirum credi habetur isto Deum displicere conatum.

Quapropter et ego ex illo loco statui animum ad repatriandum, quatenus Deo propitio, Anglia quæ me produxit seculo viuentem, usciperet morientem.

Of the Godenesse of the folk of the Yle of Bragman. Of Kyng Alisandre: and
  wherfore the Emperour of Ynde is clept Prestre John.

[Sidenote: Cap. XXIX.] And bezonde that yle, is another yle, gret and gode, and, plentyfous, where that ben gode folk and trewe, and of gode lyvynge, aftre hire beleve, and of gode feythe. And alle be it that thei ben not cristned, ne have no perfyt lawe, zit natheles of kyndely lawe, thei ben fulle of alle vertue, and thei eschewen alle vices and alle malices and alle synnes. For thei ben not proude ne coveytous ne envyous ne wrathefulle ne glotouns ne leccherous; ne thei don to no man other wise than thei wolde that other men diden to hem: and in this poynt, thei fullefillen the 10 commandementes of God: and thei zive no charge of aveer ne of ricchesse: and thei lye not, ne thei swere not, for non occasioun; but thei seyn symply, ze and nay. For thei seyn, He that swerethe, wil disceyve his neyghbore: and therfore alle that thei don, thei don it with outen othe. And men clepen that yle, the Yle of Bragman: and somme men clepen it the Lond of Feythe. And thorgh that lond runnethe a gret ryvere, that is clept Thebe. And in generalle, alle the men of tho yles and of alle the marches there abouten, ben more trewe than in ony othere contrees there abouten, and more righte fulle than othere, in alle thinges. In that yle is no thief, ne mordrere, ne comoun woman, ne pore beggere, ne nevere was man slayn in that contree. And thei ben so chast, and leden so gode lif, as tho thei weren religious men: and thei fasten alle dayes. And because thei ben so trewe and so rightfulle and so fulle of alle gode condiciouns, thei weren nevere greved with tempestes ne with thondre ne with leyt ne with hayl ne with pestylence ne with werre ne with hungre ne with non other tribulaccioun, as wee ben many tymes amonges us, for our synnes. Wherfore it semethe wel, that God lovethe hem and is plesed with hire creance, for hire gode dedes. Thei beleven wel in God, that made alle thinges; and him thei worschipen. And thei preysen non erthely ricchesse; and so thei ben alle right fulle. And thei lyven fulle ordynatly, and so sobrely in met and drynk, that thei lyven right longe. And the most part of hem dyen with outen syknesse, whan nature faylethe hem for elde. And it befelle in Kyng Alisandres tyme, that he purposed him to conquere that yle, and to maken hem to holden of him. And whan thei of the contree herden it, thei senten messangeres to him with lettres, that seyden thus: What may ben y now to that man, to whom alle the world is insuffisant: thou schalt fynde no thing in us, that may cause the to warren azenst us: for wee have no ricchesse, ne none wee coveyten: and alle the godes of our contree ben in comoun. Oure mete, that we susteyne with alle oure bodyes, is our richesse: and in stede of tresoure of gold and sylver, wee maken oure tresoure of accord and pees, and for to love every man other. And for to apparaylle with oure bodyes, wee usen a sely litylle clout, for to wrappen in oure carcynes. Oure wyfes ne ben not arrayed for to make no man plesance, but only connable array, for to eschewe folye. Whan men peynen hem to arraye the body, for to make it semen fayrere than God made it, thei don gret synne. For man scholde not devise no aske grettre beautee, than God hathe ordeyned man to ben at his birthe. The erthe mynystrethe to us 2 thynges; our liflode, that comethe of the erthe that wee lyve by, and oure sepulture aftre oure dethe. Wee have ben in perpetuelle pees tille now, that thou come to disherite us; and also wee have a kyng, nought for to do justice to every man, for he schalle fynde no forfete amonge us; but for to kepe noblesse, and for to schewe that wee ben obeyssant, wee have a kyng. For justice ne hathe not among us no place: for wee don no man otherwise than wee desiren that man don to us; so that rightwisnesse ne vengeance han nought to don amonges us; so that no thing thou may take fro us, but oure god pes, that alle weys hath dured amonge us. And whan Kyng Alisandre had rad theise lettres, he thoughte that he scholde do gret synne, for to trouble hem: and thanne he sente hem surteez, that thei scholde not ben aferd of him, and that thei scholde kepen hire gode maneres and hire gode pees, as thei hadden used before of custom; and so he let hem allone.

Another yle there is, that men clepen Oxidrate; and another yle, that men clepen Gynosophe, where there is also gode folk, and fulle of gode feythe: and thei holden for the most partye the gode condiciouns and customs and gode maneres, as men of the contree above seyd: but thei gon alle naked. In to that yle entred Kyng Alisandre, to see the manere. And when he saughe hire gret feythe and hire trouthe, that was amonges hem, he seyde that he wolde not greven hem: and bad hem aske of him, what that they wolde have of hym, ricchesse or ony thing elles; and thei scholde have it with gode wille. And thei answerden, that he was riche y now, that hadde mete and drynke to susteyne the body with. For the ricchesse of this world, that is transitorie, is not worthe: but zif it were in his power to make hem immortalle, there of wolde thei preyen him, and thanken him. And Alisandre answerde hem, that it was not in his powere to don it, because he was mortelle, as thei were. And thanne thei asked him, whi he was so proud and so fierce and so besy, for to putten alle the world undre his subieccioun, righte as thou were a god; and hast no terme of this lif, neither day ne hour; and wylnest to have alle the world at thi commandement, that schalle leve the with outen fayle, or thou leve it. And righte as it hathe ben to other men before the, right so it schalle ben to othere aftre the: and from hens schal thou bere no thyng; but as thou were born naked, righte so alle naked schalle thi body ben turned in to erthe, that thou were made of. Wherfore thou scholdest thenke and impresse it in thi mynde, that nothing is immortalle, but only God, that made alle thing. Be the whiche answere, Alisandre was gretly astoneyed and abayst; and alle confuse departe from hem. And alle be it that theyse folk han not the articles of oure feythe, as wee han, natheles for hire gode feythe naturelle, and for hire gode entent, I trowe fulle, that God lovethe hem, and that God take hire servyse to gree, right as he did of Job, that was a Paynem, and held him for his trewe servaunt. And therfore alle be it that there ben many dyverse lawes in the world, zit I trowe, that God lovethe alweys hem that loven him, and serven him mekely in trouthe; and namely, hem that dispysen the veyn glorie of this world; as this folk don, and as Job did also: and therfore seyde oure Lorde, be the mouthe of Ozee the prophete, *Ponam eis multiplices leges meas*. And also in another place, *Qui totum orbem subdit suis legibus*. And also our Lord seythe in the Gospelle, *Alias oves habeo, que non sunt ex hoc ovili*; that is to seyne, that he hadde othere servauntes, than tho that ben undre Cristene lawe. And to that acordethe the avisioun, that Seynt Petir saughe at Jaffe, how the aungel cam from Hevene, and broughte before him diverse bestes, as serpentes and other crepynge bestes of the erthe, and of other also gret plentee, and bad him take and ete. And Seynt Petir answerde; I ete never, quoth he, of unclene bestes. And thanne seyde the aungelle, *Non dices immunda, que Deus mundavit*. And that was in tokene, that no man scholde have in despite non erthely man, for here diverse lawes: for wee knowe not whom God lovethe, ne whom God hatethe. And for that ensample, whan men seyn *De profundis*, thei seyn it in comoun and in generalle, with the Cristene, *pro animabus omnium defunctorum, pro quibus sit orandum*. And therfore seye I of this folk, that ben so trewe and so feythefulle, that God lovethe hem. For he hathe amonges hem many of the prophetes, and alle weye hathe had. And in tho yles, thei prophecyed the incarnacioun of oure Lord Jesu Crist, how he scholde ben born of a mayden; 3000 zeer or more or oure Lord was born of the Virgyne Marie. And thei beleeven wel in the incarnacioun, and that fulle perfitely: but thei knowe not the manere, how be suffred his passioun and dethe for us.

And bezonde theise yles, there is another yle, that is clept Pytan. The folk of that contree ne tyle not, ne laboure not the erthe: for thei eten no manere thing: and thei ben of gode colour, and of faire schap, aftre hire gretnesse: but the smalle ben as dwerghes: but not so litylle, as ben the pigmeyes. Theise men lyven be the smelle of wylde apples, and whan thei gon ony fer weye, thei beren the apples with hem. For zif the hadde lost the savour of the apples, thei scholde dyen anon. Thei ne ben not fulle resonable: but thei ben symple and bestyalle.

Aftre that, is another yle, where the folk ben alle skynned, roughe heer, as a rough best, saf only the face and the pawme of the hond. Theise folk gon als wel undir the watir of the see, as thei don above the lond, alle drye. And thei eten bothe flessche and fissche alle raughe. In this yle is a great ryvere, that is wel a 2 myle and an half of brede, that is clept Beumare. And fro that rivere a 15 journeyes in lengthe, goynge be the desertes of the tother syde of the ryvere, (whoso myght gon it, for I was not there: but it was told us of hem of the contree, that with inne tho desertes) weren the trees of the sonne, and of the mone, that spaken to Kyng Alisandre, and warned him of his dethe. And men seyn, that the folk that kepen tho trees, and eten of the frute and of the bawme that growethe there, lyven wel 400 zeere or 500 zere, be vertue of the frut and of the bawme. For men seyn, that bawme growethe there in gret plentee, and no where elles, saf only at Babyloyne, as I have told zou before. Wee wolde han gon toward the trees fulle gladly, zif wee had myght: but I trowe, that 100000 men of armes myghte not passen the desertes safly, for the gret multytude of wylde bestes, and of grete dragouns, and of grete multytude serpentes, that there ben, that slen and devouren alle that comen aneyntes hem. In that contre ben manye white olifantes with outen nombre, and of unycornes, and of lyouns of many maneres, and many of suche bestes, that I have told before, and of many other hydouse bestes with outen nombre.

Many other yles there ben in the lond of Prestre John, and many grete marveyles, that weren to long to tellen alle, bothe of his ricchesse and of his noblesse, and of the gret plentee also of precious stones, that he hathe. I trow that zee knowe wel y now, and have herd seye, wherefore the Emperour is clept Prestre John. But nathales for hem that knowen not, I schalle seye zou the cause. It was somtyme an Emperour there, that was a worthi and a fulle noble prynce, that hadde Cristene knyghtes in his companye, as he hathe that is how. So it befelle, that he hadde gret list for to see the service in the chirche, among Cristen men. And than dured Cristendom bezonde the zee, alle Turkye, Surrye, Tartarie, Jerusalem, Palestyne, Arabye, Halappee, and alle the lond of Egypte. So it befelle, that this emperour cam, with a Cristene knyght with him, into a chirche in Egypt: and it was the Saterday in Wyttson woke. And the bishop made ordres. And he beheld and listend the servyse fulle tentyfly: and he askede the Cristene knight, what men of degree thei scholden ben prestes. And than the emperour seyde, that he wolde no longer ben clept kyng ne emperour, but preest; and that he wolde have the name of the first preest, that went out of the chirche: and his name was John. And so evere more sithens, he is cleped Prestre John.

In his lond ben manye Cristene men of gode feythe and of gode lawe; and namely of hem of the same contree; and han comounly hire prestes, that syngen the messe, and maken the sacrement of the awtier of bred, right as the Grekes don: but thei seyn not so many thinges as the messe, as men don here. For thei seye not but only that, that the apostles seyden, as oure Lord taughte hem: righte as seynt Peter and seynt Thomas and the other apostles songen the messe, seyenge the Pater-noster, and the wordes of the sacrement. But wee have many mo addiciouns, that dyverse popes han made, that thei ne knowe not offe;

Of the Hilles of Gold, that Pissemyres kepen: and of the 4 Flodes, that comen fro Paradys terrestre.

[Sidenote: Cap. XXX.] Toward the est partye of Prestre Johnes lond, is an yle gode an gret, that men clepen Taprobane, that is fulle noble and fulle fructuous: and the kyng thereof is fulle ryche, and is undre the obeyssance of Prestre John. And alle weys there thei make hire king be eleccyoun. In that ile ben 2 someres and 2 wyntres; and men harvesten the corn twyes a zeer. And in alle the cesouns of the zeer ben the gardynes florisht. There dwellen gode folke and resonable, and manye Cristene men amonges hem, that ben so riche, that thei wyte not what to done with hire godes. Of olde tyme, whan men passed from the lond of Prestre John unto that yle, men maden ordynance for to passe by schippe, 23 dayes or more: but now men passen by schippe in 7 dayes. And men may see the botme of the see in many places: for it is not fulle depe.

Besyde that yle, toward the est, ben 2 other yles: and men clepen that on Orille, and that other Argyte; of the whiche alle the lond is myne of gold and sylver. And tho yles ben right where that the Rede See departethe fro the see occean. And in tho yles men seen ther no sterres so clerly as in other places: for there apperen no sterres, but only o clere sterre, that men clepen Canapos. And there is not the mone seyn in alle the lunacioun, saf only the seconde quarteroun. In the yle also of this Taprobane ben gret hilles of gold, that Pissemyres kepen fulle diligently. And thei fynen the pured gold, and casten away the unpured. And theise Pissemyres ben gret as houndes: so that no man dar come to tho hilles: for the Pissemyres wolde assaylen hem and devouren hem anon; so that no man may gete of that gold, but be gret sleighte. And therfore whan it is gret hete, the Pissemyres resten hem in the erthe, from pryme of the day in to noon: and than the folk of the con tree taken camayles, dromedaries and hors and other bestes and gon thidre, and chargen hem in alle haste that thei may. And aftre that thei fleen away, in alle haste that the bestes may go, or the Pissemyres comen out of the erthe. And in other tymes, whan it is not so hote, and that he Pissemyres ne resten hem not in the erthe, than thei geten gold be this sotyltee: thei taken mares, that han zonge coltes or foles, and leyn upon the mares voyde vesselles made therfore; and thei ben alle open aboven, and hangynge lowe to the erthe: and thanne thei sende forth tho mares for to pasturen aboute the hilles, and with holden the foles with hem at home. And whan the Pissemyres sen tho vesselles, thei lepen in anon, and thei han this kynde, that thei lete no thing ben empty among hem, but anon thei fillen it, be it what maner of thing that it be: and so thei fillen tho vesselles with gold. And whan that the folk supposen, that the vesselle ben fulle, thei putten forthe anon the zonge foles, and maken hem to nyzen aftre hire dames; and than anon the mares retornen towardes hire foles, with hire charges of gold; and than men dischargen hem, and geten gold y now be this sotyltee. For the Pissemyres wole suffren bestes to gon and pasturen amonges hem; but no man in no wyse.

And bezonde the lond and the yles and the desertes of Prestre Johnes lordschipe, in goynge streyght toward the est, men fynde nothing but mountaynes and roches fulle grete: and there is the derke regyoun, where no man may see, nouther be day ne be nyght, as thei of the contree seyn. And that desert, and that place of derknesse, duren fro this cost unto Paradys terrestre; where that Adam oure foremost fader, and Eve weren putt, that dwelleden there but lytylle while; and that is towards the est, at the begynnynge of the erthe. But that is not that est, that wee clep oure est, on this half, where the sonne risethe to us: for whenne the sonne is est in tho partyes, toward Paradys terrestre, it is thanne mydnyght in oure parties o this half, for the rowndenesse of the erthe, of the whiche I have towched to zou before. For oure Lord God made the erthe alle round, in the mydde place of the firmament. And there as mountaynes and hilles ben, and valeyes, that is not but only of Noes flode, that wasted the softe ground and the tendre, and felle doun into valeyes: and the harde erthe, and the roche abyden mountaynes, whan the soft erthe and tendre wax nessche, throghe the water, and felle and becamen valeyes.

Of Paradys, ne can not I speken propurly: for I was not there. It is fer bezonde; and that forthinkethe me: and also I was not worthi. But as I have herd seye of wyse men bezonde, I schalle telle zou with gode wille. Paradys terrestre, as wise men seyn, is the highest place of erthe, that is in alle the world: and it is so highe, that it touchethe nyghe to the cercle of the mone, there as the mone makethe hire torn. For sche is so highe, that the flode of

Noe ne myght not come to hire, that wolde have covered alle the erthe of the world alle aboute, and aboven and benethen, saf Paradys only allone. And this Paradys is enclosed alle aboute with a walle; and men wyte not wherof it is. For the walles ben covered alle over with mosse; as it semethe. And it semethe not that the walle is ston of nature. And that walle strecchethe fro the southe to the northe; and it hathe not but on entree, that is closed with fyre brennynge; so that no man, that is mortalle, ne dar not entren. And in the moste highe place of Paradys, evene in the myddel place, is a welle, that castethe out the 4 flodes, that rennen be dyverse londes: of the whiche, the first is clept Phison or Ganges, that is alle on: and it rennethe thorghe out Ynde or Emlak: in the whiche ryvere ben manye preciouse stones, and mochel of lignum aloes, and moche gravelle of gold. And that other ryvere is clept Nilus or Gyson, that gothe be Ethiope, and aftre be Egypt. And that other is clept Tigris, that rennethe be Assirye and be Armenye the grete. And that other is clept Eufrate, that rennethe also be Medee and be Armonye and be Persye. And men there bezonde seyn, that alle the swete watres of the world aboven and benethen, taken hire begynnynge of the welle of Paradys: and out of that welle, alle watres comen and gon. The firste ryvere is clept Phison, that is to seyne in hire langage, Assemblee: for many other ryveres meten hem there, and gon in to that ryvere. And sum men clepen it Ganges; for a kyng that was in Ynde, that highte Gangeres, and that it ran thorge out his lond. And that water is in sum place clere, and in sum place trouble: in sum place hoot, and in sum place cole. The seconde ryvere is clept Nilus or Gyson: for it is alle weye trouble: and Gyson, in the langage of Ethiope, is to seye trouble: and in the langage of Egipt also. The thridde ryvere, that is clept Tigris, is as moche for to seye as faste rennynge: for he rennethe more faste than ony of the tother. And also there is a best, that is cleped Tigris, that is faste rennynge. The fourthe ryvere is clept Eufrates, that is to seyne, wel berynge: for there growen manye godes upon that ryvere, as cornes, frutes, and othere godes y nowe plentee.

And zee schulle undirstonde, that no man that is mortelle, ne may not approchen to that paradys. For be londe no man may go for wylde bestes, that ben in the desertes, and for the highe mountaynes and gret huge roches, that no man may passe by, for the derke places that ben there, and that manye: and be the ryveres may no man go; for the water rennethe so rudely and so scharply, because that it comethe doun so outrageously from the highe places aboven, that it rennethe in so grete wawes, that no schipp may not rowe ne seyle azenes it: and the watre rorethe so, and makethe so huge noyse, and so gret tempest, that no man may here other in the schipp, thoughe he cryede with alle the craft that he cowde, in the hyeste voys that he myghte. Many grete lordes han assayed with gret wille many tymes for to passen be tho ryveres toward paradys, with fulle grete companyes: but thei myghte not speden in hire viage; and manye dyeden for werynesse of rowynge azenst tho stronge wawes; and many of hem becamen blynde, and many deve, for the noyse of the water: and summe weren perisscht and loste, with inne the wawes: so that no mortelle man may approche to that place, with outen specyalle grace of God: so that of that place I can seye zou no more. And therfor I schall holde me stille, and retornen to that that I have seen.

CAPVT. 49.

In reuertendo de Cassan, et Riboth, et de diuite Epulone.

[Sidenote: Via per quam Mandeuillus redijt in Angliam.] Ex hinc de illis quæ in reuertendo vidi scribo cursim pauca, ne modum excedere videatur materia. [Sidenote: Cassan.] Reuertebar itaque quasi per Aquilonare latus Imperij Presbyteri Ioannis, et nunc terræ, non mari nos commendantes, transiuimus Deo Ductore, multas Insulas in multis diaetis, et peruenimus ad regionem magnam Cassan: haec cum sit vna de quindecim habens longitudinem diaetarum 60. et latitudinem propè 30. posset esse nominatior omnibus ibi circa prouincijs, si a nostris frequentaretur.

Notandum. Cassan (secundum Odericum) est melior prouincia de mundo, vbi strictior est, habet diaetas 50. vbi longior 60, et est vna de 12. prouincijs Imperij Grand Can. Est ista populosa, distincta ciuitatibus, vt quisque à quacunque plaga de vna exeat ciuitate nouerit aliam in media diaeta propinquam. Tenétque istam regionem Cassan rex diues et potens, pro parte de Imperio Praebyteri Ioannis, et pro parte de Imperio Grand Can.

[Sidenote: Riboth.] De ista in reuersione nostra venimus ad Regnum Riboth, quod similiter est vnum de quindecim, latum, et speciosum, in quo de multis bonis, habetur plena copia. Hoc tenetur in toto de Imperio Tartarorum.

[Sidenote: Labassi, summus idolorum pontifex.] Vna est ibi inter et super omnes ciuitas Sacerdotalis, et Regia, in qua Rex habet suum magnificum palatium, et summus Idolorum Pontifex quem Labassi appellant, cui omnes Regni obediunt et populi sicut Domino Papæ nos Christiani quoniam et iubet, et benedicit, ac confert sacerdotibus beneficia idolorum.

Ciuitatis vndique muri sunt compacti albis et nigris lapidibus conquadratis ad modum scakarij, omnesque contractæ simili pauimento sunt stratæ. Tanta est illic reuerentia sacrificiorum vt si quis vel in modica quantitate, sanguinem hominis, seu immolaticiæ pecudis fudisse deprehensus fuerit, nequaquam iudicium mortis euadet. Et inter innumeras superstitiones est illic vna talis.

Haeres cuius pater defungitur, si alicuius vult esse reputationis, mandat cognatos, amicos, Relligiosos, et sacerdotes pro posse, qui certo Die conuenientes sub magno Symphoniæ festo, corportant defuncti cadauer, in montis sublime cacumen. Ibi accedens dignior Praelatorum, funeris caput abscindit, tradens haeredi in aureo disco decantanti sub deuotione suas orationes cum suis in propria lingua. Atque interim aues regionis rapaces, et immundæ, vt corui, vultures, et aquilæ, quæ pro consuetudine optimè morem norunt, aduolant magno numero in aere: Tuncque Relligiosi cum sacerdotibus detruncant corpus in frusta velut in macello, proijcientes pecias in altum auibus, ac decantantes certam ad hoc compositam orationem, tanquam si nostri sacerdotes cantarent. Subuenite sancti Dei, etc.

Et habet eorum oratio, hunc sensum in sua lingua. Respice quàm iustus et sanctus extitit homo iste, quem Angeli Dei conueniunt accipere et in Paradisum deferre. Talique diabolico errore delusi, putant filius, et amici, quod defunctus sit in Paradisum translatus, viuat illic sempiterne beatus, quoniam, vbi plures conuenere volucrum, ibi maiorem laetantur et iactant fuisse numerum Angelorum.

Hinc deinde reuertentes, cum choris, et resonantia Musicorum, filius paratum praestat omnibus conuiuium, in cuius fine pro extremo ferculo, tradit singulis particulam, de patris capite summa cum devotione. Hanc etiam capitis caluariam filius facit postmodum debitè formari et poliri sibi pro cypho, in quo bibit in conuijs, ob recordationem amantissimi patris.

Ab hoc Regno decem dietis per potestatem Imperatoris Grand Can, inuenitur Insula delectabilis, et speciosa satis: cuius Rex est praepotens in gloria, et in diuitijs superabundans, et de multis quæ illic geruntur admirandis vnum recito solum.

[Sidenote: Diues Epulo.] Quòd est ibi homo quidam ditissimus nullius dignitatis nomine honoratus, sed bysso, ac serico adornatus, et splendide omni tempore epulatus: non ergo vult dici princeps, Dux, comes, miles, aut huiusmodi, licet superioritatem habeat super marchiones aliquos et barones. Eius possessionis valor æstimatur in anno 30. cuman de assinarijs bladi, et risi, nec quærit nisi delitiosè viuere in isto seculo, vt cum diuite Epulone sepeliatur in inferno. Cum etiam sibi derelictus sit, iste viuendi modus a retrogenitoribus, eum et ipse posteris derelinquet. Hic tanquam Imperiali residet palatio, cuius muri ambitus ad tractum leucæ tenditur, continens arbusta, vineta, rinulos, fontes et stagna, aulas, et cubicula auro strata depictaque mirè, et sculpta artificiosè, vltra quam vales explicare, et inter omnia ad medium palatium in celso vertice atrium amaenum, valdè tamen modico, sed cunctis praeciosius, ædificio, quasi ad seema nostrarum Ecclesiarium, cum turribus, pilarijs, et columnis, in quibus nihil prominet indignius auro. Nunquam vel rarò hic exit de suo palatio cum solis pulchris quos sibi conuocat et conuariat paruis pueris et puellis, non excedentibus 16. annos ætatis. Tendit dum libet pedibus, quandoque vectatur equo, interdum ducitur vehiculo, nonnunquam vult ferri gestatorio, vel certè puellaribus brachijs, et visitat saepissimè praefatum praeciosius ædificium: atque hijs et modis alijs excogitat delectare visum pulchris, auditum suauibus, olfactum redolentibus, tactum lenibus, et gustum pascere delicatis. Electas semper habet praesto 50. puellas ei, et de proximo exquisitissimè ministrantes tam ad mensam quàm ad cubiculum, et ad omne libitum.

[Sidenote: Versus.] Hæ ad prandium recumbenti afferunt processionis more pro singulo ferculo semper 5. genera dapum nobilium cum dulcisonæ resonantia cantilenæ, quarum aliquæ ei singulos detruncant genu flexo morsellos, aliquæ ponunt in ore, mundis tergentes comedentis labia mappis.

Nam ipse quidem in mensa continet iacentes manus puras et quietas. Post deseruitionem ferculi primi, seruitur pro secundo in 5. alijs dapum generibus modo quo supra, et renouatur in apponendo cantus suauior melodia.

Ista àbsque vlla Domini cura per ministros quotidiè reparantur etiam in maiori satis quam effor nobilitate, nisi dum ipse pro placito iusserit, quandoque temperari.

Deliciosius igitur quo vult deducit carnem, non curans animam, sed nec probitatem curans terrenam, pascit sterilem, et viduæ non benefacit. Et

   Quia viuit sicut porcus,
   Morientem suscipit orcus.

[Sidenote: Longitudo vnguium. Vtunturetiam in Florida principes longis vnguibus.] Porrò quod eum dixi manus tenere quietas, noueritis nimirum nil posse manibus capere vel tenere, propter longitudinem, et recuruitatem vnguium in digitis, qui sibi nullo tempore praescinduntur. Seruatur enim hoc pro nobili more patriæ, et viri diuites delicati, qui proprios possunt habere ministros nunquàm sibi dimittunt vngues resecare, vnde et nonnullis circumdantur vndique manus, acsi uiderentur armatæ.

[Sidenote: Noua historia Chinensis hoc testatur.] Foeminarum autem mos est nobilis si habeant paruos pedes, vnde et generosarum in cunis strictissimè simè obuoluuntur, vt vix ad medium debitæ quantitatis excrescere possint.

The English Version.

Of the Customs of Kynges, and othere that dwellen in the Yles costynge to Prestre Johnes Lond. And of the Worschipe that the Sone dothe to the Fader, whan he is dede.

[Sidenote: Cap. XXXI.] From tho yles, that I have spoken of before, in the lond of Prestre John, that ben undre erthe as to us, that ben o this half, and of other yles, that ben more furthere bezonde; who so wil, pursuen hem, for to comen azen right to pursuen hem, for to comen azen right to the parties that he cam fro; and so environne alle erthe: but what for the yles, what for the see, and what for strong rowynge, fewe folk assayen for to passen that passage; alle be it that men myghte don it wel, that myght ben of power to dresse him thereto; as I have seyd zou before. And therfore men returnen from tho yles aboveseyd, be other yles costynge fro the lond of Prestre John. And thanne comen men in returnynge to an yle, that is clept Casson: and that yle hathe wel 60 jorrneyes in lengthe, and more than 50 in brede. This is the beste yle, and the beste kyngdom, that is in alle tho partyes, out taken Cathay. And zif the merchauntes useden als moche that contre an thei don Cathay, it wolde ben better than Cathay, in a schort while. This contree is fulle well enhabyted, and so fulle of cytees, and of gode townes, and enhabyted with peple, that whan a man gothe out of o cytee, men seen another cytee, evene before hem: and that is what partye that a man go, in alle that contree. In that yle is gret plentee of alle godes for to lyve with, and of alle manere of spices. And there ben grete forestes of chesteynes. The kyng of that yle is fulle ryche and fulle myghty: and natheles he holt his lond of the grete Chane, and is obeyssant to hym. For it is on of the 12 provynces, that the grete Chane hathe undre him, with outen his propre lond, and with outen other lesse yles, that he hathe: for he hathe fulle manye.

From that kyngdom comen men, in returnynge, to another yle, that is clept Rybothe: and it is also under the grete Chane. That is a fulle gode contree, and fulle plentefous of alle godes and of wynes and frut, and alle other ricchesse. And the folk of that contree han none houses: but thei dwellen and lyggen all under tentes, made of black ferne, by alle the contree. And the princypalle cytee, and the most royalle, is alle walled with black ston and white. And alle the stretes also ben pathed of the same stones. In that cytee is no man so hardy, to schede Blode of no man, ne of no best, for the reverence of an ydole, that is worschipt there. And in that yle dwellethe the pope of hire lawe, that they clepen Lobassy. This Lobassy zevethe alle the benefices, and alle other dignytees, and all other thinges, that belongen to the ydole. And alle tho that holden ony thing of hire chirches, religious and othere, obeyen to him; as men don here to the Pope of Rome.

In that yle thei han a custom, be alle the contree, that whan the fader is ded of ony man, and the sone list to do gret worchipe to his fader, he sendethe to alle his frendes, and to all his kyn, and for religious men and preestes, and for mynstralle also, gret plentee. And thanne men beren the dede body unto a gret hille, with gret joye and solempnyte. And when thei han brought it thider, the chief prelate smytethe of the hede, and leythe it upon a gret platere of Gold and of sylver, zif so be he be a riche man; and than he takethe the hede to the sone; and thanne the sone and his other kyn syngen and seyn manye orisouns: and thanne the prestes, and the religious men, smyten alle the body of the dede man in peces: and thanne thei seyn certeyn orisouns. And the fowles of raveyne of alle the contree abouten knowen the custom of long tyme before, and comen fleenge aboyen in the eyr, as egles, gledes, ravenes and othere foules of raveyne, that eten flesche. And than the preestes casten the gobettes of the flesche; and than the foules eche of hem takethe that he may, and gothe a litille thens and etethe it: and so thei don whils ony pece lastethe of the dede body. And aftre that, as preestes amonges us syngen for the dede, *Subvenite sancti Dei*, &c. right so the preestes syngen with highe voys in hire langage, beholdethe how so worthi a man, and how gode a man this was, that the aungeles of God comen for to sechen him, and for to bryngen him in to paradys. And thanne semethe in to the sone, that he is highliche worschipt, whan that many briddes and foules and raveyne comen and eten his fader. And he that hathe most nombre of foules, is most worschiped. Thanne the sone bryngethe hoom with him alle his kyn, and his frendes, and alle the othere to his hows, and makethe hem a gret feste. And thanne alle his frendes maken hire avaunt and hire dalyance, how the fowles comen thider, here 5, here 6, here 10, and there 20, and so forthe: and thei rejoyssen hem hugely for to speke there of. And whan thei ben at mete, the sone let brynge forthe the hede of his fader, and there of he zevethe of the flesche to his most specyalle frendes, in stede of entre messe, or a sukkarke. And of the brayn panne, he letethe make a cuppe, and there of drynkethe he and his other frendes also, with great devocioun, in remembrance of the holy man, that the aungeles of God han eten. And that cuppe the sone schalle kepe to drynken of, alle his lif tyme, in remembrance of his fadir.

From that lond, in returnynge be 10 jorneyes thorghe out the lond of the grete Chane, is another gode yle, and a gret kyngdom, where the kyng is fulle riche and myghty. And amonges the riche men of his contree, is a passynge riche man, that is no prince, ne duke ne erl; but he hathe mo that holden of him londes and other lordschipes: for he is more riche. For he hathe every zeer of annuelle rente 300000 hors charged with corn of dyverse greynes and of ryzs: and so he ledethe a fulle noble lif, and a delycate, aftre the custom of the contree. For he hathe every day, 50 fair damyseles, alle maydenes, that serven him everemore at his mete, and for to lye be hem o nyght, and for to do with hem that is to his pleasance. And whan he is at the table, they bryngen him hys mete at every tyme, 5 and 5 to gedre. And in bryngynge hire servyse, thei syngen a song. And aftre that, thei kutten his mete, and putten it in his mouthe; for he touchethe no thing ne handlethe nought, but holdethe evere more his hondes before him, upon the table. For he hathe so long nayles, that he may take no thing, ne handle no thing. For the noblesse of that contree is to have longe nayles, and to make hem growen alle weys to ben as longe as men may. And there ben manye in that contree, that han hire nayles so longe, that thei envyronne alle the hond: and that is a gret noblesse. And the noblesse of the wommen, is for to haven smale feet and litille: and therfore anon as thei ben born, they leet bynde hire feet so streyte, that thei may not growen half as nature wolde; and alle weys theise damyseles, that I spak of beforn, syngen alle the tyme that this riche man etethe: and whan that he etethe no more of his firste cours, than other 5 and 5 of faire damyseles bryngen him his seconde cours, alle weys syngynge, as thei dide beforn. And so thei don contynuelly every day, to the ende of his mete. And in this manere he ledethe his lif. And so dide thei before him, that weren his auncestres; and so schulle thei that comen aftre him, with outen doynge of ony dedes of armes: but lyven evere more thus in ese, as a swyn, that is fedde in sty, for to ben made fatte. He hathe a fulle fair palays and fulle riche, where that he dwellethe inne: of the whiche, the walles ben in circuyt 2 myle: and he hathe with inne many faire gardynes, and many faire halles and chambres, and the pawment of his halles and chambres ben of gold and sylver. And in the myd place of on of his gardynes, is a lytylle mountayne, wher there is a litylle medewe: and in that medewe, is a litylle toothille with toures and pynacles, alle of gold: and in that litylle toothille wole he sytten often tyme, for to taken the ayr and to desporten hym: for that place is made for no thing elles, but only for his desport.

Fro that contree men comen be the lond of the grete Chane also, that I have spoken of before.

And ze schulle undirstonde, that of alle theise contrees, and of alle theise yles, and of alle the dyverse folk, that I have spoken of before, and of dyverse lawes, and of dyverse beleeves that thei han; zit is there non of hem alle, but that thei han sum resoun with in hem and undirstondynge, but zif it be the fewere: and that han certeyn articles of oure feithe and summe gode poyntes of oure beleeve: and that thei beleeven in God, that formede alle thinges and made the world; and clepen him God of Nature, aftre that the prophete seythe, *Et metuent cum omnes fines terre*: and also in another place, *Omnes gentes servient ei*; that is to seyn, *Alle folke schalle serven Him*. But zit thei cone not speken perfytly; (for there is no man to techen hem) but only that thei cone devyse be hire naturelle wytt. For thei han no knouleche of the Sone, ne of the Holy Gost: but thei cone alle speken of the Bible: and namely of Genesis, of the prophetes lawes, and of the Bokes of Moyses. And thei seyn wel, that the creatures, that thei worschipen, ne ben no goddes: but thei worschipen hem, for the vertue that is in hem, that may not be, but only be the grace of God. And of simulacres and of ydoles, thei seyn, that there ben no folk, but that thei han simulacres: and that thei seyn, for we Cristene men han ymages, as of Oure Lady, and of othere seyntes, that wee worschipen; nohte the ymages of tree or of ston, but the seyntes, in whoos name thei ben made aftre. For righte as the bokes of the Scripture of hem techen the clerkes, how and in what manere thei schulle beleeven, righte so the ymages and the peyntynges techen the lewed folk to worschipen the seyntes, and to have hem in hire mynde, in whoos name that the ymages ben made aftre. Thei seyn also, that the aungeles of God speken to hem in tho ydoles, and that thei don manye grete myracles. And thei seyn sothe, that there is an aungele with in hem: for there ben 2 maner of aungeles, a gode and an evelle; as the Grekes seyn, Cacho and Calo; this Cacho is the wykked aungelle, and Calo is the gode aungelle: but the tother is not the gode aungelle, but the wykked aungelle, that is with inne the ydoles, for to disceyven hem, and for to meyntenen hem in hire errour.

CAPVT. 50.

De compositione huius tractatus in nobili ciuitate Leodiensi.

In reuertendo igitur venitur ab hac insula per prouincias magnas Imperij Tartarorum, in quibus semper noua, semper mira, imo nonnunquam incredibilia viator potest videre, percipere, et audire.

Et Noueritis, vt praedixi, me pauca eorum vidisse, quæ in terris sunt mirabilium, sed nec hic scripsisse centessimam partem eorum quæ vidi, quod nec omnia memoriæ commendare potui, et de commendatis multa subticui, proptèr modestiam, quam decet omnibus actibus addi.

Idcirco vt et alijs, qui vel antè me in partibus illis steterunt, vel ituri sunt, maneat locus narrandi siue scribendi, modum huius pono tractatus, potius decurtans quàm complens, quoniam aliàs loquendi non esset finis, nec aures implerentur auditu.

[Sidenote: Concludit opus suum.] Itàque anno à natiuitate Domini nostri Iesu Christi 1355. in patriando, cum ad nobilem Legiæ, seu Leodij ciuitatem peruenissem, et præ grandeuitate ac artericis guttis illic decumberem in vico qui dicitur, Bassessanemi, consului causa conualescendi aliquos medicos ciuitatis: Et accidit, Dei nutu, vnum intrare physicum super alios ætate simul et canicie venerandum, ac in sua arte euidenter expertum, qui ibidem dicebatur communiter, Magister Ioannes ad barbam.

Is, dum paritèr colloqueremur, interseruit aliquid dictis, per quod tandem nostra inuicem renouabatur antiqua notitia, quam quondam habueramus in Cayr Aegypti apud Melech Mandibron Soldanum, prout suprà tetigi in 7. capitulo libri.

Qui cum in me experientiam artis suæ excellenter monstrasset, adhortabatur ac praecabatur instanter, vt de hijs quæ videram tempore peregrinationis, et itinerationis meæ per mundum, aliquid digererem in scriptis ad legendum, et audiendum pro vtilitate.

Sicque tandem illius monitu et adiutorio, compositus est iste tractatus, de quo certè nil scribere proposueram, donec saltem ad partes proprias in Anglia peruenissem. [Sidenote: Edwardus tertius.] Et credo praemissa circa me, per prouidentiam et gratiam Dei contigisse, quoniam à tempore quo recessi, duo reges nostri Angliæ, et Franciæ, non cessauerunt inuicem exercere destructiones, depraedationes, insidias, et interfectiones, inter quas, nisi à Domino custoditus, non transissem sine morte, vel mortis periculo, et sine criminum grandi cumulo. Et ecce nunc egressionis meæ anno 33. constitutus in Leodij ciuitate, quæ à mari Angliæ distat solum per duas diætas, audio dictas Dominorum inimicitias, per gartiam Dei consopitas: quapropter et spero, ac propono de reliquo secundum maturiorem ætatem me posse in proprijs, intendere corporis quieti, animaeque saluti.

Hie itaque finis sit scripti, in nomine Patris, et Filij, et spiritus sancti, AMEN.

Explicit itinerarium à terra Angliæ, in partes Hierosolimitanas, et in vlteriores transmarinas, editum primò in lingua Gallicana, à Domino Ioanne Mandeuille milite, suo authore, Anno incarnationis Domini 1355. in Ciuitate Leodiensi: Et Paulò post in eadem ciuitate, translatum in dictam formam Latinam.

The English Version.

There ben manye other dyverse contrees and manye other marveyles bezonde, that I have not seen: wherfore of hem I can not speke propurly, to telle zou the manere of hem. And also in the contrees where I have ben, ben many dyversitees of manye wondir fulle thinges, mo thanne I make mencioun of. For it were to longe thing to devyse zou the manere. And therfore that that I have devised zou of certeyn contrees, that I have spoken of before, I beseche zoure worthi and excellent noblesse, that it suffise to zou at this tyme. For zif that I devysed zou alle that is bezonde the see, another man peraunter, that wolde peynen him and travaylle his body for to go in to tho marches, for to encerche tho contrees, myghten ben blamed be my wordes, in rehercynge many straunge thynges. For he myghten not seye no thing of newe, in the whiche the hereres myghten haven outher solace or desport or lust or lykynge in the herynge. For men seyn alle weys, that newe thynges and newe tydynges ben plesant to here. Wherfore I wole holde me stille, with outen ony more rehercyng of dyversiteez or of marvaylles, that ben bezonde, to that entent and ende, that who so wil gon in to the contrees, he schalle fynde y nowe to speke of, that I have not touched of in no wyse.

And zee schulle undirstonde, zif it lyke zou, that at myn hom comynge, I cam to Rome, and schewed my lif to oure holy fadir the Pope, and was assoylled of alle that lay in my conscience, of many a dyverse grevous poynt: as men mosten nedes, that ben in company, dwellyng amonges so many a dyverse folk of dyverse secte and of beleeve, as I have ben. And amonges alle, I schewed hym this tretys, that I had made aftre informacioun of men, that knewen of thinges, that I had not seen my self; and also of marveyles and customes, that I hadde seen my self; as fer as God wolde zeve me grace: and besoughte his holy fadirhode, that my boke myghten be examyned and corrected be avys of his wyse and discreet conscille. And oure holy fadir, of his special grace, remytted my boke to ben examyned and preved be the avys of his seyd conscille. Be the whiche, my boke was preeved for trewe; in so moche that thei schewed me a boke, that my boke was examynde by, that comprehended fulle moche more, ben an hundred part; be the whiche, the *Mappa Mundi* was made after. And so my boke (alle be it that many men ne list not to zeve credence to no thing, but to that that thei seen with hire eye, ne be the auctour ne the persone never so trewe) is affermed and preved be oure holy fadir, in maner and forme as I have seyd.

And I John Maundevylle knyghte aboveseyd, (alle thoughe I ben unworthi) that departed from oure contrees and passed the see, the zeer of grace 1322, that have passed many londes and manye yles and contrees, and cerched manye fulle straunge places, and have ben in manye a fulle gode honourable comyanye, and at many a faire dede of armes, (alle be it that I dide none my self, for myn unable insuffisance) now I am comen hom (mawgree my self) to reste: for gowtes, artetykes, that me distreynen, tho diffynen the ende of my labour, azenst my wille (God knowethe). And thus takynge solace in my wrecched reste, recordynge the tyme passed, I have fulfilled theise thinges and putte hem wryten in this boke, as it wolde come in to my mynde, the zeer of grace 1356 in the 34 zeer that I departede from oure contrees. Wherfore I preye to alle the rederes and hereres of this boke, zif it plese hem, that thei wolde preyen to God for me: and I schalle preye for hem. And alle tho that seyn for me a *Pater nostre*, with an *Ave Maria*, that God forzeve me my synnes, I make hem parteneres, and graunte hem part of alle the gode pilgrymages and of alle the gode dedes, that I have don, zif ony be to his plesance: and noghte only of tho, but of alle that evere I schalle do unto my lyfes ende. And I beseche Almighty God, fro whom alle godenesse and grace comethe fro, that he vouchesaf, of his excellent mercy and habundant grace, to fulle fylle hire soules with inspiracioun of the Holy Gost, in makynge defence of alle hire gostly enemyes here in erthe, to hire salvacioun, bothe of body and soule; to worschipe and thankynge of Him, that is three and on, with outen begynnynge and withouten endynge; that is, with outen qualitee, good, and with outen quantytee, gret; that in alle places is present, and alle thinges conteynynge; the whiche that no goodnesse may amende, ne non evelle empeyre; that in perfeyte Trynytee lyvethe and regnethe God, be alle worldes and be alle tymes. Amen, Amen, Amen.

* * * * *

Richardi Hakluyti breuis admonitio ad Lectorem.

Ioannem Mandeuillum nostratem, eruditum et insignem Authorem (Balaeo, Mercatore, Ortelio, et alijs, testibus) ab innumeris Scribarum et Typographorum mendis repurgando, ex multorum, eorumque optimorum exemplarium collatione, quid praestiterim, virorum doctorum, et eorum praecipuè, qui Geographiæ et Antiquitatis periti sunt, esto iudicium. Quæ autem habet de monstriferis hominum formis itinerarij sui praecedentis capitibus trigessimo, trigessimo primo, trigessimo tertio, et sparsim in sequentibus, quanquam non negem ab illo fortasse quædam eorum alicubi visa fuisse, maiori tamen ex parte ex Caio Plinio secundo hausta videntur, vt facile patebit ca cum his Plinianis, hic ideo a me appositis, collaturo, quæ idem Plinius, singulis suis authoribus singula refert, in eorum plærisque fidem suam minimè obstringens. Vale, atque aut meliora dato, aut his vtere mecum.

* * * * *

Ex libro sexto Naturalis historiæ C. Plinij secundi. Cap. 30.

Vniuersa verò gens Ætheria appellata est, deinde Atlantia, mox à Vulcani filio Æthiope Æthiopia. Animalium hominumque effigies monstriferas circa extremitates eius gigni minimè mirum, artifici ad formanda corpora effigiésque caelandas mobilitate ignea. Ferunt certè ab Orientis parte intimatgentes esse sine naribus. æquali totius oris planitie. Alias superiore labro orbas, alias sine linguis. Pars etiam ore concreto et naribus carens, vno tantùm foramine spirat, potùmque calamis auenæ trahit, et grana eiusdem auenæ, sponte prouenientis ad vescendum; Quibusdam pro sermone nutus motùsque membrorum est, &c.

* * * * *

Ex libro eiusdem Plinij septimo. Cap. 2. cui titulus est, De Scythis, et aliarum diversitate gentium.

Esse Scytharum genera, et quidem plura, quæ corporibus humanis vescerentur, indicauimus. Idipsum incredibile fortasse, ni cogitimus in medio orbe terrarum, ac Sicilia et Italia fuisse, gentes huius monstri, Cyclopas et Laestrigonas, et nuperrimè trans Alpes hominem immolari gentium carum more solitum: quod paulum à mandendo abest. Sed et iuxta eos, qui sunt ad Septentrionem versi, haud procul ab ipso Aquilonis exortu, specuque eius dicto, quem locum Gesclitron appellant, produntur Arimaspi, duos diximus, vno oculo in fronte media insignes: quibus assiduè bellum esse circa metalla cum gryphis, ferarum volucri genere, quale vulgò traditur, eruente ex cuniculis aurum, mira cupiditate et feris custodientibus, et Arimaspis rapientibus, multi, sed maximè illustres Herodotus, et Aristeas Proconnesius scribunt. Super alios autem Anthropophagos Scythas, in quadam conualle magna Imai montis, regio est, quæ vocatur Abarimon, in qua syluestres viuunt homines, auersis post crura plantis, eximiæ velocitatis, passim cum feris vagantes. Hos in alio non spirare coelo, ideoque ad finitimos reges non pertrahi, neque ad Alexandrum magnum pertractos, Beton itinerum eius mensor prodidit. Priores Anthropophagos, quos ad Septentrionem esse diximus decem dierum itinere supra Borysthenem amnem, ossibus humanorum capitum bibere, cutibusque cum capillo pro mantelibus ante pectora vti, Isigonus Nicænsis. Idem in Albania gigni quosdam glauca oculorum acie, à pueritia statim canos, qui noctu plusquàm interdiu cernant. Idem itinere dierum x. supra Borysthenem, Sauromatas tertio die cibum capere semper. Crates Pergamenus in Hellesponto circa Parium, genus hominum fuisse tradit, quos Ophiogenes vocat serpentum ictus contactu leuare solitos, et manu imposita venena extrahere corpori. Varro etiam nunc esse paucos ibi, quorum saliuæ contra ictus serpentum medeantur. Similis et in Africa gens Psyllorum fuit, vt Agatharchides scribit, à Psyllo rege dicta, cuius sepulchrum in parte Syrtium maiorum est. Horum corpori ingenitum fuit virus exitiale serpentibus, vt cuius odore sopirent eas. Mos verò, liberos genitos protinus obijciendi saeuissimis earum, eòque genere pudicitiam coniugum experiendi, non profugientibus adulterino sanguine natos serpentibus. Haec gens ipsa quidem prope internicione sublata est à Nasamonibus, qui nunc eas tenent sedes: genus tamen hominum ex his qui profugerant, aut cùm pugnatum est, abfuerant, hodièque remanent in paucis. Simile et in Italia Marsorum gentis durat, quos à Circes filio ortos seruant, et ideo inesse ijs vim naturalem eam. Et tamen omnibus hominibus contra serpentes inest venenum: ferùntque ictas saliua, vt feruentis aquæ contactum fugere. Quòd si in fauces penetrauerit, etiam mori: idque maximè humani ieiuni oris. Supra Nasamonis confinésque illis Machlyas, Androginos esse vtriusque naturæ, inter se vicibus coeuntes, Calliphanes tradit. Aristoteles adijcit, dextram mammam ijs virilem, lacuam muliebrem esse. In eadem Africa familias quasdam effascinantium, Isigonus et Nymphodorus tradunt quarum laudatione intereant probata, arescant arbores, emoriantur infantes. Esse eiusdem generis in Triballis et Illyrijs, adijcit Isigonus, qui visu quoque effascinent, interimantque quos diutius intueantur. Iratis praecipuè oculis: quod eorum malum faciliùs sentire puberes. Notabilius esse quòd pupillas binas in oculis singulis habeant. Huius generis et foeminas in Scythia, quæ vocantur Bithyæ, prodit Apollonides. Philarchus et in Ponto Thibiorum genus, multosque alios eiusdem naturæ: quorum notas tradit in altero oculo geminam pupillam, in altero equi effigiem. Eosdem præterea non posse mergi, ne veste quidem degrauatos. Haud dissimile ijs genus Pharnacum in Æthiopia prodidit Damon, quorum sudor tabem contactis corporibus afferat. Foeminas quidem omnes vbique visu nocere, quæ duplices pupillas habeant, Cicero quoque apud nos autor est. Adeò naturæ, cùm ferarum morem vescendi humanis visceribus in homine genuisset, gignere etiam in toto corpore et in quorundam oculis quoque venena placuit: ne quid vsquam mali esset, quod in homine non esset. Haud procul vrbe Roma in Faliscorum agro familiæ sum paucæ, quæ vocantur Hirpiæ: quæ sacrificio annuo, quod fit ad montem Soractem Apollini, super ambustam ligni struem ambulantes non aduruntur. Et ob id perpetuo senatusconsulto militiæ omniumque aliorum numerum vacationem habent. Quorundam corpore partes nascuntur ad aliqua mirabiles sicut Pyrrho regi pollex in dextero pede: cuius tactu lienosis medebatur. Hunc cremari cum reliquo corpore non potuisse tradunt, conditumque loculo in templo. Præcipuè India Æthiopumque tractus, miraculis scatent. Maxima in India gignuntur animalia, Indicio sunt canes grandioris cæteris. Arbores quidem tantæ proceritatis traduntur, vt sagittis superari nequeant. Hæc facit vbertas soli, temperies coeli, aquarum abundantia (si libeat credere) vt sub vna ficu turmæ condantur equitum. Arundines verò tantæ proceritatis, vt singula internodia alueo nauigabili ternos interdum homines ferant. Multos ibi quina cubita constat longitudine excedere: non expuere: non capitis, aut dentium, aut oculorum vllo dolore affici, rarò aliarum corporis partium: tam moderato Solis vapore durari. Philosophos eorum quos Gymnosophystas vocant, ab exortu ad Occasum præstare, contuentes Solem immobilibus oculis: feruentibus harenis toto die alternis pedibus insistere. In monte cui nomen est Milo, homines esse auersis plantis, octonos digitos in singulis pedibus habentes, autor est Megasthenes. In multis autem montibus genus hominum capitibus caninis, ferarum pellibus velari, pro voce latratum edere, vnguibus armatum venatu et aucupio vesci. Horum supra centum viginti millia fuisse prodente se, Ctesias scribit: et in quadam gente Indiæ, foeminas semel in vita parere, genitosque confestim canescere. Item hominum genus, qui Monosceli vocarentur, singulis cruribus, miræ pernicitatis ad saltum: eosdemque Sciopodas vocari, quòd in maiori æstu humi iacentes resupini, vmbra se pedum protegant, non longè eos à Troglodytis abesse. Rursusque ab his Occidentem versus quosdam sine ceruice, oculos in humeris habentes. Sunt et Satyri subsolanis Indorum montibus (Cartadalorum dicitur Regio) pernicissimum animal, tum quadrupedes, tum rectè currentes humana effigie propter velocitatem, nisi senes aut ægri, non capiuntur. Choromandarum gentem vocat Tauron siluestrem sine voce, stridoris horrendi, hirtis corporibus, oculis glaucis, dentibus caninis. Eudoxus in meridianis Indiæ viris plantas esse cubitales, foeminis adeò paruas, vt Struthopodes appellentur. Megastenes gentem inter Nomadas Indos narium loco foramina tantùm habentem, anguium modo loripedem, vocarit Syrictas. Ad extremos fines Indiæ ab Oriente, circa fontem Gangis, Astomorum gentem sine ore, corpore toto hirtam vestiri frondium lanugine, halitu tantùm viuentem et odore quem naribus trahant: nullum illis cibum, nullumque potum: tantum radicum florumque varios odores et syluestrium malorum, quæ secum portant longiore itinere, ne desit olfactus, grauiore paulò odore haud difficulter examinari. Supra hos extrema in parte montium Spithamaei Pygmaei narrantur, ternas spithamas longitudine, hoc est, ternos dodrantos non excedentes, salubri caelo, sempérque vernante, montibus ab Aquilone oppositis, quos à gruibus infestari Homerus quoque prodidit: Fama est, insidentes arietum, caprarumque dorsis, armatos sagittis, veris tempore, vniuerso agmine ad mare descendere, et oua pullosque earum alitum consumere, ternis expeditionem eam mensibus confici, aliter futuris gregibus non resisti. Casas eorum luto, pennisque, et ouorum putaminibus construi. Aristotelis in cauernis viuere Pygmaeos tradit. Caetera de his, vt reliqui. Cyrnos Indorum genus Isigonus annis centenis quadragenis viuere. Item Aethiopas Marcrobios, et Seras existimat, et qui Athon montem incolant: hos quidem quia viperinis carnibus alantur, itaque nec capiti, nec vestibus eorum noxia corpori inesse animalia. Onesicritus, quibus in locis Indiæ vmbræ non sint, corpora hominum cubitorum quinum, et binorum palmorum existere, et viuere annos centum triginta, nec senescere, sed vt medio æuo mori. Crates Pergamenus Indos, qui centenos annos excedant Gymnætas appelat, non pauci Macrobios. Ctesias gentem ex his, quæ appellatur Pandore, in conuallibus sitam, annos ducenos viuere, in iuuenta candido capillo, qui in senectute nigrescat. Contra alios quadragenos non excedere annos, iunctos Macrobijs, quorum foeminæ semel pariant: idque et Agatharchides tradit, præextereà locustis eos ali, et esse pernices. Mandrorum nomen ijs dedit Clitarchus et Megastenes, trecentosque eorum vicos annumerat. Foeminas septimo ætatis anno parere, senectam quadragesimo anno accedere. Artemidorus, in Taprobana insula longissimam vitam sine vllo corporis languore traduci. Duris, Indorum quosdam cum feris coire, mistosque et semiferos esse partus. In Calingis eiusdem Indiæ gente quinquennes concipere foeminas, octauum vitæ annum non excedere, et alibi cauda villosa homines nasci pernicitatis eximiæ, alios auribus totos contegi. Oritas ab Indis Arbis fluuius disterminat. Ii nullum alium cibum nouere, quàm piscium, quos vnguibus dissectos sole torreant, atque ita panem ex his faciunt, vt refert Clitarchus. Troglodytas super Aethiopiam velociores esse equis, Pergamenus Crates. Item Aethiopas octona cubita longitudine excedere. Syrbotas vocari gentem eam Nomadum Aethiopum, secundùm flumen Astapum ad Septentrionem vregentium. [Marginal note: Vel vergentium.] Gens Menisminorum appellata, abest ab oceana dierum itinere viginti, animalium que Cynocephalos vocamus, lacte viuit, quorum armenta pacscit maribus interemptis, praeterquam sobolis causa. In Africæ solitudinibus hominum species obuiæ subinde fiunt, momentoque euanescunt. Haec atque talia, ex hominum genere ludibria sibi, nobis miracula, ingeniosa fecit natura: et singula quidem, quæ facit indies, ac propè horas, quis enumerare valeat? Ad detegendam eius potentiam, satis sit inter prodigia posuisse gentes.

END OF MANDEVILLE'S VOYAGES.

* * * * *

Anthony Beck bishop of Durisme was elected Patriarch of Hierusalem, and confirmed by Clement the fift bishop of Rome: in the 34 yere of Edward the first. Lelandus.

Antonius Beckus episcopus Dunelmensis fuit, regnante Edwardo eius appelationis ab aduentu Gulielmi magni in Angliam primo. Electus est in patriarcham Hierosolymitanum anno Christo 1305, et a Clemente quinto Rom. pontifice confirmatus. Splendidus erat supra quàm decebat episcopum. Construxit castrum Achelandæ, quatuor passuum millibus a Dunelmo in ripa Vnduglessi fluuioli. Elteshamum etiam vicinum Grenouico, ac Somaridunum castellum Lindianæ prouinciæ, ædificijs illustria reddidit. Deinde et palatium Londini erexit, quod nunc Edwardi principis est. Tandem ex splendore nimio, et potentia conflauit sibi apud nobilitatem ingentem inuidiam, quam viuens nunquam extinguere potuit. Sed de Antonio, et eius scriptis fusiùs in opere, cuius titulus de pontificibus Britannicis, dicemus. Obijt Antonius anno a nato in salutem nostram Christo, 1310, Edwardo secundo regnante.

The same in English.

Anthony Beck was bishop of Durisme in the time of the reigne of Edward the first of that name after the inuasion of William the great into England. This Anthony was elected patriarch of Ierusalem in the yeere of our Lord God 1305, and was confirmed by Clement the fift, pope of Rome. He was of greater magnificence then for the calling of a bishop. He founded also the castle of Acheland foure miles from Durisme, on the shore of a prety riuer called Vnduglesme. [Footnote: Probably Barnard Castle, on the Tees.] He much beautified with new buildings Eltham mannor nere vnto Greenwich, and the castle Somaridune in the county of Lindsey. [Footnote: Lindsey is the popular name for the north part of County Lincoln.] And lastly, he built new out of the ground the palace of London, which now is in possession of prince Edward. Insomuch, that at length, through his ouer great magnificence and power he procured to himselfe great enuy among the nobility, which he could not asswage during the rest of his life. But of this Anthony and of his writings we will speake more at large in our booke intituled of the Britain bishops. This Anthony finished his life in the yere of our Lord God, 1310, and in the reigne of king Edward the second.

* * * * *

Incipit Itinerarium fratris Odorici fratrum minorum de mirabilibus Orientalium Tartarorum.

Licet multa et varia de ritibus et conditionibus huius mundi enarrentur a multis, ego tamen frater Odoricus de foro Iulij de portu Vahonis, volens ad partes infidelium transfretare, magna et mira vidi et audiui, quæ possum veracitèr enarrare. Primò transiens Mare Maius me de Pera iuxta Constantinopolim transtuli Trapesundam, quæ antiquitùs Pontus vocabatur: Haec terra benè situata est, sicut scala quaedam Persarum et Medorum, et eorum qui sunt vltra mare. In hac terra vidi mirabile quod mihi placuit, scilicet hominem ducentem secum plusquam 4000 perdicum. Homo autem per terram gradiebatur, perdices vero volabant per aera, quas ipse ad quoddam castrum dictum Zauena duxit, distans à Trapesunda per tres dietas. Hæ perdices illius conditionis erant, cùm homo ille quiescere voluit, omnes se aptabant circa ipsum, more pullorum gallinarum, et per illum modum duxit eas vsque ad Trapesundam, et vsque ad palatium imperatoris, qui de illis sumpsit quot voluit, et residuas vir ille ad locum vnde venerat, adduxit. In hac ciuitate requiescit corpus Athanasij supra portem ciuitatis. [Sidenote: Armenis maior.] Vltra transiui vsque in Armeniam maiorem, ad quandam ciuitatem quæ vocatur Azaron, quæ erat multùm opulenta antiquitus, sed Tartari eam pro magna parte destruxterunt: In ea erat abundantia panis et carnium, et aliorum omnium victualium praeterquam vini et fructuum. Hæc ciuitas est multum frigida, et de illa dicitur quòd altius situatur quàm aliqua alia in hoc mundo: haec optimas habet aquas, nam venæ illarum aquarum oriri videntur et scaturire à flumine magno Euphrate quod per vnam dietam ab ciuitate distat: haec ciuitas via media eundi Taurisium. Vltra progressus sum ad quendam montem dictum Sobissacato. In ilia contrau est mons ille supra quem requicscit arca Noe; in quem libenter ascendissem, si societas mea me praestolare voluisset: A gente tamen illius contratæ dicitur quòd nullus vnquam illum montem ascendere potuit, quia vt dicitur, hoc Deo altissimo non placet. [Sidenote: Tauris ciuitas Persiæ.] Vltra veni Tauris ciuitatem magnam et regalem, quæ antiquitus Susis dicta est. Haec ciuitas melior pro mercenarijs reputatur, quàm aliqua quæ sit in mundo, nam nihil comestibile, nec aliquid quod ad mercimonium pertinet, reperitur, quod illic in bona copia non habetur. Haec ciuitas multum benè situatur: Nam ad eam quasi totus mundus pro mercimonijs confluere potest: De hac dicunt Christiani qui ibi sunt, quòd credunt Imperatorem plus de ea accipere, quàm Regem Franciæ de toto regno suo: Iuxta illam ciuitatem est mons salinus praebens sal ciuitati, et de illo sale vnusquisque tantum accipit, quantum vult, nihil soluendo alicui. In hac ciuitate multi Christiani de omni natione commorantur, quibus Saraceni in omnibus dominantur. [Sidenote: Sultania.] Vltra iui per decem dietas ad ciuitatem dictam Soldania, in qua imperator Persarum tempore æstiuo commoratur; In hyeme autem vadit ad ciuitatem aliam sitam supra mare vocatam Bakuc: Praedicta autem ciuitas magna est, et frigida, in se habens bonas aquas, ad quam multa mercimonia portantur. Vltra cum quadam societate Carauanorum iui versus Indiam superiorem, ad quam dum transissem per multas dietas perueni ad ciuitatem trium Magorum quæ vocatur Cassan, [Marginal note: Vel Cassibin.] quæ regia ciuitas est et nobilis, nisi quod Tartari eam in magnaparte destruxerunt: haec abundat pane, vino, et alijsbonis multis. Ab hac ciuitate vsque Ierusalem quo Magi iuerunt miraculosè, sunt L. dietiæ, et multa mirabilia sunt in hac ciuitate quæ pertranseo. [Sidenote: Gest.] Inde recessi ad quandam ciuitatem vocatam Gest a qua distat mare arenosum per vnam dietam, quod mirè est mirabile et periculosum: In hac ciuitate est abundantia omnium victualium, et ficuum potissimè, et vuarum siccarum et viridium, plus vt credo quàm in alia parte mundi. Haec est tertia cuitas melior quam Rex Persarum habet in toto regno suo: De illa dicunt Saraceni, quod in ea nullus Christianus vltra annum viuere vnquam potest. [Sidenote: Como.] Vltra per multas dietas iui ad quandam ciuitatem dictam Comum quæ maxima ciuitas antiquitùs erat, cuius ambitus erat ferè L. Miliaria, quæ magna damna intulit Romanis antiquis temporibus. In ea sunt palatia integra non habitata, tamen multis victualibus abundat. Vltra per multas terras transiens, perueni ad terram Iob nomine Hus quæ omnium victualium plenissima est, et pulcherrimè situata; iuxta eam sunt montes in quibus sunt pascua multa pro animilibus: Ibi manna in magna copia reperitur. Ibi habentur quatuor perdices pro minori, quam pro vno grosso: In ea sunt pulcherrimi senes, vbi homines nent et filant, et faeminæ non: haec terra correspondet Chaldeæ versus transmontana.

De moribus Chaldæorum, et de India.

Indè iui in Chaldaeam quæ est regnum magnum, et transiui iuxta turrim Babel: Haec regio suam linguam propriam habet, et ibi sunt homines formosi, et foeminæ turpes: et homines illius regionis vadunt compti crinibus, et ornati, vt hîc mulieres, et portant super capita sua fasciola aurea cum gemmis, et margaritis; mulieres verò solum vnam vilem camisiam attingentem vsque ad genua, habentem manicas longas et largas, quæ vsque ad terram protenduntur: Et vadunt discalceatæ portantes Serablans vsque ad terram. Triceas non portant, sed capilli earum circumquaque disperguntur: et alia multa et mirabilia sunt ibidem. Indé veni in Indiam quæ infra terram est, quam Tartari multum destruxerunt; et in ea vt plurimum homines tantum dactilos comedunt, quarum xlij, libræ habentur pro minori quam pro vno grosso. [Sidenote: Ormus.] Vltra transsiui per multas dietas ad mare oceanum, et prima terra, ad quam applicui, vocatur Ormes, quæ est optime murata, et multa mercimonia et diuitiæ in ea sunt; in ea tantus calor est, quod virilia hominum exeunt corpus et descendunt vsque ad mediam tibiarum: ideò homines illius terræ volentes viuere, faciunt vnctionum, et vngunt illa, et sic vncta in quibusdam sacculis ponunt circa se cingentes, et aliter morerentur: In hac terra homines vtuntur nauigio quæ vocatur Iase, suitium sparto. [Sidenote: Thana.] Ego autem ascendi in vnum illorum in quo nullum ferrum potui reperrire, et in viginta octo dietis perueni ad ciuitaten Thana, in qua pro fide Christi quatuor de fratribus nostris martyrizati sunt. Hæc terra est optimè situata, et in ea abundantia panis et vini, et aliorum victualium. Hæc terra antiquitus fuit valde magna, et fuit regis Pori, qui cum rege Alexandro prælium magnum commisit. Huius terræ populus Idolatrat, adorans ignem serpentes, et arbores: Et istam terram regunt Saraceni, qui vio lenter eam acceperunt, et subiacent imperio regis Daldili. Ibi sunt diuersa genera bestiarum, leones nigri in maxima quantitate: sunt et ibi simiæ, gatimaymones, et noctuae magnæ sicut hic habentur columbæ; ibi mures magni sunt, sicut sunt hîc scepi, et ideò canes capiunt ibi mures, quia murelegi non valent. Ad hæc, in illa terra quilibet homo habet ante domum suam vnum pedem fasciculorum, ita magnum sicut esset vna columna, et pes ille non desiccatur, dummodò adhibeatur sibi aqua. Multæ nouitates sunt ibi, quas pulcherrimum esset audire.

De martyrio fratrum.

Martyrium autem quatuor fratrum nostrorum in illa ciuitate Thana fuit per istum modum; dum praedicti fratres fuerant in Ormes, fecerunt pactum cum vna naui vt nauigarent vsque Polumbrum, et violentèr deportati sunt vsque Thanam vbi sunt 15. domus Christianorum, qui Nestoriani sunt et Schismatici, et cum illic essent, hospitati sunt in domo cuiusdam illorum; contigit dum ibi manerent litem oriri inter virum domus, et vxorem eius, quam sero ver fortiter verberauit, quæ suo Kadi, i. Episcopo conquesta est; à qua interrogauit Kadi, vtrum hoc probari posset? quæ dixit, quod sic; quia 4. Franchi, i. viri religiosi erant in domo hoc videntes, ipsos interrogate, qui dicent vobis veritatem: Muliere autem sic dicente, Ecce vnus de Alexandria praesens rogauit Kadi vt mitteret pro eis, dicens eos esse homines maximæ scientiæ et scripturas bene scire, et ideo dixit bonum esse cum illis de fide disputare: Qui misit pro illis, et adducti sunt isti quatuor, quorum nomina sunt frater de Tolentino de Marchia, frater Iacobus de Padua, frater Demetrius Laicus, Petrus de Senis. Dimisso autem fratre Petro, vt res suas custodiret, ad Kadi perrexerunt, qui coepit cum illis de fide nostra disputare; dicens Christum tantum hominem esse et non Deum. E contra frater Thomas rationibus et exemplis Christum verum Deum et hominem esse euidenter ostendit, et in tantum confudit Kadi, et infideles qui cum eo tenuerunt, quod non habuerunt quid rationabiliter contradicere: Tunc videns Kadi se sic confusum, incepit clamare sic; Et quid dicis de Machometo? Respondit frater Thomas: Si tibi probauimus Christum verum Deum et hominem esse, qui legem posuit inter homines, et Machometus è contrario venit, et legem contrariam docuit, si sapiens sis optime scire poteris, quid de eo dicendum sit. Iterum Kadi et alij Saraceni clamabant, Et tu quid iterum de Machometo dicis? Tunc frater T. respondit: vos omnes videre potestis, quid dico de eo. Tum ex quo vultis quod plane loquar de eo, dico quod Machometus vester filius perditionis est, et in inferno cum Diabolo patre suo. Et non solum ipse, sed omnes ibi erunt qui tenent legem hanc, quia ipsa tota pestifera est, et falsa, et contra Deum, et contra salutem animæ. Hoc audientes Saraceni, coeperunt clamare, moriatur, moriatur ille, qui sic contra Prophetam locutus est. Tunc acceperunt fratres et in sole vrente stare permiserunt, vt ex calore solis adusti, dira morte interirent. Tantus enim est calor solis ibi, quòd si homo in eo per spacium vnius missæ persisteret, moreretur; fratres tamen illi sani et hilares à tertia vsque ad nonam laudantes et glorificantes dominum in ardore solis permanserunt, quod videntes Saraceni stupefacti ad fratres venerunt, et dixerunt, volumus ignem accendere copiosum, et in illum vos proijcere, et si fides vestra sit vt dicitis, ignis non poterit vos comburere: si autem vos combusserit, patebit quòd fides vestra nulla sit. Responderunt fratres; parati sumus pro fide nostra ignem, carcerem, et vincula, et omnium tormentorum genera tolerare: verum tamen scire debetis, quòd si ignis potestatem habeat comburendi nos hoc non erit propter fidem nostram, sed propter peccata nostra: fides enim nostra perfectissima et verissima est, et non est alia in mundo in qua animsæ hominum possunt saluæ fieri; Dum autem ordinaretur quòd fratres conburerentur, rumor insonuit per totam ciuitatem, de qua omnes senes, et iuuenes, viri et mulieres, qui ire poterant, accurrerunt ad illud spectaculum intuendum. Fratres autem ducti fuerunt ad plateam ciuitatis, vbi accensus est ignis copiosus, in quen frater Thomas voluit se proijcere, sed quidam Saracenus cepit eam per caputium et retraxit dicens; Non vadus tu cum sis senex, quia carmen aliquod vel experimentum habere posses super te, quare te ignis non posset laedere, sed alium ire in ignem permittas. Tunc 4 Saraceni sumentes fratrem Iacobum, eum in ignem proijcere volebant; quibus ille, permittatis, me quia libenter pro fide mea ignem intrabo: Cui Saraceni non adquiescentes eum violentèr in ignem proiecerunt: ignis autem ita accensus erat, quòd nullus eum videre poteret, vocem tamen eius audierunt, inuocantem semper nomen virginis gloriosæ; Igne autem totalitèr consumpto stetit frater Iacobus super prunas illaesus, et laetus, manibus in modum crucis eleuatis, in coelum respiciens, et Deum laudans et glorificans, qui sic declararet fidem suam: nihil autem in eo nec pannus, nec capillus laesus per ignem inuentus est; Quod videns populus vnanimitèr conclamare coepit, sancti sunt, sancti sunt, nefas est offendere eos, modò videmus quia fides eorum bona et sancta est. Tunc clamare coepit Kadi: sanctus non est ille, quia combustus non est, quia tunica quam portat est de lana terræ Habraæ, et ideò nudus exspolietur, et in ignem proijciatur, et videbitur si comburetur vel non. Tunc Saraceni pessimi ad praeceptum Kadi ignem in duplo magis quàm priùs accenderunt, et fratrem Iacobum nudantes, corpus suum abluerunt, et oleo abundantissimè vnxerunt, insuper et oleum maximum in struem lignorum ex quibus ignis fieret, fuderunt, et igne accenso fratrem in ipsum proiecerunt. Frater autem Thomas, et frater Demetrius extra populum in loco separato flexis genibus orantes cum lachrymis deuotioni se dederunt Frater autem Iocobus iterum ignem exiuit illaesus sicut prius fecerat: quod videns omnis populus clamare coepit, peccatum est, deccatum est, offendere eos, quià sancti sunt. Hoc autem tantum miraculum videns Melich. i. potestas ciuitatis, vocauit ad se fratrem Iacobum, et fecit eum ponere indumenta, sua, et dixit, videte fratres, Ite cum gratia Dei, quia nullum malum patiemini a nobis, modò benè videmus vos sanctos esse, et fidem vestram bonam ac veram esse; et ideo consulimus vobis, vt de ista terra exeatis, quàm citiùs poteritis, quia Kadi pro posse suo vobis nocere curabit, quia sic confudistis eum: Hora autem tunc erat quasi completorij, et dixerunt illi de populo, attoniti, admirati, et stupefacti, tot, et tanta mirabilia vidimus ab istis hominibus, quòd nescimus quid tenere et obseruare debemus. Melich verò fecit duci illos tres fratres vltra vnum paruum brachium maris in quendam Burgum modicum ab illa ciuitate distantem: ad quem etiam ille in cuius iam domo fuerant hospitati associauit eos, vbi in domo cuiusdam idolatri recepti sunt. Dum haec argerenter, Kadi iuit ad Melich, dicens quid facimus? Lex Machometi destructa est, veruntamen hoc scire debes, quod Machomet praecepit in suo Alcorano, quod si quis vnum Christianum interficeret, tantum mereretur, ac si in Mecha ad ipsum peregrinaretur. Est enim Alkoranus lex Sarracenorum sicut Euangelium, Mecha, verò est locus vbi iacet Machomet. Quem locum ita visitant Saraceni, sicut Christiani sepulchram Christi. Tunc Melich respondet, vade, et fac sicut vis: quo dicto statim Kadi accepit quatuor homines armatos vt irent, et illos fratres interficerent, qui cùm aquam transijssent, facta est nox, et illo sero eos non inuenerunt, statim Melieh omnes Christianos in ciuitate capi fecit, et incarcerauit, media autem nocte fratres surrexerunt dicere matutinum, quos illi Saraceni qui missi fuerant, inuenerunt, et extra burgum, sub quadam arbore adduxerunt, dixerunt eis. Sciatis fratres nos mandatum habere a Kadi et Melich interficere vos, quod tamen faciemus inuiti, quia vos estis boni homines et sancti, sed non audemus aliter facere; quia si iussa sua non perficeremus, et nos cum liberis nostris et vxoribus moreremur. Tunc fratres responderunt, vos qui huc venistis, et tale mandatum recepistis, vt per mortem temporalem vitam æternam adipiscamur, quod vobis iniunctum est perficite; quia pro amore domini nostri Iesu Christi, qui pro nobis crucifigi et mori dignatus est, et pro fide nostra, parati sumus omnia tormenta, et etiam mortem libenter sustinere. Christianas autem qui fratres comitabatur, multum cum illis quatuor armatis altercatus est dicens, quod si gladium haberet, vel eos à nece tam sanctorum hominum impediret, vel ipse cum eis interfectus esset. Tunc armati fecerunt fratres se exspoliare, et frater Thomas primus iunctis manibus in modum crucis genuflectens capitis abscissionem suscepit: Fratrem verò Iacobum vnus percussit in capite, et eum vsque ad oculos scidit, et alio ictu totum caput abscidit. Frater autem Demetrius, primò percussus est cum gladio in pectore, et secundò caput suum abscissum est: Statim vt fratres suum martyrium compleuerunt, aer ita lucidus effectus est, quod omnes admirati sunt, et luna maximam claritatem ostendit. Statim quasi subito tanta tonitrua, et fulgura, et coruscationes, et obscuritas fiebant, quòd omnes mori crediderunt: Nauis etiam illa quæ illos debuerat deportasse submersa est cum omnibus quæ in se habuit, ita quod nunquam de illa posteà aliquid scitum est. Facto mane misit Kadi pro rebus fratrum prædictorum nostrorum, et tunc inuentus est frater Petrus de Senis quartus socius fratrum prædictorum, quem ad Kadi duxerunt: Cui Kadi, et alij Saraceni maxima promittentes persuaserunt quòd fidem suam renueret, et legem Machometi confiteretur, et teneret. Frater autem Petrus de illis truffabat, eos multum deridendo, quem de mane vsque ad meridiem diuersis pænarum ac tormentorum generibus affixerunt ipso semper constantissimè in fide, et in Dei laudibus persistente, et fidem illorum Machometi deridente et destruente. Videntes autem Saraceni eum non posse a suo proposito euelli, eum super quandam arborem suspenderunt, in qua de nona vsque ad noctem viuus et illaesus pependit: nocte verò ipsum de arbore sumpserunt, et videntes illum laetum, viuum et illaesum per medium suum corpus diuiserunt, mane autem facto nihil de corpore eius inuentum est, vni tamen personæ fide dignæ reuelatum est, quod Deus corpus eius occultauerat reuelandum in certo tempore, quandò Deo placuerit Sanctorum corpora manifestare. Vt autem Deus ostenderet animas suorum martyrum iam in coelis consistere, et congaudere cum Deo et Angelis et alijs Sanctis eius, die sequenti post martyrium fratrum praedictorum Melich dormitioni se dedit, et ecce apparuerunt sibi isti fratres gloriosi, et sicut Sol, lucidi, singulos enses tenentes in manibus, et supra eum eos sic vibrantes, quod vt si eum perfodere ac diuidere vellent: qui excitatus horribilitèr exclamauit sic, quòd totam familiam terruit: quæ sibi accurrens quaesiuit, quid sibi esset? quibus ille, Illi Raban Franchi quos interfici iussi, venerunt hac ad me cum ensibus, volentes me interficere. Et statim Melich misit pro Kadi, referens sibi visionem et petens consilium, et consolationem, quia timuit per eos finaliter interire. Tunc Kadi sibi consuluit, vt illis maximas eleemosynas faceret, si de manibus interfectorum euadere vellet. Tunc misit pro Christianis quos in carcere intrudi praeceperat: A quibus cum ad eum venissent indulgentiam petijt pro facto suo, dicens se esse amodo socium eorum, et confratrem: Praecepit autem et legem statuit, quòd pro tempore suo, si quis aliquem Christianum offenderet, statim moreretur, et sic omnes illaesos, et indemnes abire permisit: Pro illis autem quatuor fratribus interfectis quatuor mosquetas. (i.) Ecclesias ædificari fecit, quas per Sacerdotes Saracenorum inhabitari fecit. Audiens autem imperator Dodsi istos tres fratres talem sententiam subijsse, misit pro Melich, vt vinctus ad eum duceretur, A quo cùm adductus esset, quaesiuit imperator, quare ita crudeliter illos fratres iusserat interfici, respondit, quia subuertere volebant legem nostram, et malum et blasphemiam de propheta nostro dicebant: et imperator ad eum; O crudelissime canis, cùm videres quod Deus omnipotens bis ab igne eos liberauerit, quo modo ausus fuisti illis mortem inferre tam crudelem. Et edicta sententia, ipsum Melich cum tota sua familia per medium scindi fecit, sicut ipse talem mortem fratri inflixerat. Kadi verò audiens, de terra illa, et etiam de imperatoris illius dominio clàm fugit, et sic euasit.

De miraculis quatuor fratrum occisorum

Est autem consuetudo in terra illa, quòd corpora mortua non traduntur sepulturæ, sed in campis dimittuntur, et ex calore Solis citò resoluuntur, et sic consumantur: Corpora autem trium fratrum praedictorum per 14. dies illic in fuerore Solis iacuerunt, et ita recentia et redolentia inuenta fuerunt sicut illa die quandò martirizati erant: quod videntes Christiani qui in illa terra habitabant, praedicta corpora ceperunt, et honorificè sepelierunt. Ego autem Odoricus audiens factum et martyrium illorum fratrum, iui illuc, et corpora eorum effodi, et ossa omnia mecum accepi, et in pulchris towallijs colligaui, et in Indiam superiorem ad vnum locum fratrum nostrorum ea deportaui, habens mecum socium, et vnum famulum. Cum autem essemus in via, hospitabamus in domo cuiusdam hospitarij, et ipsa ossa capiti meo supposui, et dormiui: Et dùm dormirem domus illa à Saracenis subitò accendebatur, vt me cum domo comburerent. Domo autem sic accensa, socius meus et famulus de domo exierunt, et me solum cum ossibus dimiserunt, qui videns ignem supra me, ossa accepi et cum illis in angulos domus recollegi. Tres autem anguli domus statim combusti fuerunt, angulo in quo steti cum ossibus saluo remanente: Supra me autem ignis se tenuit in modum aeris lucidi, nec descendit quamdiu ibi persistebam; quàm citò autem cum ossibus exiui, statim tota pars illa sicut aliæ priores igne consumpta est, et multa alia loca circumadiacentia combusta sunt. Aliud miraculum contigit, me cum ossibus per mare proficiente ad ciuitatem Polumbrum vbi piper nascitur abundantèr, quia nobis ventus totaliter defecit: quapropter venerunt Idolatræ adorantes Deos suos pro vento prospero, quem tamen non obtinuerunt: Tunc Saraceni suas inuocationes, et adorationes laboriose fecerunt, sed nihil profecerunt: Et praeceptum est mihi et socio meo vt orationes funderemus Deo nostro: Et dixit rector nauis in Armenico mihi, quod alij non intelligerent: quòd nisi possemus ventum prosperum à Deo nostro impetrare, nos cum ossibus in mare proijcerent: Tunc ego et socius fecimus orationes, vouentes multas missas de beata virgine celebrare, sic quòd ventum placeret sibi nobis impetrare. Cum autem tempus transiret, et ventus non veniret, accepi vnum de ossibus, et dedi famulo, vt ad caput nauis iret, et clàm in mare proijceret; quo proiecto statim affuit ventus prosper qui nunquam nobis defecit, vsquequò peruenimus ad portum, meritis istorum martyrum cum salute. Deinde ascendimus aliam nauem vt in Indiam superiorem iremus; Et venimus ad quandam ciuitatem vocatam Carchan in qua sunt duo loca fratrum nostrorum, et ibi reponere istas reliquias volebamus. In naui autem illa erant plus 700. mercatores et alij: Nunc illi Idolatræ istam consuetudinem habebant, quòd semper antequàm ad portum applicuerint, totam nauem perquirerent, si isti aliqua ossa mortuorum animalium inuenirent, qui reperta statim in mare proijcerent, et per hoc bonum portum attingere, et mortis periculum euadere crederent. Cùm autem frequentèr perquirerent, et illa ossa frequenter tangerent, semper oculi delusi fuerunt, sic quòd illa non perpenderunt; et sic ad locum fratrum deportauimus cum omni reuerentia, vbi in pace requiescunt; vbi etiam inter idolatras Deus continuè miracula operatur. Cum enim aliquo morbo grauantur, in terra illa vbi fratres passi sunt ipsi vadunt; et de terra vbi corpora sanguinolenta iacuerunt sumunt quam abluunt, et ablutionem bibunt, et sic ab infirmitatibus suis liberantur.

Quo modo habetur Piper, et vbi nascitur.

[Sidenote: Malabar.] Vt autem videatur quo modo habetur piper, sciendum quòd in quodam imperio ad quod applicui, nomine Minibar, nascitur, et in nulla parte mundi tantum, quantum ibi; Nemus enim in quo nascitur, continet octodecim dietas, et in ipso nemore sunt duæ ciuitates vna nomine Flandrini, alia nomine Cyncilim: In Flandrina habitant Iudaei aliqui et aliqui Christiani, inter quos est bellum frequenter, sed Christiani vincunt Iudaeos semper: In isto nemore habetur piper per istum modum. Nam primò nascitur in folijs olerum, quæ iuxta magnas arbores plantantur, sicut nos ponimus vites; et producunt fructum, sicut racemi nostri producunt vuas; sed quandò maturescunt sunt viridis coloris, et sic vindemiantur vt inter nos vindemiantut vuæ, et ponuntur grana ad solem vt desiccentur: quæ desiccata reponuntur in vasis terreis, et sic fit piper, et custoditur. In isto autem nemore sunt flumina multa in quibus sunt Crocodili multi, et multi alij serpentes sunt in illo nemore, quos homines per stupam et paleas comburunt, et sic ad colligendum piper securé accedunt. [Sidenote: Polumbrum ciuitas. Adoratio bouis.] A capite illius nemoris versus meridiem est ciuitas Polumbrum in qua maxima mercimonia cuiuscunque generis reperiuntur Omnes autem de terra illa bouem viuum sicut Deum suum adorant, quem 6. annis faciunt laborare, et in septimo faciunt ipsum quiescere ab omni opere; ponentes ipsum in loco solemni, et communi, et dicentes ipsum esse animal sanctum. Hunc autem ritum obseruant: quolibet mane accipiunt duas pelues de auro, vel de argento, et vnam submittunt vrinæ bouis, et aliam stercori, de vrina lauant sibi faciem et oculos, et omnes 5. sensus: de stercore verò ponunt in vtròque oculo, posteà liniunt summitates genarum, et tertiò pectus, et ex tunc dicunt se sanctificatos pro toto die illo: et sicut facit populus, ita etiam facit rex et regina. Isti etiam aliud idolum mortuum adorant, quod in medietate vna superior est homo, et in alia est bos, et iliud idolum dat eis responsa, et aliquotièns pro stipendio petit sanguinem, 40. virginum: et ideo homines illius regionis ita vouent filias suas et filios, sicut Christiani aliqui alicui religioni, vel sancto in coelis. Et per istum modum immolant filios et filias, et multi homines per istum ritum moriuntur ante idolum illud, et multa alia abominabilia facit populus iste bestialis, et multa mirabilia vidi inter eos quæ nolui hic inserere. [Sidenote: Combustio mortuorum.] Aliam consuetudinem vilissimam habet gens illa: Nam quamdo homo moritur, comburunt ipsum mortuum, et si vxorem habet, ipsam comburunt viuam, quia dicunt quod ipsa ibit in aratura, et cultura cum viro suo in alio mundo: si autem vxor illa habeat liberos ex viro suo, potest manere cum eis si velit sine verecundia et improperio, communiter tamen omnes praeeligunt comburi cum marito; si autem vxor praemoriatur viro, lex illa non obligat virum, sed potest aliam vxorem ducere. Aliam consuetudinem habet gens illa, quòd foeminæ ibi bibunt vinum, et homines non: foeminæ etiam faciunt sibi radi cilia, et supercilia, et barbam, et homines non: et sic de multis alijs vilibus contra naturam sexus eorum. [Sidenote: Mobar regnum vel Maliapor.] Ab isto regno iui decem dietas ad iliud regnum dictum Mobar, quod habet in se multas ciuitates, et in illo requiescit in vna ecclesia corpus beati Thomæ Apostoli, et est ecclesia illa plena idolis, et in circuitu ecclesiæ simul Cononici viuunt in 15 domibus Nestoriani, id est, mali Christiani, et schismatici.

De quodam idolo mirabili, et de quibusdam ritibus eorum.

In hoc regno est vnum Idolum mirabile, quod omnes Indi reuerentur: et est statura hominis ita magni, sicut noster Christophorus depictus, et est totum de auro purissimo et splendidissimo, et circa collum habet vnam chordulam sericam cum lapidibus pretiosissimis, quorum aliquis valet plus quàm vnum regnum: Domus idoli est tota de auro, scilicet in tecto, et pauimento, et superficie parietum interius et exterius. Ad illud idolum peregrinantur Indi, sicut nos ad S. Petrum: Alij veniunt cum chorda ad collum, alij cum manibus retro ligatis, alij cum cultello in brachio vel tibia defixo, et si post peregrinationem fiat brachium marcidum, illum reputant sanctum, et benè cum Deo suo. Iuxta ecclesiam illius idoli est lacus vnus manufactus, et manifestus, in quem peregrini proijciunt aurum et argentum, et lapides pretiosos in honorem Idoli, et ad ædificationem ecclesiæ suæ, et ideo quando aliquid debet ornari, vel reparari, vadunt homines ad hunc lacum, et proiecta extrahunt: die autem annua constructionis illius idoli, rex et regina, cum toto populo et omnibus peregrinis accedunt, et ponunt illud idolum in vno curru pretiosissimo ipsum de ecclesia educentes cum Canticis, et omni genere musicorum, et multae virgines antecedunt ipsum binæ et binæ, processionaliter combinatæ modulantes: [Sidenote: Crudelissima Satanæ tyrannis, et carnificina.] Peregrini etiam multi ponunt se sub curru, vt transeat Deus supra eos; et omnes super quos currus transit, comminuit, et per medium scindit, et interficit, et per hoc reputant se mori pro deo suo, sanctè et securè: et in omni anno hoc modo moriuntur in via sub idolo plusquam 500. homines, quorum corpora comburuntur, et cineres sicut reliquiæ custodiuntur, quia sic pro Deo suo moriuntur. Alium ritum habent, quando aliquis homo offert se mori pro deo suo, conueniunt omnes amici eius et parentes cum histrionibus multis, facientes sibi festum magnum, et post festum appendunt collo eius 5 cultellos acutissimos ducentes eum ante idolum, quo cum peruenerit, sumit vnum ex cultellis, et clamat alta voce, pro deo meo incido mihi de carne mea, et frustum incisum proijcit in faciem idoli: vltima vero incisione per quam seipsum interficit, dicit, me mori pro deo meo permitto, quo mortuo corpus eius comburitur, et sanctum fore ab omnibus creditur. Rex illius regionis est ditissimus in auro et argento, et gemmis pretiosis; ibi etiam sunt margaritæ pulchriores de mundo. Indè transiens iui per mare oceanum versus meridiem per 50 dietas ad unam terram vocatam Lammori, in qua ex immensitate caloris, tam viri quam foeminæ omnes incedunt nudi in toto corpore: Qui videntes me vestitum, deridebant me, dicentes Deum, Adam et Euam fecisse nudos. In illa regione omnes mulieres sunt communes, ita quod nullus potest dicere, haec est vxor mea, et cùm mulier aliqua parit filium vel filiam dat cui vult de hijs qui concubuerunt: Tota etiam terra illius regionis habetur in communi, ita quod non meum et tuum in diuisione terrarum, domos tamen habent speciales: Carnes humanæ quando homo est pinguis ita benè comeduntur, sicut inter nos bouinæ: et licet gens sit pestifera, tamen terra optima est, et abundat in omnibus bonis, carnibus, bladis, riso, auro, argento, et lignis Aloe, canfari, et multis alijs. Mercatores autem cum accedunt ad hanc regionem ducunt secum homines pingues vendentes illos genti illius regionis, sicut nos vendimus porcos, qui statim occidunt eos et comedunt. [Sidenote: Simoltra vel Samotra.] In hac insula versus meridiem est aliud regnum vocatum Symolcra, in quo tam viri quam mulieres signant se ferro calido in facie, in 12. partibus, Et hij semper bellant cum hominibus nudis in alia regione. Vltra transiú ad aliam insulam quæ vocatur Iaua cuius ambitus per mare est trium millium milliarium, et rex illius insulæ habet sub se 7. reges coronatos, et haec insula optimè inhabitatur, et melior secunda de mundo reputatur. In ea nascuntur in copia garyophylli, cubibez, et nuces muscatæ: et breuiter omnes species ibi sunt, et maxima abundantia omnium victualium praeterquam vini. Rex illius terræ habet palatium nobilissimum inter omnia quæ vidi altissime stat, et gradus et scalas habet altissimos, quorum semper vnus gradus est aureus, alius argenteus: Pauimentum vero vnum laterem habet de auro, alium de argento. Parietes vero omnes interius sunt laminati laminis aureis, in quibus sculpti sunt Equites de auro habentes circa caput circulum aureum plenum lapidibus pretiosis: Tectum est de auro puro. Cum isto rege ille magnus Canis de Katay frequenter fuit in bello: Quem tamen semper ille Rex vicit et superauit.

De arboribus dantibus farinam, et mel, et venenum.

Iuxta istam Insulam est alia contrata vocata Panten, vel alio nomine Tathalamasim, [Marginal note: Vel Malasmi.] et Rex illius contratæ multas insulas habet sub se. In illa terra sunt arbores dantes farinam, et mel, et vinum, et etiam venenum periculosius quod sit in mundo, quia contra illud non est remedium, nisi vnum solum, et est illud. Si aliquis illud venenum sumpsisset, si velit liberari, sumat stercus hominis et cum aqua temperet, et in bona quantitate bíbat, et statim fugat venenum faciens exire per inferiores partes. Farinam autem faciunt arbores hoc modo, sunt magnæ et bassæ, et quandò inciduntur cum securi propè terram, exit de stipite liquor quidam secut gummæ, quem accipiunt homines et ponunt in sacculis de folijs factis, et per quindecim dies in sole dimittunt, et in fine decimi quinti diei ex isto liquore desiccato fit farina, quam primò ponunt in aqua maris, posteà lauant eam cum aqua dulci, et fit pasta valdè bona et odorifera, de qua faciunt cibos vel panes sicut placet eis. De quibus panibus ego comedi, et est panis exterius pulcher, sed interius aliquantulum niger. [Sidenote: Mare quod semper currit versus meridiem.] In hac contrata est mare mortuum quod semper currit versus meridiem, in quod si homo ceciderit, nunquam posteà comparet. In contrata illa inueniuntur Cannæ longissimæ plures passus habentes quàm 60 et sunt magnæ vt arbores. Aliæ etiam Cannæ sunt ibi quæ vocantur Cassan quæ per terram diriguntur vt gramen, et in quolibet nodo earum ramuli producuntur qui etiam prolongantur super terram per vnum miliare ferè: in hijs Cannis reperiuntur lapides, quorum si quis vnum super se portauerit, hon poterit incidi aliquo ferro, et ideò, communiter homines illius contratæ portant illos lapides super: Multi etiam faciunt pueros suos dum sunt parui incidi in vno brachio, et in vulnere ponunt vnum de illis lapidibus, et faciunt vulnus recludere se per vnum puluerem de quodam pisce, cuius nomen ignoro, qui puluis statim vulnus consolidat et sanat: et virtute illorum lapidum communitèr isti homines triumphant in bellis, et in mari, nec possent isti homines laedi per aliqua arma ferra: Vnum tamen remedium est, quod aduersarij illius gentis scientes virtutem lapidum, prouident sibi propugnacula ferrea contra spicula illorum, et arma venenata de veneno arborum, et in manu portant palos ligneos accutissimos et ita duros in extremitate sicut esset ferrum: Similitér sagittant cum sagittis sino ferro, et sic confundunt aliquos et perforant inermes ex lapidum securitate. [Sidenote: Vela ex arundinibus facta.] De istis etiam Cannis Cassan faciunt sibi vela pro suis nauibus et domunculas paruas, et multa sibi necessaria. [Sidenote: Campa.] Inde recessi per multas dietas ad aliud regnum vocatum Campa, pulcherrimum, et opulentissimum in omnibus victualibus. Cuius rex quamdo fui ibi tot habuit vxores, et alias mulieres, quod de illis 300. filios et filias habuit. Iste rex habet decies millesies et quatuor elephantum domesticorum, quos ita facit custodiri sicut inter nos custodiunt boues, vel greges in pascuis.

De multitudine Piscium, qui se proijciunt in aridam.

In hac contrata vnum mirabile valde reperitur, quod vnaquaeque generatio piscium in mari ad istam contratam venit in tanta quantitate, quod per magnum spatium maris nil videtur nisi dorsa piscium, et super aridam se proijciunt quando prope ripam sunt, et permittunt homines per tres dies venire, et de illis sumere quantum placuerint, et tunc redeunt ad mare: Post illam speciem per illum modum venit alia species, et offert se, et sic de omnibus speciebus, semel tamen tantum hoc faciunt in anno. Et quaesiui à gente illa quomodo et qualiter hoc possit fieri? responderunt quod hoc modo pisces per naturam docentur venire, et imperatorem suum reuereri. [Sidenote: Testitudines magnæ.] Ibi etiam sunt testudines ita magnæ sicut est vnus furnus, et multa alia vidi quæ incredibilia forent, nisi homo illa vidisset. In illa etiam contrata homo mortuus conburitur, et vxor viua cum eo, sicut superius de alia contrata dictum est, quia dicunt homines illi quod illa vadit ad alium mundum ad morandum cum eo, ne ibi aliam vxorem accipiat. [Sidenote: Moumoran.] Vltra transiui per mare Oceanum versus meridiem, et transiui per multas contratas et insulas, quarum vna vocatur Moumoran, et habet in circuitu 2000. milliaria, in qua homines portant facies caninas et mulieres similitèr, et vnum bouem adorant pro Deo suo, et ideo quilibet vnum bouem aureum vel argenteum in fronte portat: Homines illius contratæ et mulieres vadunt totaliter nudi, nisi quod vnum pannum lineum portant ante verenda sua. Homines illius regionis sunt maximi et fortissimi, et quia vadunt nudi, quando debent bellare, portant vnum scutum de ferro, quod cooperit eos à capite vsque ad pedes, et si contingat eos aliquem de aduersarijs capere in bello qui pecunia non possit redimi, statim comedunt eum; si autem possit se redimere pecunia, illum abire permittunt: Rex eorum portat 300. margaritas ad collum suum maximas et pulcherrimas, et 300. orationes omni die dicit Deo suo: Hic etiam portat in digito suo vnum lapidem longitudinis vnius spansæ, et dum habet illum videtur ab alijs quasi vna flamma ignis, et ideò nullus audet sibi appropinquare, et dicitur quòd non est lapis in mundo pretiosior illo. Magnus autem imperator Tartarorum de Katai, nunquam vi, nec pecunia, nec ingenio illum obtinere potuit, cùm tamen circa hoc laborauerit.

De Insula Ceilan, et de monte vbi Adam planxit Abel filium suum.

[Sidenote: Ceilan insula.] Transiui per aliam insulam vocatam Ceilan, quæ habet in ambitu plusquam duo millia milliaria, in qua sunt serpentes quasi infiniti, et maxima multitudo leonum, vrsarum, et omnium animalium rapacium, et siluestrium, et potissimè elephantum. In illa contrata est mons maximus, in quo dicunt gentes illius regionis quod Adam planxit Abel filium suum 500. annis. In medio illius montis est planicies pulcherrima, in qua est lacus paruus multum habens de aqua, et homines illi dicunt aquam illam fuisse de lachrymis Adæ et Euæ, sed probaui hoc falsum esse, quia vidi aquam in lacu scaturire: haec aqua plena est hirudinibus et sanguisugis, et lapidibus pretiosis; istos lapides rex non accepit sibi, sed semel vel bis in anno permittit pauperes sub aqua ire pro lapidibus, et omnes quot possunt colligere illis concedit, vt orent pro anima sua. Vt autem possint sub aqua ire accipiunt lymones, et cum illis vngunt se valdè benè, et sic nudos se in aquam submergunt, et sanguisugæ illis nocere non possunt. Ab isto lacu aqua exit et currit vsque ad mare, et in transitu quando retrahit se, fodiuntur Rubiæ, et adamantes, et margaritæ, et aliæ gemmæ pretiosæ: vndè opinio est quod rex ille magis abundat lapidibus pretiosis, quàm aliquis in mundo. In contrata illa sunt quasi omnia genera animalium et auium; et dixerunt mihi gentes illæ quod animalia illa nullum forensem inuadunt, nec offendunt, sed tantum homines illius regionis. Vidi in illa insula aues ita magnas sicut sunt hic anseres, habentes duo capita, et alia mirabilia quæ non scribo. [Sidenote: Bodin Insula.] Vltra versus meridiem transiui, et applicui, ad insulam quandam quæ vocatur Bodin, quod idem est quod immundum in lingua nostra. In ea morantur pessimi homines, qui comedunt carnes crudas, et omnem immunditiam faciunt quæ quasi excogitari non poterit; nam pater comedit filium et filius patrem, et maritus vxorem, et è contrario, et hoc per hunc modum: si pater alicuius infirmetur, filius vadet ad Astrologum sacerdotem, scz. rogans eum quod consulat Deum suum, si pater de tali infirmitate euadat, vel non. Tunc ambo vadunt ad idolum aureum, vel argenteum, facientes orationes in hac forma. Domine, tu es Deus noster, te adoramus, et rogamus vt nobis respondeas, debetnè talis à tali infirmitate mori vel liberari? Tunc Daemon respondet, et si dicat, viuet, filius vadit et ministrat illi vsque ad plenam conualescentiam: Si autem dicat, morietur, Sacerdos ibit ad eum, et vnum pannum super os eius ponet, et suffocabit eum, et ipsum mortuum incidet in frusta, et inuitabuntur omnes amici, et parentes eius ad comedendum eum cum canticis, et omni laetitia, ossa tamen eius honorificè sepelient. Cum autem ego eos de tali ritu reprehendi, quaerens causam: Respondit vnus mihi, hoc facimus ne vermes carnes eius comedant, tunc eius anima magnam poenam sustinerit, nec poteram euellere eos ab isto errore: et multæ aliæ nouitates sunt ibi, quas non crederent, nisi qui viderent. Ego autem coram Deo nihil hic refero, nisi illud de quo certus sum sicut homo certificari poterit. De ista insula inquisiui à multis expertis, qui omnes vno ore responderunt mihi, dicentes, quod ista India 4400. insulas continet sub se, siue in se, in qua etiam sunt 64. reges coronati, et etiam dicunt quod maior pars illius insulæ benè inhabitatur. Et hic istius Indiæ facio finem.

De india superiori, et de Prouincia Manci.

In primis refero, quòd cum transirem per mare Oceanum per multas dietas versus Orientem, perueni ad illam magnam prouinciam Manci, quæ India vocatur à Latinis. De ista India superiori inquisiui à Christianis, Saracenis, idolatris, et omnibus, qui officiales sunt domini Canis magni, qui omnes vno ore responderunt, quod hæ prouincia Manci habet plusquam 2000, magnarum ciuitatum, et in ipsa est maxima copia omnium victualium, puta, panis, vini, risi, carnium, piscium, &c. Omnes homines istius prouinciæ sunt artifices et mercatores, qui pro quacunque penuria, dummodo proprijs manibus iuuare se possent per labores, nunquam ab aliquo eleemosynam peterent. Viri istius prouinciæ sunt satis formosi, sed pallidi, et rasas et paruas barbas habentes; foeminæ vero sunt pulcherrimæ inter omnes do mundo. Prima ciuitas ad quam veni de ista India vocatur Ceuskalon, [Marginal note: Vel Ceuscala.] et distat à mari per vnam dietam, positaque est super flumen, cuius aqua propè mare cui contignatur, ascendit super terram per 12. dietas. Totus populus illius Indiæ idolatrat. Ista autem ciuitas tantum nauigium habet, quod incredibile foret nisi videnti. [Sidenote: Hi sunt alcatrarsi vel onocratoli.] In hac ciuitate vidi quod 300. libræ de bono et recenti zinzibero habentur pro minori quam pro vno grosso: Ibi sunt anseres grossiores et pulchriores, et maius forum de illis, quam sit in mundo, vt credo, et sunt albissimi sicut lac, et habent vnum os super caput quantitatis oui, et habet colorem sanguineum, sub gula habent vnam pellem pendentem semipedalem: Pinguissimi sunt, et optimi fori: et ita est de anatibus, et gallinis, quæ magnæ sunt valdé in illa terra plusquam duæ de nostris. Ibi sunt serpentes maximi, et capiuntur et a gente illa comeduntur: vnde qui faceret festum solemne, et non daret serpentes, nihil reputaret se facere; breuiter in hac ciuitate sunt omnia victualia in maxima abundantia. Indè transiui per ciuitates multas, et veni ad ciuitatem nomine Kaitan, [Marginal note: Vel Zaiton.] in qua fratres Minores habent duo loca, ad quæ portaui de ossibus fratrum nostrorum pro fidi Christi interfectorum, de quibus supra. In hac est copia omnium victualium pro leuissimo foro, haec ciuitas ita magna est, sicut bis Bononia, et in ea multa monasteria religiosorum, qui omnes idolis seruiunt. In vno autem istorum monasteriorum ego fui, et dictum est mihi quòd inerant 3000. religiosorum habentium 11000. idoloram, et vnum illorum, quod quasi paruum inter caetera mihi videbatur, est ita magnum sicut Christophorus noster. Isti religiosi omni die pascunt Deos suos, vnde semel iui ad videntum comestionem illam, et vidi quòd illa quæ detulerunt sibi comestibilia sunt, et calidissima, et multum fumigantia, ita quòd fumus ascendit ad idola, et dixerunt Deos illo fumo recreari. Totum autem cibum illi reportauerunt et comederunt, et sic de fumo tantum Deos suos pauerunt.

De Ciuitate Fuko.

Vltra versus Orientem veni ad ciuitatem quæ vocatur Fuko, [Marginal note: Vel Foqaien.] cuius circuitus continet 30. milliaria, in qua sunt Galli maximi et pulcherrimi, et gallinæ ita albæ sicut nix, lanam solum pro pennis habentes sicut pecudes. Haec ciuitas pulcherrima est, et sita supra mare. Vltra iui per 18. dietas, et pertransij multas terras et ciuitates, et in transitu veni ad quendam montem magnum, et vidi quod in vno latere montis omnia animalia erant nigra vt carbo, et homines et mulieres diuersum modum viuendi habent: ab alio autem latere omnia animalia erant alba sicut nix, et homines totaliter diuersè ab alijs vixerunt. Ibi omnes foeminæ quæ sunt desponsatæ portant in signum quod habent maritos vnum magnum barile de cornu in capita. [Sidenote: Magnum flumen.] Inde transiui per 18. dietas alias, et veni ad quoddam magnum flumen, et intraui ciuitatem vnam, quæ transuersum illius fluminis habet pontem maximum, et hospitabar in domo vnius hospitarij, qui volens mihi complacere, dixit mihi: si velis videre piscari, veni mecum; et duxit me super pontem, et vidi in brachijs suis mergos ligatos super perticas, ad quorum gulam vbi ille ligauit vnum filum, ne illi capientes pisces, comederent eos: Postea in brachio vno posuit 3. cistas magnas, et tunc dissoluit mergos de perticis, qui statim in aquam intrauerunt, et pisces ceperunt, et cistas illas repleuerunt in pania hora, quibus repletis vir ille dissoluit fila à collis eorum, et ipsi reintrantes flumen se de piscibus recreauerunt, et recreati ad perticas redierunt, et se ligari sicut priùs permiserunt: Ego autem de illis piscibus comedi, et optimi mihi videbantur. [Sidenote: Aliâs Cansai, vel Quinzai.] Inde transiens per multas dietas veni ad vnam ciuitatem quæ vocatur Kanasia, quæ sonat in lingua nostro ciuitas coeli: Nunquam ita magnam ciuitatem vidi, Circuitus enim eus continet 100. millaria, nec in ea vidi spatium quin benè inhabitaretur; Imo vidi multas domus habentes 10. vel 12. solaria vnum supra aliud: haec habet suburbia maxima continentia maiorem populum quàm ipsa ciuitas contineat 12. portas habet principales, et in via de qualibet illarum portarum ad 8. milliaria sunt ciuitates fortè maiores vt æstimo, quàm est ciuitas Venetiarum, et Padua. Haec ciuitas sita est in aquis quæ semper stant, et nec fluunt, nec refluunt, vallum tamen habet propter ventum sicut ciuitas Venetiarum. In ea sunt plus decem mille et 2. pontium, quorum multos numeraui et transiui, et in qualibet ponte stant custodes ciuitatis continuè custodientes ciuitatem pro magno Cane imperatore Catai. Vnum mandatum dicunt gentes illius ciuitatis a domino se recepisse. Nam quilibet ignis soluit vnum balis, i. 5. cartas bombicis, qui unum florenum cum dimidio valent, et 10. vel 12. supellectiles facient vnum ignem, et sic pro vno igne soluent. Isti ignes sunt benè 85. Thuman, eum alijs 4. Saracenorum quæ faciunt 89. Thuma vero vnum decem milia ignium facit, reliqui autem de populo ciuitatis sunt alij Christiani, alij mercatores, et alij transeuntes per terram, vndè maximè fui miratus quo modo tot corpora hominum poterant simul habitare: in ea est maxima copia victualium, scz. panis et vini, et carnium de porco praecipué cum alijs necessarijs.

De monasterio vbi sunt multa animalia diuersa in quodam monte.

In illa ciuitate 4. fratres nostri conuerterant vnum potentem ad fidem Christi, in cuius hospitio continué habitabam, dum fui ibi, qui semèl dixit mihi, Ara, i. pater, vis tu venire et videre ciuitatem istam: et dixi quòd sic, et ascendimus vnam barcham, et iuimus ad vnum monasterium maximum, de quo vocauit vnum religiosum sibi notum, et dixit sibi de me. Iste Raban Francus, i. religiosus venit de indé vbi sol occidit, et nunc vadit Cambaleth, vt deprecetur vitam pro magno Cane, et ideò ostendas sibi aliquid, quòd si reuertatur ad contratas suas possit referre quod tale quid nouum vidi in Canasia ciuitate: tunc sumpsit ille religiosus duos mastellos magnos repletos reliquijs quæ supererant de mensa, et duxit me ad vnam perclusam paruam, quam aperuit cum claue, et aparuit, viridarium gratiosum et magnum in quod intrauimus, et in illo viridario stat vnas monticulus sicut vnum campanile, repletus amoenis herbis et arboribus, et dum staremus ibi, ipse sumpsit cymbalum, et incoepit percutere ipsum sicut percutitur quando monachi intrant refectorium, ad cuius sonitum multa animalia diuersa descenderunt de monte illo, aliqua vt simiæ, aliqua vt Cati, Maymones, et aliqua faciem hominis habentia, et dum sic starem congregauerunt se circa ipsum, 4000. de illis animalibus, et se in ordinibus collocauerunt, coram quibus posuit paropsidem et dabat eis comedere, et cum comedissent iterum cymbalum percussit, et omnia ad loca propria redierunt. Tunc admiratus inquisiui quæ essent animalia ista? Et respondit mihi quod sunt animæ nobilium virorum, quas nos hic pascimus amore Dei, qui regit orbem, et sicut vnus homo fuit nobilis, ita anima eius post mortem in corpus nobilis animalis intrat. Animæ verò simplicium et rusticorum, corpora vilium animalium intrant. Incoepi istam abusionem improbare, sed nihil valuit sibi, non enim poterat credere, quòd aliqua anima posset sine corpore manere. [Sidenote: Chilenso.] Indè transiui ad quandam ciuitatem nomine Chilenso, cuius muri per 40. milliaria circuerunt. In ista ciuitate sunt 360. pontes lapidei pulchriores quàm vnquam viderim, et benè inhabitatur, et nauigium maxinium habet, et copiam omnium victualium et aliorum bonorum. [Sidenote: Thalay. Kakam.] Inde iui ad quoddam flumen dictum

Thalay, quod vbi est strictius habet in latitudine 7. milliaria, et illud flumen per medium terræ Pygmæorum transit, quorum ciuitas vocatur Kakam, quæ de pulchrioribus ciuitatibus mundi est. Isti Pigmaei habent longitudinem trium spansarum mearum, et faciunt maiora et meliora goton, et bombicinam quàm aliqui homines in mundo. Indè per illud flumen transiens, veni ad vnam ciuitatem Ianzu, in qua est vnus locus fratrum nostrorum, et sunt in ea tres ecclesiæ Nestorianorum: haec ciuitas nobilis est, et magna, habens in se 48. Thuman ignium, et in ea omnia victualia, et animalia in magna copia, de quo Christiani viuunt: Dominus istius ciuitatis solum de sale habet in redditibus 50. Thuman Balisi, et valet balisus vnum florenum cum dimidio: Ita quod vnum Thuman facit 15. millia florenorum, vnam tamen gratiam facit dominus populo, quia dimittit ei, ne sit caristia in eo, 200. Thuman. Habet haec ciuitas consuetudinem, quod quando vnus vult facere conuiuium amicis suis, ad hoc sunt hospitia deputata, et vbi ille circuit per hospites, dicens sibi tales amicos meos habebis, quos festabis nomine meo, et tantum in festo volo expendere, et per illum modum meliùs conuiuant amici in pluribus hospitijs quam facerent in vno. [Sidenote: Montu.] Per 10. milliaria ab ista ciuitate in capite fluminis Thalay est vna ciuitas vocata Montu, quæ maius nauigium habet, quàm viderim in toto mundo; Et omnes naues ibi sunt albæ sicùt nix, et in ipsis sunt hospitia, et multa alia quæ nullus homo crederet nisi viderentur.

De ciuitate Cambaleth.

[Sidenote: Caramoran.] Indè transiui per 8. dietas per multas terras et ciuitates, et veni tandem per aquam dulcem ad quandam ciuitatem nomine Leneyn, quæ est posita super flumen vocatum Caramoran, quod per medium Catai transit, et magnum damnum sibi infert, quando erumpit. Indè transiens per flumen versus Orientem per multas dietas et ciuitates, veni ad vnam ciuitatem nomine Sumacoto, quæ maiorem copiam habet de serico, quàm aliqua ciuitas in mundo: Quando enim est maior caristia Serici, ibi 40. libræ habentur pro minori quàm pro 8. grossis. In ea est copia omnium mercimoniorum et omnium victualium, panis, vini, carnium, piscium, et omnium specierum electarum. [Sidenote: Cambalec.] Inde transiui versus Orientem per multas ciuitates, et veni ad illam nobilem, et nominatam Cambaleth quæ est ciuitas multum antiqua, et veni ad Catai, et eam ceperunt Tartari: Et iuxta eam ad dimidium miliare aliam ciuitatem fecerunt, quæ vocatur Caido et haec 12. portas habet, et semper inter vnam et aliam sunt duo miliaria, et medium inter illas ciuitates benè inhabitatur, ita quòd faciunt quasi vnam ciuitatem; Et ambitus istarum duarum ciuitatum est plusquàm 40. milliaria. [Sidenote: Mandeuil cap. 33.] In hac ciuitate magnus imperator Canis habet sedem suam principalem, et suum magnum palatium, cuius muri bene 4. miliaria continent; et infra illud palatium sunt multa alia palatia dominorum de familia sua. In palatio etiam illo est vnus mons pulcherrimus consitus arboribus, propter quod mons viridis nominatur, et in monte palatium amoenissimum in quo communitèr Canis residet: A latere autem montis est vnus lacus magnus, supra quem pons pulcherrimus est factus, et in illo lacu est magna copia anserum et anatum, et omnium auium aquaticarum; et in silua montis copia omnium auium et ferarum siluestrium, et ideo quando dominus Canis vult venari non oportet eum exire palatium suum. Palatium vero principale, in quo sedes sua est, est magnum valde, et habet interius 14. columnas aureas, et omnes muri eius cooperti sunt pellibus rubeis quæ dicuntur nobiliores pelles de mundo: Et in medio palatij est vna pigna altitudinis duorum passuum, quæ tota est de vno lapide pretioso nomine merdochas; et est tota circumligata auro, et in quolibet angulo eius est vnum serpens de auro qui verberatos fortissimé: Habet etiam haec pignaretia de margaritis, et per istam pignam defertur potus per meatus et conductus qui in curia regis habetur; et iuxta eam pendent multa vasa aurea cum quibus volentes bibere possunt. In hoc autem palatio sunt multi pauones de auro; et cùm aliquis Tartarus facit festum domino suo, tunc quando conuiuantes collidunt manus suas præ gaudio et læticia, pauones emittunt alas suas, et expandunt caudas, et videntur tripudiare; Et hoc credo factura arte Magica, vel aliqua cautela subterranea.

De gloria magni Canis.

Qvando autem magnus ille Imperator Canis in sede sua imperiali residet, tunc a sinistro latere sedet Regina, et per vnum gradum inferius duo mulieres quas ipse tenet pro se; quando non potest ad Reginam accedere: In infimo autem gradu resident omnes dominae de sua parentela. Omnes autem mulieres nuptæ portant supra caput suum vnum pedem hominis, longitudinis vnius brachij cum dimidio; et subter illum pedem sunt pennæ gruis, et totus ille pes ornatur maximis margaritis. A latero verò dextro ipsius Canis resident filius eius primogenitus, regnaturus post ipsum, et inferius ipso omnes qui sunt de sanguine regio: Ibi etiam sunt 4. scriptores scribentes omnia verba quæ dicit rex; Ante cuius conspectum sunt Barones sui, et multi alij nobiles cum sua gente maxima, quorum nullus audet loqui nisi a domino licentia petatur exceptis fatuis et histrionibus, qui suum dominum consolari habent; Illi etiam nihil audent facere, nisi secundum quod Dominus voluerit eis legem imponere. Ante portam palatij sunt Barones custodientes, ne aliquis limen portæ tangat. Cùm autem ille Canis voluerit facere conuiuium, habet secum 14000. Barones portantes circulos, et coronulas in capite, et domino suo seruientes; Et quilibet portat vnam vestem de auro et margaritis tot quot valent plus quam decies millies florenorum. Curia eius optime ordinatur per denarios, centenarios, et millenarios, et taliter quòd quilibet in suo ordine peragit officium sibi deputatum, nec aliquis defectus reperitur. Ego frater Odoricus fui ibi per tres annos, et multotiens in istis festis suis fui, quià nos fratres minores in sua curia habemus locum nobis deputatum, et oportet nos semper ire, et dare sibi nostram benedictionem: et inquisiui ab illis de curia, de numero illorum qui sunt in curia domini, et responderunt mihi quod de histrionibus sunt bene 18. Thuman; Custodes autem canum et bestiarum, et auium sunt. 15. Thuman; Medici vero pro corpore Regis sunt 400. Christiani autem 8. et vnus Saracenus. Et ego quando fui ibi, hij omnes omnia necessaria tam ad victum, quam ad vestitum habebant de Curia domini Canis. Quando autem vult equitare de vna terra ad aliam, habet 4. exercitus equitum, et vnus per vnam dietam ipsum antecedit, secundus aliam, et tertius similitèr, et quartus; ita quod semper ipse se tenet in medio in modum crucis; et ita omnes exercitus habent omnes dietas suas ordinatas, quod inueniunt omnia victualia parata sine defectu. Illémet autem dominus Canis per illum modum vadit; Sedet in curru cum duabus rotis in quo facta est pulcherrima sella tota de lignis Aloe, et auro ornata, et margaritis maximis, et lapidibus pretiosis; et 4. Elephantes bene ordinati ducunt istum currum, quos praecedunt 4. equi altissimi optime cooperti. Iuxta currum à lateribus sunt 4. Barones tenentes currum, ne aliquis appropinquet domino suo. Supra currum sedent duo Gerfalcones albissimi, et dùm videt aues quos vult capere, dimittit Falcones volare, et capiunt eas; Et sic habet solatium suum equitando, et per iactum vnius lapidis nullus audet appropinquare currui nisi populus assignatus: vnde incredibile esset homini qui non vidisset de numero gentis suæ, et reginæ, et primogeniei sui. Istæ Dominus Canis imperium suum diuisit in 12. partes, et vna habet sub se 200. magnarum ciuitatum: vnde ita latum et longum est suum imperium, quod ad quamcunque partem iret, satis haberes facere in sex mensibus, exceptis insulis, quæ sunt bene 5000.

De hospitijs paratis per totum imperium pro transeuntibus.

Iste Dominus, vt transeuntes habeant omnia necessaria sua per totum suum imperium, fecit hospitia praeparari vbique per vias; in quibus sunt omnia parata quæ ad victualia pertinent: Cum autem aliqua nouitas oritur in imperio suo, tunc si distat, ambassiatores super equos vel dromedarios festinant, et cùm lassantur in cursu, pulsant cornu, et proximum hospitium parat vnum similitèr, equum, qui quando alius venit fessus accipit literam, et currit ad hospitium, et sic per hospitia, et per diuersos cursores rumor per 30. dietas, vno die naturali venit ad imperatorem; et ideò nihil ponderis potest fieri in imperio suo, quin statim scitur ab eo. Cum autem ipse Canis vult ire venatum; istum modum habet. Extra Cambaleth ad 20. dietas, est vna foresta quæ 6. dietas continet in ambitu; in qua sunt tot genera animalium et auium quòd mirabile est dicere: Ad illud nemus vadit in fine trium annorum vel quatuor cum tota gente, cum qua ipsum circuit, et canes intrare permittit, qui animalia, scilicet leones, ceruos, et alia animalia reducunt ad vnam planitiem pulcherrimam in medio nemoris, quia ex clamoribus canum maximè tremunt omnes bestiæ syluæ. Tunc accedit magnus Canis super tres elephantes et 5. sagittas mittit in totam multitudinem animalium, et post ipsum omnes Barones, et post ipsos alij de familia sua emittunt sagittas suas; et omnes sagittæ sunt signatæ certis signis et diuersis: Tunc vadit ad animalia interfecta, dimittens viua nemus reintrare vt aliàs habeat ex eis venationem suam, et quilibet illud animal habebit in cuius corpere inuenit sagittam suam quam iaciebat.

De quatuor festis quæ tenet in anno Canis in curia.

Quatuor magna festa in anno facit Dominus Canis, scilicet festum natiuitatis, festum circumcisionis, coronationis, et desponsationis suæ; et ad ista festa conuocat omnes Barones, et histriones, et omnes de parentela sua. Tunc domino Cane in suo throno sedente, accedunt Barones cum circulis et coronis in capite, vestiti vario modo, quia aliqui de viridi, scilicet primi, secundi de sanguineo, et tertij de croceo, et tenent in manibus vnam tabulam eburneam de dentibus Elephantum, et cinguntur cingulis aureis vno semisse latis, et stant pedibus silentium tenentes. Circa illos stant histriones cum suis instrumentis: In vno autem angulo cuiusdam magni palatij resident Philosophi omnes ad certas horas, et puncta attendentes: et cum deuenitur ad punctumn et horam petitam à philosopho, vnus praeco clamat valentèr. Inclinetis vos omnes imperatori vestro: tunc omnes Barones cadunt ad terram; et iterum clamat, Surgite omnes, et illi statim surgunt. Iterum philosophi ad aliud punctum attendunt, et cùm peruentum fuerit, iterum praeco clamat; ponite digitum in aurem, et statim dicit, extrahite ipsum; iterùm ad aliud punctum clamat, Buratate farinam: et multa alia faciunt, quæ omnia dicunt certam signifcationem habere, quæ scriberi nolui, nec curaui, quia vana sunt et risu digna. Cùm autem peruentum fuerit ad horam histrionum, time Philosophi dicunt, facite festum domino, et omnes pulsant instrumenta sua, et faciunt maximum sonitum; et statim alius clamat; Taceant omnes, et omnes tacent: Tunc accedunt histrionatrices ante dominum dulcitèr modulantes, quod mihi plus placuit. Tunc veniunt leones, et faciunt reuerentiam domino Cani; Et tunc histriones faciunt ciphos aureos plenos vino volare per aerem, et ad ora hominum se applicare vt bibant. Haec et multa alia mirabilia in curia illius Canis vidi, quæ nullus crederet nisi videret; et ideò dimitto ea. De alio mirabili audiui à fide dignis, quòd in vno regno istius Canis in quo sunt montes Kapsei (et dicitur illud regnum Kalor) nascuntur pepones maximi, qui quando sunt maturi aperiuntur, et intùs inuenitur vna bestiola similis vni agnello: sicut audiui quòd in mari Hybernico stant arbores supra ripam maris et portant fructum sicut essent cucurbitæ, quæ certo tempore cadunt in aquam et fiunt aues vocatæ Bernakles, et illud est verum.

De diuersis Prouincijs et ciuitatibus.

De isto imperio Katay recessi post tres annos, et transiui 50. dietas versus Occidentem; et tandem veni ad terram Pretegoani, cuius ciuitas principalis Kosan vocatur, quæ multas habet sub se ciuitates. [Sidenote: Casan.] Vltra per multas dietas iui, et perueni ad vnam prouinciam vocatam Kasan; et haec est secunda melior prouincia mundi, vt dicitur, et est optimè habitata: Sic quod quando exitur à porta vnius ciuitatis, videntur portæ alterius ciuitatis, sicut egomet vidi de multis. Latitudo Prouinciæ est 50. dietarum, et longitudo plusquam 60. In ea est maxima copia omnium victualium, et maximè castaneorum; et haec est vna de 12. prouincijs magni Canis. [Sidenote: Tibec regio aliàs Tebet Guillielmo de Rubricis.] Vltra veni ad vnum regnum vocatum Tibek quod est subiectum Cani, in quo est maior copia panis et vini, quam sit in toto mundo vt credo. Gens illius terræ moratur communiter in tenorijs factis ex feltris nigris: Principalis ciuitas sua murata est pulcherrimè ex lapidibus albissimis, et nigerrimis interescalariter dispositis et curiosè compositis, et omnes viæ eius optimè pouatæ. In ista contrata nullus audet effundere sanguinem hominis, nec alicuius animalis, ob reuerentiam vnius Idoli. In ista ciuitate moratur Abassi i. Papa eorum, qui est caput et princeps omnium Idolatrarum; quibus dat et distribuit beneficia secundum morem eorum; sicut noster Papa Romanus est caput omnium Christianorum. Foeminæ in hoc regno portant plusquam centum tricas, et habent duos dentes in ore ita longos sicut apri. Quando etiam pater alicuius moritur, tunc filius conuocat omnes sacerdotes et histriones, et dicit se velle patrem suum honorare, et facit eum ad campum duci sequentibus parentibus omnibus, amicis, et vicinis, vbi sacerdotes cum magna solemnitate amputant caput suum, dantes illud filio suo, et tunc totum corpus in frusta concidunt, et ibi dimittunt, cum orationibus cum eo redeuntes; [Sidenote: Eadem historia de eodem populo apud Guilielmum de Rubricis.] Tunc veniunt vultures, de monte assuefacti ad huiusmodi, et carnes omnes asportant: Et ex tunc currit fama de eo quòd sanctus est, quia angeli domini ipsum portant in paradisum: Et iste est maximus honor, quem reputat filius posse fieri patri suo mortuo: Tunc filius sumit caput patris, et coquit ipsum, et comedit, de testa eius faciens ciphum in quo ipse cum omnibus de domo et cognatione eius bibunt cum solemnitate et laetitia in memoriam patris comesti. Et multa vilia et abominabilia facit gens illa quæ non scribo, quia non valent, nec homines crederent nisi viderent.

De diuite qui pascitur à 50. Virginibus.

Dum fui in prouincia Manzi transiui iuxta palatium vnius hominis popularis, qui habuit 50. domicellas virgines sibi continuè ministrantes, in omnibus pascentes eum sicut auis auiculas, et habet semper 5. fercula triplicata; et quando pascunt eum, continuè cantant dulcissimè: Iste habet in redditibus Tagaris risi 30. Thuman, quorum quodlibet decies millies facit: vnum autem Tagar pondus est asini. Palatium suum duo millaria tenet in ambitu; cuius pauimentum semper vnum laterem habet aureum, alium argenteum: Iuxta ambitum istius palatij est vnus monticulus artificialis de auro et argento, super quo stant Monasteria, et campanilia, et alia delectabilia pro solatio illius popularis; Et dictum fuit mihi, quòd quatuor tales homines sunt in regno illo. [Sidenote: Mulierum parui pedes.] Nobilitas virorum est longos habere vngues in digitis, praecipue pollicis quibus circueunt sibi manus: Nobilitas autem et pulchritudo mulierum est pauos habere pedes: Et ideò matres quando filiæ suæ sunt tenellæ ligant pedes earum, et non dimittunt crescere. [Sidenote: Milestorite.] Vltra transiens versus meridiem applicui ad quandam contratam, quæ vocatur Milestorite, quæ pulchra est valdè et fertilis: Et in ista contrata erat vnus vocatus Senex de monte, qui inter duos montes fecerat sibi vnum murum circumuentem istos montes. Infra istum murum erant fontes pulcherrimi de mundo; Et iuxta fontes erant pulcherrimæ virgines in maximo numero, et equi pulcherrimi, et omni illud quod ad suauitatem, et delectationem corporis fieri poterit, et ideo illum locum vocant homines illius contratæ Paradisum. Iste senex cùm viderit aliquem iuuenem formosum et robustum, posuit eum in illo paradiso; Per quosdam autem conductus descendere facit vinum et lac abundantèr. Iste Senex cùm voluerit se vindicare, vel interficere regem aliquem vel Baronem, dicit illi qui præerat illi paradiso vt aliquem de notis illius regis, vel Baronis introduceret in paradisum illum, et illum delicijs frui permitteret, et tunc daret sibi potionem vnam, quæ ipsum sopiebat in tantum, quòd insensibilem redderet, et ipsum sic dormientem faceret extra paradisum deportari: qui excitatus et se extra paradisum conspiciens, in tanta tristitia positus foret, quòd nesciret quid faceret: Tunc ad illum senem iret, rogans eum, vt interùm in paradisum introduceretur: qui sibi dicit, tu illic introduci non poteris, nisi talem vel talem interficias; et siue interfeceris, siue non, reponam te in paradiso, et ibidem poteris semper manere; Tunc ille sic faceret, et omnes seni odiosos interficeret; Et ideò omnes reges orientales illum senem timuerunt, et sibi tributum magnum dederunt.

De morte Senis de monte.

Cum autem Tartari magnam partem mundi cepissent, venerunt ad istum Senem, et dominium illius Paradisi ab eo abstulerunt, qui multos sicarios de Paradiso illo emisit, et nobiliores Tartarorum interfici fecit. Tartari autem hoc videntes ciuitatem, in qua erat senex obsederunt, eum ceperunt, et pessima morte interfecerunt. Hanc gratiam habent fratres ibidem, quod citissimè per virtutem nominis Christi Iesu, et in virtute illius sanguinis pretiosi, quem effudit in cruce pro salute generis humani, daemonia ab obsessis corporibus expellunt; et quia multi ibidem sum obsessi, ducuntur per decem dietas ad fratres ligati, qui liberati statim credunt in Christum, qui liberauit ebs habentes ipsum pro Deo suo, et baptizati sunt, et idola sua, et pecorum suorum statim dant fratribus, quæ sunt communitèr de feltro, et de crinibus mulierum et fratres ignem in communi loci faciunt ad quem populus confluit, vt videat Deos vicinorum suorum comburi et fratres coram populo Idola in ignem proijciunt; Et prima vice de igne exierunt; Tunc fratres ignem cum aqua benedicta conspercerunt, et interùm Idola in ignem proiecerunt, et daemones in effigie fumi nigerrimi fugerunt, et Idola remanserunt, et combusta sunt. Posteà auditor clamor per aerem talis, vide, vide, quo modo de habitatione mea expulsus sum. Et per istum modum fratres maximam multitudinem baptizant, qui citò recidiuant ad idola pecorum: qui fratres continuò quasi stent cum illis, et illos informent. Aliud terribile fuit quod ego vidi ibi. Nam cùm irem per vnam vallem quæ sita est iuxta fluuium deliciarum, multa corpora mortua vidi, et in illa valle audiui sonos musicos dulces et diuersos, et maximè de cytharis, vndè multum timui. Haec vallis habet longitudinem septem, vel octo milliarium ad plus, in quam si quis intrat, moritur, et nunquam viuus potest transire per medium illius vallis, et ideò omnes de contrata declinant à latere: Et tentatus eram intrare, et videre, quid hoc esset. Tandem oratis et Deo me recommendans, et cruce signans, in nomine Iesu intraui, et vidi tot corpora mortua ibi, quòd nullus crederet nisi videret In hac valle ab vno eius latere, in vno saxo vnam faciem hominis vidi, quæ ita terribilitèr me respexit, quòd omnino credidi ibi fuisse mortuus: Sed semper hoc verbum (verbum caro factum est et habitauit in nobis) protuli, et cruce me signaui, nec propiùs quàm per 7. passus, vel 8. accedere capiti ausus fui: Iui autem fugiens ad aliud caput vallis, et super vnum monticulum arenosum ascendi, in quo vndique circumspiciens nihil vidi nisi cytharas illas, quas per se (vt mihi videbatur) pulsari et resonare mirabiliter audiui. Cùm vero fui in cacumine montis, inueni ibi argentum in maxima quantitate, quasi fuissent squamæ piscium. Congregans autem inde in gremio meo pro mirabili ostendendo, sed ductus conscientia, in terram proieci, nihil mecum reseruans, et sic per gratiam Dei liber exiui. Cùm autem homines illius contratæ sciuerunt me viuum exisse, reuerebantur me multum, dicentes me baptizatum et sanctum: et corpora illa fuisse daemonum infernalium qui pulsant cytharas vt homines alliciant intare, et interficiant. Haec de visis certudinalitér ego frater Odoricus hic inscripsi; et multa mirabilia omisi ponere, quia homines hon credidissent nisi vidissent.

De honore et reuerentia factis Domino Cani.

Vnum tantùm referam de magno Cane quod vidi. Consuetudo est in partibus illis quòd quando praedictus dominus per aliquam contratam transit, homines ante ostia sua accendunt ignem et apponunt aromata, ac faciunt fumum, vt dominus transiens suauem sentiat adorem, et multi obuiam sibi vadunt. Dum autem semel veniret in Cambeleth, et fama vndique diuulgaretur de suo aduentu, vnus noster Episcopus, et aliqui nostri minores fratres et ego iuimus obuiàm sibi benè per duas dietas: Et dum appropinquaremus ad eum, posuimus crucem super lignum, et ego habebam mecum in manu thuribulum, et incepimus cantare alta voce dicentes: Veni creator spiritus: Et dum sic cantaremus audiuit voces, nostras, fecítque nos vocari, ac iussit nos ad eum accedere; cùm vt suprà dictum est, nullus audeat appropinquare currui suo ad iactum lapidis, nisi vocatus, exceptis illis qui currum custodiunt. Et dum iuissemus ad eum, ipse deposuit galerum suum, sine capellum inestimabilis quasi valoris, et fecit reuerentiam Cruci; et statim incensum posui in thuribulo; Episcopus noster accepit thuribulum, et thurificauit eum; ac sibi praedictus Episcopus dedit benedictionem suam. Accedentes verò ad praedictum dominum, sempèr sibi aliquid offerendum deferunt; secum illam antiquam legem obseruantes; Non apparebis in conspectu meo vacuus; Idcirco portauimus nobiscum poma, et ea sibi super vnum incisorium reuerentèr obtulimus; et ipse duo accepit, et de vno aliquantulum comedit: Et tunc fecit nobis signum quod recederemus, ne equi venientes in aliquo nos offenderent; statimque ab eo discessimus, atque diuertimus, et iuimus ad aliquos Barones per fratres nostri ordinis ad fidem conuersos, qui in exercitu eius erant, et eis obtulimus de pomis praedictis, qui cum maximo gaudio ipsa accipientes ita videbantur laetari, ac si praebuissemus eis familiaritèr magnum munus. Haec praedicta frater Guilelmus de Solangna in scriptis redegit, sicùt praedictus frater Odoricus ore tenus exprimebat. Anno Domini 1330, mense Maij in loco Sancti Antonij de Padua; Nec curauit de latino difficili, et stilo ornato; Sed sicut ipse narrabat ad hoc vt homines faciliùs intelligerent quæ dicuntur. Ego frater Odoricus de Foro Iulij de quadam terra quæ dicitur Portus Vahonis de ordine minorum testificor, et testimonium perhibeo reuerendo patri Guidoto ministro prouinciæ Sancti Antonij in Marchia Triuisana, cùm ab eo fuerim per obedientiam requisitus, quòd haec omnia quæ superiùs scripta sunt, aut proprijs oculis ego vidi, aut a fide dignis audiui: Communis etiam loquutio illarum terrarum illa quæ nec vidi testatur esse; Multa etiam alia ego dimisissem, nisi illa proprijs oculis conspexissem. Ego autem de die in diem me propono contratas seu terras accedere, in quibus mori, et viuere me dispono, si placuerit Deo meo.

De morte fratris Odorici.

Anno igitur Domini 1331. disponente se praedicto fratre Odorico ad perficiendum iter suæ peregrinationis, prout mente conceperat, et etiam vt via et labor esset sibi magnis ad meritum, decreuit primò praesentiam adire Domini et patris omnium summi Pontificis Domini Ioannis Papæ 22: cuius benedictione obedientiaque recepta cum societate fratrum secum ire volentium ad partes infidelium se transferret: Cùmque sic eundo versus summum Pontificem, non multum distaret à ciuitate Pisana, in quadam via occurrit sibi quidam senex in habitu peregrini eum salutans ex nomine, Aue (inquiens) frater Odorice: Et cùm frater quaereret quo modo ipsius haberet noticiam? Respondit, Dum eras in India noui te, tuùm qui noui sanctum propositum; Sed et tu modò ad conuentum vndè venisti reuertere, quia die sequenti decimo ex hoc mundo migrabis. Verbis igitur senis attonitus et stupefactus, praesertim cùm Senex ille statim post dictum ab eius aspectu disparuit; reuerti decreuit; Et reuersus est in bona prosperitate nullam sentiens grauedinem corporis, seu aliquam infirmitatem; Cùmque esset in conuentu suo Vtinensi. N. in prouincia Paduana decimo die, prout facti sibi fuir reuelatio, accepta communione, ipsoque ad Deum disponente, etiam corpore existens incolumis in Domino foeliciter requieuit: Cuius sacer obitus Domino summo Pontifici praefato sub manu Notarij publici transmittitur; qui sic scribet.

Anno Domini 1331. decima quarta die mensis Ianuarij obijt in Christo Beatus Odoricus ordinis fratrum Minorum, cuius precibus omnipotens Deus multa, et varia miracula demonstrauit; quæ ego Guetelus notarius communis Vtini, filius domini Damiani de portu Gruario, de mandato et voluntate nobilis viri Domini Conradi de Buardigio Castaldionis, et consilij Vtini, scripsi, sicut potui, bona fide, et fratribus Minoribus exemplum dedi; sed non de omnibus, quià sunt innumerabilia, et mihi difficilia ad scribendum.

The same in English.

Here beginneth the iournall of Frier Odoricus, one of the order of the Minorites, concerning strange things which hee sawe among the Tarters of the East.

Albeit many and sundry things are reported by diuers authors concerning the fashions and conditions of this world: notwithstanding I frier Odoricus of Friuli, de portu Vahonis being desirous to trauel vnto the foreign and remote nations of infidels, sawe and heard great and miraculous things, which I am able truely to auoch. [Sidenote: Pera. Trapesunda.] First of al therefore sayling from Pera by Constantinople, I arriued at Trapesunda. This place is right commodiously situate, as being an hauen for the Persians and Medes, and other countreis beyonde the sea. In this lande I behelde with great delight a very strange spectacle, namely a certaine man leading about with him more then foure thousande partriges. The man himselfe walked vpon the ground, and the partriges flew in the aire, which he ledde vnto a certaine castle called Zauena, being three dayes iourney distant from Trapesunda. The saide partriges were so tame, that when the man was desirous to lie downe and rest, they would all come flocking about him like chickens. And so hee led them vnto Trapesunda, and vnto the palace of the Emperour, who tooke as many of them as he pleased, and the rest the saide man carried vnto the place from whence he came. In this citie lyeth the body of Athanasius, vpon the gate of the citie. [Sidenote: The citie of

Azaron in Armenia maior.] And then I passed on further vnto Armenia maior, to a certaine citie called Azaron, which had bene very rich in olde time, but nowe the Tarters haue almost layde it waste. In the saide citie there was abundance of bread and flesh, and of all other victuals except wine and fruites. This citie also is very colde, and is reported to be higher situated, then any other city in the world. It hath most holesome and sweete waters about it: for the veines of the said waters seeme to spring and flow from the mighty riuer of Euphrates, which is but a dayes iourney from the saide city. Also, the said citie stands directly in the way to Tauris. [Sidenote: Sobissacalo.] And I passed on vnto a certaine mountaine called Sobissacalo. In the foresaide countrey there is the very same mountalne whereupon the Arke of Noah rested: vnto the which I would willingly haue ascended, if my company would haue stayed for me. Howbeit the people of that countrey report, that no man could euer ascend the said mountaine, because (say they) it pleaseth not the highest God. [Sidenote: Tauris a citie of Persia.] And I trauailed on further vnto Tauris that great and royal city, which was in old time called Susis. This city is accompted for traffique of marchandize the chiefe city of the world: for there is no kinde of victuals, nor anything else belonging vnto marchandize, which is not to be had there in great abundance. This city stands very commodiously: for vnto it all the nations of the whole worlde in a maner may resort for traffique. Concerning the saide citie, the Christians in those parts are of opinion, that the Persian Emperour receiues more tribute out of it, then the King of France out of all his dominions. Neare vnto the said city there is a salt-hill yeelding salt vnto the city: and of that salt ech man may take what pleaseth him, not paying ought to any man therefore. In this city many Christians of all nations do inhabite, ouer whom the Saracens beare rule in alle things. Then I traueiled on further vnto a city called Soldania, [Marginal note: Or, Sultania.] wherein the Persian Emperour lieth all Sommer time: but in winter hee takes his progresse vnto another city standing upon the sea called Baku. [Marginal note: The Caspian sea.] Also the foresaid city is very great and colde, hauing good and holesome waters therein, vnto the which also store of marchandize is brought. Moreouer I trauelled with a certaine company of Carauans toward vpper India: and in the way, after many days iourney, I came vnto the citie of the three wise men called Cassan [Marginal Note: Or Cassibin.], which is a noble and renowmed city, sauing that the Tartars haue destroyed a great part thereof, and it aboundeth with bread, wine, and many other commodities. From this city vnto Ierusalem (whither the three foresaid wise-men were miraculously led) it is fiftie days iourney. There be many wonders in this citie also, which, for breuities sake, I omit [Sidenote: Geste.] From thence I departed vnto a certaine city called Geste, whence the Sea of Sand is distant, one dayes iourney, which is a most wonderful and dangerous thing. In this city there is abundance of all kinds of victuals, and especially of figs, reisins, and grapes; more (as I suppose) then in any part of the whole world besides. This is one of the three principall cities in all the Persian Empire. Of this city the Saracens report, that no Christian can by any meanes liue therein aboue a yeere. [Sidenote: Como.] Then passing many dayes iourney on forward, I came vnto a certaine citie called Comum, which was an huge and mightie Citie in olde time, conteyning well nigh fiftie miles in circuite, and hath done in times past great damage vnto the Romanes. In it there are stately palaces altogether destitute of inhabitants, notwithstanding it aboundeth with great store of victuals. From hence traueiling through many countreys, at length I came vnto the land of Iob named Hus, which is fulle of all kinde of victuals, and very pleasantly situated. Thereabouts are certaine mountains hauing good pastures for cattell upon them. Here also Manna is found in great aboundance. Four partriges are here solde for lesse than a groat In this countrey there are most comely olde men. Here also the men spin and card, and not the women. This land bordereth vpon the North part of Chalddæa.

Of the maners of the Chaldaeans, and of India.

[Sidenote: The Tower of Babel.] From thence I traueled into Chaldæa which is a great kingdome, and I passed by the tower of Babel. This region hath a language peculiar vnto it selfe, and there are beautifull men, and deformed women. The men of the same countrey vse to haue their haire kempt, and trimmed like vnto our women: and they weare golden turbants vpon their heades richly set with pearle, and pretious stones. The women are clad in a coarse smock onely reaching to their knees, and hauing long sleeues hanging downe to the ground. And they goe bare-footed, wearing breeches which reach to the ground also. Thei weare no attire vpon their heads, but their haire hangs disheaueled about their eares: and there be many other strange things also. From thence I came into the lower India, which the Tartars ouerran and wasted. And in this countrey the people eat dates for the most part, whereof 42. li. are there sold for lesse than a groat. [Sidenote: Ormus.] I passed further also many dayes iourney vnto the Ocean sea, and the first land where I arriued, is called Ormes, being well fortified, and hauing great store of marchandize and treasure therein. Such and so extreme is the heat in that countrey, that the priuities of men come out of their bodies and hang down euen vnto their mid-legs. And therefore the inhabitants of the same place, to preserue their own liues, do make a certaine ointment, and anointing their priuie members therewith, do lap them up in certaine bags fastened vnto their bodies, for otherwise they must needs die. Here also they vse a kinde of Bark or shippe called Iase being compact together onely with hempe. [Sidenote: Thana, whereof Frederick Cæsar maketh mention.] And I went on bourd into one of them, wherein I could not finde any yron at all, and in the space of 28 dayes I arriued at the city of Thana, wherein foure of our friers were martyred for the faith of Christ. This countrey is well situate, hauing abundance of bread and wine, and of other victuals therein. This kingdome in olde time was very large and vnder the dominion of king Porus, who fought a great battell with Alexander the great. The people of this countrey are idolaters worshipping fire, serpents and trees. And ouer all this land the Saracen do beare rule, who tooke it by maine force, and they themselues are in subjection vnto King Daldilus. There be diuers kinds of beasts, as namely blacke lyouns in great abundance, and apes also, and monkeis, and battes as bigge as our doues. Also there are mise as bigge as our countrey dogs, because cats are not able to incounter them. Moreouer in the same countrey euery man hath a bundle of great boughs standing in a water-pot before his doore, which bundle is as great as a pillar, and it will not wither, so long as water is applied thereunto: with many other nouelties and strange things, the relation whereof would breed great delight.

How peper is had: and where it groweth.

[Sidenote: Malabar.] Moreouer, that it may be manifest how peper is had, it is to be vnderstood that it groweth in a certaine kingdome whereat I my selfe arriued, being called Minibar, and it is not so plentifull in any other part of the worlde as it is there. For the wood wherein it growes conteineth in circuit 18 dayes iourney. And in the said wood or forrest there are two cities, one called Flandrina, and the other Cyncilim. In Flandrina both Iewes and Christians doe inhabite, betweene whom there is often contention and warre: howbeit the Christians ouercome the Iewes at all times. In the foresaid wood pepper is had after this maner: first it groweth in leaues like vnto pot-hearbs, which they plant neere vnto great trees as we do our vines, and they bring forth pepper in clusters, as our vines doe yeeld grapes, but being ripe, they are of a greene colour, and are gathered as we gather grapes, and then the graines are layed in the Sunne to be dried, and being dried are put into earthen vessels: and thus is pepper made and kept. Now, in the same wood there be many riuers, wherein are great store of Crocodiles, and of other serpents, which the inhabitants thereabout do burne vp with straw and with other dry fewel, and so they go to gather their pepper without danger. [Sidenote: Polumbrum.] At the South end of the said forrest stands the city of Polumbrum, which aboundeth with marchandize of all kinds. All the inhabitants of that countrey do worship a liuing oxe, as their god, whom they put to labour for sixe yeres, and in the seuenth yere they cause him to rest from al his worke, placing him in a solemne and publique place, and calling him an holy beast Moreouer they vse this foolish ceremonie: Euery morning they take two basons, either of siluer, or of gold, and with one they receiue the vrine of the oxe, and with the other his dung. With the vrine they wash their face, their eyes, and all their fiue senses. Of the dung they put into both their eyes, then they anoint the bals of the cheeks therewith, and thirdly their breast: and then they say that they are sanctified for all that day; And as the, people doe, euen so doe their King and Queene. This people worshippeth also a dead idole, which, from the nauel vpward, resembleth a man, and from the nauel downeward an oxe. The very same Idol deliuers oracles vnto them, and sometimes requireth the blood of fourtie virgins for his hire. And therefore the men of that region do consecrate their daughters and their sonnes vnto their idols, euen as Christians do their children vnto some Religion or Saint in heauen. Likewise they sacrifice their sonnes and their daughters, and so, much people is put to death before the said Idol by reason of that accursed ceremony. Also, many other hainous and abominable villanies doeth that brutish beastly people commit: and I sawe many moe strange things among them which I meane not here to insert. [Sidenote: The burning of their dead.] Another most vile custome the foresaide nation doeth retaine: for when any man dieth they burne his dead corps to ashes: and if his wife suruiueth him, her they burne quicke, because (say they) she shall accompany her husband in his tilthe and husbandry, when he is come into a new world. Howbeit the said wife hauing children by her husband, may if she will, remain with them, without shame or reproach; notwithstanding, for the most part, they all of them make choice to be burnt with their husbands. Now, albeit the wife dieth before her husband, that law bindeth not the husband to any such inconuenience, but he may mary another wife also. Likewise, the said nation hath another strange custome, in that their women drink wine, but their men do not. Also the Women haue the lids and brows of their eyes and beards shauen, but the men haue not: with many other base and filthy fashions which the said women do vse contrary to the nature of their sexe. [Sidenote: Mobar, or Maliapor.] From that kingdom I traueiled 10. daies iourney vnto another kingdome called Mobar, which containeth many cities. Within a certaine church of the same countrey, the body of S. Thomas the Apostle is interred, the very same church being full of idols: and in 15. houses round about the said Church, there dwell certaine priests who are Nestorians, that is to say, false, and bad Christians, and schismatiques.

Of a strange and vncouth idole: and of certaine customes and ceremonies.

In the said kingdome of Mobar there is a wonderfull strange idole, being made after the shape and resemblance of a man, as big as the image of our Christopher, et [sic passim—KTH] consisting all of most pure and glittering gold. And about the neck thereof hangeth a silke riband, ful of most rich and precious stones, some one of which is of more value then a whole kingdome. The house of this idol is all of beaten gold, namely the roofe, the pauement, and the sieling of the wall within and without. Vnto this idol the Indians go on pilgrimage, as we do vnto S. Peter. Some go with halters about their necks, some with their hands bound behind them, some others with kniues sticking on their armes or legs: and if after their peregrination, the flesh of their wounded arme festereth or corrupteth, they esteeme that limme to be holy, and thinke that their God is wel pleased with them. Neare vnto the temple of that idol is a lake made by the hands of men in an open et common place, whereinto the pilgrimes cast gold, siluer, and precious stones, for the honour of the idol and the repairing of his temple. And therefore when any thing is to be adorned or mended, they go vnto this lake taking vp the treasure which was cast in. Moreouer at euery yerely feast of the making or repairing of the said idol, the king and queene, with the whole multitude of the people, and all the pilgrimes assemble themselues, and placing the said idol in a most stately and rich chariot, they cary him out of their temple with songs, and with all kind of musical harmonie, and a great company of virgins go procession-wise two and two in a rank singing before him. Many pilgrims also put themselues vnder the chariot wheeles, to the end that their false god may go ouer them: and al they ouer whom the chariot runneth, are crushed in pieces, and diuided asunder in the midst, and slaine right out. Yea, and in doing this, they think themselues to die most holily and securely, in the seruice of their god. And by this meanes euery yere, there die vnder the said filthy idol, mo then 500. persons, whose carkases are burned, and their ashes are kept for reliques, because they died in that sort for their god. Moreouer they haue another detestable ceremony. For when any man offers to die in the seruice of his false god, his parents, and all his friends assemble themselues together with a consort of musicians, making him a great and solemne feast: which feast being ended, they hange 5. sharpe kniues about his neck carying him before the idol, and so soone as he is come thither, he taketh one of his kniues crying with a loud voice, For the worship of my god do I cut this my flesh, and then he casteth the morsel which is cut, at the face of his idol: but at the very last wound wherewith he murthereth himselfe, he vttereth these words: Now do I yeeld my self to death in the behalfe of my god, and being dead, his body is burned, and is esteemed by al men to be holy. The king of the said region is most rich in gold, siluer, and precious stones, and there be the fairest vnions in al the world. Traueling from thence by the Ocean sea 50. daies iourney southward, I came vnto a certain land named Lammori, [Marginal note: Perhaps he meaneth Comori.] where, in regard of extreeme heat, the people both men and women go stark-naked from top to toe: who seeing me apparelled scoffed at me, saying that God made Adam et Eue naked. In this countrey al women are common, so that no man can say, this is my wife. Also when any of the said women beareth a son or a daughter, she bestowes it vpon any one that hath lien with her, whom she pleaseth. Likewise al the land of that region is possessed in common, so that there is not mine and thine, or any propriety of possession in the diuision of lands: howbeit euery man hath is owne house peculiar vnto himselfe. Mans flesh, if it be fat, is eaten as ordinarily there, as beefe in our country. And albeit the people are most lewd, yet the country is exceedingly good, abounding with al commodities, as flesh, corne, rise, siluer, gold, wood of aloes, Campheir, and many other things. Marchants comming vnto this region for traffique do vsually bring with them fat men, selling them vnto the inhabitants as we sel hogs, who immediatly kil and eat them. [Sidenote: Sumatra.] In this island towards south, there is the another kingdome called Simoltra, where both men and women marke themselues with red-hot yron in 12. sundry spots of their faces: and this nation is at continual warre with certaine naked people in another region. [Sidenote: Iaffa.] Then I traueled further vnto another island called Iaua, the compasse whereof by sea is 3000. miles. The king of this Iland hath 7. other crowned kings vnder his iurisdiction. The said Island is throughly inhabited, and is thought to be one of the principall Ilands of the whole world. In the same Iland there groweth great plenty of cloues, cubibez, and nutmegs, and in a word all kinds of spices are there to be had, and great abundance of all victuals except wine. The king of the said land of Iaua hath a most braue and sumptuous pallace, the most loftily built, that euer I saw any, and it hath most high greeses and stayers to ascend vp to the roomes therein contained, one stayre being of siluer, and another of gold, throughout the whole building. Also the lower roomes were paued all ouer with one square plate of siluer, and another of gold. All the wals vpon the inner side were seeled ouer with plates of beaten gold, whereupon were engrauen the pictures of knights, hauing about their temples, ech of them a wreath of golde, adorned with precious stones. The roofe of the palace was of pure gold. With this king of Iaua the great Can of Catay hath had many conflictes in war: whom notwithstanding the said king hath always ouercome and vanquished.

Of certaine trees yeelding meale, hony, and poyson.

Nere vnto the said Iland is another countrey called Panten, or Tathalamasin. And the king of the same country hath many Ilands vnder his dominion: In this land there are trees yeelding meale, hony, and wine, and the most deadly poison in all the whole world: for against it there is but one only remedy: and that is this: if any man hath taken of the poyson, and would be deliuered from the danger thereof, let him temper the dung of a man in water, and so drinke a good quantitie thereof, and it expels the poyson immediatly, making it to auoid at the fundament. Meale is produced out of the said trees after this maner. They be mighty huge trees, and when they are cut with an axe by the ground, there issueth out of the stocke a certain licour like vnto gumme, which they take and put into bags made of leaues, laying them for 15 daies together abroad in the sun, and at the end of those 15 dayes, when the said licour is throughly parched, it becommeth meale. Then they steepe it first in sea water, washing it afterward with fresh water, and so it is made very good and sauorie paste, whereof they make either meat or bread, as they thinke good. Of which bread I my selfe did eate, and it is fayrer without and somewhat browne within. [Sidenote: A sea running still Southward.] By this countrey is the sea called Mare mortuum, which runneth continually Southward, into the which whoseuer falleth is neuer seene after. In this countrey also are found canes of an incredible length, namely 60 paces high or more, and they are as bigge as trees. Other canes there be also called Cassan, which overspread the earth like grasse, and out of euery knot of them spring foorth certaine branches, which are continued vpon the ground almost for the space of a mile. In the sayd canes there are found certaine stones, one of which stones, whoseuer carryeth about with him, cannot be wounded with any yron: and therefore the men of that countrey for most part, carry such stones with them, whithersoeuer they goe. Many also cause one of the armes of their children, while they are yong, to be launced, putting one of the said stones in the wound, healing also, and closing vp the said wound with the powder of a certaine fish (the name whereof I do not know) which powder doth immediatly consolidate and cure the said wound. And by the vertue of these stones, the people aforesaid doe for the most part triumph both on sea and land. Howbeit there is one kind of stratageme, which the enemies of this nation, knowing the vertue of the sayd stones, doe practise against them: namely, they prouide themselues armour of yron or steele against their arrowes, and weapons also poisoned with the poyson of trees, and they carry in their hands wooden stakes most sharpe and hard-pointed, as if they were yron: likewise they shoot arrowes without yron heads, and so they confound and slay some of their vnarmed foes trusting too securely vnto the vertue of their stones. [Sidenote: Sayles made of reedes.] Also Of the foresayd canes called Cassan they make sayles for their ships, and litle houses, and many other necessaries. [Sidenote: Campa.] From thence after many dayes trauell, I arrived at another kingdome called Campa, a most beautiful and rich countrey, and abounding with all kind of victuals: the king whereof, at my being there, had so many wiues and concubines, that he had 300 sonnes and daughters by them. This king hath 10004 tame Elephants, which are kept euen as we keepe droues of oxen, or flocks of sheepe in pasture.

Of the abundance of fishes, which cast themselues vpon the shore.

In this countrey there is one strange thing to be obserued, that euery seueral kind of fishes in those seas come swimming towards the said countrey in such abundance, that, for a great distance into the sea, nothing can be seene but the backs of fishes: which, casting themselues vpon the shore when they come neare vnto it, do suffer men, for the space of 3. daies, to come and to take as many of them as they please, and then they returne againe vnto the sea. After that kind of fishes comes another kind, offering it selfe after the same maner, and so in like sort all other kinds whatsoeuer: notwithstanding they do this but once in a yere. And I demaunded of the inhabitants there, how, or by what meanes this strange accident could come to passe: They answered, that fishes were taught, euen by nature, to come and to do homage vnto their Emperour. [Sidenote: Tortoises.] There be Tortoises also as bigge as an ouen. Many other things I saw which are incredible, vnlesse a man should see them with his own eies. In this country also dead men are burned, and their wiues are burned aliue with them, as in the city of Polumbrum above mentioned: for the men of that country say that she goeth to accompany him in another world, that he should take none other wife in marriage. [Sidenote: Moumoran.] Moreouer I traueled on further by the ocean-sea towards the south, and passed through many countries and islands, whereof one is called Moumoran, and it containeth in compasse ii. M. miles, wherein men and women haue dog faces, and worship an oxe for their god: and therefore euery one of them cary the image of an oxe of gold or siluer vpon their foreheads. The men and the women of this country go all naked, sauing that they hang a linen cloth before their priuities. The men of the said country are very tall and mighty, and by reason that they goe naked, when they are to make battell, they cary yron or steele targets before them, which do couer and defend their bodies from top to toe: and whomsoeuer of their foes they take in battel not being able to ransom himselfe for money, they presently deuoure him: but if he be able to redeeme himselfe for money, they let him go free. Their king weareth about his necke 300. great and most beautifull vnions, and saith euery day 300. prayers vnto his god. He weareth vpon his finger also a stone of a span long which seemeth to be a flame of fire, and therefore when he weareth it, no man dare once approch vnto him: and they say that there is not any stone in the whole world of more value then it. Neither could at any time the great Tartarian Emperour of Katay either by force, money, or policie obtaine it at his hands: notwithstanding that he hath done the vtmost of his indeuour for this purpose.

Of the Island of Sylan: and of the mountaine where Adam mourned for his sonne Abel.

I passed also by another island called Sylan, which conteineth in compasse aboue ii. M. miles: wherein are an infinit number of serpents, and great store of lions, beares, and al kinds of rauening and wild beasts, and especially of elephants. In the said country there is an huge mountaine, whereupon the inhabitants of that region do report that Adam mourned for his son Abel the space of 500. yeres. In the midst of this mountain there is a most beautiful plain, wherin is a litle lake conteining great plenty of water, which water the inhabitants report to haue proceeded from the teares of Adam and Eue: howbeit I proued that to be false, because I saw the water flow in the lake. This water is ful of hors-leeches, and blood-suckers, and of precious stones also: which precious stones the king taketh not vnto his owne vse, but once or twise euery yere he permitteth certaine poore people to diue vnder the water for the said stones, and al that they can get he bestoweth vpon them, to the end they may pray for his soule. But that they may with lesse danger diue vnder the water, they take limons which they pil, anointing themselues throughly with the iuice therof, and so they may diue naked vnder the water, the hors-leeches not being able to hurt them. From this lake the water runneth euen vnto the sea, and at a low ebbe the inhabitants dig rubies, diamonds, pearls, and other pretious stones out of the shore: wherupon it is thought, that the king of this island hath greater abundance of pretious stones, then any other monarch in the whole earth besides. In the said country there be al kinds of beasts and foules: and the people told me, that those beasts would not inuade nor hurt any stranger, but only the natural inhabitants. I saw in this island fouls as big as our countrey geese, hauing two heads, and other miraculous things, which I will not here write off. Traueling on further toward the south, I arriued at a certain island called Bodin, [Marginal note: Or, Dadin.] which signifieth in our language vnclean. In this island there do inhabit most wicked persons, who deuour and eat raw flesh committing al kinds of vncleannes and abominations in such sort, as it is incredible. For the father eateth his son, and the son his father, the husbande his owne wife, and the wife her husband: and that after this maner. If any mans father be sick, the son straight goes vnto the soothsaying or prognosticating priest, requesting him to demand of his god, whether his father shall recouer of that infirmity of no: Then both of them go vnto an idol of gold or of siluer, making their praiers vnto it in maner folowing: Lord, thou art our God, and thee we do adore, beseeching thee to resolue vs, whether such a man must die, or recouer of such an infirmity or no: Then the diuel answereth out of the foresaid idol: if he saith (he shal liue) then returneth his son and ministreth things necessary vnto him, til he hath attained vnto his former health: but if he saith (he shal die) then goes the priest vnto him, and putting a cloth into his mouth doth strangle him therewith: which being done, he cuts his dead body into morsels, and al his friends and kinsfolks are inuited vnto the eating thereof, with musique and all kinde of mirth: howbeit his bones are solemnely buried. And when I found fault with that custome demanding a reason thereof, one of them gaue me this answer: this we doe, least the wormes should eat his flesh, for then his soule should suffer great torments, neither could I by any meanes remooue them from that errour. Many other nouelties and strange things there bee in this countrey, which no man would credite, vnles he saw them with his owne eyes. Howbeit, I (before almighty God) do here make relation of nothing but of that only, whereof I am as sure, as a man may be sure. Concerning the foresaid islands I inquired of diuers wel-experienced persons, who al of them, as it were with one consent, answered me saying, That this India contained 4400. islands vnder it, or within it: in which islands there are sixtie and foure crowned kings: and they say moreouer, that the greater part of those islands are wel inhabited. And here I conclude concerning that part of India.

Of the vpper India: and of the prouince of Mancy.

First of al therefore, hauing traueled many dayes iourney vpon the Ocean-sea toward the East, at length I arriued at a certaine great prouince called Mancy, being in Latine named India. Concerning this India I inquired of Christians, of Saracens, and of Idolaters, and of al such as bare any office vnder the great Can. Who all of them with one consent answered, that this prouince of Mancy hath mo then 2000. great cities within the precincts thereof, and that it aboundeth with all plenty of victuals, as namely with bread, wine, rise, flesh, and fish. All the men of this prouince be artificers and marchants, who, though they be in neuer so extreme penurie, so long as they can helpe themselues by the labor of their hands, wil neuer beg almes of any man. The men of this prouince are of a faire and comely personage, but somewhat pale, hauing their heads shauen but a litle: but the women are the most beautiful vnder the sunne. The first city of the said India which I came vnto, is called Ceuskalon, [Marginal note: Or, Ceuskala.] which being a daies iourney distant from the sea, stands vpon a riuer, the water whereof, nere vnto the mouth, where it exonerateth it selfe into the sea, doth ouerflow the land for the space of 12. daies iourney. All the inhabitants of this India are worshippers of idols. The foresaid city of Ceuskalon hath such an huge nauy belonging thereunto, that no man would beleeue it vnlesse he should see it. In this city I saw 300. li. of good and new ginger sold for lesse than a groat. There are the greatest, and the fairest geese, and most plenty of them to be sold in al the whole world, as I suppose: [Sidenote: He meaneth Pellicans, which the Spaniards cal Alcatrarzi.] they are as white as milke, and haue a bone vpon the crowne of their heads as bigge as an egge, being of the colour of blood: vnder their throat they haue a skin or bag hanging downe halfe a foot. They are exceeding fat and wel sold. Also they haue ducks and hens in that country, one as big as two of ours. There be monstrous great serpents likewise, which are taken by the inhabitants and eaten: whereupon a solemne feast among them without serpents is not set by: and to be briefe, in this city there are al kinds of victuals in great abundance. From thence I passed by many cities, and at length I came vnto a city named Caitan, [Marginal note:

Or, Zaiton.] wherin the friers Minorites haue two places of aboad, vnto the which I transported the bones of the dead friers, which suffred martyrdom for the faith of Christ, as it is aboue mentioned. In this city there is abundance of al kind of victuals very cheap. The said city is as big as two of Bononia, and in it are many monasteries of religious persons, al which do worship idols. I my selfe was in one of those Monasteries, and it was told me, that there were in it iii. M. religious men, hauing xi. M. idols: and one of the said idols which seemed vnto me but litle in regard of the rest, was as big as our Christopher. These religious men euery day do feed their idol-gods: wherupon at a certeine time I went to behold the banquet: and indeed those things which they brought vnto them were good to eat, and fuming hote, insomuch that the steame of the smoke thereof ascended vp vnto their idols, and they said that their gods were refreshed with the smoke: howbeit all the meat they conueyed away, eating it vp their owne selues, and so they fed their dumb gods with the smoke onely.

Of the citie Fuco.

Traueling more eastward, I came vnto a city named Fuco, which conteineth 30. miles in circuit, wherin be exceeding great and faire cocks, and al their hens are as white as the very snow, hauing wol in stead of feathers, like vnto sheep. It is a most stately and beautiful city, and standeth vpon the sea. Then I went 18. dates iourney on further, and passed by many prouinces and cities, and in the way I went ouer a certain great mountaine, vpon the one side whereof I beheld al liuing creatures to be as black as a cole, and the men and women on that side differed somwhat in maner of liuing from others: howbeit, on the other side of the said hil euery liuing thing was snow-white, and the inhabitants in their maner of liuing, were altogether vnlike vnto others. There, all maried women cary in token that they haue husbands, a great trunke of horne vpon their heads. [Sidenote: A great riuer.] From thence I trauelled 18. dayes journey further, and came vnto a certaine great riuer, and entered also into a city, whereunto belongeth a mighty bridge, to passe the said riuer. And mine hoste, with whom I soiourned, being desirous to shew me some sport, said vnto me: Sir, if you will see any fish taken, goe with me. [Sidenote: Foules catching fish.] Then he led me vnto the foresaid bridge, carying in his armes with him certaine diue-doppers or water-foules, bound vnto a company of poles, and about euery one of their necks he tied a threed, lest they should eat the fish as fast as they tooke them: and he carried 3. great baskets with him also: then loosed he the diue doppers from the poles, which presently went into the water, and within lesse then the space of one houre, caught as many fishes as filled the 3. baskets: which being full, mine hoste vntyed the threeds from about their neckes, and entering the second time into the riuer they fed themselues with fish, and being satisfied they returned and suffered themselues to be bound vnto the saide poles as they were before. And when I did eate of those fishes, me thought they were exceeding good. Trauailing thence many dayes iourneys, at length I arriued at another city called Canasia, [Marginal note: Or Cansai, or Quinzai.] which signifieth in our language, the city of heauen. Neuer in all my life did I see so great a citie; for it conteineth in circuit an hundreth miles: neither sawe I any plot thereof, which was not throughly inhabited: yea, I sawe many houses of tenne or twelue stories high, one aboue another. It hath mightie large suburbs containing more people than the city it selfe. Also it hath twelue principall gates: and about the distance of eight miles, in the high way vnto euery one of the saide gates standeth a city as big by estimation as Venice, and Padua. The foresaid city of Canasia is situated in waters or marshes, which alwayes stand still, neither ebbing nor flowing: howbeit it hath a defence for the winde like vnto Venice. In this city there are mo than 10002. bridges, many whereof I numbred and passed ouer them: [Sidenote: The Italian copy in Ramusius, hath 11000. bridges.] and vpon euery of those bridges stand certaine watchmen of the citie, keeping continuall watch and ward about the said city, for the great Can the Emperour of Catay. The people of this countrey say, that they haue one duetie inioyned vnto them by their lord: for euery fire payeth one Balis in regard of tribute: and a Balis is fiue papers or pieces of silke, which are worth one floren and an halfe of our coine. Tenne or twelue housholds are accompted for one fire, and so pay tribute but for one fire onely. Al those tributary fires amount vnto the number of 85. Thuman, with other foure Thuman of the Saracens, which make 89. in al; And one Thuman consisteth of 10000. fires. The residue of the people of the city are some of them Christians, some marchants, and some traueilers through the countrey: whereupon I marueiled much howe such an infinite number of persons could inhabite and liue together. There is great aboundance of victuals in this citie, as namely of bread and wine, and especially of hogs-flesh, with other necessaries.

Of a Monastery where many strange beastes of diuers kindes doe liue vpon an hill.

In the foresaide citie foure of our friers had conuerted a mighty and riche man vnto the faith of Christ, at whose house I continually abode, for so long time as I remained in the citie. Who vpon a certaine time saide vnto me: Ara, that is to say, Father, will you goe and beholde the citie? And I said, yea. Then embarqued we our selues, and directed our course vnto a certaine great Monastery: where being arrived, he called a religious person with whom he was acquainted, saying vnto him concerning me: this Raban Francus, that is to say, this religious Frenchman commeth from the Westerne parts of the world, and is now going to the city of Cambaleth to pray for the life of the great Can, and therefore you must shew him some rare thing, that when hee returnes into his owne countrey, he may say, this strange sight or nouelty haue I seene in the city of Canasia. Then the said religious man tooke two great baskets full of broken reliques which remained of the table, and led me vnto a little walled parke, the doore whereof he vnlocked with his key, and there appeared vnto vs a pleasant faire green plot, into the which we entred. In the said greene stands a litle mount in forme of a steeple, replenished with fragrant herbes and fine shady trees. And while we stood there, he tooke a cymball or bell, and rang therewith, as they vse to ring to dinner or beuoir in cloisters, at the sound whereof many creatures of diuers kinds came downe from the mount, some like apes, some like cats, some like monkeys and some hauing faces like men. And while I stood beholding of them, they gathered themselues together about him, to the number of 4200. of those creatures, putting themselues in good order, before whom he set a platter, and gaue them the said fragments to eate. And when they had eaten he rang vpon his cymbal the second time, and they al returned vnto their former places. Then, wondring greatly at the matter, I demanded what kind of creatures those might be? They are (quoth he) the soules of noble men which we do here feed, for the loue of God who gouerneth the world: and as a man was honorable or noble in this life, so his soule after death, entreth into the body of some excellent beast or other, but the soules of simple and rusticall people do possesse the bodies of more vile and brutish creatures. Then I began to refute that foule error: howbeit my speach did nothing at all preuaile with him: for he could not be perswaded that any soule might remaine without a body. [Sidenote: Chilenso.] From thence I departed vhto a certaine citie named Chilenso, the walls whereof conteined 40. miles in circuit. In this city there are 360. bridges of stone, the fairest that euer I saw: and it is wel inhabited, hauing a great nauie belonging thereunto, and abounding with all kinds of victuals and other commodities. [Sidenote: Thalay.] And thence I went vnto a certaine riuer called Thalay, which where it is most narrow, is 7. miles broad: [Sidenote: Cakam.] and it runneth through the midst of the land of Pygmæi, whose chiefe city is called Cakam, and is one of the goodliest cities in the world. These Pigmæans are three of my spans high, and they make larger and better cloth of cotten and silke, then any other nation vnder the sunne. [Sidenote: Ianzu.] And coasting along by the saide riuer, I came vnto a certaine citie named Ianzu, in which citie there is one receptacle for the Friers of our order, and there be also three Churches of the Nestorians. This Ianzu is a noble and great citie, containing 48 Thuman of tributarie fiers, and in it are all kindes of victuals, and great plenty of such beastes, foules and fishes, as Christians doe vsually liue vpon. The lord of the same citie hath in yeerely reuenues for salt onely, fiftie Thuman of balis, and one balis is worth a floren and a halfe of our coyne: insomuch that one Thuman of balis amounteth vnto the value of fifteene thousand florens. Howbeit the sayd lord fauoureth his people in one respect, for sometimes he forgiueth them freely two hundred Thuman, least there should be any scarcity or dearth among them. There is a custome in this citie, that when any man is determined to banquet his friends, going about vnto certaine tauernes or cookes houses appointed for the same purpose, he sayth vnto euery particular hoste, you shall haue such, and such of my friendes, whom you must intertaine in my name, and so much I will bestowe vpon the banquet. And by that means his friendes are better feasted at diuerse places, then they should haue beene at one. Tenne miles from the sayde citie, about the head of the foresayd riuer of Thalay, there is a certaine other citie called Montu, which hath the greatest nauy that I saw in the whole world. All their ships are as white as snow, and they haue banqueting houses in them, and many other rare things also, which no man would beleeue, vnlesse he had seene them with his owne eyes.

Of the citie of Cambaleth.

[Sidenote: Karamoron.] Traueiling eight dayes iourney further by diuers territories and cities, at length I came by fresh water vnto a certaine citie named Lencyn, standing vpon the riuer of Karauoran, which runneth through the midst of Cataie, and doeth great harme in the countrey when it ouerfloweth the bankes, or breaketh foorth of the chanell. [Sidenote: Sumacoto.] From thence passing along the riuer Eastward, after many dayes trauell, and the sight of the diuers cities, I arriued at a citie called Sumakoto, which aboundeth more with silke then any other citie in the world: for when there is great scarcitie of silke, fortie pound is sold for lesse then eight groates. In this citie there is abundance of all merchandize, and all kindes of victuals also, as of bread, wine, flesh, fish, with all choise and delicate spices. Then traueiling on still towards the East by many cities, I came vnto the noble and renowmed citie of Cambaleth, which is of great antiquitie being situate in the prouince of Cataie. This citie the Tartars tooke, and neare vnto it within the space of halfe a mile, they built another citie called Caido. The citie of Caido hath twelue gates, being each of them two miles distant from another. Also the space lying in the midst betweene the two foresayd cities is very well and throughly inhabited, so that they make as it were but one citie betweene them both. The whole compasse or circuit of both cities together, is 40. miles. In this citie the great emperour Can hath his principall seat, and his Imperiall palace, the wals of which palace containe foure miles in circuit: and neere vnto this his palace are many other palaces and houses, of his nobles which belong vnto his court. Within the precincts of the sayd palace Imperiall, there is a most beautiful mount, set and replenished with trees, for which cause it is called the Greene mount, hauing a most royall and sumptuous palace standing thereupon, in which, for the most part, the great Can is resident. Vpon the one side of the sayd mount there is a great lake, whereupon a most stately bridge is built, in which lake is great abundance of geese, ducks, and all kindes of water foules: and in the wood growing vpon the mount there is great store of all birds, and wilde beasts. And therefore when the great Can will solace himselfe with hunting or hauking, he needs not so much as once to step forth of his palace. Moreouer, the principall palace, wherein he maketh his abode, is very large, hauing within it 14 pillers of golde, and all the walles thereof are hanged with red skinnes, which are sayd to be the most costly skinnes in all the world. In the midst of the palace standes a cisterne of two yards high, which consisteth of a precious stone called Merdochas, and is wreathed about with golde, and at ech corner thereof is the golden image of a serpent, as it were, furiously shaking and casting forth his head. This cisterne also hath a kind of networke of pearle wrought about it. Likewise by the sayd cisterne there is drinke conueyed thorow certeine pipes and conducts, such as vseth to be drunke in the emperors court, vpon the which also there hang many vessels of golde, wherein, whosoeuer will may drinke of the sayd licour. In the foresayd palace there are many peacocks of golde: and when any Tartar maketh a banquet vnto his lord, if the guests chance to clap their hands for ioy and mirth, the sayd golden peacocks also will spread abroad their wings, and lift vp their traines, seeming as if they danced: and this I suppose to be done by arte magike or by some secret engine vnder the ground.

Of the glory and magnificence of the great Can.

Moreouer, when the great emperor Can sitteth in his imperiall throne of estate, on his left hand sitteth his queene or empresse, and vpon another inferior seate there sit two other women, which are to accompany the emperor, when his spouse is absent, but in the lowest place of all, there sit all the ladies of his kindred. All the maried women weare vpon their heads a kind of ornament in shape like vnto a mans foote, of a cubite and a halfe in length, and the lower part of the sayd foote is adorned with cranes feathers, and is all ouer thicke set with great and orient pearles. Vpon the right hand of the great Can sitteth his first begotten sonne and heire apparent vnto his empire, and vnder him sit all the nobles of the blood royall. There bee also foure Secretaries, which put all things in writing that the emperor speaketh. In whose presence likewise stand his Barons and diuers others of his nobilitie, with great traines of folowers after them, of whom none dare speake so much as one word, vnlease they haue obtained licence of the emperor so to doe, except his iesters and stage-players, who are appointed of purpose to solace their lord. Neither yet dare they attempt to doe ought, but onely according to the pleasure of their emperor, and as hee inioineth them by lawe. About the palace gate stand certaine Barons to keepe all men from treading vpon the threshold of the sayd gate. When it pleassth the great Can to solemnize a feast, he hath about him 14000. Barons, carying wreathes and litle crownes vpon their heads, and giuing attendance vpon their lord, and euery one of them weareth a garment of gold and precious stones, which is woorth ten thousand Florens. His court is kept in very good order, by gouernours of tens, gouernours of hundreds, and gouernours of thousands, insomuch that euery one in his place performeth his duetie committed vnto him, neither is there any defect to bee found. I Frier Odoricus was there present in person for the space of three yeeres, and was often at the sayd banquets; for we friers Minorites haue a place of aboad appointed out for vs in the emperors court, and are enioined to goe and to bestow our blessing vpon him. And I enquired of certaine Courtiers concerning the number of persons pertaining to the emperors court? And they answered mee that of stage-players, musicians, and such like, there were eighteene Thuman at the least, and that the keepers of dogs, beasts and foules were fifteene Thuman, and the physicians for the emperours body were foure hundred; the Christians also were eight in number, together with one Saracen. At my being there, all the foresayd number of persons had all kind of necessaries both for apparell and victuals out of the emperors court. Moreouer, when he will make his progresse from one countrey to another, hee hath foure troupes of horsemen, one being appointed to goe a dayes iourney before, and another to come a dayes iourney after him, the third to march on his right hand, and the fourth on his left, in the manner of a crosse, he himselfe being in the midst, and so euery particular troupe haue their daily iourneys limited vnto them, to the ende they may prouide sufficient victuals without defect. Nowe the great Can himselfe is caried in maner following; hee rideth in a chariot with two wheeles, vpon which a maiesticall throne is built of the wood of Aloe, being adorned with gold and great pearles, and precious stones, and foure elephants brauely furnished doe drawe the sayd chariot, before which elephants, foure great horses richly trapped and couered doe lead the way. Hard by the chariot on both sides thereof, are foure Barons laying hold and attending thereupon, to keepe all persons from approaching neere vnto their emperour. Vpon the chariot also two milke-white Ier-falcons doe sit, and seeing any game which hee would take, hee letteth them flie, and so they take it, and after this maner doeth hee solace himselfe as hee rideth. Moreover, no man dare come within a stones cast of the chariot, but such as are appointed. The number of his owne followers, of his wiues attendants, and of the traine of his first begotten sonne and heire apparent, would seeme incredible vnto any man, vnlesse hee had seene it with his owne eyes. The foresayd great Can hath diuided his Empire into twelue partes or Prouinces, and one of the sayd prouinces hath two thousand great cities within the precincts thereof. Whereupon his empire is of that length and breadth, that vnto whatsoeuer part thereof he intendeth his iourny, he hath space enough for six moneths continual progresse, except his Islands which are at the least 5000.

Of certaine Innes or hospitals appointed for trauailers throughout the whole empire.

The foresayd Emperor (to the end that trauailers may haue all things necessary throughout his whole empire) hath caused certaine Innes to be prouided in sundry places vpon the high wayes, where all things pertaining vnto victuals are in a continuall readinesse. And when any alteration or newes happen in any part of his Empire, if he chance to be farre absent from that part, his ambassadors vpon horses or dromedaries ride post vnto him, and when themselues and their beasts are weary, they blow their horne, at the noise whereof, the next Inne likewise prouideth a horse and a man, who takes the letter of him that is weary and runneth vnto another Inne: and so by diuers Innes, and diuers postes, the report, which ordinarily could skarce come in 30. dayes, is in one naturall day brought vnto the emperor: and therefore no matter of any moment can be done in his empire, but straightway he hath intelligence thereof. Moreouer, when the great Can himselfe will go on hunting, he vseth this custome. Some twenty dayes iourney from the citie of Kambaleth there is a forrest containing six dayes iourney in circuit, in which forrest there are so many kinds of beasts and birds, as it is incredible to report. Vnto this forrest, at the ende of euery third or fourth yere, himselfe with his whole traine resorteth, and they all of them together enuiron the sayd forrest, sending dogs into the same, which by hunting do bring foorth the beasts: namely, lions and stags, and other creatures, vnto a most beautifull plaine in the midst of the forrest, because all the beasts of the forrest doe tremble, especially at the cry of hounds. Then commeth the great Can himselfe, being caried vpon three elephants, and shooteth fine arrowes into the whole herd of beasts, and after him all his Barons, and after them the rest of his courtiers and family doe all in like maner discharge their arrowes also, and euery mans arrow hath a sundry marke. Then they all goe vnto the beasts which are slaine (suffering the liuing beasts to returne into the wood that they may haue more sport with them another time) and euery man enjoyeth that beast as his owne, wherein he findeth his arrow sticking.

Of the foure feasts which the great Can solemnizeth euery yeere in his Court.

Foure great feasts in a yeere doeth the emperor Can celebrate: namely the feast of his birth, the feast of his circumcision, the feast of his coronation, and the feast of his mariage. And vnto these feasts he inuiteth all his Barons, his stage-players, and all such as are of his kinred. Then the great

Can sitting in his throne, all his Barons present themselues before him, with wreaths and crownes vpon their heads, being diuersly attired, for some of them are in greene, namely the principall: the second are in red, and the third in yellow, and they hold each man in his hand a little Iuorie table of elephants tooth, and they are girt with golden girdles of halfe a foote broad, and they stand vpon their feete keeping silence. About them stand the stage-players or musicians with their instruments. And in one of the corners of a certaine great pallace, all the Philosophers or Magicians remaine for certaine howers, and doe attend vpon points or characters: and when the point and hower which the sayd Philosophers expected for, is come, a certaine crier crieth out with a loud voyce, saying, Incline or bowe your selues before your Emperour: with that all the Barons fall flat vpon the earth. Then hee crieth out againe; Arise all, and immediately they all arise. Likewise the Philosophers attend vpon a point or character the second time, and when it is fulfilled, the crier crieth out amaine; Put your fingers in your eares: and foorthwith againe he saieth; Plucke them out. Againe, at the third point he crieth, Boult this meale. Many other circumstances also doe they performe, all which they say haue some certaine signification: howbeit, neither would I write them, nor giue any heed vnto them, because they are vaine and ridiculous. And when the musicians hower is come, then the Philosophers say, Solemnize a feast vnto your Lord: with that all of them sound their instruments, making a great and a melodious noyse. And immediately another crieth, Peace, peace, and they are all whist. Then come the women-musicians and sing sweetly before the Emperour, which musike was more delightfull vnto me. After them come in the lions and doe their obeisance vnto the great Can. Then the iuglers cause golden cups full of wine to flie vp and downe in the ayre, and to apply themselues vnto mens mouthes that they may drinke of them. These and many other strange things I sawe in the court of the great Can, which no man would beleeue vnlesse he had seen with his owne eies, and therefore I omit to speake of them. [Sidenote: A lambe in a gourd.] I was informed also by certaine credible persons, of another miraculous thing, namely, that in a certaine kingdome of the sayd Can, wherein stand the mountains called Kapsei (the kingdomes name is Kalor) there grewe great Gourds or Pompions, which being ripe, doe open at the tops, and within them is found a little beast like vnto a yong lambe, euen as I my selfe haue heard reported, that there stand certaine trees vpon the shore of the Irish sea, bearing fruit like vnto a gourd, which, at a certaine time of the yeere doe fall into the water, and become birds called Bernacles, and this is most true. [Footnote: This report is first found in the writings of Giraldus Cambreusis, tutor to King John.]

Of diuers prouinces and cities.

And after three yeeres I departed out of the empire of Cataie, trauailing fiftie dayes iourney towards the West. [Sidenote: His returne Westward.] And at length I came vnto the empire of Pretegoani, whose principall citie is Kosan, which hath many other cities vnder it. [Sidenote: Casan] From thence passing many dayes trauell, I came vnto a prouince called Casan, which is for good commodities, one of the onely prouinces vnder the Sunne, and is very well inhabited, insomuch that when we depart out of the gates of one city we may beholde the gates of another city, as I my selfe saw in diuers of them. The breadth of the sayd prouince is fifty dayes iourney, and the length aboue sixty. In it there is great plenty of all victuals, and especially of chesnuts, and it is one of the twelue prouinces of the great Can. Going on further, I came vnto a certaine kingdome called Tebek, [Marginal note: Or Thebet.] which is in subiection vnto the great Can also, wherein I thinke there is more plenty of bread and wine then in any other part of the whole world besides. The people of the sayd countrey do, for the most part, inhabit in tents made of blacke felt. Their principall city is inuironed with faire and beautifull walles, being built of most white and blacke stones, which are disposed chekerwise one by another, and curiously compiled together: likewise all the high wayes in this countrey are exceedingly well paued. In the sayd countrey none dare shed the bloud of a man, or of any beast, for the reuerence of a certaine idole. In the foresayd city their Abassi, that is to say, their Pope is resident, being the head and prince of all idolaters (vpon whom he bestoweth and distributeth gifts after his maner) euen as our pope of Rome accounts himselfe to be the head of all Christians. The women of this countrey weare aboue an hundreth tricks and trifles about them, and they haue two teeth in their mouthes as long as the tushes of a boare. When any mans father deceaseth among them, his sonne assembleth together all the priests and musicians that he can get, saying that he is determined to honour his father: then causeth he him to be caried into the field (all his kinsfolks, friends, and neighbours, accompanying him in the sayd action) where the priests with great solemnity cut off the father's head, giuing it vnto his sonne, which being done, they diuide the whole body into morsels, and so leaue it behinde them, returning home with prayers in the company of the sayd sonne. So soone as they are departed, certaine vultures, which are accustomed to such bankets, come flying from the mountaines, and cary away all the sayd morsels of flesh: and from thenceforth a fame is spread abroad, that the sayd party deceased was holy, because the angels of God carried him into paradise. And this is the greatest and highest honour, that the sonne can deuise to performe vnto his deceased father. [Sidenote: The same story concerning the very same people is in William de Rubricis.] Then the sayd sonne taketh his fathers head, seething it and eating the flesh thereof, but of the skull he makes a drinking cup, wherein himselfe with all his family and kindred do drinke with great solemnity and mirth, in the remembrance of his dead and deuoured father. Many other vile and abominable things doth the said nation commit, which I meane not to write, because men neither can nor will beleeue, except they should haue the sight of them.

Of a certaine rich man, who is fed and nourished by fiftie virgins.

While I was in the prouince of Mancy, I passed by the palace of a certaine famous man, which hath fifty virgin damosels continually attending vpon him, feeding him euery meale, as a bird feeds her yoong ones. Also he hath sundry kindes of meat serued in at his table, and three dishes of ech kinde; and when the sayd virgins feed him, they sing most sweetly. This man hath in yeerely reuenues thirty thuman of tagars of rise, euery of which thuman yeeldeth tenne thousand tagars, and one tagar is the burthen of an asse. His palace is two miles in circuit, the pauement whereof is one plate of golde, and another of siluer. Neere vnto the wall of the sayd palace there is a mount artificially wrought with golde and siluer, whereupon stand turrets and steeples and other delectable things for the solace and recreation of the foresayd great man. And it was tolde me that there were foure such men in the sayd kingdome. [Sidenote: Long nailes.] It is accounted a great grace for the men of that countrey to haue long nailes vpon their fingers, and especially vpon their thumbes which nailes they may fold about their hands: but the grace and beauty of their women is to haue small and slender feet: and therefore the mothers when their daughters are yoong, do binde vp their feet, that they may not grow great. [Sidenote: Melistorte.] Trauelling on further towards the South, I arriued at a certaine countrey called Melistorte, which is a pleasant and fertile place. And in this countrey there was a certeine man called Senex de monte, who round about two mountaines had built a wall to inclose the sayd mountaines. Within this wall there were the fairest and most chrystall fountaines in the whole world: and about the sayd fountaines there were most beautifull virgins in great number, and goodly horses also, and in a word, euery thing that could be deuised for bodily solace and delight, and therefore the inhabitants of the countrey call the same place by the name of Paradise.

The sayd olde Senex, when he saw any proper and valiant yoong man, he would admit him into his paradise. Moreouer, by certaine conducts he makes, wine and milke to flow abundantly. This Senex, when he hath a minde to reuenge himselfe or to slay any king or baron, commandeth him that is gouernor of the sayd paradise, to bring thereunto some of the acquaintance of the sayd king or baron, permitting him a while to take his pleasure therein, and then to giue him a certaine potion being of force, to cast him into such a slumber as should make him quite voide of all sense, and so being in a profound sleepe to conuey him out of his paradise: who being awaked, and seeing himselfe thrust out of the paradise would become so sorrowfull, that he could not in the world deuise what to do, or whither to turne him. Then would he goe vnto the foresaid old man, beseeching him that he might be admitted againe into his paradise: who saith vnto him, You cannot be admitted thither, vnlesse you will slay such or such a man for my sake, and if you will giue the attempt onely, whether you kill him or no, I will place you againe in paradise, that there you may remaine alwayes: then would the party without faile put the same in execution, indeuouring to murther all those against whom the sayd olde man had conceiued any hatred. And therefore all the kings of the east stood in awe of the sayd olde man, and gaue vnto him great tribute.

Of the death of Senex de monte.

And when the Tartars had subdued a great part of the world, they came vnto the sayd olde man, and tooke from him the custody of his paradise: who being incensed thereat, sent abroad diuers desperate and resolute persons out of his forenamed paradise, and caused many of the Tartarian nobles to be slaine. The Tartars seeing this, went and besieged the city wherein the said olde man was, tooke him, and put him to a most cruell and ignominious death. The friers in that place haue this speciall gift and prerogatiue: namely, that by the vertue of the name of Christ Iesu, and in the vertue of his pretious bloud, which he shedde vpon the crosse for the saluation of mankinde, they doe cast foorth deuils out of them that are possessed. And because there are many possessed men in those parts, they are bound and brought ten dayes iourney unto the sayd friers, who being dispossessed of the vncleane spirits, do presently beleeue in Christ who deliuered them, accounting him for their God, and being baptized in his name, and also deliuering immediatly vnto the friers all their idols, and the idols of their cattell, which are commonly made of felt or of womens haire: then the sayd friers kindle a fire in a publike place (whereunto the people resort, that they may see the false gods of their neighbors burnt) and cast the sayd idols thereinto: howbeit at the first those idols came out of the fire againe. Then the friers sprinkled the sayd fire with holy water, casting the idols into it the second time, and with that the deuils fled in the likenesse of blacke smoake, and the idols still remained till they were consumed vnto ashes. Afterward, this noise and outcry was heard in the ayre: Beholde and see how I am expelled out of my habitation. And by these meanes the friers doe baptize great multitudes, who presently reuolt againe vnto their idols: insomuch that the sayd friers must eftsoones, as it were, vnderprop them, and informe them anew. There was another terrible thing which I saw there: for passing by a certaine valley, which is situate beside a pleasant riuer, I saw many dead bodies, and in the sayd valley also I heard diuers sweet sounds and harmonies of musike, especially the noise of citherns, whereat I was greatly amazed. This valley conteineth in length seuen or eight miles at the least; into the which whosoeuer entreth, dieth presently, and can by no meanes passe aliue thorow the middest thereof: for which cause all the inhabitants thereabout decline vnto the one side. Moreouer, I was tempted to go in, and to see what it was. At length, making my prayers, and recommending my selfe to God in the name of Iesu, I entred, and saw such swarmes of dead bodies there, as no man would beleeue vnlesse he were an eye witnesse thereof. At the one side of the foresayd valley vpon a certaine stone, I saw the visage of a man, which beheld me with such a terrible aspect, that I thought verily I should haue died in the same place. But always this sentence, the word became flesh, and dwelt amongst vs, I ceased not to pronounce, signing my selfe with the signe of the crosse, and neerer then seuen or eight pases I durst not approach vnto the said head: but I departed and fled vnto another place in the sayd valley, ascending vp into a little sand mountaine, where looking round about, I saw nothing but the sayd citherns, which me thought I heard miraculously sounding and playing by themselues without the help of musicians. And being vpon the toppe of the mountaine, I found siluer there like the scales of fishes in great abundance: and I gathered some part thereof into my bosome to shew for a wonder, but my conscience rebuking me, I cast it vpon the earth, reseruing no whit at all vnto my selfe, and so, by Gods grace I departed without danger. And when the men of the countrey knew that I was returned out of the valley aliue, they reuerenced me much, saying that I was baptised and holy, and that the foresayd bodies were men subiect vnto the deuils infernall, who vsed to play vpon citherns, to the end they might allure people to enter, and so murther them. Thus much concerning those things which I beheld most certainely with mine eyes, I frier Odoricus haue heere written: many strange things also I haue of purpose omitted, because men will not beleeue them vnlesse they should see them.

Of the honour and reuerence done vnto the great Can.

I will report one thing more, which I saw, concerning the great Can. It is an vsuall custome in those parts, that when the forsayd Can traueileth thorow any countrey, his subiects kindle fires before their doores, casting spices thereinto to make a perfume, that their lord passing by may smell the sweet and delectable odours thereof, and much people come forth to meet him. And vpon a certaine time when he was cumming towardes Cambaleth, the fame of his approch being published, a bishop of ours with certaine of our minorite friers and my selfe went two dayes iourney to meet him: and being come nigh vnto him, we put a crosse vpon wood, I my selfe hauing a censer in my hand, and began to sing with a loud voice: Veni creator spiritus. And as we were singing on this wise, he caused vs to be called, commanding vs to come vnto him: notwithstanding (as it is aboue mentioned) that no man dare approach within a stones cast of his chariot, vnlesse he be called, but such onely as keepe his chariot. And when we came neere vnto him, he vailed his hat or bonet being of an inestimable price, doing reuerance vnto the crosse. And immediatly I put incense into the censer, and our bishop taking the censer perfumed him, and gaue him his benediction. Moreouer, they that come before the sayd Can do always bring some oblation to present vnto him, obseruing the antient law: Thou shall not appeare in my presence with an empty hand. And for that cause we carried apples with vs, and offered them in a platter with reuerence vnto him: and taking out two of them he did eat some part of one. And then he signified vnto vs, that we should go apart, least the horses comming on might in ought offend vs. With that we departed from him, and turned aside, going vnto certaine of his barons, which had bene conuerted to the faith by certeine friers of our order, being at the same time in his army: and we offered vnto them of the foresayd apples, who receiued them at our hands with great ioy, seeming vnto vs to be as glad, as if we had giuen them some great gift.

All the premisses abouewritten friar William de Solanga hath put downe in writing euen as the foresayd frier Odoricus vttered them by word of mouth, in the yeere of our Lord 1330. in the moneth of May, and in the place of S. Anthony of Padua. Neither did he regard to write them in difficult Latine or in an eloquent stile, but euen as Odoricus himselfe rehearsed them, to the end that men might the more easily vnderstand the things reported. I frier Odoricus of Friuli, of a certaine territory called Portus Vahonis, and of the order of the minorites, do testifie and beare wimesse vnto the reuerend father Guidotus minister of the prouince of S. Anthony, in the marquesate of Treuiso (being by him required vpon mine obedience so to doe) that all the premisses aboue written, either I saw with mine owne eyes, or heard the same reported by credible and substantiall persons. The common report also of the countreyes where I was, testifieth those things, which I saw, to be true. Many other things I haue omitted, because I beheld them not with mine owne eyes. Howbeit from day to day I purpose with my selfe to trauell countreyes or lands, in which action I dispose myselfe to die or to liue, as it shall please my God.

Of the death of frier Odoricus.

In the yeere therefore of our Lord 1331 the foresayd frier Odoricus preparing himselfe for the performance of his intended iourney, that his trauel and labour might be to greater purpose, he determined to present himselfe vnto Pope Iohn the two and twentieth, whose benediction and obedience being receiued, he with a certaine number of friers willing to beare him company, might conuey himselfe vnto all the countreyes of infidels. And as he was trauelling towards the pope, and not farre distant from the city of Pisa, there meets him by the waye a certaine olde man, in the habit and attire of a pilgrime, saluting him by name, and saying: All haile frier Odoricus. And when the frier demaunded how he had knowledge of him: he answered: Whiles, you were in India I knew you full well, yea, and I knew your holy purpose also: but see that you returne immediatly vnto the couer from whence you came, for tenne dayes hence you shall depart out of this present world. Wherefore being astonished and amazed at these wordes (especially the olde man vanishing out of his sight, presently after he had spoken them) he determined to returne. And so he returned in perfect health, feeling no crazednesse nor infirmity of body. And being in his couen at Vdene in the prouince of Padua, the tenth day after the foresayd vision, hauing receiued the Communion, and preparing himselfe vnto God, yea, being strong and sound of body, hee happily rested in the Lord; whose sacred departure was signified vnto the Pope aforesaid, vnder the hand of the publique notary in these words following.

In the yeere of our Lord 1331, the 14. day of Ianuarie, Beatus Odoricus a Frier minorite deceased in Christ, at whose prayers God shewed many and sundry miracles, which I Guetelus publique notarie of Vtina, sonne of M. Damianus de Porto Gruaro, at the commandement and direction of the honorable Conradus of the Borough of Gastaldion, and one of the Councell of Vtina, haue written as faithfully as I could, and haue deliuered a copie thereof vnto the Friers minorites: howbeit not of all, because they are innumerable, and too difficult for me to write.

* * * * *

The voyage of the Lord Iohn of Holland, Earle of Huntington, brother by the mothers side to King Richard the second, to Ierusalem and Saint Katherins mount.

[Sidenote: 1394. Froyssart.] The Lord Iohn of Holland, Earle of Huntington, was as then on his way to Ierusalem, and to Saint Katherins mount, and purposed to returne by the Realme of Hungarie. For as he passed through France (where he had great cheere of the King, and of his brother and vncles) hee heard how the king of Hungary and the great Turke should haue battell together: therefore he thought surely to be at that iourney.

* * * * *

The voiage of Thomas lord Moubray duke of Norfolke to Ierusalem, in the yeere of our Lord 1399. written by Holinshed, pag. 1233.

Thomas lord Moubray, second sonne of Elizabeth Segraue and Iohn lord Moubray her husband, was advanced to the dukedome of Norfolke in the 21. yeere of the reigne of Richard the 2. Shortly after which, hee was appealed by Henry earle of Bullingbroke of treason; and caried to the castle of Windsore, where he was strongly and safely garded, hauing a time of combate granted to determine the cause betweene the two dukes, the 16. day of September, in the 22. of the sayd king, being the yeere of our redemption 1398. But in the end the matter was so ordered, that this duke of Norfolke was banished for euer: whereupon taking his iourney to Ierusalem, he died at Venice in his returne from the said citie of Ierusalem, in the first yeere of King Henry the 4. about the yeere of our redemption, 1399.

* * * * *

The Voiage of the bishop of Winchester to Ierusalem, in the sixt yeere of the reigne of Henry the fift, which was the yeere of our Lord, 1417. Thomas Walsingham.

Vltimo die mensis Octobris, episcopus Wintoniensis accessit ad concilium Constanciense, peregrinaturus Hierosolymam post electionem summi pontificis celebratam, vbi tantum valuit eius facunda persuasio, vt et excitaret dominos Cardinales ad concordiam, et ad electionem summi pontificis se ocyùs præpararent.

The same in English.

The last day of October the bishop of Winchester came to the Councell of Constance, which after the chusing of the Pope determined to take his iourney to Ierusalem: where his eloquent perswasion so much preuailed, that he both perswaded my lords the Cardinals to vnity and concord, and also moued them to proceed more speedily to the election of the Pope.

* * * * *

A preparation of a voyage of King Henrie the fourth to the Holy land against the infidels in the yere 1413, being the last yere of his reigne: wherein he was preuented by death: written by Walsingham, Fabian, Polydore Virgile, and Holenshed.

[Sidenote: Order taken for building of ships and gallies.] In this fourteenth and last yere of king Henries reigne a councell was holden in the White friers in London, at the which among other things, order was taken for ships and gallies to be builded and made ready, and all other things necessary to be prouided for a voyage, which he meant to make into the Holy land, there to recouer the city of Ierusalem from the infidels: for it grieued him to consider the great malice of Christian princes, that were bent vpon a mischieuous purpose to destroy one another, to the perill of their owne soules, rather than to make warre against the enemies of the Christian faith, as in conscience, it seemed to him, they were bound. We finde, sayeth Fabian in his Chronicle, that he was taken with his last sickeness, while he was making his prayers at Saint Edwards shrine, there as it were, to take his leaue, and so to proceede foorth on his iourney. He was so suddenly and grieuously taken, that such as were about him feared least he would haue died presently: wherefore to relieue him, if it were possible, they bare him into a chamber that was next at hand, belonging to the Abbot of Westminster, where they layd him on a pallet before the fire, and vsed all remedies to reuiue him. At length he recouered his speech, and perceiuing himselfe in a strange place which he knew not, he willed to knowe if the chamber had any particular name, whereunto answere was made, that it was called Ierusalem. Then sayde the king, Laudes be giuen to the father of heauen: for now I knowe that I shall die here in this chamber, according to the prophesie of mee declared, that I should depart this life in Ierusalem.

* * * * *

Of this intended voyage Polydore Virgile writeth in manner following.

Post haec Henricus Rex memor nihil homini debere esse antiquius, quàm ad officium iustitiæ, quæ ad hominum vtilitatem pertinet, omne suum studium conferre, protinùs omisso ciuili bello, quo pudebat videre Christianos omni tempore turpitèr occupari, de republica Anglica benè gubernanda, de bello in hostes communes sumendo, de Hierosolymis tandem aliquando recipiendis plura destinabat, classemque iam parabat, cum ei talia agenti atque meditanti casus mortem attulit: subito enim morbo tentatus, nulla medicina subleuari potuit. Mortuus est apud Westmonasterium, annum agens quadragesimum sextum, qui fuit annus salutis humanæ, 1413.

The same in English.

Afterward, King Henry calling to minde, that nothing ought to be more highly esteemed by any man, then to doe the vtmost of his indeuour for the performance of iustice, which tendeth to the good and benefite of mankinde; altogether abondoning ciuill warre (wherewith he was ashamed to see, how Christians at all times were dishonourably busied) entered into a more deepe consideration of well gouerning his Realme of England, of waging warre against the common enemie, and of recouering, in processe of time the citie of Ierusalem, yea, and was prouiding a nauie for the same purpose, whenas in the very midst of this his heroicall action and enterprise, he was surprised with death: for falling into a sudden disease, he could not be cured by any kinde of physicke. He deceased at Westminster in the 46 yeare of his age, which was in the yeere of our Lord, 1413.

* * * * *

The voyage of M. Iohn Locke to Ierusalem.

In my voyage to Ierusalem, I imbarked my selfe the 26 of March 1553 in the good shippe called the Mathew Gonson, which was bound for Liuorno, or Legorne and Candia. It fell out that we touched in the beginning of Aprill next ensuing at Cades in Andalozia, where the Spaniardes, according to their accustomed maner with all shippes of extraordinarie goodnes and burden, picked a quarell against the company, meaning to haue forfeited, or at least to haue arrested the sayd shippe. And they grew so malicious in their wrongfull purpose that I being vtterly out of hope of any speedie release, to the ende that my intention should not be ouerthrowen, was inforced to take this course following. Notwithstanding this hard beginning, it fell out so luckily, that I found in the roade a great shippe called the Caualla of Venice, wherein after agreement made with the patron, I shipped my selfe the 24. of May in the said yere 1553. and the 25 by reason of the winde blowing hard and contrary, we were not able to enter the straits of Gibraltar, but were put to the coast of Barbarie, where we ankered in the maine sea 2. leagues from shore, and continued so vntill two houres before sunne set, and then we weighed againe, and turned our course towards the Straits, where we entered the 26 day aforesayd, the winde being calme, but the current of the straites very fauourable. The same day the winde beganne to rise somewhat, and blew a furthering gale, and so continued at Northwest vntill we arriued at Legorne the third of Iune. And from thence riding ouer land vnto Venice, I prepared for my voyage to Ierusalem in the Pilgrimes shippe.

[Sidenote: The ship Fila Cauena departeth for Ierusalem. Rouigno a port in Istria.] I John Locke, accompanied with Maister Anthony Rastwold, and diuers other, Hollanders, Zelanders, Almaines and French pilgrimes entered the good shippe called Fila Cauena of Venice, the 16 of July 1553. and the 17 in the morning we weighed our anker and sailed towardes the coast of Istria, to the port of Rouigno, and the said day there came aboard of our ship the Perceuena of the shippe named Tamisari, for to receiue the rest of all the pilgrimes money, which was in all after the rate of 55. Crownes for euery man for that voyage, after the rate of fiue shillings starling to the crowne: This done, he returned to Venice.

[Sidenote: Sancta Eufemia.] The 19 day we tooke fresh victuals aboard, and with the bote that brought the fresh provision we went on land to the Towne, and went to see the Church of Sancta Eufemia, where we sawe the bodie of the sayd Saint.

[Sidenote: Monte de Ancona.] The 20 day wee departed from Rouignio, and about noone we had sight of Monte de Ancona, and the hilles of Dalmatia, or else of Sclauonia both at one time, and by report they are 100. miles distant from ech other, and more.

[Sidenote: Il Pomo.] The 21 we sayled still in sight of Dalmatia, and a little before noone, we had a sight of a rocke in the midst of the sea, called in the Italian il Pomo, it appeareth a farre off to be in shape like a sugarloafe. [Sidenote: Sant Andrea.] Also we sawe another rocke about two miles compasse called Sant Andrea; on this rocke is only one Monasterie of Friers: [Sidenote: Lissa an Iland.] we sayled betweene them both, and left S. Andrea on the left hand of vs, and we had also kenning of another Iland called Lissa, all on the left hande, these three Ilands lie East and West in the sea, and at the sunne setting we had passed them. [Sidenote: Lezina Iland.] Il pomo is distant from Sant Andrea 18 miles, and S. Andrea from Lissa ten miles, and Lissa from another Iland called Lezina, which standeth betweene the maine of Dalmatia and Lissa, tenne miles. This Iland is inhabited and hath great plentie of wine and frutes and hereagainst we were becalmed.

[Sidenote: Catza. Pelagosa.] The 22. we had sight of another small Iland called Catza, which is desolate and on the left hand, and on the right hand, a very dangerous Iland called Pelagosa, this is also desolate, and lyeth in the midst of the sea betweene both the maines: it is very dangerous and low land, and it hath a long ledge of rockes lying out six miles into the sea, so that many ships by night are cast away vpon them. There is betweene Catza and Pelagosa 30 miles, and these two Ilands are distant from Venice 400. miles. [Sidenote: Augusta.] There is also about twelue miles eastward, a great Iland called Augusta, about 14 miles in length, somewhat hillie, and well inhabited, and fruitfull of vines, corne and other fruit, this also we left on the left hand: and we haue hitherto kept our course from Rouignio East southeast. [Sidenote: Meleda. Mount Sant Angelo.] This Iland is vnder the Signiorie or gouernement of Ragusa, it is distant from Ragusa 50 miles, and there is by that Iland a greater, named Meleda, which is also vnder the gouernement of Ragusa, it is about 30 miles in length, and inhabited, and hath good portes, it lyeth by East from Augusta, and ouer against this Iland lyeth a hill called Monte S. Angelo, vpon the coast of Puglia in Italy, and we had sight of both landes at one time.

The 23 we sayled all the day long by the bowline alongst the coast of Ragusa, and towardes night we were within 7. or 8. miles of Ragusa, that we might see the white walles, but because it was night, we cast about to the sea, minding at the second watch, to beare in againe to Ragusa, for to know the newes of the Turkes armie, but the winde blew so hard and contrary, that we could not. [Sidenote: Ragusa paieth 14000. Sechinos to the Turke yerely.] This citie of Ragusa paieth tribute to the Turke yerely fourteene thousand Sechinos, and euery Sechino is of Venetian money eight liuers and two soldes, besides other presents which they giue to the Turkes Bassas when they come thither. The Venetians haue a rocke or cragge within a mile of the said towne, for the which the Raguseos would giue much money, but they doe keepe it more for the namesake, then for profite. This rocke lieth on the Southside of the towne, and is called Il Cromo, there is nothing on it but onely a Monasterie called Sant Ieronimo. The maine of the Turkes countrie is bordering on it within one mile, for the which cause they are in great subiection. This night we were put backe by contrarie winds, and ankered at Melleda.

The 24 being at an anker vnder Melleda, we would haue gone on land, but the winde came so faire that we presently set sayle and went our course, and left on the right hand of vs the forenamed Iland, and on the left hand betweene vs and the maine the Iland of Zupanna, and within a mile of that vnder the maine by East, another Iland called Isola de Mezo. This Iland hath two Monasteries in it, one called Santa Maria de Bizo, and the other Sant Nicholo. Also there is a third rocke with a Frierie called Sant Andrea: these Ilands are from the maine but two miles, and the channell betweene Melleda and Zupanna is but foure or fiue miles ouer by gesse, but very deepe, for we had at an anker fortie fathoms. The two Ilands of Zupanno and Mezo are well inhabited, and very faire buildings, but nothing plentie saue wine onely. This night toward sunne set it waxed calme, and we sayled little or nothing.

The 24 we were past Ragusa 14 miles, and there we mette with two Venetian ships, which came from Cyprus, we thought they would haue spoken with vs, for we were desirous to talke with them, to knowe the newes of the Turkes armie, and to haue sent some letters by them to Venice. About noone, we had scant sight of Castel nouo, which Castell a fewe yeeres past the Turke tooke from the Emperour, in which fight were slaine three hundred Spanish souldiers, besides the rest which were taken prisoners, and made gallie slaues. This Castell is hard at the mouth of a channell called Boca de Cataro. The Venetians haue a hold within the channell called Cataro, this channell goeth vp to Budoa, and further vp into the countrey. About sunne set we were ouer against the hilles of Antiueri in Sclauonia, in the which hilles the Venetians haue a towne called Antiueri, and the Turkes haue another against it called Marcheuetti, the which two townes continually skirmish together with much slaughter. At the end of these hils endeth the Countrey of Sclauonia, and Albania beginneth. These hilles are thirtie miles distant from Ragusa.

The 27 we kept our course towards Puglia, and left Albania on the left hand. The 28. we had sight of both the maines, but we were neere the coast of Puglia, for feare of Foystes. It is betweene Cape Chimera in Albania and Cape Otranto in Puglia 60 miles. Puglia is a plaine low lande, and Chimera in Albania is very high land, so that it is seene the further. Thus sayling our course along the coast of Puglia, we saw diuerse white Towers, which serue for sea-markes. About three of the clocke in the after noone, we had sight of a rocke called Il fano, 48 miles from Corfu, and by sunne set we discouered Corfu. Thus we kept on our course with a prosperous winde, and made our way after twelue mile euery houre. Most part of this way we were accompanied with certaine fishes called in the Italian tongue Palomide, it is a fish three quarters of a yard in length, in colour, eating, and making like a Makarell, somewhat bigge and thick in body, and the tayle forked like a halfe moone, for the which cause it is said that the Turke will not suffer them to be taken in all his dominions.

The 29 in the morning we were in sight of an Iland, which we left on our left hande called Cephalonia, it is vnder the Venetians, and well inhabited, with a faire towne strongly situated on a hill of which hill the Iland beareth her name, it hath also a very strong fortresse or Castle, and plentie of corne and wine, their language is Greek, it is distant from the maine of Morea, thirtie miles, it is in compasse 80 miles. One hour within night we sayled by the towne standing on the South cape of Cephalonia, whereby we might perceiue their lights. There come oftentimes into the creeks and riuers, the Turkes foystes and gallies where at their arriual, the Countrey people doe signifie vnto their neighbours by so many lights, as there are foistes or gallies in the Iland, and thus they doe from one to another the whole Iland ouer. Aboute three of the clocke in the afternoone the winde scanted, and wee minded to haue gone to Zante, but we could not for that night. [Sidenote: Zante.] This Iland of Zante is distant from Cephalonia, 12 or 14 miles, but the towne of Cephalonia, from the towne of Zante, is distant fortie miles. This night we went but little forward.

The 30 day we remained still turning vp and downe because the winde was contrary, and towards night the winde mended, so that we entered the channell betweene Cephalonia, and Zante, the which chanell is about eight or tenne miles ouer, and these two beare East and by South, and West and by North from the other. The towne of Zante lieth within a point of the land, where we came to an anker, at nine of the clocke at night.

[Sidenote: Iohn Locke, and fiue Hollanders goe on land.] The 31 about sixe of the clocke in the morning, I with fiue Hollanders went on land, and hosted at the house of Pedro de Venetia. After breakfast we went to see the towne, and passing along we went into some of the Greeke churches, wherein we sawe their Altares, images, and other ornaments. [Sidenote: Santa Maria de la Croce.] This done, wee went to a Monasterie of Friers called Sancta Maria de la Croce, these are westerne Christians, for the Greekes haue nothing to doe with them, nor they with the Greekes, for they differ very much in religion. There are but 2. Friers in this Friery. [Sidenote: The tombe of M. T. Cicero.] In this Monasterie we saw the tombe that M. T. Cicero was buried in, with Terentia Antonia, his wife. This tombe was founde about sixe yeeres since, when the Monastery was built, there was in time past a streete where the tombe stoode. At the finding of the tombe there was also found a yard vnder ground, a square stone somewhat longer then broad, vpon which stone was found a writing of two seuerall handes writing, the one as it seemed, for himselfe, and the other for his wife, and vnder the same stone was found a glasse somewhat proportioned like an vrinall, but that it was eight square and very thicke, wherein were the ashes of the head and right arme of Mar. T. Cicero, for as stories make mention he was beheaded as I remember at Capua, for insurrection. And his wife hauing got his head and right arme, (which was brought to Rome to the Emperor) went from Rome, and came to Zante, and there buried his head and arme, and wrote vpon his tombe this style M. T Cicero. Haue. [Marginal note: Or, Aue.] Then followeth in other letters, *Et tu Terentia Antonia*, which difference of letters declare that they were not written both at one time. [Sidenote: The Description of the tombe.] The tombe is long and narrowe, and deepe, walled on euery side like a graue, in the botome whereof was found the sayd stone with the writing on it, and the said glasse of ashes, and also another litle glasse of the same proportion, wherein, as they say, are the teares of his friendes, and in those dayes they did vse to gather and bury with them, as they did vse in Italy and Spaine to teare their haire, to bury with their friendes. In the sayde tombe were a fewe bones. After dinner we rested vntill it drew towards euening by reason of the heat. [Sidenote: Sant Elia, but one Frier.] And about foure of the clocke we walked to another Frierie a mile out of the towne called Sant Elia, these are white Friers, there were two, but one is dead, not six dayes since. This Frierie hath a garden very pleasant, and well furnished with Orenges, Lemons, pomegranates, and diuers other good fruites. The way to it is somewhat ragged, vp hill and downe, and very stonie, and in winter very durtie. It standeth very plesantly in a clift betweene two hilles, with a good prospect. From thence we ascended the hill to the Castle, which is situated on the very toppe of a hill. [Sidenote: The description of the Castle of Zante.] This Castle is very strong, in compasse a large mile and a halfe, which being victualed, (as it is neuer vnfurnished) and manned with men of trust, it may defende itselfe against any Princes power. This Castle taketh the iust compasse of the hill, and no other hill neere it, it is so steepe downe, and so high and ragged, that it will tyre any man or euer he be halfe way vp. Very nature hath fortified the walles and bulwarkes: It is by nature foure square, and it commandeth the towne and porte. The Venetians haue alwayes their Podesta, or Gouernour, with his two Counsellours resident therein. The towne is welle inhabited, and hath great quantity of housholders. The Iland by report is threescore and tenne miles about, it is able to make twentie thousand fighting men. They say they have alwayes fiue or six hundred horsemen readie at an houres warning. They saye the Turke hath assayed it with 100. Gallies, but he could neuer bring his purpose to passe. It is strange to mee how they should maintains so many men in this Iland, for their best sustenance is wine, and the rest but miserable.

The first of August we were warned aboord by the patron, and towards euening we set sayle, and had sight of a Castle called Torneste, which is the Turkes, and is ten miles from Zante, it did belong to the Venetians, but they haue now lost it, it standeth also on a hill on the sea side in Morea. All that night we bare into the sea, because we had newes at Zante of twelue of the Turkes gallies, that came from Rhodes, which were about Modon, Coron, and Candia, for which cause we kept at the sea.

The second of August, we had no sight of land, but kept our course, and about the thirde watch the winde scanted, so that we bare with the shore, and had sight of Modon and Coron.

The third we had sight of Cauo Mattapan, and all that day by reason of contrary windes, which blew somewhat hard, we lay a hull vntill morning.

The fourth we were still vnder the sayd Cape, and so continued that day, and towardes night there grewe a contention in the ship amongst the Hollanders, and it had like to haue bene a great inconuenience, for we had all our weapons, yea euen our kniues, taken from vs that night.

The fift, we sayled by the Bowline, and out of the toppe we had sight of the Iland of Candia, and towardes noone we might see it plaine, and towards night the winde waxed calme.

The sixt toward the breake of day we saw two small Ilands called Gozi, and towards noone we were betweene them: the one of these Ilands is fifteene miles about, and the other 10. miles. In those Ilands are nourished store of cattell for butter and cheese. There are to the number of fiftie or sixtie inhabitants, which are Greekes, and they liue chiefly on milke and cheese. The Iland of Candia is 700 miles about, it is in length, from Cape Spada, to Cape Salomon, 300 miles, it is as they say, able to make one hundred thousand fighting men. We sayled betweene the Gozi, and Candia, and they are distant from Candia 5 or 6 miles. The Candiots are strong men, and very good archers, and shoot neere the marke. This Ilande is from Zante 300 miles.

The seuenth we sayled all along the sayd Iland with little winde and vnstable, and the eight day towards night we drew to the East end of the Iland.

The 9 and 10 we sayled along with a prosperous winde and saw no land.

The 11 in the morning, we had sight of the Iland of Cyprus, and towards noone we were thwart the Cape called Ponta Malota, and about foure of the clocke we were as farre as Baffo, and about sunne set we passed Cauo Bianco, and towards nine of the clocke at night we doubled Cauo de la gatte, and ankered afore Limisso, but the wind blew so hard, that we could not come neere the towne, neither durst any man goe on land. The towne is from Cauo de le gatte twelue miles distant.

The 12. of August in the morning wee went on land to Limisso: this towne is ruinated and nothing in it worth writing, saue onely in the midst of the towne there hath bene a fortresse, which is now decayed, and the wals part ouerthrowen, which a Turkish Rouer with certaine gallies did destroy about 10. or 12. yeeres past. [Sidenote: Caualette is a certaine vermine in the Island of Cyprus.] This day walking to see the towne, we chanced to see in the market place, a great quantitie of certaine vermine called in the Italian tongue Caualette. It is as I can learne, both in shape and bignesse like a grassehopper, for I can iudge but little difference. Of these many yeeres they haue had such quantitie that they destroy all their corne. They are so plagued with them, that almost euery yeere they doe well nie loose halfe their corne, whether it be the nature of the countrey, or the plague of God, that let them iudge that can best define. But that there may no default be laied to their negligence for the destruction of them, they haue throughout the whole land a constituted order, that euery Farmor or husbandmen (which are euen as slaues bought and sold to their lord) shall euery yeere pay according to his territorie, a measure full of the seede or egges of these forenamed Caualette, the which they are bound to bring to the market, and present to the officer appointed for the same, the which officer taketh of them very straight measure, and writeth the names of the presenters, and putteth the sayd egges or seed, into a house appointed for the same, and hauing the house full, they beate them to pouder, and cast them into the sea, and by this pollicie they doe as much as in them lieth for the destruction of them. This vermine breedeth or ingendereth at the time of corne being ripe, and the corne beyng had away, in the clods of the same ground do the husbandmen find the nestes, or, as I may rather terme them, cases of the egges, of the same vermine. Their nests are much like to the keies of a hasel-nut tree, when they be dried, and of the same length, but somewhat bigger, which case being broken you shall see the egges lie much like vnto antes egges, but somewhat lesser. This much I haue written at this time, because I had no more time of knowledge, but I trust at my returne to note more of this island, with the commodities of the same at large.

[Sidenote: The pilgrimes going to the Greeke churches.] The 13. day we went in the morning to the Greeks church, to see the order of their ceremonies, and of their communion, of the which to declare the whole order with the number of their ceremonious crossings, it were to long. Wherefore least I should offend any man, I leaue it vnwritten: but onely that I noted well, that in all their Communion or seruice, not one did euer kneele, nor yet in any of their Churches could I euer see any grauen images, but painted or portrayed. Also they haue store of lampes alight, almost for euery image one. Their women are always separated from the men, and generally they are in the lower ende of the Church. This night we went aboord the ship, although the wind were contrary, we did it because the patrone should not find any lacke of vs, as sometimes he did: when as tarying vpon his owne businesse, he would colour it with the delay of the pilgrimes.

The 14. day in the morning we set saile, and lost sight of the Island of Cyprus, and the 15. day we were likewise at Sea, and sawe no land: and the 16. day towards night, we looked for land, but we sawe none. But because we supposed our selues to be neere our port, we tooke in all our sailes except onely the foresaile and the mizzen, and so we remained all that night.

The 17. day in the morning, we kept by report of the Mariners, some sixe miles from Iaffa, but it prooued contrary. But because we would be sure, wee made to an anker seuen miles from the shore, and sent the skiffe with the Pilot and the master gunner, to learne the coast, but they returned, not hauing seen tree nor house, nor spoken with any man. But when they came to the sea side againe, they went vp a little hill standing hard by the brinke, whereon as they thought, they sawe the hill of Ierusalem, by the which the Pilot knew (after his iudgement) that we were past our port. And so this place where we rode was, as the mariners sayd, about 50. mile from Iaffa. This coast all alongst is very lowe, plaine, white, sandie, and desert, for which cause it hath fewe markes or none, so that we rode here as it were in a gulfe betweene two Capes.

[Sidenote: A great currant.] The 18. day we abode still at anker, looking for a gale to returne backe, but it was contrary: and the 19. we set saile, but the currant hauing more force then the winde, we were driuen backe, insomuch that the ship being vnder saile, we cast the sounding lead, and (notwithstanding the wind) it remained before the shippe, there wee had muddie ground at fifteene fadome. The same day about 4. of the clocke, wee set saile againe, and sayled West alongst the coast with a fresh side-winde. [Sidenote: A Cat fallen into the sea and recouered.] It chanced by fortune that the shippes Cat lept into the Sea, which being downe, kept her selfe very valiauntly aboue water, notwithstanding the great waues, still swimming, the which the master knowing, he caused the Skiffe with halfe a dozen men to goe towards her and fetch her againe, when she was almost halfe a mile from the shippe, and all this while the ship lay on staies. I hardly beleeue they would haue made such haste and meanes if one of the company had bene in the like perill. They made the more haste because it was the patrons cat. This I haue written onely to note the estimation that cats are in, among the Italians, for generally they esteeme their cattes, as in England we esteeme a good Spaniell. The same night about tenne of the clocke the winde calmed, and because none of the shippe knewe where we were, we let fall an anker about 6 mile from the place we were at before, and there wee had muddie ground at twelue fathome.

The 20 it was still calme, and the current so strong still one way, that we were not able to stemme the streame: moreouer we knew not where we were, whereupon doubting whither wee were past, or short of our port, the Master, Pilot, and other Officers of the shippe entered into counsell what was best to doe, wherevpon they agreed to sende the bote on lande againe, to seeke some man to speake with all, but they returned as wise as they went. Then we set sayle againe and sounded euery mile or halfe mile, and found still one depth, so we not knowing where we were, came againe to an anker, seuen or eight miles by West from the place we were at. Thus still doubting where we were, the bote went on land againe, and brought newes that wee were short 80 miles of the place, whereas we thought wee had beene ouershot by east fiftie miles. Thus in these doubts we lost foure dayes, and neuer a man in the shippe able to tell where we were, notwithstanding there were diuerse in the shippe that had beene there before. [Sidenote: They met with two Moores on land.] Then sayd the Pylot, that at his comming to the shore, by chance he saw two wayfaring men, which were Moores, and he cryed to them in Turkish, insomuch that the Moores, partly for feare, and partly for lacke of vnderstanding, (seeing them to be Christians) beganne to flie, yet in the end with much a doe, they stayed to speake with them, which men when they came together, were not able to vnderstand ech other, but our men made to them the signe of the Crosse on the sande, to giue them to vnderstand that they were of the shippe that brought the pilgrims. Then the Moores knowing (as al the country else doth) that it was the vse of Christians to go to Ierusalem, shewed them to be yet by west of Iaffa. Thus we remained ail that night at anker, and the farther west that we sayled, the lesse water we had.

The 21 we set sayle againe and kept our course Northeast, but because we would not goe along the shore by night, wee came to an anker in foure and twentie fathome water. [Sidenote: The two towers of Iaffa. Scolio di Santo Petro.] Then the next morning being the 22 we set sayle againe, and kept our course as before, and about three of the clocke in the afternoone, wee had sight of the two towers of Iaffa, and about fiue of the clocke, wee were with a rocke, called in the Italian tongue, Scolio di Santo Petro, on the which rocke they say he fished, when Christ bid him cast his net on the right side, and caught so many fishes. This rocke is now almost worne away. It is from Iaffa two or three mile: here before the two towers we came to an anker. Then the pilgrimes after supper, in salutation of the holy lande, sang to the prayse of God, Te Deum laudamus, with Magnificat, and Benedictus, but in the shippe was a Frier of Santo Francisco, who for anger because he was not called and warned, would not sing with vs, so that he stood so much vpon his dignitie, that he forgot his simplicitie, and neglected his deuotion to the holy land for that time, saying that first they ought to haue called him yer they did beginne, because he was a Fryer, and had beene there, and knewe the orders.

[Sidenote: A messenger departeth for Ierusalem.] The 23 we sent the bote on land with a messenger to the Padre Guardian of Ierusalem. [Sidenote: Mahomet is clothed in green.] This day it was notified vnto mee by one of the shippe that had beene a slaue in Turkie, that no man might weare greene in this land, because their prophet Mahomet went in greene. This came to my knowledge by reason of the Scriuanello, who had a greene cap, which was forbidden him to weare on the land.

The 24. 25. and 26 we taryed in the shippe still looking for the comming of the Padre guardian, and the 26 at night we had a storme which lasted all the next day.

[Sidenote: The Guardian of Ierusalem commeth to Iaffa, with the Cady, and Subassi.] The 27 in the morning, came the Cadi, the Subassi, and the Meniwe, with the Padre guardian, but they could not come at vs by reason of the stormy weather: in the afternoone we assayed to send the bote on land, but the weather would not suffer us. Then againe towards night the bote went a shore, but it returned not that night. [Sidenote: A cloud called of the Italians Cion most dangerous.] The same day in the afternoone we sawe in the element, a cloud with a long tayle, like vnto the tayle of a serpent, which cloud is called in Italian Cion, the tayle of this cloud did hang as it were into the sea: and we did see the water vnder the sayde cloude ascend, as it were like a smoke or myste, the which this Cion drew vp to it. The Marriners reported to vs that it had this propertie, that if it should happen to haue lighted on any part of the shippe, that it would rent and wreth sayles, mast, shroudes and shippe and all in manner like a wyth: on the land, trees, houses, in whatsoeuer else it lighteth on, it would rent and wreth. [Sidenote: A coniuration.] These marriners did vse a certaine coniuration to breake the said tayle, or cut it in two, which as they say doth preuaile. They did take a blacke hafted knife, and with the edge of the same did crosse the said taile as if they would cut it in twain, saying these words, Hold thou Cion, eat this, and then they stucke the knife on the ship side with the edge towards the said cloude, and I saw it therewith vanish in lesse than one quarter of an houre. But whether it was then consumed, or whether by vertue of the Inchantment it did vanish I knowe not, but it was gone. Hereof let them iudge that know more then I. This afternoone we had no winde, but the sea very stormy, insomuch that neither cheste, pot, nor any thing else could stand in the shippe, and wee were driuen to keepe our meate in one hand, and the pot in the other, and so sit downe vpon the hatches to eate, for stand we could not, for that the Seas in the very port at an anker went so high as if wee had bene in the bay of Portugall with stormy weather. The reason is, as the Mariners said to me, because that there meete all the waues from all places of the Straights of Gibralter, and there breake, and that in most calmes there go greatest seas, whether the winde blow or not.

The 28. the weather growing somewhat calme, we went on land and rested our selues for that day, and the next day we set forward toward the city of Ierusalem.

What I did, and what places of deuotion I visited in Ierusalem, and other parts of the Holy land, from this my departure from Iaffa, vntill my returne to the said port, may briefly be seene in my Testimoniall, vnder the hand and seale of the Vicar generall of Mount Sion, which for the contentment of the Reader I thought good here to interlace.

Vniuersis et singulis præsentes litteras inspecturis salutem in Domino nostro Iesu Christo. Attestamur vobis ac alijs quibuscunque qualiter honorabilis vir Iohannes Lok ciuis Londoniensis, filius honorabilis viri Guilhelmi Lok equitis aurati, ad sacratissima terræ sanctæ loca personaliter se contulit, sanctissimum Domini nostri Iesu Christi sepulchrum, equo die tertia gloriosus à mortuis resurrexit, sacratissimum Caluariæ montem, in quo pro nobis omnibus cruci affixus mori dignatus est, Sion etiam montem vbi coenam illam mirificam cum discipulis suis fecit, et vbi spiritus sanctus in die sancto Pentecostes in discipulos eosdem in linguis igneis descendit, Oliuetique montem vbi mirabiliter coelos ascendit, intemeratæ virginis Mariæ Mausoleum in Iosaphat vallis medio situm, Bethaniam quoque Bethlehem ciuitatem Dauid in qua de purissima virgine Maria natus est, ibique inter animalia reclinatus, pluraque loca alia tam in Hierusalem ciuitate sancta terre Iudææ, quàm extra, à modernis peregrinis visitari solita, deuotissimè visitauit, pariterque adorauit. In quorum fidem, ego frater Anthonius de Bergamo ordinis fratrum minorum regularis obseruantiæ prouinciæ diui Anthonij Sacri conuentus montis Sion vicarius (licet indignus) necnon aliorum locorum terræ Sanctæ, apostolica authoritate comissarius et rector, has Sigillo maiori nostri officij nostraque subscriptione muniri volui. Datum Hierosolymis apud sacratissimum domini coenaculum in sæpè memorato monte Sion, Anno Domini millesimo quingentesimo, quinquagesimo tertio, die vero sexto mensis Septembris.

Frater Antonius qui supra.

[Sidenote: The pilgrims returne from Ierusalem. Mount Carmel.] The 15. of September being come from our pilgrimage, we went aborde our shippe, and set saile, and kept our course West toward the Island of Cyprus, but al that night it was calme, and the 16. the winde freshed, and we passed by Mount Carmel.

The 17. the winde was very scant, yet we kept the sea, and towards night wee had a guste of raine whereby wee were constrained to strike our sailes, but it was not very stormie, nor lasted very long.

The 18. 19. 20. and 21. we kept still the sea and saw no land because we had very little winde, and that not very fauourable.

The 22. at noone the Boatswaine sent some of the Mariners into the boat, (which we toed asterne from Iaffa) for certaine necessaries belonging to the ship, wherein the Mariners found a certaine fish in proportion like a Dace, about 6 inches long (yet the Mariners said they had seene the like a foote long and more) the which fish had on euery side a wing, and toward the taile two other lesser as it were finnes, on either side one, but in proportion they were wings and of a good length. These wings grow out betweene the gils and the carkasse of the same fish. [Sidenote: Pesce columbini.] They are called in the Italian tongue Pesce columbini, for in deede, the wings being spred it is like to a flying doue, they say it will flie farre and very high. So it seemeth that being weary of her flight she fell into the boate, and not being able to rise againe died there.

The 23. 24. and 25. we sailed our direct course with a small gale of winde, and this day we had sight of the Island of Cyprus. [Sidenote: Cauo de la Griega.] The first land that we discouered was a headland called Cauo de la Criega, and about midnight we ankered by North of the Gape. This cape is a high hil, long and square, and on the East corner it hath a high cop, that appeareth vnto those at the sea, like a white cloud, for toward the sea it is white, and it lieth into the sea Southwest. This coast of Cyprus is high declining toward the sea, but it hath no cliffes.

The 26. we set saile againe, and toward noone we came into the port of Salini, where we went on land and lodged that night at a towne one mile from thence called Arnacho di Salini, this is but a village called in Italian, Casalia. This is distant from Iaffa 250. Italian miles.

The 27. we rested, and the 28. we hired horses to ride from Arnacho to Sulina, which is a good mile. The salt pit is very neere two miles in compasse, very plaine and leuell, into the which they let runne at the time of raine a quantitie of water comming from the mountaines, which water is let in vntil the pit be full to a certaine marke, which when it is full, the rest is conueyed by a trench into the sea. The water is let runne in about

October, or sooner or later, as the time of the yeere doth afforde. There they let it remaine vntill the ende of Iuly or the middest of August, out of which pits at that time, in stead of water that they let in they gather very faire white salt, without any further art or labour, for it is only done by the great heate of the sunne. This the Venetians haue, and doe maintaine to the vse of S. Marke, and the Venetian ships that come to this Island are bound to cast out their ballast, and to lade with salt for Venice. Also there may none in all the Iland buy salt but of these men, who maintaine these pits for S. Marke. This place is watched by night with 6. horsemen to the end it be not stolne by night. Also vnder the Venetians dominions no towne may spende any salt, but they must buy it of Saint Marke, neither may any man buy any salt at one towne to carie to another, but euery one must buy his salt in the towne where he dwelleth. Neither may any man in Venice buy more salt then he spendeth in the city, for if he be knowen to carte but one ounce out of the due and be accused, hee looseth an eare. The most part of all the salt they haue in Venice commeth from these Salines, and they have it so plentifull, that they are not able, neuer a yeere to gather the one halfe, for they onely gather in Iuly, August, and September, and not fully these three moneths. Yet notwithstanding the abundance that the shippes carie away yeerely, there remaine heapes like hilles, some heapes able to lade nine or tenne shippes, and there are heapes of two yeeres gathering, some of three and some of nine or tenne yeeres making, to the value of a great somme of golde, and when the ships do lade, they neuer take it by measure, but when they come at Venice they measure it. This salt as it lyeth in the pit is like so much ice, and it is sixe inches thicke: they digge it with axes, and cause their slaues to cary it to the heapes. This night at midnight we rode to Famagusta, which is eight leagues from Salina, which is 24 English miles.

The 29 about two houres before day we alighted at Famagusta, and after we were refreshed we went to see the towne. This is a very faire strong holde, and the strongest and greatest in the Iland. The walks are faire and new, and strongly rampired with foure principall bulwarkes, and bettweene them turrions responding one to another, these walks did the Venetians make. They haue also on the hauen side of it a Castle, and the hauen is chained, the citie hath onely two gates, to say, one for the lande and another for the sea, they haue in the towne continually, be it peace or warres, 800 souldiers, and fortie and six gunners, besides Captaines, petie Captaines, Gouernour and Generall The lande gate hath always fiftie souldiers, pikes and gunners with their harnes, watching thereat night and day. At the sea gate fiue and twenties upon the walles euery night doe watch fifteene men in watch houses, for euery watch house fiue men, and in the market place 30 souldiers continually. There may no souldier serue there aboue 5 yeres, neither will they without friendship suffer them to depart afore 5. yeres be expired, and there may serue of all nations except Greekes. [Sidenote:

Morenigo.] They haue euery pay which is 45 dayes, 15 Morenigos, which is 15 shillings sterling. [Sidenote: Solde of Venice] Their horsemen haue only sixe soldes Venetian a day, and prouender for their horses, but truth I maruell how they liue being so hardly fed, for all the sommer they feede only vpon chopt strawe and barley, for hay they haue none, and yet they be faire, fat and seruiceable. [Sidenote: Castellani] The Venetians send euery two yeres new rulers, which they call Castellani. The towne hath allotted it also two gallies continually armed and furnished.

[Sidenote: Saint Katherens Chappel in old Famagusta.] The 30. in the morning we ridde to a chappell, where they say Saint Katherin was borne. This Chappell is in olde Famagusta, the which was destroyed by Englishmen, and is cleane ouerthrowne to the ground, to this day desolate and not inhabited by any person, it was of a great circuit, and there be to this day mountaines of faire, great, and strong buildings, and not onely there, but also in many places of the Iland. [Sidenote: Diuvers coines vnder ground.] Moreouer when they digge, plowe, or trench they finde sometimes olde antient coines, some of golde, some of siluer, and some of copper, yea and many tombes and vautes with sepulchers in them. This olde Famagusta is from the other, foure miles, and standeth on a hill, but the new towne on a plaine. [Sidenote: Cornari, a family of Venice maried to king Iaques.] Thence we returned to new Famagusta againe to dinner, and toward euening we went about the towne, and in the great Church we sawe the tombe of king Iaques, which was the last king of Cyprus, and was buried in the yere of Christ one thousand foure hundred seuentie and three, and had to wife one of the daughters of Venice, of the house of Cornari, the which family at this day hath great reuenues in this Island, and by means of that mariage the Venetians, chalenge the kingdome of Cyprus.

The first of October in the morning, we went to see the reliefe of the watches. That done, we went to one of the Greekes Churches to see a pot or Iarre of stone, which is sayd to bee one of the seuen Iarres of water, the which the Lord God at the mariage conuerted into wine. It is a pot of earth very faire, white enamelled, and faireiy wrought vpon with drawen worke, and hath on either side of it, instead of handles, eares made in fourme as the painters make angels wings, it was about an elle high, and small at the bottome, with a long necke and correspondent in circuit to the botome, the belly very great and round, it holdeth full twelue gallons, and hath a taphole to drawe wine out thereat, the Iarre is very auncient, but whether it be one of them or no, I know not. The aire of Famagusta is very vnwholesome, as they say, by reason of certaine marish ground adioyning vnto it. They haue also a certaine yeerely sicknesse raigning in the same towne, aboue all the rest of the Island: yet neuerthelesse, they haue it in other townes, but not so much. It is a certaine rednesse and paine of the eyes, the which if it bee not quickly holpen, it taketh away their sight, so that yeerely almost in that towne, they haue about twentie that lose their sight, either of one eye or both, and it commeth for the most part in this moneth of October, and the last moneth: for I haue met diuers times three and foure at once in companies, both men and women. [Sidenote: No vitailes must be sold out of the city of Famagusta.] Their liuing is better cheape in Famagusta then in any other place of the Island, because there may no kinde of prouision within their libertie bee solde out of the Citie.

The second of October we returned to Arnacho, where wee rested vntill the sixt day. [Sidenote: Greate ruines in Cyprus.] This towne is a pretie Village, there are thereby toward the Sea side diuers monuments, that there hath bene great ouerthrow of buildings, for to this day there is no yere when they finde not, digging vnder ground, either coines, caues, and sepulcres of antiquities, as we walking, did see many, so that in effect, all alongst the Sea coast, throughout the whole Island, there is much ruine and ouerthrow of buildings, [Sidenote: Cyprus 36. yeres disinhabited for lacke of water.] for as they say, it was disinhabited sixe and thirtie yeres, before Saint Helens time for lacke of water. [Sidenote: Cypr. ruinated by Rich. the I.] And since that time it hath bene ruinated and ouerthrowen by Richard the first of that name king of England, which he did in reuenge of his sisters rauishment comming to Ierusalem, the which inforcement was done to her by the king of Famagusta.

The sixt day we rid to Nicosia, which is from Arnacho seuen Cyprus miles, which are one and twentie Italian miles. This is the ancientest citie of the Iland, and is walled about, but it is not strong neither of walles nor situation: It is by report three Cyprus miles about, it is not throughly inhabited, but hath many great gardens in it, and also very many Date trees, and plentie of Pomegranates and other fruites. There dwell all the Gentilitie of the Island, and there hath euery Cauallier or Conte of the Island an habitation. [Sidenote: A fountaine that watereth al the gardens in the citie.] There is in this citie one fountaine rented by saint Marke, which is bound euery eight dayes once, to water all the gardens in the towne, and the keeper of this fountaine hath for euery tree a Bizantin, which is twelue soldes Venice, and sixpence sterling. [Sidenote: A Bizantin is 6. d. sterling.] He that hath that to farme, with a faire and profitable garden thereto belonging, paieth euery yeere to saint Marke, fifteene hundred crownes. The streetes of the citie are not paued, which maketh it with the quantitie of the gardens, to seeme but a rurall habitation. But there be many faire buildings in the Citie, there be also Monasteries both of Franks and Greekes. [Sidenote: S. Sophia is a Cathedral church of Nicosia.] The Cathedrall church is called Santa Sophia, in the which there is an old tombe of Iaspis stone, all of one piece, made in forme of a cariage coffer, twelue spannes long, sixe spannes broad, and seuen spannes high, which they say was found vnder ground. It is as faire a stone as euer I haue seene.

The seuenth day we rid to a Greeke Frierie halfe a mile without the towne. It is a very pleasaunt place, and the Friers feasted vs according to their abilitie. These Friers are such as haue bene Priests, and their wiues dying they must become Friers of this place, and neuer after eate flesh, for if they do, they are depriued from saying masse: neither, after they haue taken vpon them this order, may they marry againe, but they may keepe a single woman. These Greekish Friers are very continent and chast, and surely I haue seldome seen (which I haue well noted) any of them fat.

The 8. day we returned to Arnacho, and rested there. [Sidenote: Monte de la Croce.] The 9. after midnight my company rid to the hill called Monte de la Croce (but I not disposed would not go) which hill is from Arnacho 15. Italian miles. Vpon the sayd hill is a certaine crosse, which is, they say, a holy Crosse. This Crosse in times past did by their report of the Island, hang in the ayre, but by a certaine earthquake, the crosse and the chappeil it hung in, were ouerthrowen, so that neuer since it would hang againe in the aire. But it is now couered with siluer, and hath 3. drops of our lordes blood on it (as they say) and there is in the midst of the great crosse, a little crosse made of the crosse of Christ; but it is closed in the siluer, you must (if you will) beleeue it is so, for see it you cannot. This crosse hangeth nowe by both endes in the wall, that you may swing it vp and downe, in token that it did once hang in the aire. This was told me by my fellow pilgrimes, for I sawe it not.

The 10. at night we went aboard by warning of the patron: and the 11. in the morning we set saile, and crept along the shore, but at night we ankered by reason of contrary windes.

[Sidenote: Limisso.] The 12. we set saile toward Limisso, which is from Salines 50. miles, and there we went on land that night.

The 13. and 14. we remained still on land, and the 15. the patrone sent for vs; but by reason that one of our company was not well, we went not presently, but we were forced afterward to hire a boate, and to ouertake the ship tenne miles into the sea. At this Limisso all the Venetian ships lade wine for their prouision, and some for to sell, and also vineger. [Sidenote: Carrobi.] They lade also great store of Carrobi: for all the countrey thereabout adioning, and all the mountaines are full of Carrobi trees, they lade also cotton wooll there. [Sidenote: Vulture.] In the sayd towne we did see a certaine foule of the land (whereof there are many in this Island) named in the Italian tongue Vulture. It is a foule that is as big as a Swanne, and it liueth vpon carion. The skinne is full of soft doune, like to a fine furre, which they vse to occupie when they haue euill stomocks, and it maketh good digestion. This bird (as they say) will eat as much at one meale as shall serue him fortie dayes after, and within the compasse of that time careth for no more meate. The countrey people, when they haue any dead beast, they cary it into the mountaines, or where they suppose the sayd Vultures to haunt, they seeing the carion doe immediately greedily seize vpon it, and doe so ingraft their talents, that they cannot speedily rise agayne, by reason whereof the people come and kill them: sometimes they kill them with dogs, and sometimes with such weapons as they haue. This foule is very great and hardy, much like an Eagle in the feathers of her wings and backe, but vnder her great feathers she is onely doune, her necke also long and full of doune. She hath on the necke bone, betweene the necke and the shoulders a heape of fethers like a Tassell, her thighs vnto her knees are couered with doune, her legs strong and great, and dareth with her talents assault a man. [Sidenote: Great pleny of very fat birds.] They haue also in this Island a certaine small bird, much like vnto a Wagtaile in fethers and making, these are so extreme fat that you can perceiue nothing els in all their bodies: these birds are now in season. They take great quantitie of them, and they vse to pickle them with vineger and salt, and to put them in pots and send them to Venice and other places of Italy for presents of great estimation. They say they send almost 1200. Iarres or pots to Venice, besides those which are consumed in the Island, which are a great number. These are so plentifull that when there is no shipping, you may buy then for 10. Carchies, which coine are 4. to a Venetian Soldo, which is peny farthing the dozen, and when there is store of shipping, 2 pence the dozen, after that rate of their money. [Sidenote: The Famagustans obserue the French statutes.] They of the limites of Famagusta do keep the statutes of the Frenchmen which sometimes did rule there. And the people of Nicosia, obserue the order of the Genoueses, who sometimes also did rule them. All this day we lay in the sea with little wind.

The 16. we met a Venetian ship, and they willing to speake with vs, and we with them, made towards each other, but by reason of the euil stirrage of the other ship, we had almost boorded each other to our great danger. [Sidenote: Cauo Bianco.] Toward night we ankered vnder Cauo Bianco, but because the winde grew faire, we set saile againe presently.

[Sidenote: Another Cion.] The 17. 18. 19, and 20 we were at sea with calme sommer weather, and the 20. we had some raine, and saw another Cion in the element. [Sidenote: A ship called el Bonna.] This day also we sawe, and spake with a Venetian ship called el Bonna, bound for ciprus.

The 21. we sailed with a reasonable gale, and saw no land vntil the 4. of Nouember. [Sidenote: A great tempest.] This day we had raine, thunder, lightening, and much wind and stormie weather, but God be praised we escaped all dangers.

[Sidenote: Candia, Gozi.] The 4. of Nouember we had sight of the Island of Candia, and we fell with the Islands called Gozi, by south of Candia. [Sidenote: Antonie Gelber departed this life.] This day departed this present life, one of our company named Anthonie Gelber of Prussia, who onely tooke his surfet of Cyprus wine. This night we determined to ride a trie, because the wind was contrary, and the weather troublesome.

The 5. we had very rough stormie weather. This day was the sayd Anthonie Gelber sowed in a Chauina filled with stones and throwen into the sea. By reason of the freshnes of the wind we would haue made toward the shore, but the wind put vs to the sea, where we endured a great storme and a troublesome night.

The 6. 7. and 8. we were continually at the sea, and this day at noone the wind came faire, whereby we recouered the way which we had lost, and sayled out of sight of Candia.

[Sidenote: Cauo Matapan. Modon.] The 9. we sailed all day with a prosperous wind after 14. mile an houre: and the 10. in the morning, wee had sight of Cauo Matapan, and by noone of Cauo Gallo, in Morea, with which land we made by reason of contrary wind, likewise we had sight of Modon, vnder the which place we ankered. This Modon is a strong towne, and built into the sea, with a peere for litle ships and galleis to harbour in. [Sidenote: Sapientia.] It hath on the South side of the chanell, the Iland of Sapientia, with other litle Ilands all disinhabited. The chanell lieth Southwest and Northeast betweene the Islands and Morea, which is firme land. This Modon was built by the Venetians, but as some say it was taken from them by force of the Turke, and others say by composition: [Sidenote: Coron. Napolis de Romania.] in like case Coron, and Napolis de Romania, which is also in Morea. This night the Flemmish pilgrimes being drunke, would have slaine the patrone because he ankered here.

The 11. day we set saile againe, and as we passed by Modon, we saluted them with ordinance, for they that passe by this place, must salute with ordinance, (if they haue) or els by striking their top sailes, for if they doe not, the towne will shoot at them. [Sidenote: Prodeno. Zante and Cephalonia.] This day toward 2. of the clocke wee passed by the Island of Prodeno, which is but litle, and desert, vnder the Turke. About 2. houres before night, we had sight of the Islands of Zante and Cephalonia, which are from Modon one hundreth miles.

The 12. day in the morning, with the wind at West, we doubled between Castle Torneste, and the Island of Zante. [Sidenote: Castle Torneste vnder the Turke.] This castle is on the firme land vnder the Turke. This night we ankered afore the towne of Zante, where we that night went on land, and rested there the 13. 14. and 15. at night we were warned aboord by the patrone. This night the ship tooke in vitailes and other necessaries.

The 16. in the morning we set saile with a prosperous wind, and the 17. we had sight of Cauo de santa Maria in Albania on our right hand, and Corfu on the left hand. This night we ankered before the castles of Corfu, and went on land and refreshed our selues.

[Sidenote: The description of the force of Corfu.] The 18. by meanes of a friend we were licenced to enter the castle or fortresse of Corfu, which is not onely of situation the strongest I haue seene, but also of edification. It hath for the Inner warde two strong castles situated on the top of two high cragges of a rocke, a bow shoot distant the one from the other: the rocke is vnassaultable, for the second warde it hath strong walles with rampiers and trenches made as well as any arte can deuise. For the third warde and vttermost, it hath very strong walles with rampires of the rocke it selfe cut out by force and trenched about with the sea. The bulwarkes of the vttermost warde are not yet finished, which are in number but two: there are continually in the castle seuen hundred souldiours. Also it hath continually foure wardes, to wit, for the land entrie one, for the sea entrie another, and two other wardes. Artillerie and other munition of defence always readie planted it hath sufficient, besides the store remaining in their storehouses. The Venetians hold this for the key of all their dominions, and for strength it may be no lesse. This Island is very fruitfull and plentifull of wine and corne very good, and oliues great store. This Island is parted from Albania with a chanell, in some places eight and ten, and in other but three miles. Albania is vnder the Turke, but in it are many Christians. All the horseman of Corfu are Albaneses; the Island is not aboue 80. or 90. miles in compasse.

The 19. 20. and 21. we remained in the towne of Corfu.

The 22. day wee went aboord and set saile, the wind being very calme wee toed the ship all that day, and toward Sunne set, the castle sent a Fragatta vnto us to giue vs warning of three Foistes comming after vs, for whose comming wee prepared and watched all night, but they came not.

The 23. day in the morning being calme, wee toed out of the Streight, vntill wee came to the olde towne, whereof there is no thing standing but the walles. There is also a new Church of the Greekes called Santa Maria di Cassopo, and the townes name is called Cassopo. It is a good porte. About noone wee passed the Streight, and drew toward the ende of the Iland, hauing almost no wind. This night after supper, by reason of a certaine Hollander that was drunke, there arose in the ship such a troublesome disturbance, that all the ship was in an vprore with weapons, and had it not bene rather by Gods helpe, and the wisedome and patience of the patrone, more then by our procurement, there had bene that night a great slaughter. But as God would, there was no hurt, but onely the beginner was put vnder hatches, and with the fall hurt his face very sore. All that night the wind blew at Southeast, and sent vs forward.

The 24. in the morning wee found ourselues before an Island called Saseno, which is in the entrie to Valona, and the wind prosperous.

The 25. day we were before the hils of Antiueri, and about sunne set wee passed Ragusa, and three houres within night we ankered within Meleda, hauing Sclauonia or Dalmatia on the right hand of vs, and the winde Southwest.

The 26. in the morning we set sayle, and passed the chanell between Sclauonia and Meleda, which may be eight mile ouer at the most. This Iland is vnder the Raguses. At after noone with a hard gale at west and by north we entered the chanell betweene the Iland Curzola and the hilles of Dalmatia, in which channell be many rockes, and the channell not past 3 miles ouer, and we ankered before the towne of Curzolo. This is a pretie towne walled about and built vpon the sea side, hauing on the toppe of a round hill a faire Church. This Iland is vnder the Venetians, there grow very good vines, also that part toward Dalmatia is well peopled and husbanded, especially for wines. In the said Iland we met with the Venetian armie, to wit, tennie gallies, and three foystes. All that night we remained there.

The 27 we set sayle and passed along the Iland, and towards afternoone we passed in before the Iland of Augusta, and about sunne set before the towne of Lesina, whereas I am informed by the Italians, they take all the Sardinas that they spend in Italy. This day we had a prosperous winde at Southeast. The Iland of Lesina is vnder the Venetians, a very fruitfull Iland adioyning to the maine of Dalmatia, we left it on our right hand, and passed along.

[Sidenote: The gulfe of Quernero. Rouigno.] The 28 in the morning we were in the Gulfe of Quernero, and about two houres after noone we were before the cape of Istria, and at sunne set we were at anker afore Rouignio which is also in Istria and vnder the Venetians, where all ships Venetian and others are bound by order from Venice to take in their pilots to goe for Venice. All the sommer the Pilots lie at Rouignio, and in winter at Parenzo, which is from Rouignio 18 miles by West.

[Sidenote: Parenzo.] The 29 we set sayle and went as farre as Parenzo, and ankered there that day, and went no further.

[Sidenote: S. Nicolo an Iland.] The 30 in the morning we rowed to Sant Nicolo a litle Island hard by vninhabited, but only it hath a Monastery, and is full of Oliue trees, after masse wee returned and went aboord. This day we hired a Barke to imbarke the pilgrims for Venice, but they departed not. In the afternoone we went to see the towne of Parenzo, it is a pretie handsome towne, vnder the Venetians. After supper wee imbarked our selues againe, and that night wee sayled towardes Venice.

The first of December we past a towne of the Venetians, standing on the entery to the Palude or marshes of Venice: which towne is called Caorle, and by contrary windes we were driuen thither to take port. This is 60 miles from Parenzo, and forty from Venice, there we remayned that night.

The second two houres before day, with the winde at Southeast, we sayled towards Venice, where we arriued (God be praysed) at two of the clocke after dinner, and landed about foure, we were kept so long from landing, because we durst not land vntill we had presented to the Prouidor de la Sanita, our letter of health.

* * * * *

The first voyage or iourney, made by Master Laurence Aldersey, Marchant of
  London, to the Cities of Ierusalem, and Tripolis, &c. in the yeere 1581. Penned and set downe by himselfe.

I departed from London the first day of April in the yeere of our Lord 1581, passing through the Nether-land and vp the riuer Rhene by Colen, and other cities of Germanie. And vpon Thursday, the thirde day of May, I came to Augusta, where I deliuered the letter I had to Master Ienise, and Master Castler, whom I found very willing to pleasure me, in any thing that I could or would reasonably demaund. He first furnished me with a horse to Venice, for my money, and then tooke me with him a walking, to shew me the Citie, for that I had a day to tary there, for him that was to be my guide. He shewed me first the Statehouse, which is very faire, and beautiful: then be brought mee to the finest garden, and orchard, that euer I sawe in my life: for there was in it a place for Canarie birdes, as large as a faire Chamber, trimmed with wier both aboue and beneath, with fine little branches of trees for them to sit in, vhich was full of those Canarie birdes. There was such an other for Turtle dooues: also there were two pigeon houses ioyning to them, hauing in them store of Turtle dooues and pigeons. In the same garden also were sixe or seuen fishponds, all railed about, and full of very good fish. Also, seuen or eight fine fountaines, or water springs, of diuers fashions: as for fruite, there wanted none of all sorts, as Orenges, figges, raisons, wallnuts, grapes, besides apples, peares, fillbirds, small nuts, and such other fruite, as wee haue in England.

Then did hee bring mee to the water tower of the same Citie, that by a sleight and deuise hath the water brought vp as high as any Church in the towne, and to tel you the strange deuises of all, it passeth my capacitie. Then he brought me to another faire garden, called the Shooters hoose, where are buts for the long bowe, the cross bowe, the stone bowe, the long peece, and for diuers other exercises more.

After this, we walked about the walles of the Citie, where is a great, broade, and deepe ditch, vpon one side of the towne, so full of fish, as euer I saw any pond in my life, and it is reserued onely for the States of the Citie. And vpon the other side of the Citie is also a deepe place all greene, wherein Deere are kept, and when it pleaseth the States to hunt for their pleasure, thither they resort, and haue their courses with grayhounds, which are kept for that purpose.

The fift of May, I departed from Augusta towards Venice, and came thither vpon Whitsunday the thirteenth of the same moneth. It is needlesse to speake of the height of the mountaines that I passed ouer, and of the danger thereof, it is so wel knowen already to the world: the heigth of them is marueilous, and I was the space of sixe dayes in passing them.

I came to Venice at the time of a Faire, which lasted foureteene dayes, wherein I sawe very many, and faire shewes of wares. I came thither too short for the first passage, which went away from Venice about the seuenth or eight of May, and with them about three score pilgrims, which shippe was cast away at a towne called Estria, two miles from Venice, and all the men in her, sauing thirtie, or thereabout, lost.

Within eight dayes after fell Corpus Christi day, which was a day amongst them of procession, in which was shewed the plate and treasure of Venice, which is esteemed to be worth two millions of pounds, but I do not accompt it woorth halfe a quarter of that money, except there be more than I sawe. To speake of the sumptuousnesse of the Copes and Vestments of the Church, I leaue, but the trueth is, they be very sumptuous, many of them set all ouer with pearle, and made of cloth of golde. And for the Iesuits, I thinke there be as many at Venice, as there be in Colen.

The number of Iewes is there thought to be 1000, who dwell in a certaine place of the Citie, and haue also a place, to which they resort to pray, which is called the Iewes Sinagogue. They all, and their offspring vse to weare red caps, (for so they are commaunded) because they may thereby be knowen from other men. For my further knowledge of these people, I went into their Sinagogue vpon a Saturday, which is their Sabbath day: and I found them in their seruice or prayers, very deuoute: they receiue the fiue bookes of Moses, and honour them by carying them about their Church, as the Papists doe their crosse.

Their Synagogue is in forme round, and the people sit round about it, and in the midst, there is a place for him that readeth to the rest: as for their apparell, all of them weare a large white lawne ouer their garments, which reacheth from their head, downe to the ground.

The Psalmes they sing as wee doe, hauing no image, nor vsing any maner of idolatrie: their error is, that they beleeue not in Christ, nor yet receiue the New Testament. This Citie of Venice is very faire, and greatly to bee commended, wherein is good order for all things: and also it is very strong and populous: it standeth vpon the maine Sea, and hath many Islands about it, that belong to it.

To tell you of the duke of Venice, and of the Seigniory: there is one chosen that euer beareth the name of a duke, but in trueth hee is but seruant of his Seigniorie, for of himselfe hee can doe litle: it is no otherwise with him, then with a Priest that is at Masse vpon a festiual day, which putting on his golden garment, seemeth to be a great man, but if any man come vnto him, and craue some friendship at his handes, hee will say, you must goe to the Masters of the Parish, for I cannot pleasure you, otherwise then by preferring to your suite: and so it is with the duke of Venice, if any man hauing a suite, come to him and make his complaint, and deliuer his supplication, it is not in him to helpe him, but hee will tell him, You must come this day, or that day, and then I will preferre your suite to the Seigniorie, and doe you the best friendship that I may. Furthermore, if any man bring a letter vnto him, hee may not open it, but in the presence of the Seigniorie, and they are to see it first, which being read, perhaps they will deliuer it to him, perhaps not. Of the Seigniory there be about three hundreth, and about fourtie of the priuie Counsell of Venice, who vsually are arayed in gownes of crimsen Satten, or crimsen Damaske, when they sit in Counsell.

In the citie of Venice, no man may weare a weapon, except he be a souldier for the Seigniorie, or a scholler of Padua, or a gentleman of great countenance, and yet he may not do that without licence.

As for the women of Venice, they be rather monsters then women. Euery Shoomakers or Taylors wife will haue a gowne of silke, and one to carie vp her traine, wearing their shooes very neere halfe a yarde high from the ground: if a stranger meete one of them, he will surely thinke by the state that she goeth with, that he meeteth a Lady.

I departed from this citie of Venice, vpon Midsommer day, being the foure and twentieth of Iune, and thinking that the ship would the next day depart, I stayed, and lay a shippeboord all night, and we were made beleeue from time to time, that we should this day, and that day depart, but we taried still, till the fourteenth of July, and then with scant winde we set sayle, and sayled that day and that night, not aboue fiftie Italian miles: and vpon the sixteene day at night the winde turned flat contrary, so that the Master knewe not what to doe: and about the fift houre of the night, which we reckon to be about one of the clocke after midnight, the Pilot descried a saile, and at last perceiued it to be a Gallie of the Turkes, whereupon we were in great feare.

The Master being a wise fellowe, and a good sayler, beganne to deuise howe to escape the danger, and to loose litle of our way: and while both he, and all of vs were in our dumps, God sent vs a merry gale of winde, that we ranne threescore and tenne leagues before it was twelue a clocke the next day, and in six dayes after we were seuen leagues past Zante. And vpon Munday morning, being the three and twentie of the same moneth, we came in the sight of Candia which day the winde came contrary, with great blasts and stormes, vntill the eight and twentie of the same moneth: in which time, the Mariners cried out vpon me, because I was an English man, and sayd, I was no good Christian, and wished that I were in the middest of the Sea, saying, that they, and the shippe, were the worse for me. I answered, truely it may well be, for I thinke my selfe the worst creature in the worlde, and consider you your selues also, as I doe my selfe, and then vse your discretion. The Frier preached, and the sermon being done, I was demaunded whether I did vnderstand him: I answered, yea, and tolde the Frier himselfe, thus you saide in your sermon, that we were not all good Christians, or else it were not possible for vs to haue such weather: to which I answered, be you well assured, that we are not indeede all good Christians, for there are in the ship some that hold very vnchristian opinions: so for that time I satisfied him, although (they said) that I would not see, when they said the procession, and honoured their images, and prayed to our Lady and S. Marke.

There was also a Gentleman, an Italian, which was a passenger in the ship, and he tolde me what they said of me, because I would not sing, Salue Regina and Aue Maria, as they did: I told them, that they that praied to so many, or sought helpe of any other, then of God the Father, or of Iesus Christ his onely sonne, goe a wrong way to worke, and robbed God of his honour, and wrought their owne destructions.

All this was told of the Friers, but I heard nothing of it in three daies after: and then at euening prayer, they sent the purser about with the image of our Lady to euery one to kisse, and I perceiuing it went another way from him, and would not see it: yet at last he fetched his course about, so that he came to me, and offered it to me as he did to others, but I refused it: whereupon there was a great stirre: the patron and all the friers were told of it, and euery one saide I was a Lutheran, and so called me: but two of the friers that were of greatest authoritie, seemed to beare me better good will then the rest, and trauelled to the patron in my behalfe, and made all well againe.

The second day of August we arriued in Cyprus, at a towne called Missagh: the people there be very rude, and like beasts, and no better they eat their meat sitting vpon the ground, with their legges a crosse like tailors, their beds for the most part be hard stones, but yet some of them haue faire mattraces to lie vpon.

Vpon Thursday the eight of August we came to Ioppa in a small barke, which we hired betwixt Missagh and Salina, and could not be suffered to come on land till noone the next day, and then we were permitted by the great Basha, who sate vpon the top of a hill to see vs sent away. Being come on land, we might not enter into any house for victuals, but were to content our selues with our owne prouision, and that which we bought to carie with vs was taken from vs. I had a paire of stirrops, which I bought at Venice to serue me in my journey, and trying to make them fit for me, when the Basha saw me vp before the rest of the companie, he sent one to dismount me, and to strike me, whereupon I turned me to the Basha, and made a long legge, saying, Grand mercie Signior: and after a while we were horsed vpon litle asses, and sent away, with about fiftie light horsemen to be our conduct through the wildernesse, called Deserta foelix, who made vs good sport by the way with their pikes, gunnes, and fauchins.

That day being S. Laurence day we came to Rama, which is tenne Italian miles from Ioppa, and there we stayed that night, and payed to the captaine of the castell euery man a chekin, which is seuen shillings and two pence sterling. So then we had a new gard of souldiers, and left the other.

The house we lodged in at Rama had a doore so low to enter into, that I was faine to creepe in, as it were vpon my knees, and within it are three roomes to lodge trauellers that come that way: there are no beds, except a man buy a mat, and lay it on the ground, that is all the prouision, without stooles or benches to sit vpon. Our victuals were brought vs out of the towne, as hennes, egges, bread, great store of fruite, as pomgranates, figges, grapes, oringes, and such like, and drinke we drue out of the well. The towne it selfe is so ruinated that I take it rather to be a heape of stones then a towne.

Then the next morning we thought to haue gone away, but we could not be permitted that day, so we stayed there till two of the clocke the next morning, and then with a fresh gard of souldiers we departed toward Ierusalem. We had not ridde fiue English miles, but we were incountred with a great number of the Arabians, who stayed vs, and would not suffer vs to passe till they had somewhat, so it cost vs for all our gard aboue twentie shillings a man betwixt Ioppa and Ierusalem. These Arabians troubled vs oftentimes. Our Truchman that payed the money for vs was striken down, and had his head broken because be would not giue them as much as they asked: and they that should haue rescued both him and vs, stood sill and durst do nothing, which was to our cost.

Being come within sight of Ierusalem, the maner is to kneele downe, and giue God thankes, that it hath pleased him to bring vs to that holy place, where he himselfe had beene: and there we leaue our horses and go on foote to the towne, and being come to the gates, there they tooke our names, and our fathers names, and so we were permitted to go to our lodgings.

The gouernour of the house met vs a mile out of the towne, and very curteously bade vs all welcome, and brought vs to the monasterie. The gates of the citie are all couered with yron, the entrance into the house of the Christians is a very low and narrow doore, barred or plated with yron, and then come we into a very darke entry: the place is a monastery: there we lay, and dieted of free cost, we fared reasonable well, the bread and wine was excellent good, the chambers cleane, and all the meat well serued in, with cleane linnen.

We lay at the monasterie two days, Friday and Saturday, and then we went to Bethlem with two or three of the friers of the house with vs: in the way thither we saw many monuments, as:

The mountaine where the Angell tooke vp Abacuck by the haire, and brought him to Daniel in the Lions denne.

The fountaine of the prophet Ieremie.

The place where the wise men met that went to Bethlem to worship Christ, where is a fountaine of stone.

Being come to Bethlem we sawe the place where Christ was borne, which is now a chappell with two altars, whereupon they say masse: the place is built with gray marble, and hath bene beautifull, but now it is partly decayed.

Neere thereto is the sepulchre of the innocents slaine by Herod, the sepulchres of Paul, of Ierome, and of Eusebius.

Also a little from this monasterie is a place vnder the ground, where the virgine Mary abode with Christ when Herod sought him to destroy him.

We stayed at Bethlem that night, and the next day we went from thence to the mountaines of Iudea, which are about eight miles from Ierusalem, where are the ruines of an olde monasterie. In the mid way from the monasterie to Ierusalem is the place where Iohn Baptist was borne, being now an olde monasterie, and cattell kept in it. Also a mile from Ierusalem is a place called Inuentio sanctæ crucis, where the wood was found that made the crosse.

In the citie of Ierusalem we saw the hall where Pilate sate in iudgement when Christ was condemned, the staires whereof are at Rome, as they told vs. A litle from thence is the house where the virgin Mary was borne.

There is also the piscina or fishpoole where the sicke folkes were healed, which is by the wals of Ierusalem. But the poole is now dry.

The mount of Caluaria is a great church, and within the doore thereof, which is litle, and barred with yron, and fiue great holes in it to looke in, like the holes of taverne doores in London, they sit that are appointed to receiue our money with a carpet vnder them vpon a banke of stone, and their legges a crosse like tailors: hauing paid our money, we are permitted to go into the church: right against the church doore is the graue where Christ was buried, with a great long stone of white marble ouer it, and rayled about, the outside of the sepulchre is very foule, by meanes that euery man scrapes his name and marke vpon it, and is ill kept.

Within the sepulchre is a partition, and in the further part thereof is a place like an altar, where they say masse, and at the doore thereof is the stone whereupon the Angell sate when he sayde to Marie, He is risen, which stone was also rowled to the doore of the sepulchre.

The altar stone within the sepulchre is of white marble, the place able to confeine but foure persons, right ouer the sepulchre is a deuise or lanterne for light, and ouer that a great louer such as are in England in ancient houses. There is also the chappell of the sepulchre, and in the mids thereof is a canopie as it were of a bed, with a great sort of Estridge egges hanging at it, with tassels of silke and lampes.

Behinde the sepulchre is a litle chappell for the Chaldeans and Syrians.

Vpon the right hand comming into the church is the tombe of Baldwine king of France, and of his sonne: and in the same place the tombe of Melchisedech.

There is a chappell also in the same church erected to S. Helen, through which we go vp to the place where Christ was crucified: the stayres are fiftie steps high, there are two altars in it: before the high altar is the place where the crosse stood, the hole whereof is trimmed about with siluer, and the depth of it is halfe a mans arme deepe: the rent also of the mountaine is there to be seene in the creuis, wherein a man may put his arme.

Vpon the other side of the mount of Caluarie is the place where Abraham would haue sacrificed his sonne. Where also is a chapell, and the place paued with stones of diuers colours.

There is also the house of Annas the high Priest, and the Oliue tree whereunto Christ was bound to when he was whipt. Also the house of Caiphas, and by it the prison where Christ was kept, which is but the roome of one man, and hath no light but the opening of the doore.

Without Ierusalem in the vally of Iosaphat is a church vnder the ground, like to the shrouds in Pauls, where the sepulchre of the virgin Mary is: the staires be very broad, and vpon the staires going downe are two sepulchres: vpon the left hand lieth Iosaphat, and vpon the right hand lieth Ioachim and Anna, the father and mother of the virgin Mary.

Going out of the valley of Iosaphat we came to mount Oliuet, where Christ praied vnto his father before his death: and there is to be seene (as they tolde me) the water and blood that fell from the eyes of Christ. A litle higher vpon the same mount is the place where the Apostles slept, and watched not. At the foot of the mount is the place where Christ was imprisoned.

Vpon the mountaine also is the place where Christ stood when he wept ouer
Ierusalem, and where he ascended into heauen.

Now hauing seene all these monuments, I with my company set from Ierusalem, the 20 day of August, and came againe to Ioppa the 22 of the same moneth, where wee tooke shipping presently for Tripolis, and in foure dayes we came to Mecina the place where the ships lie that come for Tripolis.

The citie of Tripolis is a mile and a halfe within the land, so that no ship can come further then Mecina: so that night I came thither, where I lay nine daies for passage, and at last we imbarked our selues in a good ship of Venice called the Naue Ragasona. We entred the ship the second of September, the fourth we set saile, the seuenth we came to Salina, which is 140 miles from Tripolis: there we stayed foure dayes to take in more lading, in which meane time I fell sicke of an ague, but recouered againe, I praise God.

Salina is a ruinated citie, and was destroyed by the Turke ten yeeres past: there are in it now but seuenteene persons, women and children. A litle from this citie of Salina is a salt piece of ground, where the water groweth salt that raineth vpon it.

Thursday the 21 of September, we came to Missagh, and there we stayed eight dayes for our lading: the 18 of September before we came to Missagh, and within ten miles of the towne, as we lay at an anker, because the winde was contrary, there came a great boat full of men to boord vs, they made an excuse to seeke for foure men which (they said) our ship had taken from theirs about Tripolis, but our captaine would not suffer any of them to come into vs.

The next morning they came to vs againe with a great gally, manned with 500 men at the least, whereupon our captaine sent the boat to them with twelue men to know their pleasure: they said they sought for 4 men, and therefore would talke with our maister: so then the maisters mate was sent them, and him they kept, and went their way; the next morning they came againe with him, and with three other gallies, and then would needes speake with our captaine, who went to them in a gowne of crimson damaske, and other very braue apparell, and fiue or sixe other gentlemen richly apparelled also. They hauing the Turkes safe conduct, shewed it to the captaine of the gallies, and laid it vpon his head, charging him to obey it: so with much adoe, and with the gift of 100 pieces of golde we were quit of them, and had our man againe.

That day as aforesaid, we came to Missagh, and there stayed eight dayes, and at last departed towards Candie, with a scant winde.

The 11 day of October we were boorded with foure gallies, manned with 1200 men, which also made a sleeuelesse arrant, and troubled us very much, but our captaines pasport, and the gift of 100 chekins discharged all.

The 27 of October we passed by Zante with a merrie winde, the 29 by Corfu, and the third of Nouember we arriued at Istria, and there we left our great ship, and tooke small boates to bring vs to Venice.

The 9 of Nouember I arriued again at Venice in good health, where I staied nine daies, and the 25 of the same moneth I came to Augusta, and staied there but one day.

The 27 of Nouember I set towards Nuremberg where I came the 29, and there staied till the 9 of December, and was very well interteined of the English marchants there: and the gouernors of the towne sent me and my company sixteene gallons of excellent good wine.

From thence I went to Frankford, from Frankford to Collen, from Collen to Arnam, from Arnam to Vtreight, from Vtreight to Dort, from Dort to Antwerpe, from Antwerpe to Flushing, from Flushing to London, where I arriued vpon Twelue eue in safetie, and gaue thanks to God, hauing finished my iourney to Ierusalem and home againe, in the space of nine moneths and fiue dayes.

* * * * *

The passeport made by the great Maister of Malta vnto the Englishmen in the barke Raynolds. 1582.

Frere Hugo de Loubeux Verdala, Dei gratia sacræ domus hospitalis sancti Ioannis Hierosolymitani, magister humilis, pauperumque Iesu Christi custos, vniuersis et singulis principibus ecclesiasticis et secularibus, archiepiscopis, episcopis, ducibus, marchionibus, baronibus, nobilibus, capitaneis, vicedominis, præfectis, castellanis, admiralijs, et quibuscunque triremium vel aliorum nauigiorum patronis, ac ciuitatum rectoribus, potestatibus ac magistratibus, cæterisque officialibus, et quibuscunque personis cuiusuis dignitatis, gradus, status et conditionis fuerint, vbilibet locorum et terrarum constitutis, salutem.

Notum facimus et in verbo veritatis attestamur, come nel mese di Maggio prossime passato le nostre galere vennero dal viaggio di Barberia, doue hauendo mandato per socorrere a vn galionetto de Christiani che hauea dato trauerso in quelle parti, essendo arriuati sopra questa isola alla parte de ponente trouarono vno naue Inglesa, sopra cargo de essa il magnifico Giouanni Keale, et Dauid Filly patrono, volendo la reconoscere che naue fosse, han visto, che se metteua in ordine per defendersi, dubitando che dette nostre galere fossero de inimici: et per che vn marinaro riuoltose contra la volonta de detti magnifico Giouanni Keale et Dauid Filly, habbi tirato vn tiro di artiglieria verso vna de dette galere, et che non se amangnaua la vela de la Maiestra secondo la volonta de detti magnifico Giouanni Keale et Dauid Filly patrono, furimensata detta naue nel presente general porto di Malta, secondo l'ordine del venerando Generale de dette galere, et essendo qua, monsignor Inquisitore ha impedita quella per conto del sancto officio, et si diede parte alla santita di nostro signor Gregorio papa xiij. A la fin fu licenciata per andarsene al suo viaggio. Han donque humilmente supplicato detti magnifico Giouanni Keale et Dauid Filly per nome et parte delli magnifici Edwardo Osborn senatore et Richardo Staper merchanti Inglesi della nobile citta di Londra, et anco di Tomaso Wilkinson scriuano, piloti, nocheri, et marinari, gli volessimo dare le nostre lettere patente et saluo condutto, accioche potranno andare et ritornare quando gli parera commodo con alcuna roba et mercantia a loro benuista: si come noi, essendo cosa giusta et che retornera commoda a nostra relligione et a questi forrestieri, per tenor de li presenti se gli habiamo concesse con le conditione però infra scritte, videlicet:

Che ogni volta che detti mercadanti con sopradetta naue o con altra non porterano mercantie de contrabando, et che constara per fede authentica et con lettere patente de sanita, poteran liberalmente victualiarse de tutte le victuarie necessarie, et praticare in questa isola et dominij, et poi partisene et seguire suo viaggio per doue volessero in leuante o altroue, come tutti altri vaselli et specialmente de Francesi et aitri nationi, et die venderi et comprare qual si voglia mercantia a loro benuista.

Item, che potera portare poluere de canone et di archibuso, salnitro, carboni di petra rosetta, platine de rame, stagno, acciale, ferro, carisée commune, tela grossa bianca per far tende de galere, balle de ferro de calibro, petre de molino fine, arbore et antenne de galere, bastardi et alteri. Et in conclusione, hauenda visto che loro per il tempo che restarano qua, si portorno da fideli et Catholici Christiani, et che sua sanctita habbia trouata bono il saluo condutto del gran Turko a loro concesso, per il timor della armata Turkesca et di altri vaselli de inimici, inherendo alla volonta di sua sanctità, et massime per che hauera de andare et passare per diuersi lochi et tanto lontani come Ingilterra, Flandra, et tutti patri di ponente, et in altroue, a noi ha parso farle le presente nostre lettere patente com fidele conuersatore nostro, accio piu securamente et sensa obstaculo possa andare et ritornare quando li parera con detta naue o con altre, a loro benuista. Per tanto donque tutti et ciascun di voi sudetti affecutosamente pregamo, che per qual si voglia de vostra iurisditione, alla quale detto magnifico Giouanni Keale et Dauid Filly anome quo supra con la naue et marinari de detti loro principali o altri caschera, nauigare, passare, et venire sicuramente, alla libera, sensa alcuno disturbo o altro impedimento li lasciate, et facciate lasciare, stare, et passare, tornare, et quando li parera partire, talmente che per amore et contemplatione nostra il detto magnifico Giouanni Keale a nome quo supra con le naue, marinari, et mercantia non habbi difficulta, fastidio et ritentione alcuna, anzi se gli dia ogni agiuto et fauore, cosa degnadi voi, giusta, et a noi gratissima, de recompensaruila con vagule et maggior seruitio, quando dall'occasione ne saremo rechiesti. Et finalmente commandammo a tutti et qual si voglia relligiosi et frati de nostra relligione di qual si voglia conditione, grado et stato che siano, et a tutti riceuitori et procuratori nostri in tutti et qual si voglia priorati nostri deputati et deputandi in vertu di santa obedientia, et attuti nostri vassalli et alla giurisditione di nostri relligione sogetti, che in tale et per tale tenghino et reputino il detto magnifico Giouanni Keale a nome vt supra, naue, marinari, et mercantia, sensa permittere, che nel detto suo viaggio, o in alcun altro Iuogo sia molestato, o in qual si voglia manera impedito, anzi rutte le cose sue et negotij loro sian da voi agioutati et continuamente fauoriti. In cuius rei testimonium Bulla nostra magistralis in cera nigra præsentibus est impressa. Datæ Melitæ in conuentu nostro die duodecimo Mensis Iulij. 1582.

The same in English

Frier Hugo of Loubeux Verdala, by the grace of God, master of the holy house, the hospital of S. Iohn at Ierusalem, and an humble keeper of the poore of Iesus Christ, to all and euery prince ecclesiastical and secular, archbishops, bishops, Dukes, Marqueses, Barons, Capteines, Vicelords, Maiors, Castellanes, Admirals, and whatsoeuer patrons of Gallies, or other greater officers and persons whatsoeuer, of what dignitie, degree, state and condition soeuer they be, dwelling in all places and landes, greeting.

We make it knowne, and in the word of truth do witnesse, that in the moneth of May last past, our gallies came on the voyage from Barbarie, where hauing commandement to succour a little ship of the Christians which was driuen ouer into that part being arriued vpon this Iland on the West part they found one English ship vnder the charge of the worshipfull Iohn Keele, and Dauid Fillie master: and our men willing to know what ship it was, they seemed to put themselues in order for their defence, doubting that the said our gallies were of the enemies, and therefore one mariner attempted contrary to the will of the worshipfull Iohn Keele, and Dauid Fillie maister: and had shot off a piece of artillerie against one of the said gallies, and because she would not strike amaine her sayle, according to the will of the saide worshipfull Iohn Keele, and Dauid Fillie master, the said ship was brought backe again vnto the present port of Malta, according to the order of the reuerend generall of the said gallies: and in being there maister Inquisitor staid it by authoritie of the holy office, and in that behalfe by the holinesse of our Lord pope Gregorie the thirteenth, in the end was licenced to depart on her voyage. They therefore the said worshipfull Iohn Keele and Dauid Fillie, in the name and behalfe of the worshipfull master Edward Osborne and Alderman, and Richard Staper, English marchants of the noble citie of London, haue humbly besought together with Thomas Wilkinson the purser, pilots, master and mariners, that we would giue our letters patents, and safe conducts, that they might goe and returne, when they shall see opportunitie, with their goods and marchandizes at their pleasure: whereupon the thing seeming vnto vs iust, and that it might be for the profite of our religion, and of these strangers, by the tenor of these presents we haue graunted the same to them: yet, with the conditions hereunder written, viz.

That euery time the said marchants of the said ship, or with any other, shall not bring such merchandize as is forbidden, and that sufficient proofe and letters testimonial it appeareth that they are free from the infections of the plague, they may vituall themselues with all necessarie victuals, and traffike with vs, and in this Iland and dominion, and afterwarde may depart and follow their voyage whither they will into the Luant or else where, as all other vessels, and especially of France and other nations do, and sell and buy whatsoeuer marchandize they shal thinke good.

Item, that they may bring powder for cannon and harquebush, saltpeeter, cole of Newcastle, plates of lattin, tinne, steele, yron, common karsies white, course canuas to make saile for the gallies, balles of yron for shot, fine milstones, trees and masts for gallies, litle and others, and in conclusion, hauing seene that they for the time of their abode here, did behaue themselues like faithfull and catholike Christians, and that his holines hath allowed the safeconduct of the great Turke to them granted for feare of the Turkish armie, and other vessels of the enemie, submitting our selues to the pleasures of his holinesse, and especially because our people haue occasion to passe by diuers places so farre off, as England, Flanders, and all parts Westwards, and in other places, we haue vouchsafed to make these our letters patents, as our faithfull assistant, so as more surely, and with let they may go and returne when they shall thinke good, with the said ship or with others at their pleasure. We therefore pray all and euery of your subiects effectually that by what part soeuer of your iurisdiction, vnto the which the said worshipful Iohn Keele and Daniel Fillie by name abouesaid, with the ship and mariners of the said principall place or other, shall haue accesse, saile, and passe, and come safely with libertie without any disturbance or other impediment, that you giue leaue, and cause leaue to be giuen that they may passe, stay and returne, and when they please, depart, in such sort, that for loue and contention the said worshipfull Iohn Keele, with the ship and mariners haue no let, hinderance, or retention, also that you giue all helpe and fauour, a thing worthy of your iustice, and to vs most acceptable, to be recompenced with equall and greater seruice, when vpon occasion it shalbe required.

And finally, we command all, and whatsoeuer religious people, and brothers of our religion, of whatsoeuer condition, degree, and state they be, and all other receiuers and procurators, in all and whatsoeuer our priories deputed, and to be deputed by vertue of the holy obedience, and all our people, and all that are subiect to the iurisdiction of our religion, that in, and by the same they hold, and repute the said worshipfull Iohn Keele in the name as abouesaid, the ship, mariners, and merchandize, without let in the same their voyage, or in any other place, that they be not molested, not in any wise hindered, but that in all their causes and businesse they be of you holpen, and furthered continually. In witnesse whereof, our seale of gouernment is impressed to these presents in blacke waxe. Giuen at Malta in our Conuent, the twelfth of the moneth of Iuly, in the yeere 1582.

* * * * *

Commission giuen by M. William Harebourne the English Ambassadour, to Richard Foster, authorising him Consul of the English nation in the parts of Alepo, Damasco, Aman, Tripolis, Ierusalem, &c.

I William Harborne, her Maiesties Ambassadour, Ligier with the Grand Signior, for the affaires of the Leuant doe in her Maiesties name confirme and appoint Richart Foster Gentleman, my Deputie and Consull in the parts of Alepo, Damasco, Aman, Tripolis, Ierusalem and all other ports whatsoeuer in the prouinces of Syria, Palestina, and Iurie, to execute the office of Consull ouer all our Nation her Maiesties subiects, of what estate or quality soeuer: giuing him hereby full power to defend, protect, and maintaine all such her Maiesties subiects as to him shall be obedient, in all honest and iest causes whatsoeuer: and in like case no lesse power to imprison, punish, and correct any and all such as he shall finde disobedient to him in the like causes, euen in such order as I myselfe might doe by virtue to her Maiesties Commission giuen me the 26 of Nouember 1582, the copie whereof I haue annexed to this present vnder her Maiesties Seale deliuered me to that vse. Straightly charging and commanding all her Maiesties subiects in those parts, as they will auoid her Highnesse displeasure and their owne harmes, to honour his authoritie, and haue due respect vnto the same, aiding and assisting him there with their persons and goods in any cause requisit to her Maiesties good seruice and commoditie of her dominions. In witnesse whereof I haue confirmed and sealed these these presents at Rapamat my house by Pera ouer against Constantinople, to 20 of Iune 1583.

* * * * *

A letter of directions of the English Ambassadour to M. Richard Forster, appointed the first English Consull at Tripolis in Syria.

Cousin Forster, these few words are for your remembrance when it shall please the Almighty to send you safe arriuall in Tripolis of Syria. When it shall please God to send you thither, you are to certifie our Nation at Tripolis of the certaine day of your landing, to the end they both may haue their house in a readinesse, and also meet you personally at your entrance to accompany you, being your selfe apparelled in the best manner. The next, second, or third day, after your comming, giue it out that you be crazed and not well disposed, by meanes of your trauell at Sea, during which time, you and those there are most wisely to determine in what manner your are to present your selfe to the Beglerbi, Cadi, and other officers: who euery of them are to be presented according to the order accustomed of others formerly in like office: which after the note of Iohn Blanke, late Viceconsull of Tripolis for the French, deliuered you heerewith, is very much: and therefore, if thereof you can saue any thing, I pray you doe it, as I doubt not but you will. They are to giue you there also another Ianizarie according as the French hath: whose outward procedings you are to imitate and follow, in such sort as you be not his inferour, according as those of our Nation heeretofore with him resident can informe you. Touching your demeanour after your placing, your [sic—KTH] are wisely to proceede considering both French and Venetian will haue an enuious eye on you: whome if they perceiue wise and well aduised, they will feare to offer you any iniurie. But if they shall perceiue any insufficiencie in you, they will not omitte any occasion to harme you. They are subtile, malicious, and disembling people, wherefore you must alwayes haue their doings for suspected, and warily walke in all your actions: wherein if you call for Gods diuine assistance, as doth become euery faithfull good Christian, the same shall in such sort direct you as he shall be glorified, your selfe preserued, your doings blessed, and your enemies confounded. Which if contrarywise you omit and forget, your enemies malice shalbe satisfied with your confusion, which God defend, and for his mercies sake keepe you. Touching any outlopers of our nation, which may happen to come thither to traffike, you are not to suffer, but to imprison the chiefe officers, and suffer the rest not to traffike at any time, and together enter in such bonds as you thinke meete, that both they shall not deale in the Grand Signiors dominions, and also not harme, during their voyage, any his subiects shippes, vessels, or whatsoeuer other, but quitely depart out of the same country without any harme doing. And touching those there for the company, your are to defend them according to your priuiledge and such commandements as you haue had hence, in the best order you may. In all and euery your actions, at any hand, beware of rashnesse and anger, after both which repentance followeth. Touching your dealings in their affaires of marchandise, you are not to deale otherwise then in secret and counsell. You are carefully to foresee the charge of the house, that the same may be in all honest measure to the companies profit and your owne health through moderation in diet, and at the best hand, and in due time to prouide things needfull to saue what may be: for he that buyeth euery thing when he needed it, harmeth his owne house, and helpeth the retailer. So as it is, in mine opinion, wisdome to foresee the buying of all things in their natiue soile, in due time, and at the first hand euery yeere, as you are to send the company the particular accounts of the same expenses. Touching your selfe, your [sic—KTH] are to cause to be employed fifty or threescore ducats, videlicet, twenty in Sope, and the rest in Spices, whereof the most part to be Pepper, whereof we spend very much. The Spices are to be prouided by our friend William Barrat, and the Sope buy you at your first arriuall, for that this shippe lading the same commodity will cause it to amount in price. From our mansion Rapamat, the fift of September 1583.

* * * * *

A commandement for Chio.

Vobis, Beg et Cadi et Ermini, qui estis in Chio, significamus: quòd serenissimæ Reginæ Maiestatis Angliæ orator, qui est in excelsa porta per literas significauit nobis, quod ex nauibus Anglicis vna nauis venisset ad portum Chico, et illinc Constantinopolim recto cursu voluisset venire, et contra priuilegium detenuistis, et non siuistis venire. Hæc prædictus orator significauit nobis: et petiuit a nobis in hoc negocio hoc mandatum, vt naues Anglicæ veniant et rediant in nostras ditiones Cæsareas. Priuilegium datum et concessum est ex parte Serenitatis Cæsareæ nostræ: et huius priuilegij copia data est sub insigni nostro: Et contra nostrum priuilegium Cæsareum quod ita agitur, quæ est causa? Quando cum hoc mandato nostro homines illorum ad vos venerint ex prædicta Anglia, si nauis venerit ad portum vestrum, et si res et merces ex naue exemerint, et vendiderint, et tricessimam secundam partem reddiderint, et res quæ manserint Constantinopolim auferre velint, patiantur: Et si aliquis contra priuilegium et articulos eius aliquid ageret, non sinatis, nec vos facite: et impediri non sinatis eos, vt rectà Constantinopolim venientes in suis negotiationibus sine molestia esse possint. Et quicunque contra hoc mandatum et priuilegium nostrum aliquid fecerit, nobis significate. Huic mandato nostro et insigni fidem adhibete. In principio mensis Decembris.

* * * * *

A description of the yeerely voyage or pilgrimage of the Mahumitans, Turkes and Moores vnto Mecca in Arabia.

Of the Citie of Alexandria.

Alexandria the most ancient citie in Africa situated by the seaside containeth seuen miles in circuite, and is enuironed with two walles one neere to the other with high towers, but the walles within be farre higher than those without, with a great ditch round about the same: yet is not this Citie very strong by reason of the great antiquitie, being almost halfe destroyed and ruinated. The greatnesse of this Citie is such, that if it were of double habitation, as it is compassed with a double wall, it might be truely said, that there were two Alexandrias one builded vpon another, because vnder the foundations of the said City are great habitations, and incredible huge pillers. True it is, that this part vnderneath remaineth at this day inhabitable, because of the corrupt aire, as also for that by time, which consumeth all things, it is greately ruinated. It might well be sayd, that the founder hereof, as he was worthy in all his enterprises, so likewise in building hereof he did a worke worthy of himselfe, naming it after his owne name. This Citie hath one defect, for it is subiect to an euill ayre, which onely proceedeth of that hollownesse vnderneath, out of the which issueth infinite moisture: and that this is true the ayre without doth evidently testifie, which is more subtile and holesome then that beneath. The waters hereof be salt, by reason that the soile of it selfe is likewise so. And therefore the inhabitants, at such time as the riuer Nilus floweth, are accustomed to open a great ditch, the head wherof extendeth into the said riuer, and from thence they conueigh the same within halfe a mile of Alexandria, and so consequently by meanes of conduct-pipes the water commeth vnto the cesternes of Alexandria, which being full serue the citie from one inundation to another. Within the citie is a Pyramide mentioned of in Histories, but not of great importance. Without the citie is La colonna di Pompeio, or the pillar of Pompey, being of such height and thicknesse, that it is supposed there is not the like in the whole world besides. Within the citie there is nothing of importance saue a litle castle which is guarded with 60 Ianizaries. Alexandria hath three portes, one towardes Rossetto, another to the land ward, and the third to the sea ward, which is called Babelbar, without which appeareth a broad Iland called Ghesira in the Moores tongue, which is not wholy an Iland, because a litle point or corner thereof toucheth the firme lande, and therefore may be called Peninsula, that is to say, almost an Iland. Hereupon are builded many houses of the Iewes, in respect of the aire. This Peninsula is situate betweene two very good ports, one of them being much more safe then the other, called The old port, into the which only the vessels of Barbarie, and the sixe Gallies of the Grand Signior deputeth for the guard of Alexandria doe enter. And this port hath vpon the right hand at the mouth or enterance thereof a castle of small importance, and guarded but with fifteene men or thereabouts On the other side of this Iland is the other called The new port, which name is not vnfitly giuen vnto it, for that in all mens iudgement in times past there hath not beene water there, because in the midst of this port, where the water is very deepe, there are discouered and found great sepulchres and other buildings, out of the which are dayly digged with engines Iaspar and Porphyrie stones of great value, of the which great store are sent to Constantinople for the ornament of the Mesquitas or Turkish Temples, and of other buildings of the Grand Signior. Into this port enter all such vessels as traffique to this place. This port hath on ech side a castle, whereof that vpon the Peninsula is called Faraone, vpon the toppe whereof euery night there is a light set in a great lanterne for direction of the ships, and for the guard thereof are appointed 200 Ianizaries: the other on the other side is but a litle castle kept by 18. men. It is certeine, that this hauen of Alexandria is one of the chiefest hauens in the world: for hither come to traffique people of euery Nation, and all sorts of vessels which goe round about the citie. It is more inhabited by strangers, marchants, and Christians, then by men of the countrey which are but a few in number. [Sidenote: Fontecho signifieth an house of trafique, as the Stilyard.] Within the citie are fiue Fontechi, that is to say, one of the Frenchmen, where the Consul is resident, and this is the fairest and most commodious of all the rest. Of the other foure, two belong to the Venetians, one to the Raguseans, and the fourth to the Genoueses. And all strangers which come to traffique there, except the Venetians, are vnder the French Consull. It is also to be vnderstood, that all the Christians dwell within their Fontechi, and euery euening at the going downe of the sunne, they which are appointed for that office goe about and shut all the gates of the saide Fontechi outward, and the Christians shut the same within: and so likewise they doe on the Friday (which is the Moores and the Turkes Sabboth) till their deuotions be expired. And by this meanes all parties are secure and voide of feare: for in so doing the Christians may sleepe quietly and not feare robbing, and the Moores neede not doubt whiles they sleepe or pray, that the Christians should make any tumult, as in times past hath happened.

Of the coast of Alexandria.

[Sidenote: Bichier.] On the side towardes Barbarie along the sea-coast for a great space there is founde neither hold, nor any thing worthy of mention: but on the other side towards Syria 13 miles from Alexandria standeth a litle castle called Bichier kept by fiftie Turkes, which castle is very olde and weake, and hath a port which in times past was good, but at this present is vtterly decayed and full of sand, so that the vessels which come thither dare not come neere the shoare, but ride far off into the sea. [Sidenote: Rossetto] Fortie miles further is Rossetto, which is a litle towne without walles, and is situate vpon the banke of Nilus three miles from the sea, at which place many times they build ships and other vessels, for gouernement whereof is appointed a Saniacbey, without any other guard: it is a place of traffique, and the inhabitants are very rich, but naughtie varlets and traytours. Further downe along the sea-side and the riuer banke is another litle castle like vnto the abouesayde, and because the Moores beleeue, that Mecca will in short time be conquered by the Christians, they holde opinion, that the same being lost shall be renued in this place of Rossetto, namely, that all their prayers, vowes, and pilgrimages shall be transported to Rossetto, as the religious order of Saint Iohn of the Rhodes is translated thence to Malta. Further forwarde thirtie miles standes another castle of small importance called Brulles, kept continually by fourtie Turkes, which hath a good and secure port, in forme like to a very great lake or ponde, wherein is taken great quantitie of fish, whith they salt, and the marchants of Candie and Cyprus come thither to lade the same, and it is greatly esteemed, especially of the Candiots, who hauing great abundance of wine aduenture abroad to seeke meate fitte for the taste of the sayd wine. Distant from Brulles fiue and thirtie miles there is anothet castle like vnto the abouesayd kept by an Aga with fourtie men or thereabout. More within the lande by the riuers side is Damiata an auncient citie enuironed with walles contayning fiue miles in circuit, and but of small strength. For the gouernement of this place is a Sanjaco with all his housholde and no other companie. This citie is very large, delightfull, and pleasant, abounding with gardens and faire fountaines. Other fortie miles further is Latma, a castle of very small importance, and kept as other with fortie Turkes vnder an Aga. In this place is no port, but a roade very daungerous, and without other habitation. Passing this place we enter Iudea. But because our intent is to reason simply of the voyage to Mecca, we will proceede no further this way, but returning to our first way, let it suffice to say, that from Alexandria to Cairo are two hundred miles, in which way I finde nothing woorthie of memorie.

Of the mightie Citie of Cairo.

Cairo containeth in circuit eighteene miles, being so inhabited and replenished with people, that almost it cannot receiue more; and therefore they haue begunne to builde newe houses without the citie and about the walles. In Cairo are people of all Nations, as Christians, Armenians, Abexins, Turkes, Moores, Iewes, Indians, Medians, Persians, Arabians, and other sortes of people, which resort thither by reason of the great traffique. This citie is gouerned by a Basha, which ministreth iustice, together with the Cadie throughout the whole kingdome. Also there are two and twentie Saniackes, whose office is onely to ouersee and guarde the kingdome of euery good respect. There are also seuen thousand Turkes in pay, to wit, three thousand Ianizaries, and foure thousand horsemen: The rest of the people in Cairo are for the most part marchants which goe and come, and the remnant are Moores and other base people. About two miles from Cairo there is another little Cairo called The olde Cairo, which containeth in circuit litle more then tenne miles, and the better halfe is not inhabited, but destroyed, whereof I neede not make any other mention. The new Cairo answereth euery yeere in tribute to the grand Signior, 600000 ducates of gold, neat and free of all charges growing on the same, which money is sent to Constantinople, about the fine of September, by the way of Aleppo, alwayes by lande, vnder the custodie of three hundred horsemen, and two hundred Ianizaries footmen. The citie of Cairo is adorned with many faire Mesquitas rich, great, and of goodly and gorgeous building, among which are fiue principall. The first is called Morastano, that is to say, The hospitall, which hath of rent fiue hundred ducats of golde euery day left vnto it by a king of Damasco from auncient times; which king hauing conquered Cairo, for the space of fiue daies continually put the people thereof to the sword, and in the end repenting him of so great manslaughter, caused this cruelty to cease, and to obtaine remission for this sinne committed, caused this hospitall to be built, enriching it as is abouesaid. The second famous monument of Cairo is called Neffisa, of one Neffisa buried there, who was a Dame of honour, and mooued by lust, yeelded her body voluntarily without rewarde, to any that required the same, and sayde she bestowed this almes for the loue of her Prophet Mahomet, and therefore at this day they adore her, reuerence her, and finally haue canonized her for a Saint, affirming that shee did many miracles. The third is called Zauia della Innachari, who was one of the foure Doctors in the law. The fourth is called Imamsciafij, where is buried Sciafij the second Doctor of this law. Of the other two Doctors one is buried in Damasco, the other in Aleppo. The fift and last famous monument is Giamalazar, that is, the house of Lazarus:

and this is the generall Vniuersity of the whole kingdome of Egypt. [Sidenote: 1566.] In this place Anno 1566 in the moneth of Ianuary by misfortune of fire were burned nine thousand bookes of great value, as well for that they were written by hand, as also wrought so richly with golde, that they were worth 300 and 400 ducats a piece, one with another. And because it could neuer be knowen yet how this fire beganne, they haue and doe holde the same for a most sinister augurie, and an euident and manifest signe of their vtter ruine. The houses of Cairo without are very faire, and within the greater number richly adorned with hangings wrought with golde. Euery person which resorteth to this place for traffiques sake, is bound to pay halfe a duckat, except the gentlemen Venetians, Siotes, and Rhaguseans, because they are tributarie to the Grand Signior. [Sidenote: The description of Cairo.] Cairo is distant from the riuer Nilus a mile and more, being situate on a plaine, saue that on the one side it hath a faire little hill, on the toppe, whereof stands a faire castle, but not strong, for that it may be battered on euery side, but very rich and large, compassed about with faire gardens into the which they conueigh water for their necessitie out of Nilus, with certaine wheeles and other like engines. This magnificent citie is adorned with very fruitfull gardens both pleasant and commodious, with great plenty of pondes to water the same. Notwithstanding the great pleasures of Cairo are in the moneth of August, when by meanes of the great raine in Ethiopia the riuer Nilus ouerfloweth apd watereth all the countrey, and then they open the mouth of a great ditch, which extendeth into the riuer, and passeth through the midst of the citie, and entring there are innumerable barkes rowing too and fro laden with gallant girles and beautifull dames, which with singing, eating, drinking and feasting, take their solace. The women of this countrey are most beautifull, and goe in rich attire bedeked with gold, pretious stones, and iewels of great value, but chiefely perfumed with odours, and are very libidinous, and the men likewise, but foule and hard fauoured. The soile is very fertile and abundant, the flesh fat which they sell without bones, their candles they make of the marowe of cattell, because the Moores eate the tallow. They vse also certaine litle furnaces made of purpose, vnder the which they make fire, putting into the furnace foure or fiue hundred egges, and the said fire they nourish by litle and litle, vntill the chickens be hatched, which after they be hatched, and become somewhat bigger, they sell them by measure in such sort, as we sell and measure nuts and chestnuts and such like.

Of certaine notable monuments without the citie of Cairo.

Without the Citie, sixe miles higher into the land, are to be seene neere vnto the riuer diuerse Piramides, among which are three marueilous great, and very artificially wrought. Out of one of these are dayly digged the bodies of auncient men, not rotten, but all whole, the cause whereof is the qualitie of the Egyptian soile, which will not consume the flesh of man, but rather dry and harden the same, and so alwayes conserueth it. And these dead bodies are the Mummie which the Phisitians and Apothecaries doe against our willes make vs to swallow. Also by digging in these Pyramides oftentimes are found certaine Idoles or Images of gold, siluer, and other mettall, but vnder the other piramides the bodies are not taken vp so whole as in this, but there are found legges and armes comparable to the limmes of giants. Neare to these piramides appeareth out of the sand a great head of stone somewhat like marble, which is discouered so farre as the necke ioyneth with the shoulders, being all whole, sauing that it wanteth a little tippe of the nose. The necke of this head contayneth in circuit about sixe and thirty foot, so that it may be according to the necke considered, what greatnesse the head is of. The riuer Nilus is a mile broad, wherein are very many great Croccodiles from Cairo vpward, but lower than Cairo passeth no such creature: and this, they say, is by reason of an inchantment made long since which hindereth their passage for comming any lower then Cairo. Moreouer of these creatures there are sometimes found some of an incredible bignesse, that is to say, of fourtie foot about. The males haue their members like to a man, and the females like to a woman. These monsters oftentimes issue out of the water to feede, and finding any small beasts, as sheepe, lambes, goates, or other like, doe great harme. And whiles they are foorth of the water, if they happen at vnawares vpon any man, woman or childe, whom they can ouercome, they spare not their liues. In the yeere of our Lord one thousand fiue hundred and sixtie it happened, that certaine poore Christians trauelling by Cairo towardes the countrey of Prete Ianni to rescue certaine slaues, were guided by a Chaus, and iourneyed alongst the banke of the said riuer. The Chaus remained lingering alone behinde to make his prayers (as their custome is) at a place called Tana, whom being busie in his double deuotion one of these Crocodiles ceazed by the shoulders, and drew him vnder water, so that he was neuer after seene. And for this cause they haue made in sundry places certaine hedges as bankes within the water, so that betwixt the hedge and banke of the riuer there remaineth so much water, that the women washing may take water without danger at their pleasure. This countrey is so fruitfull, that it causeth the women as other creatures to bring foorth one, two, and oft-times three at a birth. Fiue miles southwarde of Cairo is a place called Matarea, where the balme is refined: and therefore some will say, that the trees which beare the balme growe in the said place, wherein they are deceiued: for the sayde trees growe two dayes iourney from Mecca, in a place called Bedrihone, which yeeldeth balme in great plenty, but saluage, wilde, and without vertue, and therefore the Moores carying the same within litle chests from Bedrihone to Matarea, where the trees being replanted (be it by vertue of the soyle, or the water, aire, or any other thing whatsoeuer) it sufficeth that heare they beare the true balme and licour so much in these dayes esteemed of. In this place of Matarea there are certaine little houses, with most goodly gardens, and a chappell of antiquity, where the very Moores themselues affirme, that the mother of the blessed Christ fleeing from the fury of wicked Herode there saued her selfe with the childe, wherein that saying of the Prophet was fulfilled, Ex Ægypto vocaui fillium meum. The which Chappell in the yeare of our Lorde one thousand fiue hundred and foure, the Magnifico Daniel Barbaro first Consull of that place went to visite, and caused it to be renued and reedified, so that in these dayes there resort thither many Christians, who oftentimes bring with them a Priest, to say masse there. Also about an Harque-buz-shotte from Matarea is a spire of great height like to that at Rome, and more beautifull to beholde. Neere vnto the olde Cairo are yet twelue storehouses of great antiquitie, but now very much decayed, and these till late dayes serued to keepe corne for behoofe of the kingdome, concerning which many are of opinion, that the founder hereof was Ioseph the sonne of Iacob, for consideration of the seuen deare yeares. [Sidenote: Olde Thebes.] Also passing higher vp by the banke of Nilus, there is to bee seene a fayre Citie ouerflowed with water, the which at such time as Nilus floweth lyeth vnder water, but when the water returneth to the marke, there plainely appeare princely palaces, and stately pillars, being of some called Thebes, where they say that Pharao was resident. Moroeuer three dayes iourney higher vp are two great images of speckled marble, all whole, and somewhat sunke into the earth, being things wonderfull to consider of, for the nose of either is two spannes and a halfe long, and the space from one eare to the other conteineth tenne spannes, the bodies being correspondent to their heads, and grauen in excellent proportion, so that they are shapes of maruellous hugenesse, and these they call The wife, and The daughter of Pharao.

Of the patriarke of Greece.

In Cairo are two Patriarkes, one of the Greekes, and another of the Iacobites. The Greeke Patriarke called Gioechni, being about the age of one hundred and thirteene yeeres, was a very good and holy man. They say, that when Soldan Gauri of Egypt reigned, there was done this miracle following; this good patriarke being enuied at by the Iewes of the countrey, for none other cause, but for his good workes, and holy life, it happened (I say) that being in disputation with certaine of the Hebrewes in presence of the Sultan, and reasoning of their lawe and faith, it was sayd vnto him by one of these Miscreants: sith thou beleeuest in the faith of Christ, take and drinke this potion which I will giue thee; and if thy Christ be true Messias and true God, he will (sayd he) deliuer thee from daunger. To whom the auncient patriarke answered, that he was content: whereupon that cursed Iewe brought him a cuppe of the most venemous and deadly poyson that could be found, which the holy Patriarke hauing perceiued, said: In the name of the father, of the sonne, and of the holy Ghost: and hauing so sayde he dranke it quite vp; which done, he tooke a droppe of pure water, putting it into that very cup, and gaue it vnto the Iewe, saying vnto him, I in the name of my Christe haue drunke thy poyson, and therefore in the name of thy expected Messias drinke this water of mine within thine owne cuppe. Whereupon the Iewe tooke the cup out of the hand of the Patriarke, and hauing drunke the water, within halfe an houre burst a sunder. And the Patriarke had none other hurt, saue that he became somewhat pale in sight, and so remained euer after. And this miracle (which meriteth to be called no lesse) was done to the great commendation of the holy Patriarke in the presence of a thousand persons, and namely of the Soldan of Egypt: who seeing the despight of the Iewes, vnto their owne cost and confusion compelled them to make the conduct, which with so many engines commeth into the castle from Nilus aboue mentioned. And this triumphant Patriarke not long since was aliue, and in perfect health, which God continue long time.

Of the preparation of the Carouan to goe to Mecca.

As touching the Carouan which goeth to Mecca, it is to be vnderstoode, that the Mahometans obserue a kinde of lent continuing one whole moone, and being a moueable ceremonie, which sometimes falleth high, sometimes lowe in the yeere called in their tongue Ramazan, and their feast is called Bairam. During this time of lent all they which intende to goe vnto Mecca resort vnto Cairo, because that twentie dayes after the feast the Carouan is readie to depart on the voyage: and thither resort a great multitude of people from Asia, Grecia, and Barbaria to goe on this voyage, some mooued by deuotion, and some for traffiques sake, and some to passe away the time. Nowe, within fewe dayes after the feast they which goe on the voyage depart out of the citie two leagues vnto a place called Birca, where they expect the Captaine of the Carouan. This place hath a great pond caused by the inundation of Nilus, and so made that the camels and other beastes may drinke therein: whereof, namely, of Mules, Camels, and Dromedaries there are at least fortie thousand, and the persons which followe the Carouan euerie yeere are about fiftie thousand, fewe more or lesse, according to the times. Moreouer euery three yeeres they renue the Captaine of the Carouan, called in the Arabian tongue Amarilla Haggi, that is, the Captaine of the Pilgrimes, to whom the Grand Signior giueth euery voyage eighteene purses, conteyning each of them six hundred twentie and fiue ducates of golde, and these be for the behoofe of the Carouan, and also to doe almes vnto the needfull pilgrimes. This Captaine, besides other seruingmen which follow him, hath also foure Chausi to serue him. Likewise he hath with him for the securitie of the Carouan foure hundred souldiers, to wit, two hundred Spachi or horsemen mounted on Dromedaries, and two hundred Ianizaries riding vpon Camels. The Chausi and the Spachi are at the charge of the Captaine, but the Ianizaries not so, for their prouision is made them from Cairo. The Spachi weare caps or bonnets like to the caps of Sergeants, but the Ianizaries after another sort, with a lappe falling downe behinde like a French-hoode, and hauing before a great piece of wrought siluer on their heads. The charge of these is to cause the Carouan to march in good array when neede requireth; these are not at the commaundement of any but of the Captaine of the Carouan. Moreouer the Captaine hath for his guide eight pilots, the office of whom is alwayes stable and firme from heire to heire, and these goe before guiding the Carouan, and shewing the way, as being well experienced in the place, and in the night they gouerne them as the mariners, by the starre. [Sidenote: Pieces of dry wood in stead of torches.] These also vse to sende before foure or fiue men carying pieces of dry wood which giue light, because they should not goe out of the way, and if at any time through their ill hap they wander astray out of the way, they are caste downe and beaten with so many bastonadoes vpon the soles of their feete, as serue them for a perpetuall remembrance. The Captaine of the Carouan hath his Lieutenant accompanied continually with fifteene Spachi, and he hath the charge to set the Carouan in order, and to cause them to depart on their iourney when neede requireth: and during the voyage their office is some whiles to goe before with the forewarde, sometimes to come behinde with the rereward, sometimes to march on the one side, and sometimes on the other, to spy, that the coast be cleare. The Carouan carrieth with it sixe pieces of ordinance drawen by 12 camels, which serue to terrifie the Arabians, as also to make triumph at Mecca, and other places. The marchants which followe the Carouan, some carry for marchandise cloth of silke, some Corall, some tinne, others wheat, rise, and all sorts of graine. Some sell by the way, some at Mecca, so that euery one bringeth something to gaine by, because all marchandise that goeth by land payeth no custome, but that which goeth by sea is bound to pay tenne in the hundred.

The beginning of the voyage.

The feast before the Carouan setteth forth, the Captaine with all his retinue and officers resort vnto the castle of Cairo before the Basha, which giueth vnto euery man a garment, and that of the Captaine is wrought with golde, and the others are serued according to their degree. Moreouer he deliuereth vnto him the Chisua Talnabi, which signifieth in the Arabian tongue, The garment of the Prophet: this vesture is of silke, wrought in the midst with letters of golde, which signifie: La illa ill'alla Mahumet Resullala: that is to say, There are no gods but God, and his ambassadour Mahumet. This garment is made of purpose to couer from top to botome a litle house in

Mecca standing in the midst of the Mesquita, the which house (they say) was builded by Abraham or by his sonne Ismael. After this he deliuereth to him a gate made of purpose for the foresaid house of Abraham wrought all with fine golde, and being of excellent workmanship, and it is a thing of great value. Besides, he deliuereth vnto him a couering of greene veluet made in maner of a pyramis, about nine palmes high, and artificially wrought with most fine golde, and this is to couer the tombe of their prophet within Medina, which tombe is built in manner of a pyramis: and besides that couering there are brought many others of golde and silke, for the ornament of the sayde tombe. Which things being consigned, the Basha departeth not from his place; but the Captaine of the Carouan taketh his leaue with all his officers and souldiers, and departeth accompanied with all the people of Cairo orderly in manner of a procession, with singing, shouting and a thousand other ceremonies too long to recite. From the castle they goe to a gate of the citie called Bab-Nassera, without the which standes a Mosquita, and therein they lay vp the sayd vestures very well kept and guarded. And of this ceremony they make so great account, that the world commeth to see this sight, yea the women great with childe, and others with children in their armes, neither is it lawfull for any man to forbid his wife the going to this feast, for that in so doing the wife may separate her selfe from her husband, and may lie with any other man, in regard of so great a trespasse. Now this procession proceeding from the castle towardes the Mosquita, the Camels which bring the vestures are all adorned with cloth of golde, with many little belles, and passing along the streete you may see the multitude casting vpon the said vesture thousands of beautifull flowers of diuers colours, and sweete water, others bringing towels and fine cloth touch the same, which euer after they keepe as reliques with great reuerence. Afterward hauing left the vesture in the Mosquita, as is aforesaid, they returne againe into the citie, where they remaine the space of 20 dayes, and then the captaine departeth with his company, and taking the vestures out of the Mosquita, carieth the same to the foresaid place of Birca, where the Captaine hauing pitched his tent with the standard of the grand Signior ouer the gate, and the other principall tents standing about his, stayeth there some tenne dayes and no more: in which time all those resort thither that meane to follow the Carouan in this voyage to Mecca. Where you shall see certaine women which intend to goe on this voiage accompanied with their parents and friends mounted vpon Camels, adorned with so many tryfles, tassels, and knots, that in beholding the same a man cannot refraine from laughter. The last night before their departure they make great feasting and triumph within the Carouan, with castles and other infinite deuises of fireworke, the Ianizaries alwayes standing round about the tent of the Captaine with such shouting and ioy, that on euery side the earth resoundeth, and this night they discharge all their ordinance, foure or sixe times, and after at the breake of the day vpon the sound of a trumpet they march forward on their way.

What times the Carouan trauelleth, and when it resteth.

It is to be noted, that from Cairo to Mecca they make 40 dayes iourney or thereabout, and the same great dayes iourneies. For the custome of the Carouan is to trauell much and rest little, and ordinarily they iourney in this maner: They trauell from two a clock in the morning vntill the sunne rising, then hauing rested till noone, they set forward, and so continue till night, and then also rest againe, as is abouesaid, till two of the clocke; and this order they obserue vntill the end of the voiage, neuer changing the same, except in some places, whereof we will hereafter speake, where for respect of water they rest sometimes a day and an halfe, and this they obserue to refresh themselues, otherwise both man and beast would die.

In what order the Carouan trauelleth.

The maner and order which the Carouan obserueth in marching is this. It goeth diuided into three parts, to wit, the foreward, the maine battell, and the rereward. In the foreward go the 8 Pilots before with a Chaus, which hath foure knaues, and ech knaue carrieth a sinew of a bul, to the end that if occasion requireth, the bastonado may be giuen to such as deserue the same. These knaues cast offendours downe, turning vp the soles of their feete made fast to a staffe, giuing them a perpetuall remembrance for them and the beholders. This Chaus is as the Captaine of the foreward, which commandeth lights to be carried before when they trauell in the night. Also there go in this foreward 6 Santones with red turbants vpon their heads, and these eat and ride at the cost of the Captaine of the Carouan. These Santones when the Carouan arriueth at any good lodging, suddenly after they haue escried the place, cry with an horrible voyce saying, good cheare, good cheare, we are neere to the wished lodging. For which good newes the chiefe of the company bestow their beneuolence vpon them. In this foreward goeth very neere the third part of the people of the Carouan, behind whom go alwayes 25 Spachi armed with swords, bowes and arrowes to defend them from thieues. Next vnto the foreward, within a quarter of a mile, followeth the maine battell, and before the same are drawen the sayd sixe pieces of ordinance, with their gunners, and fifteene Spachi Archers. And next vnto these commeth the chiefe physicion, who is an olde man of authoritie, hauing with him many medicines, oyntments, salues, and other like refreshings for the sicke, hauing also camels with him for the sicke to ride on, which haue no horse nor beast. Next vnto him goeth one Camell alone, the fairest that can be found: for with great industrie is sought the greatest and fairest which may be found within the dominions of the Grand Signior. This camell also is decked with cloth of golde and silke, and carieth a little chest made of pure Legmame made in likenesse of the arke of the olde Testament: but, as is abouesayd, made of pure Legmame, without golde or any other thing of cost. Within this chest is the Alcoran all written with great letters of golde, bound betweene two tables of massie golde, and the chest during their voyage is couered with Silke, but at their entring into Mecca it is all couered with cloth of golde adorned with iewels, and the like at the enterance into Medina. The Camell aforesayd which carrieth the chest, is compassed about with many Arabian singers and musicians, alwayes singing and playing vpon instruments. After this folow fiftene other most faire Camels, euery one carying one of the abouesayd vestures, being couered from toppe to toe with silke. Behind these goe twentie other Camels which carrie the money, apparell, and prouision of the Amir el Cheggi captaine of the Carouan. After foloweth the royall Standard of the Grand Signior, accompanied continually with the musicians of the captaine, and fiue and twentie Spachi archers, with a Chaus before them, and about these marueilous things goe all the people and Camels which follow the Carouan. Behind these, lesse then a mile, foloweth the rerereward, whereof the greater part are pilgrimes: the occasion whereof is, for that the merchants seeke alwayes to be in the foreward for the securitie of their goods, but the pilgrimes which haue litle to loose care not though they come behind. Behind these alwayes goe fiue and twentie other Spachi well armed with another Chaus their captaine, and fortie Arabians all Archers for guard of the rerereward. And because the Carouan goeth alwayes along the red sea banke, which in going forth they haue on their right hand, therfore the two hundred Ianissaries parted into three companies goe vpon their left hand well armed and mounted vpon Camels bound one to another, for vpon that side is all the danger of thieues, and on the other no danger at all, the captaine of the Carouan alwayes going about his people, sometimes on the one side, and sometimes on the other, neuer keeping any firme place, being continually accompanied with a Chaus and 25. Spachi, armed and mounted vpon Dromedaries, and 8. musicians with violes in their handes, which cease not sounding till the captaine take his rest, vpon whom they attend, till such time as he entreth his pauillion, and then licencing all his attendants and folowers to depart, they goe each man to their lodging.

Of things notable which are seene in this voyage by the way.

Because in the way there are not many things found woorthy memorie, for that the Carouan seldome resteth in places of habitation, of which in the way there are but fewe, yea rather the Carouan resteth altogether in the field: therefore in this our voyage wee will onely make mention of certaine Castles found in the way, which bee these, namely Agerut, Nachel, Acba, Biritem, Muel and Ezlem. Of which fiue the two first are kept of Moores, and the other three of Turkes, and for guard they haue eight men or tenne at the most in euery Castle, with foure or fiue Smerigli, which serue to keepe the water from the Arabians, so that the Carouan comming thither may haue wherewithall to refresh it selfe. Agerut is distant from Suez a port of the red sea eight miles, where are always resident fiue and twentie gallies of the Grand Signior for the keeping of that Sea. Nachel is distant from the Sea a dayes iourney. The walles of Acba are founded vpon the red Sea banke. Biritem and Muel likewise are dashed by the waues of the Sea. Ezlem is distant from thence aboue a dayes iourney. These fiue Castles abouesayd are not of force altogether to defend themselues agaynst an hundred men. The Carouan departing from Birca vntill Agerut findeth no water by the way to drinke, neither from Agerut till Nachel, nor from Nachel till Acba, but betweene Acba and Biritem are found two waters, one called Agiam el Cassap, and the other Magarraxiaibi, that is to say, the riuer of Iethro the father in lawe of Moses, for this is the place mentioned in the second chapter of Exodus, whither it is sayd that Moses fledde from the anger of Pharao, who would haue killed him, because hee had slaine the Ægyptian, which fought with the Hebrew, in which place stoode the citie of Midian; and there are yet the pondes, neere vnto the which Moses sate downe. And from that place forward they finde more store of water by the way, and in more places, though not so good. It is also to bee noted, that in this voiage it is needfull and an vsuall thing, that the captaine put his hand to his purse, in these places, and bestow presents, garments, and turbants vpon certaine of the chiefe of the Arabians, to the ende they may giue him and his Carouan, free passage: who also promise, that their followers likewise shall doe no damage to the Carouan, and bind themselues to accomplish the same, promising also by worde of mouth, that if the Carouan bee robbed, they will make restitution of such things as are stollen: but notwithstanding the Carouan is by them oftentimes damnified, and those which are robbed haue no other restitution at the Arabians handes then the shewing of them a paire of heeles, flying into such places as it is impossible to finde them. Nowe the Carouan continuing her accustomed iourneys, and hauing passed the abouesayd castles, and others not woorthie mention, at length commeth to a place called Iehbir, which is the beginning and confine of the state and realme of Serifo the king of Mecca: where, at their approching issueth out to meete them the gouernour of the land, with all his people to receiue the Carouan, with such shouting and triumph, as is impossible to expresse, where they staie one whole day. This place aboundeth with fresh and cleare waters, which with streames fall downe from the high mountaines. Moreouer, in this place are great store of dates, and flesh great store and good cheape, and especially laced muttons which willingly fall downe, and here the weary pilgrimes haue cummoditie to refresh themselues, saying, that this wicked fact purgeth them from a multitude of sinnes, and besides increaseth deuotion to prosecute the voiage. Touching the building in these places, it is to bee iudged by the houses halfe ruinated, that it hath bene a magnificent citie: but because it was in times past inhabited more with thieues then true men, it was therefore altogether destroyed by Soldan Gauri king of Ægypt, who going on pilgrimage vnto Mecca, and passing by this place, there was by the inhabitants hereof some iniurie done vnto his Carauan, which he vnderstandeng of, dissembled till his returne from Mecca, and then caused it to bee burned and destroyed in pitifull sort for reuenge of the iniurie done vnto the Carouan. The Carouan hauing rested and being refreshed as is abouesayd, the next day departed on the way, and the first place they arriue at woorthy mention is called Bedrihonem, in which place (as is aforesayd) grow those little shrubbes whereout Balme issueth. And before the Carouan arriueth at this place a mile from the citie is a large and great field enuironed about with most high and huge mountaines. And in this field, according to the Alcoran, their prophet Mahomet had a most fierce and cruel battell giuen by the Christians of the countrey and other people which set themselues agaynst them, and withstood his opinion, so that hee was ouercome and vanquished of the Christians, and almost halfe of his people slaine in the battell. Whereupon the Phrophet seeing himselfe in such extremitie, fell to his prayers, and they say, that God hauing compassion vpon his deare friend and prophet, heard him, and sent him infinite thousands of angels, wherewith returning to the battell, they conquered and ouercame the conquerour. And therefore in memorie of this victorie, the Carouan lodgeth euery yeere one night in this place, making great bonefires with great mirth. And they say that as yet there is heard vpon the mountaines a litle drumme, which while the Carouan passeth, neuer ceaseth sounding. And they say further, that the sayd drumme is sounded by the angels in signe of that great victory graunted of God to their prophet. Also the Mahumetan writings affirme, that after the ende of the sayd battell, the prophet commaunded certaine of his people to goe and burie all the Mahumetans which were dead in the fields, who going, knew not the one from the other, because as yet they vsed not circumcision, so they returned vnto him, answering, that they had bene to doe his commaundement, but they knew not the Musulmans from the Christians. To whom the prophet answered, saying. Turne againe, and all those which you shall finde with their faces downeward, leaue them, because all they are misbeleeuers: and the other which you shall finde with their faces turned vpward, them burie, for they are the true Musulmani, and so his commaundement was done.

The next morning by Sunne rising, the Carouan arriueth at Bedrihomen, in which place euery man washeth himselfe from toppe to toe, as well men as women, and leauing off their apparell, hauing each a cloth about their priuities, called in their tongue Photah, and another white one vpon their shoulders, all which can goe to Mecca in this habite, doe so, and are thought to merite more then the other, but they which cannot doe so make a vowe to sacrifice a Ramme at the mountaine of pardons; and after they bee washed, it is not lawfull for any man or women, to kill either flea or lowse with their handes, neither yet to take them with their nailes, vntill they haue accomplished their vowed orations in the mountaine of pardons abouesayd: and therefore they cary with them certaine stickes made of purpose in maner of a File, called in their language Arca, Cassah Guch, with which they grate their shoulders. And so the Carouan marching, commeth within two miles of Mecca, where they rest that night. In the morning at the breake of day, with all pompe possible they set forward toward Mecca, and drawing neere thereunto, the Seripho issueth foorth of the citie with his guard, accompanied with an infinite number of people, shouting, and making great triumph. And being come out of the citie a boweshoote into a faire field, where a great multitude of tents are pitched, and in the middest the pauillion of the captaine, who meeting with the Serifo, after salutations on each side, they light from their horses and enter the pauillion, where the king of Mecca depriueth himselfe of all authoritie and power, and committeth the same to the aboue named captaine, giuing him full licence and authoritie to commaund, gouerne, and minister Justice during his aboad in Mecca with his company, and on the other side the captaine to requite this liberalitie vsed toward him by the Serifo giueth him a garment of cloth of gold of great value, with certaine iewels and other like things. After this, sitting downe together vpon carpets and hides they eate together, and rising from thence with certaine of the chiefest, and taking with them the gate abouesayd, they goe directly to the Mosxuita, attended on but with a fewe, and being entered, they cause the olde to be pulled downe, and put the newe couerture vpon the house of Abraham, and the olde vesture is the eunuchs which serue in the sayde Mosquita, who after sell it vnto the pilgrimes at foure or fiue serafines the pike: and happy doth that man thinke himselfe, which can get neuer so litle a piece thereof, to conserue euer after as a most holy relique: and they say, that putting the same vnder the head of a man at the houre of his death, through vertue thereof all his sinnes are forgiuen. Also they take away the old doore, setting in the place the new doore, and the old by custome they giue vnto the Serifo. After hauing made their praiers with certaine ordinarie and woonted ceremonies, the Serifo rematneth in the citie, and the captaine of the pilgrimage returneth vnto his pauillion.

Of the Serifo the king of Mecca.

The Serifo is descended of the prophet Mahomet by Fatma daughter of that good prophet, and Alli husband to her, and sonne in lawe to Mahumet, who had no issue male, saue this stocke of the Serifo, to the eldest sonne whereof the realme commeth by succession. This realme hath of reuenues royall, euery yeere halfe a million of golde, or litle more: and all such as are of the prophets kinred, or descended of that blood (which are almost innumerable) are called Emyri, that is to say, lordes. These all goe clothed in greene, or at the least haue their turbant greene, to bee knowen from the other. Neither is it permitted that any of those Christians which dwell or traffique in their Countrey goe clothed in greene, neither may they haue any thing of green about them: for they say it is not lawfull for misbeleeuers to weare that colour, wherein that great friend the prophet of God Mahomet was woont to be apparelled.

Of the citie of Mecca.

The Citie of Mecca in the Arabian tongue is called Macca, that is to say, an habitation. This citie is inuironed about with exceeding high and barren mountaines, and in the plaine betweene the sayde mountaines and the citie are many pleasant gardens, where groweth great abundaunce of figges, grapes, apples, and melons. There is also great abundance of good water and fleshe, but not of bread. This citie hath no walles about it, and containeth in circuite fiue miles. The houses are very handsome and commodious, and are built like to the houses in Italie. The palace of the Serifo is sumptuous and gorgeously adorned. The women of the place are courteous, iocund, and louely, faire, with alluring eyes, being hote and libidinous, and the most of them naughtie packes. The men of this place are giuen to that abhominable, cursed, and opprobrious vice, whereof both men and women make but small account by reason of the pond Zun Zun, wherein hauing washed themselues, their opinion is, that although like the dog they returne to their vomite, yet they are clensed from all sinne whatsoeuer, of which sin we will hereafter more largely discourse. In the midst of the city is the great Mosquita, with the house of Abraham standing in the very middest thereof, which Mosquita was built in the time when their prophet liued. It is foure square, and so great, that it containeth two miles in circuit, that is to say, halfe a mile each side. Also it is made in maner of a cloister, for that in the midst thereof separate from the rest, is the abouesayd house of Abraham, also the galleries round about are in maner of 4. streetes, and the partitions which diuide the one street from the other are pillars, whereof some are of marble, and others of lime and stone. This famous and sumptuous Mosquita hath 99. gates, and 5. steeples, from whence the Talismani call the people to the Mosquita. And the pilgrimes which are not prouided of tents, resort hither, and for more deuotion the men and women lie together aloft and beneath, one vpon another, so that their house of praier becommeth worse sometimes then a den of thieues.

Of the house of Abraham.

The house of Abraham is also foure square, and made of speckled stone, 20. paces high, and 40 in circuit. And vpon one side of this house within the wall, there is a stone of a span long, and halfe a span broad, which stone (as they say) before this house was builded, fell downe from heauen, at the fall whereof was heard a voyce, that wheresoeuer this stone fell, there should be built the house of God, wherein God will heare sinners. Moreouer, they say that when this stone fell from heauen, it was not blacke as now, but as white as the whitest snow, and by reason it hath bene so oft kissed by sinners, it is therewith become blacke: for all the pilgrimes are bound to kisse this stone, otherwise they cary their sinnes home with them again. The entrance into this house is very small, made in maner of a window, and as high from the ground as a man can reach, so that it is painful to enter. This house hath without 31. pillars of brasse, set vpon cubike or square stones being red and greene, the which pillars sustaine not ought els saue a threed of copper, which reacheth from one to another, whereunto are fastened many burning lampes. These pillars of brasse were caused to be made by Sultan Soliman grandfather to Sultan Amurath now Emperor. After this, hauing entred with the difficultie abouesayd, there stand at the entrance two pillars of marble, to wit, on each side one. In the midst there are three of Aloes-wood not very thicke, and couered with tiles of India 1000. colours which serue to vnderproppe the Terratza. It is so darke, that they can hardly see within for want of light, not without an euill smell. Without the gate fiue pases is the abouesayd pond Zun Zun, which is that blessed pond that the angell of the Lord shewed vnto Agar whiles she went seeking water for her sonne Ismael to drinke.

Of the ceremonies of the pilgrimes.

In the beginning we haue sayd how the Mahumetans haue two feasts in the yeere. The one they call Pascha di Ramazaco, that is to say, The feast of fasting, and this feast of fasting is holden thirtie dayes after the feast, wherein the Carouan trauelleth to Mecca. The other is called the feast of the Ramme, wherin all they which are of abilitie are bound to sacrifice a Ramme, and this they call Bine Bairam, that is to say, The great feast. And as the Carouan departeth from Cairo, thirtie dayes after the little feast, so likewise they come hither fiue or sixe dayes before the great feast, to the ende the pilgrimes may haue time before the feast to finish their rites and ceremonies, which are these. Departing from the Carouan, and being guided by such as are experienced in the way, they goe vnto the citie twentie or thirtie in a company as they thinke good, walking through a streete which ascendeth by litle and litle till they come vnto a certaine gate, whereupon is written on each side in marble stone, Babel Salema, which in the Arabian tongue signifieth, the gate of health. And from this place is descried the great Mosquita, which enuironeth the house of Abraham, which being descried, they reuerently salute twise, saying, Salem Alech Iara sul Alia, that is to say, Peace to thee, ambassadour of God. This salutation being ended, proceeding on the way, they finde an arche vpon their right hand, whereon they ascend fiue steps, vpon the which is a great voyd place made of stone: after, descending other fiue steps, and proceeding the space of a flight-shoot, they finde another arche like vnto the first, and this way from the one arche to the other they go and come 7. times, saying alwaies some of their prayers, which (they say) the afflicted Agar sayd, whiles she sought and found not water for her sonne Ismael to drinke. This ceremonie being ended, the pilgrimes enter into the Mosquita, and drawing neere vnto the house of Abraham, they goe round about it other seuen times, always saying: This is the house of God, and of his seruant Abraham: This done they goe to kisse the black stone abouesayd. After they go vnto the pond Zun Zun, and in their apparell as they be, they wash themselues from head to foote, saying, Tobah Allah, Tobah Allah, that is to say, Pardon Lord, Pardon Lord, drinking also of that waier, which is both mudie, filthie, and of an ill sauour, and in this wise washed and watered, euery one returneth to his place of abode, and these ceremonies euery one is bound to doe once at the least. But those which haue a mind to ouergoe their fellowes, and to goe into paradise before the rest, doe the same once a day while the Carouan remaineth there.

What the Carouan doeth after hauing rested at Mecca.

[Sidenote: The mountaine of pardons.] The Carouan hauing abode within the citie of Mecca fiue dayes, the night before the euening of their feast, the captaine with all his company setteth forward towards the mountaine of pardons, which they call in the Arabian tongue, Iabel Arafata. This mountaine is distant from Mecca 15. miles, and in the mid way thereto is a place called Mina, that is to say, The hauen, and a litle from thence are 4. great pillars, of which hereafter we will speake. Now first touching the mountaine of Pardons, which is rather to be called a litle hill, then a mountain, for that it is low, litle, delightful and pleasant, containing in circuit two miles, and enuironed round about with the goodliest plaine that euer with mans eie could be seen, and the plaine likewise compassed with exceeding high mountains, in such sort that this is one of the goodliest situations in the world: and it seemeth verily, that nature hath therein shewed all her cunning, in making this place vnder the mountaine of pardons so broad and pleasant. Vpon the side towards Mecca there are many pipes of water cleare, faire, and fresh, and aboue all most wholesome, falling down into certaine vessels made of purpose, where the people refresh and wash themselues, and water their cattel. And when Adam and Euah were cast out of paradise by the angel of the Lord, the Mahumetans say, they came to inhabite this litle mountaine of pardons. Also they say, that they had lost one another, and were separated for the space of 40. yeeres, and in the end met at this place with great ioy and gladnesse, and builded a litle house vpon the top of this mountaine, the which at this day they call Beyt Adam, that is to say, the house of Adam.

Of the three Carouans.

The same day that the Carouan of Cairo commeth to this place, hither come 2. Carouans also, one of Damasco, the other of Arabia, and in like maner all the inhabitants for ten dayes iourney round about, so that at one time there is to be seene aboue 200000. persons, and more then 300000. cattell. Now all this company meeting together in this place the night before the feast, the three hostes cast themselues into a triangle, setting the mountaine in the midst of them: and all that night there is nothing to be heard nor seene, but gunshot and fireworkes of sundry sortes, with such singing, sounding, shouting, halowing, rumors, feasting, and triumphing, as is wonderfull. After this, the day of the feast being come, they are all at rest and silence, and that day they attend on no other thing, then to sacrifice oblations and prayers vnto God, and in the euening all they which haue horses mount thereon, and approch as nigh vnto the mountaine as they can, and those which haue no horses make the best shift they can on foote, giuing euer vnto the captaine of Cairo the chiefe place, the second to the captaine of Damasco, and the third to the captaine of Arabia, and being all approched as is abouesayd, there commeth a square squire, one of the Santones, mounted on a camell well furnished, who at the other side of the mountain ascendeth fiue steps into a pulpit made for that purpose, and all being silent, turning his face towards the people he maketh a short sermon of the tenour folowing.

The summe of the Santones sermon.

The summe of this double doctors sermon is thus much in briefe. He sheweth them how many and how great benefits God hath giuen to the Mahumetan people by the hand of his beloued friend and prophet Mahomet, hauing deliuered them from the seruitude of sinne and from idolatry, in which before time they were drowned, and how he gaue vnto them the house of Abraham wherein they should be heard, and likewise the mountaine of pardons, by meanes whereof they might obtaine grace and remission of their sinnes: adding, that the mercifull God, who is a liberall giuer of all good things, commaunded his secretarie Abraham to build him an house in Mecca, where his successours might make their prayers vnto him and bee heard, at which time all the mountains in the world came together thither with sufficiencie of stones for building hereof, except that litle and low hill, which for pouertie could not go to discharge this debt, for the which it became sorrowful, weeping beyond all measure for the space of thirtie yeeres, at the ende whereof the eternall God hauing pitie and compassion vpon this poore Mountaine, saide vnto it: Weepe no more (my daughter) for thy bitter plaints haue ascended vp into mine eares, therefore comfort thy selfe: for I will cause all those that shall goe to visite the house of my friend Abraham, that they shall not be absolued from their sinnes, vnlesse they first come to doe thee reuerence, and to keepe in this place their holiest feast. And this I haue commanded vnto my people by the mouth of my friend and prophet Mahumet. This said, he exhorteth them vnto the loue of God, and to prayer and almes. The sermon being done at the Sunne-setting they make 3. prayers, namely the first for the Serifo, the second for the Grand Signior with his hoste, and the third for all the people: to which prayers all with one voice cry saying; Amni Ia Alla, Amni Ia Alla, that is to say, Be it so lord, be it so Lord. Thus hauing had the Santones blessing and saluted the Mountaine of pardons, they returne the way they came vnto Mina, whereof wee haue made mention. In returning at the end of the plaine are the abouesaid 4. pillers, to wit, two on ech side of the way, through the midst whereof they say it is needfull that euery one passe, saying, that who so passeth without looseth all that merit which in his pilgrimage he had gotten. Also from the mountaine of pardons vntill they be passed the said pillers none dare looke backward, for feare least the sinnes which he hath left in the mountains returne to him againe. Being past these pillers eueryone lighteth downe, seeking in this sandy field 50. or 60. litle stones, which being gathered and bound in an hankerchiffe they carry to the abouesaid place of Mina, where they stay 5. dayes, because at that time there is a faire free and franke of al custome. And in this place are other 3. pillers, not together, but set in diuers places, where (as their prophet saith) were the three apparitions which the diuel made vnto Abraham, and to Ismael his sonne; for amongst them they make no mention of Isaac, as if he had neuer bene borne. So they say, that the blessed God hauing commanded Abraham his faithfull seruant to sacrifice his first begotten Ismael, the old Abraham went to do according to God's wil, and met with the infernall enemie in the shape of a man, and being of him demanded whither he went, he answered, that he went to sacrifice his sonne Ismael, as God had commanded him. Against whom the diuel exclaiming said: Oh doting old man, sith God in thine old age hath marueilously giuen thee this son (in whom all nations shalbe blessed) wherefore giuing credite vnto vaine dreames, wilt thou kill him whom so much thou hast desired, and so intirely loued. But Abraham shaking him off proceeded on his way, whereupon the diuel seeing his words could not preuaile with the father attempted the sonne, saying; Ismael, haue regard vnto thyselfe betimes in this thing which is so dangerous. Wherefore? answered the childe. Because (saith the diuel) thy doting father seeketh to take away thy life. For what occasion, said Ismael? Because (saith the enemie) he saith, that God hath commanded him. Which Ismael hearing hee tooke vp stones and threw at him, saying, Auzu billahi minal scia itanil ragini, which is to say, I defend me with God from the diuel the offender, as who would say, wee ought to obey the commandement of God and resist the diuel with al our force. But to returne to our purpose, the pilgrimes during their abode there goe to visite these three pillers, throwing away the little stones which before they gathered, whiles they repeat the same words which they say, that Ismael said to the diuell, when he withstoode him. From hence halfe a mile is a mountaine, whither Abraham went to sacrifice his sonne, as is abouesaid. In this mountaine is a great den whither the pilgrims resort to make their prayers, and there is a great stone naturally separated in the midst; and they say, that Ismael, while his father Abraham was busie about the sacrifice, tooke the knife in hand to prooue how it would cut, and making triall diuided the stone in two parts. The fiue dayes being expired, the captaine ariseth with all the Carouan, and returneth againe to Mecca, where they remaine other fiue dayes. And while these rest, we will treat of the city and port of Grida vpon the Red Sea.

Of Grida.

[Grida a port neere Mecca.] Therefore wee say that from Mecca to Grida they make two small dayes iourney: and because in those places it is ill traueiling in the day-time by reason of the great heat of the Sunne, therefore they depart in the euening from Mecca, and in the morning before Sunne-rising they are arriued halfe way, where there certaine habitations well furnished, and good Innes to lodge in, but especially women ynough which voluntarily bestowe their almes vpon the poore pilgrims: likewise departing the next euening, the morning after, they come vnto Grida. This citie is founded vpon the Red Sea banke, enuironed with wals and towers to the land-ward, but through continuance of time almost consumed and wasted: on the side to seaward it stands vnwalled. Grida hath three gates, one on eche side, and the thirde in the midst towarde the lande, which is called the port of Mecca, neere vnto which are 6. or 7. Turks vpon the old towers for guard thereof with foure faulcons vpon one of the corners of the city to the land-ward. Also to sea-ward where the wall ioyneth with the water, there is lately made a fort like vnto a bulwarke, where they haue planted 25 pieces of the best ordinance that might be had, which are very well kept and guarded. More outward towards the sea vpon the farthest olde tower are other fiue good pieces with 30 men to guard them. [Sidenote: The Portugals greatly feared in the Red Sea.] On the other side of the city at the end of the wall there is lately builded a bulwarke strong and well guarded by a Saniaccho with 150 Turks wel prouided with ordinance and all other necessaries and munition, and all these fortifyings are for none other cause then for feare and suspition of the Portugals. And if the port were good this were in vaine: but the port cannot be worse nor more dangerous; being all full of rocks and sands, in such wise, that the ships cannot come neere, but perforce ride at the least two miles off. [Sidenote: Forty or fifty rich ships arriue yeerely at Grida.] At this port arriue euery yeere forty or fifty great shippes laden with spices and other rich marchandize which yeeld in custome 150000 ducats, the halfe whereof goeth vnto the Grand Signior, and the other halfe to the Serifo. And because there is none other thing worthy mention in Grida we wil returne to our Carouan which hath almost rested enough.

Of their going to Medina.

The Carouan departeth for Medina returning the same way they came vnto Bedrihonem abouesayd, where they leaue their ordinance and other cariages, whereof they haue no need, with the pilgrims which haue seene Medina aforetime, and desire not to see it againe, but stay in that place, expecting the carouan, and resting vntill the carouan go from Bedrihonem to Medina, where they always finde goodly habitations, with abundance of sweet waters, and dates enough, and being within foureteene miles of Medina they come vnto a great plaine called by them Iabel el salema, that is to say, the mountaine of health, from which they begin to descry the citie and tombe of Mahomet, at which sight they light from their horses in token of reuerence. And being ascended vp the sayd mountaine with shouting which pierceth the skies they say, Sala tuua salema Alaccha Iarah sul Allah. Sala tuua Salema Alaccha Ianabi Allah, Sala tuua Salema Allaccha Iahabit Allah: which words in the Arabian tongue signifie: Prayer and health be vnto thee, oh prophet of God: prayer and health be vpon thee, oh beloued of God. And hauing pronounced this salutacion, they proceed on their iourney, so that they lodge that night within three miles of Medina: and the next morning the captaine of the pilgrimage ariseth, and proceeding towards the city, and drawing neere, there commeth the gouernour vnder the Serifo, accompanied with his people to receiue the Carouan, hauing pitched their tents in the midst of a goodly field where they lodge.

Of Medina.

Medina is a little city of great antiquity, containing in circuit not aboue two miles, hauing therein but one castle, which is olde and weake, guarded by an Aga with fifty pieces of artillery, but not very good. The houses thereof are faire and well situated, built of lime and stone, and in the midst of the city stands a fouresquare Mosquita, not so great as that of Mecca, but more goodly, rich, and sumptuous in building. Within the same in a corner thereof is a tombe built vpon foure pillers with a vault, as if it were vnder a pauement, which bindeth all the foure pillers together. The tombe is so high, that it farre exceedeth in heighth the Mosquita, being couered with lead, and the top all inamelled with golde, with an halfe moone vpon the top: and within the pauement it is all very artificially wrought with golde. Below there are round about very great staires of yron ascending vp vntill the midst of the pillers, and in the very midst thereof is buried the body of Mahomet, and not in a chest of yron cleauing to the adamant, as many affirme that know not the trueth thereof. Moreouer, ouer the body they haue built a tombe of speckled stone a brace and a halfe high, [Marginal note: Or, a fathom.] and ouer the same another of Legmame fouresquare in maner of a pyramis. After this, round about the sepulture there hangeth a curtaine of silke, which letteth the sight of those without that they cannot see the sepulture. Beyond this in the same Mosquita are other two sepulchres couered with greene cloth, and in the one of them is buried Fatma the daughter of Mahomet, and Alli is buried in the other, who was the husband of the sayd Fatma. The attendants vpon these sepulchres are fifty eunuches white and tawny, neither is it granted to any of them to enter within the tombe, sauing to three white eunuches the oldest and best of credit; vnto whom it is lawfull to enter but twise in the day, to light the lamps, and to doe other seruices. All the other eunuchs attend without to the seruice of the Mosquita, and the other two sepulchres of Fatma, and Alli, where euery one may go and touch at his pleasure, and take of the earth for deuotion, as many do.

Of things without the City.

Without the city and on euery side are most faire gardens, with many fountaines of most sweet water, infinite pondes, abundance of fruit, with much honest liuing, so that this place is very pleasant and delightfull. This city hath three gates, one of which is an hospitall caused to be built by Cassachi, called the Rosel who was wife to Sultan Solimam grandfather to this emperour. The sayd Hospitall hath nought els woorthy mention, saue that it is fairely built, and hath large reuenues belonging thereunto, and nourisheth many poore people. A mile from the city are certaine houses whereof they affirme one to be the same, where Mahumet in his lifetime dwelt. This house hath on euery side very many faire date trees, amongst which there are two which grow out of one stocke exceeding high, and these, they say, their Prophet graffed with his owne hand: the fruit thereof is alwayes sent to Constantinople, to be presented vnto the Grand Signior, and is sayd to be that blessed fruit of the Prophet. Nere vnto the date trees is a faire fountaine of cleere and sweet water, the which by a conduct pipe is brought into the city of Medina. Also there is a little Mosquita, wherein three places are counted holy, and greatly reuerenced: the first they affirme, that their Prophet made his first prayer in, after he knew God: the second is that whither he went when he would see the holy house of Abraham, where when he sate down to that intent, they say the mountaines opened from toppe to bottome to shew him the house, and after closed againe as before: the third holy place is in the midst of the sayd Mosquita, where is a tombe made of lime and stone fouresquare, and full of sand, wherein, they say, was buried that blessed camel which Mahumet was alwayes woont to ride vpon. On the other side of the city are other tombes of holy Mahumetans, and euery one or them hath a tombe built vpon foure pillers, amongst which three were the companions of Mahumet, to wit, Abubacar; Ottoman, and Omar; all which are visited of the pilgrims as holy places.

The offering of the vestures vnto the sepulchres.

The Carouan being come to Medina two houres before day, and resting there till the euening, the captaine then with his company and other pilgrims setteth forward, with the greatest pompe possible: and taking with him the vesture which is made in maner of a pyramis, with many other of golde and silke, departeth, going thorow the midst of the city, vntill he come to the Mosquita, where hauing praied, he presenteth vnto the tombe of his prophet (where the eunuchs receiuing hands are ready) the vesture for the sayd tombe: and certaine eunuchs entring in take away the old vesture, and lay on the new, burning the olde one, and diuiding the golde thereof into equall portions. After this are presented other vestures for the ornament of the Mosquita. Also the people without deliuer vnto the eunuchs ech man somewhat to touch the tombe therewith, which they keepe as a relique with great deuotion. This ceremony being ended, the captaine resteth in Medina two dayes, to the end the pilgrims may finish their deuotion and ceremonies: and after they depart to Iambor. A good dayes iourney thence is a steepe mountaine, ouer which is no passage, sauing by one narrow path called Demir Capi, which was in times past called the yron gate. Of this gate the Mahumetans say, that Ally the companion and sonne in law of Mahumet, being here pursued by many Christians, and comming vnto this mountaine, not seeing any way whereby to flee, drew out his sword, and striking the said mountaine, diuided it in sunder, and passing thorow saued his life on the other side. Moreouer, this Alli among the Persians is had in greater reuerence than Mahumet, who affirme, that the sayd Alli hath done greater things and more miraculous than Mahumet, and therefore they esteeme him for God almighty his fellow. But to returne to our matter, the captaine with the carouan within two dayes after returneth for Cairo, and comming to Ezlem, findeth there a captaine with threescore horses come thither to bring refreshments to the said captaine of the pilgrimage, as also to sell vnto the pilgrims some victuals. From thence they set forward, and comming to Birca within two leagues of Cairo, there is the master of the house of the Bassha of Cairo with all his horsemen come thither to receiue him with a sumptuous and costly banket made at the cost of the Basha for the captaine and his retinue, who after he is well refreshed departeth toward the castle of Cairo to salute the Basha, who receiuing him with great ioy and gladnesse in token of good wil presenteth him with a garment of cloth of golde very rich: and the captaine taking the Alcaron out of the chest presenteth it to the Basha, who hauing kissed it, commandeth to lay it vp againe. Some there are which affirme, that being arriued at Cairo, they kill that goodly camell which caried the Alcaron, and eate him; which is nothing so: for they are so superstitious to the contrary, that to gaine all the world they would not kill him. But if by casuality he should die, in this case happy and blessed they thinke themselues, which can get a morsell to eat. And thus much concerning the voyage of the captaine of the carouan of Cairo.

* * * * *

The voyage and trauell of M. Cæsar Fredericke, Marchant of Venice, into the East India, and beyond the Indies. Wherein are conteined the customes and rites of those countries, the merchandises and commodities, as well of golde and siluer, as spices, drugges, pearles, and other iewels: translated out of Italian by M. Thomas Hickocke.

Cæsare Fredericke to the Reader.

[Sidenote: Cæsare Fredericke trauelled eighteene yeeres in the East Indies.] I hauing (gentle Reader) for the space of eighteene yeeres continually coasted and trauelled, as it were, all the East Indies, and many other countreys beyond the Indies, wherein I haue had both good and ill successe in my trauels: and hauing seene and vnderstood many things woorthy the noting, and to be knowen to all the world, the which were neuer as yet written of any: I thought it good (seeing the Almighty had giuen me grace, after so long perils in passing such a long voyage to returne into mine owne countrey, the noble city of Venice) I say, I thought it good, as briefly as I could, to write and set forth this voyage made by me, with the maruellous things I haue seene in my trauels in the Indies: The mighty Princes that gouerne those countreys, their religion and faith that they haue, the rites and customes which they vse, and liue by, of the diuers successe that happened vnto me, and how many of these countreys are abounding with spices, drugs, and iewels, giuing also profitable aduertisement to all those that haue a desire to make such a voyage. And because that the whole world may more commodiously reioyce at this my trauell, I haue caused it to be printed in this order: and now I present it vnto you (gentle and louing Readers) to whom for the varieties of things heerein contented, I hope that it shall be with great delight receiued. And thus God of his goodnesse keepe you.

A voyage to the East Indies, and beyond the Indies, &c.

[Sidenote: The authours going from Venice to Cyprus and Tripoly.] In the yere of our Lord God 1653, I Cæsar Fredericke being in Venice, and very desirous to see the East parts of the world, shipped my selfe in a shippe called the Gradaige of Venice, with certaine marchandise, gouerned by M. Iacomo Vatica, which was bound to Cyprus with his ship, with whom I went: and when we were arriued in Cyprus, I left that ship, and went in a lesser to Tripoly in Soria, where I stayed a while. Afterward, I tooke my iourney to Alepo, and there I acquainted my selfe with marchants of Armenia, and Moores, that were marchants, and consorted to go with them to Ormus, and wee departed from Alepo, and in two dayes iourney and a halfe, we came to a city called Bir.

Of the city called Bir.

Bir is a small city very scarse of all maner of victuals, and nere vnto the walles of the city runneth the riuer of Euphrates. [Sidenote: The river Euphrates.] In this city the marchants diuide themselues into companies, according to their merchandise that they haue, and there either they buy or make a boat to carry them and their goods to Babylon downe the riuer Euphrates, with charge of a master and mariners to conduct the boat in the voyage: these boats are in a maner flat bottomed, yet they be very strong: and for all that they are so strong, they will serue but for one voyage. They are made according to the sholdnesse of the riuer, because that the riuer is in many places full of great stones, which greatly hinder and trouble those that goe downe the riuer. These boats serue but for one voyage downe the riuer vnto a village called Feluchia, because it is impossible to bring them vp the riuer backe againe. [Sidenote: Feluchia a small city on Euphrates.] At Feluchia the marchants plucke their boats in pieces, or else sell them for a small price, for that at Bir they cost the marchants forty or fifty chickens a piece, and they sell them at Feluchia for seuen or eight chickens a piece, because that when the marchants returne from Babylon backe againe, if they haue marchandise or goods that oweth custome, then they make their returne in forty dayes thorow the wildernesse, passing that way with a great deale lesser charges then the other way. [Sidenote: Mosul.] And if they haue not marchandise that oweth custome, then they goe by the way of Mosul, where it costeth them great charges both the Carouan and company. From Bir where the marchants imbarke themselues to Feluchia ouer agains Babylon, if the riuer haue good store of water, they shall make their voyage in fifteene or eighteene dayes downe the riuer, and if the water be lowe, and it hath not rained, then it is much trouble, and it will be forty or fifty dayes journey downe, because that when the barks strike on the stones that be in the riuer, then they must vnlade them, which is great trouble, and then lade them againe when they haue mended them: therefore it is not necessary, neither doe the marchants go with one boat alone, but with two or three, that if one boat split and be lost with striking on the sholdes, they may haue another ready to take in their goods, vntil such time as they haue mended the broken boat, and if they draw the broken boat on land to mend her, it is hard to defend her in the night from the great multitude of Arabians that will come downe there to robbe you: [Sidenote: The Arabian theeues are in number like to Ants.] and in the riuers euery night, when you make fast your boat to the banckeside, you must keepe good watch against the Arabians which are theeues in number like to ants, yet when they come to robbe, they will not kill, but steale and run away. Harquebuzes are very good weapons against them, for that they stand greatly in feare of the shot. And as you passe the riuer Euphrates from Bir to Feluchia, there are certein places which you must passe by, where you pay custome certaine medines vpon a bale, which custome is belonging to the sonne of Aborise king of the Arabians and of the desert, who hath certaine cities and villages on the riuer Euphrates.

Feluchia and Babylon.

[Sidenote: The olde Babylon hath great trade with marchants still.] Feluchia is a village where they that come from Bir doe vnbarke themselues and vnlade their goods, and it is distant from Babylon a dayes iourney and an halfe by land: Babylon is no great city but it is very populous, and of great trade of strangers because it is a great thorowfare for Persia, Turkia, and Arabia: and very often times there goe out from thence Carouans into diuers countreys: and the city is very copious of victuals, which comme out of Armenia downe the riuer of Tygris, on certaine Zattares or Raffes made of blowen hides or skinnes called Vtrij. This riuer Tygris doeth wash the walles of the city. These Raffes are bound fast together, and then they lay boards on the aforesayd blowen skinnes, and on the boards they lade the commodities, and so come they to Babylon, where they vnlade them, and being vnladen, they let out the winde out of the skinnes, and lade them on cammels to make another voyage. This city of Babylon is situate in the kingdome of Persia, but now gouerned by the Turks. On the other side of the riuer towards Arabia, ouer against the city, there is a faire place or towne, and in it a faire Bazarro for marchants, with very many lodgings, where the greatest part of the marchants strangers which come to Babylon do lie with their marchandize. [Sidenote: A bridge made of boats.] The passing ouer Tygris from Babylon to this Borough is by a long bridge made of boates chained together with great chaines: prouided, that when the riuer waxeth great with the abundance of raine that falleth, then they open the bridge in the middle, where the one halfe of the bridge falleth to the walles of Babylon, and the other to the brinks of this Borough, on the other side of the riuer: and as long as the bridge is open, they passe the riuer in small boats with great danger, because of the smalnesse of the boats, and the ouerlading of them, that with the fiercenesse of the streame they be ouerthrowen, or els the streame doth cary them away, so that by this meanes, many people are lost and drowned: this thing by proofe I haue many times seene.

Of the tower of Babylon.

The Tower of Nimrod or Babel is situate on that side of Tygris that Arabia is, and in a very great plaine distant from Babylon seuen or eight miles: which tower is ruinated on euery side, and with the falling of it there is made a great mountaine, so that it hath no forme at all, yet there is a great part of it standing which is compassed and almost couered with the aforesayd fallings: this Tower was builded and made of foure square Brickes, which Brickes were made of earth, and dried in the Sunne in maner and forme following: first they layed a lay of Brickes, [Footnote: These bricks be in thicknes six or seuen inches, and a foot and a halfe square.] then a Mat made of Canes, square as the Brickes, and in stead of lime, they daubed it with earth: these Mats of Canes are at this time so strong, that it is a thing woonderfull to beholde, being of such great antiquity: I haue gone round about it, and haue not found any place where there hath bene any doore or entrance: it may be in my iudgement in circuit about a mile, and rather lesse then more.

This Tower in effect is contrary to all other things which are seene afar off, for they seeme small, and the more nere a man commeth to them the bigger they be: but this tower afar off seemeth a very great thing, and the nerer you come to it the lesser. My iudgment and reason of this is, that because the Tower is set in a very great plaine, and hath nothing more about to make any shew sauing the ruines of it which it hath made round about, and for this respect descrying it a farre off, that piece of the Tower which yet standeth with the mountaine that is made of the substance that hath fallen from it, maketh a greater shew then you shall finde comming neere to it.

Babylon and Basora.

From Babylon I departed for Basora, shipping my selfe in one of the barks that vse to go in the riuer Tigris from Babylon to Basora, and from Basora to Babylon: which barks are made after the maner of Fusts or Galliots with a Speron and a couered poope: they haue no pumpe in them because of the great abundance of pitch which they haue to pitch them with all: which pitch they haue in abundance two dayes iourney from Babylon. Nere vnto the riuer Euphrates, there is a city called Heit, nere vnto which city there is a great plaine full of pitch, very maruellous to beholde, a thing almost incredible, that out of a hole [Footnote: This hole where out commeth this pitch is most true, and the water and pitch runneth into the valley or Iland where the pitch resteth, and the water runneth into the riuer Euphrates, and it maketh all the riuer to be as it were brackish with the smell of pitch and brimstone.] in the earth, which continually throweth out pitch into the aire with continuall smoake, this pitch is throwen with such force, that being hot it falleth like as it were sprinckled ouer all the plaine, in such abundance that the plaine is always full of pitch: the Mores and Arabians of that place say, that that hole is the mouth of hell: and in trueth, it is a thing very notable to be marked: and by this pitch the whole people haue great benefit to pitch their barks, which barks they call Daneck and Saffin. When the riuer of Tygris is well replenished with water, you may passe from Babylon to Basora in eight or nine dayes, and sometimes more and sometimes lesse: we were halfe so much more which is 14 or 15 daies, because the waters were low: they may saile day and night, and there are some places in this way where you pay so many medins on a baile: if the waters be lowe, it is 18 dayes iourney.

Basora.

[Sidenote: Zizarij an ancient people.] Basora is a city of the Arabians, which of olde time was gouerned by those Arabians called Zizarij, but now it is gouerned by the great Turke where he keepeth an army to his great charges.

The Arabians called Zizarij haue the possession of a great countrey, and cannot be ouercome by the Turke, because that the sea hath deuided their countrey into an Iland by channels with the ebbing and flowing of the sea, and for that cause the Turke cannot bring an army against them, neither by sea nor by land, and another reason is, the inhabitants of that Iland are very strong and warlike men. [Sidenote: At the castle of Corna the riuer Euphrates and Tygris do meet.] A dayes iourney before you come to Basora, you shall haue a little castle or fort, which is set on that point of the land where the riuers of Euphrates and Tygris meet together, and the castle is called Corna: at this point, the two riuers make a monstrous great riuer, that runneth into the sea, which is called the gulfe of Persia, which is towards the South: Basora is distant from the sea fifteene miles, and it is a city of great trade of spices and drugges which come from Ormus. Also there is a great store of corne, Rice, and Dates, which the countrey doth yeeld. [Sidenote: Ormus is the barrenest Iland in all the world.] I shipped my selfe in Basora to go for Ormus, and so we sailed, thorow the Persian sea six hundred miles, which is the distance from Basora to Ormus, and we sailed in small ships made of boards, bound together with small cords or ropes, and in stead of calking they lay betweene euery board certaine straw which they haue, and so they sowe board and board together, with the straw beweene, wherethorow there commeth much water, and they are very dangerous. [Sidenote: Carichij an Iland in the gulfe of Persia.] Departing from Basora we passed 200 miles with the sea on our right hand, along the gulfe, vntil at length we arriued at an Iland called Carichij, fro whence we sailed to Ormus in sight of the Persian shore on the left side, and on the right side towards Arabia we discouered infinite Ilands.

Ormus.

Ormus [Footnote: Ormus is alwayes replenished with abundance of victuall, and yet there is none that groweth in the Iland.] is an Iland in circuit fiue and twenty or thirty miles, and it is the barrenest and most drie Iland in all the world, because that in it there is nothing to be had, but salt water, and wood, all other things necessary for mans life are brought out of Persia twelue miles off, and out of other Ilands neere thereunto adioyning, in such abundance and quantity, that the city is alwayes replenished with all maner of store: there is standing neere vnto the waters side a very faire castell, in the which the captaine of the king of Portugall is alwayes resident with a good band of Portugalles, and before this castell is a very faire prospect: in the city dwell the maried men, souldiers and marchants of euery nation, amongst whom there are Moores and Gentiles. [Sidenote: Great trade of merchandise in Ormus.] In this city there is very great trade for all sorts of spices, drugges, silke, cloth of silke, brocardo, and diuers other sorts of marchandise come out of Persia: and amongst all other trades of marchandise, the trade of Horses is very great there, which they carry from thence into the Indies. This Iland hath a Moore king of the race of the Persians, who is created and made king by the Captaine of the castle, in the name of the king of Portugall. At the creation of this king I was there, and saw the ceremonies that they vse in it, which are as followeth. The olde King being dead, the Captaine of the Portugals chuseth another of the blood royall, and maketh this election in the castle with great ceremonies, and when hee is elected, the Captaine sweareth him to be true and faithfull to the King of Portugall, as his Lord and Gouernour, and then he giueth him the Scepter regall. After this with great feasting and pompe, and with great company, he is brought into the royall palace in the city. This King keepeth a good traine, and hath sufficient reuenues to maintaine himselfe without troubling of any, because the Captaine of the castle doth mainteine and defend his right, and when that the Captaine and he ride together, he is honoured as a king, yet be cannot ride abroad with his traine, without the consent of the Captaine first had: it behooueth them to doe this, and it is necessary, because of the great trade that is in the city: their proper language is the Persian tongue. There I shipped my selfe to goe for Goa, a city in the Indies, in a shippe that had fourescore horses in her. [Sidenote: A priuilege for Marchants.] This is to aduertise those Marchants that go from Ormus to Goa to shippe themselues in those shippes that carry horses, because euery shippe that carrieth twenty horses and vpwards is priuileged, that all the marchandise whatsoeuer they carry shall pay no custome, whereas the shippes that carry no horses are bound to pay eight per cento of all goods they bring.

Goa, Diu, and Cambaia.

Goa is the principall city that the Portugals haue in the Indies, where is resident the Viceroy with his Court and ministers of the King of Portugall. From Ormus to Goa is nine hundred foure score and ten miles distance, in which passage the first city that you come to in the Indies, is called Diu, [Footnote: Off South extremity of Kathiawar Peninsula, Bombay Presidency.] and is situate in a little Iland in the kingdome of Cambaia, which is the greatest strength that the Portugals haue in all the Indies, yet a small city, but of great trade, because there they lade very many great ships for the straights of Mecca and Ormus with merchandise, and these shippes belong to the Moores and Christians, but the Moores can not trade neither saile into those seas without the licence of the Viceroy of the King of Portugall, otherwise they are taken and made good prises. The marchandise that they lade these ships withall commeth from Cambaietta a port in the kingdome of Cambaia, which they bring from thence in small barks, because there can no great shippes come thither, by reason of the sholdnesse of the water thereabouts, and these sholds are an hundred or fourescore miles about in a straight or gulfe, which they call Macareo, which is as much as to say, as a race of a tide, because the waters there run out of that place without measure, so that there is no place like to it, vnlesse it be in the kingdome of Pegu, where there is another Macareo, where the waters run out with more force than these doe. The principall city in Cambaia is called Amadauar, it is a dayes iourney and an halfe from Cambaietta, it is a very great city and very populous, and for a city of the Gentiles it is very well made and builded with faire houses and large streets, with a faire place in it with many shippes, and in shew like to Cairo, but not so great: also Cambaietta is situate on the seas side, and is a very faire city. The time that I was there, the city was in great calamity and scarsenesse, so that I haue seene the men of the countrey that were Gentiles take their children, their sonnes and their daughters, and haue desired the Portugals to buy them, and I haue seene them sold for eight or ten larines a piece, which may be of our money x.s. or xiii.s. iiii.d. For all this if I had not seene it, I could not haue beleeued that there should be such a trade at Cambaietta as there is: for in the time of euery new Moone and euery full Moone, the small barks (innumerable) come in and out, for at those times of the Moone the tides and waters are higher then at other times they be. These barkes be laden with all sorts of spices, with silke of China, with Sandols, with Elephants teeth, Veluets of Vercini, great quantity of Pannina, which commeth from Mecca, Chickinos which be pieces of golde woorth seuen shillings a piece sterling, with money, and with diuers sorts of other marchandize. Also these barks lade out, as it were, an infinite quantity of cloth made of Bumbast of all sorts, as white stamped and painted, with great quantity of Indico, dried ginger and conserued, Myrabolans drie and condite, Boraso in paste, great store of sugar, great quantity of Cotton, abundance of Opium, Assa Fetida, Puchio, with many other sorts of drugges, turbants made in Diu, great stones like to Corneolaes, Granats, Agats, Diaspry, Calcidonij, Hematists, and some kinde of naturall diamonds. There is in the city of Cambaietta an order, but no man is bound to keepe it, but they that will; but all the Portugall marchants keepe it, the which is this. There are in this city certain Brokers which are Gentiles and of great authority, and haue euery one of them fifteene or twenty seruants, and the Marchants that vse that countrey haue their Brokers, with which they be serued: and they that haue not bene there are informed by their friends of the order, and of what Broker they shall be serued. [Sidenote: Marchants that trauell to the Indies must cary their prouision of houshold with them.] Now euery fifteene dayes (as abouesayd) that the fleet of small shippes entreth into the port, the Brokers come to the water side, and these Marchants assoone as they are come on land, do giue the cargason of all their goods to that Broker that they will haue to do their businesse for them, with the marks of all the fardles and packs they haue; and the marchant hauing taken on land all his furniture for his house, because it is needful that the Marchants that trade to the Indies carry prouision of housholde with them, because that in euery place where they come they must haue a new house, the Broker that hath receiued his cargason, commandeth his seruants to carry the Marchants furniture for his house home, and load it on some cart, and carry it into the city, where the Brokers haue diuers empty houses meet for the lodging of Marchants, furnished onely with bedsteads, tables, chaires, and empty iarres for water: then the Broker sayth to the Marchant, Goe and repose your selfe, and take your rest in the city. The Broker tarrieth at the water side with the cargason, and causeth all his goods to be discharged out of the ship, and payeth the custome, and causeth it to be brought into the house where the marchant lieth, the Marchant not knowing any thing thereof, neither custome, nor charges. These goods being brought to this passe into the house of the Marchant, the Broker demandeth of the Marchant if he haue any desire to sell his goods or marchandise, at the prises that such wares are worth at that present time? And if he hath a desire to sell his goods presently, then at that instant the Broker selleth them away. After this the Broker sayth to the Marchant, you haue so much of euery sort of marchandise neat and cleare of euery charge, and so much ready money. And if the Marchant will employ his money in other commodities, then the Broker telleth him that such and such commodities will cost so much, put aboord without any maner of charges. The Marchant vnderstanding the effect, maketh his account; and if he thinke to buy or sell at the prices currant, he giueth order to make his marchandise away: and if he hath commodity for 20000 dukets, all shalbe bartred or solde away in fifteene dayes without any care or trouble: and when as the Marchant thinketh that he cannot sell his goods at the prise currant, he may tary as long as he will, but they cannot be solde by any man but by that Broker that hath taken them on land and payed the custome: and purchance tarying sometimes for sale of their commodity, they make good profit, and sometimes losse: but those marchandise that come not ordinarily euery fifteene dayes, in tarying for the sale of them, there is great profit. [Sidenote: Great store of men of warre and rouers on the coast of Cambaia.] The barks that lade in Cambaietta go for Diu to lade the ships that go from thence for the streights of Mecca and Ormus, and some go to Chaul and Goa: and these ships be very well appointed, or els are guarded by the Armada of the Portugals, for that there are many Corsaires or Pyrats which goe coursing alongst that coast, robbing and spoiling: and for feare of these theeues there is no safe sailing in those seas, but with ships very well appointed and armed, or els with the fleet of the Portugals, as is aforesayd. In fine the kingdome of Cambaia is a place of great trade, and hath much doings and traffique with all men, although hitherto it hath bene in the hands of tyrants, because that at 75 yeeres of age the true king being at the assault of Diu, was there slaine: whose name Sultan Badu. At that time foure or fiue captaines of the army diuided the kingdome amongst themselues, and euery one of them shewed in his countrey what tyranny he could: but twelue yeeres ago the great Mogul a Moore king of Agra and Delly, forty dayes iourny within the land of Amadauar, became the gouernour of all the kingdome of Cambaia without any resistance, because he being of great power and force, deuising which way to enter the land with his people, there was not any man that would make him any resistance, although they were tyrants and a beastly people, they were soone brought vnder obedience. [Sidenote: A maruellous fond delight in women.] During the time I dwelt in Cambaietta I saw very maruellous things: there were an infinite number of artificers that made bracelets called Mannij, or bracelets of elephants teeth, of diuers colours, for the women of the Gentiles, which haue their armes full decked with them. And in this occupation there are spent euery yeere many thousands of crownes: the reason whereof is this, that when there dieth any whatsoeuer of their kindred, then in signe and token of mourning and sorrow, they breake all their bracelets from their armes, and presently they go and buy new againe, because that they had rather be without their meat then without their bracelets.

Daman. Basan. Tana.

Hauing passed Diu, I came to the second city that the Portugals haue, called Daman, situated in the territory of Cambaia, distant from Diu an hundred and twenty miles: it is no towne of merchandise, saue Rice and corne, and hath many villages vnder it, where in time of peace the Portugals take their pleasure, but in time of warre the enemies haue the spoile of them; in such wise that the Portugals haue little benefit by them. Next vnto Daman you shall haue Basan, which is a filthy place in respect of Daman: in this place is Rice, Corne, and Timber to make shippes and gallies. And a small distance beyond Bassan is a little Iland called Tana, a place very populous with Portugals, Moores, and Gentiles: these haue nothing but Rice, there are many makers of Armesie, and weauers of girdles of wooll and bumbast blacke and redde like to Moocharies.

Of the cities of Chaul, and of the Palmer tree.

Beyond this Iland you shall finde Chaul in the firme land; and they are two cities, one of the Portugals, and the other of the Moores: that city which the Portugals haue is situate lower then the other, and gouerneth the mouth of the harbour, and is very strongly walled: and as it were a mile and an halfe distant from this is the city of Moores, gouerned by their king Zamalluco. In the time of warres there cannot any great ships come to the city of the Moores, because the Portugals with their ordinance will sincke them, for that they must perforce passe by the castles of the Portugals: both the cities are ports of the sea, and are great cities, and haue vnto them great traffique and trade of merchandise, of all sorts of spices, drugges, silke, cloth of silke, Sandols, Marsine, Versin, Porcelane of China, Veluets and Scarlets that come from Portugall and from Meca: with many other sortes of merchandise. There come euery yeere from Cochin, and from Cananor tenne or fifteene great shippes laden with great Nuts cured, and with sugar made of the selfe same Nuts called Giagra: the tree whereon these Nuts doe grow is called the Palmer tree: and thorowout all the Indies, and especially from this place to Goa there is great abundance of them, and it is like to the Date tree. In the whole world there is not a tree more profitable and of more goodnesse then this tree is, neither doe men reape so much benefit of any other tree as they doe of this, there is not any part of it but serueth for some vse, and none of it is woorthy to be burnt. With the timber of this tree they make shippes without the mixture of any other tree, and with the leaues thereof they make sailes, and with the fruit thereof, which be a kinde of Nuts, they make wine, and of the wine they make Sugar and Placetto, which wine they gather in the spring of the yeere: out of the middle of the tree where continually there goeth or runneth out white liquour like vnto water, in that time of the yeere they put a vessel vnder euery tree, and euery euening and morning they take it away full, and then distilling it with fire it maketh a very strong liquour: and then they put it into buts, with a quantity of Zibibbo, white or blacke and in short time it is made a perfect wine. After this they make of the Nuts great store of oile: of the tree they make great quantity of boordes and quarters for buildings. Of the barke of this tree they make cables, ropes, and other furniture for shippes, and, as they say, these ropes be better then they that are made of Hempe. They make of the bowes, bedsteds, after the Indies fashion, and Scauasches for merchandise. The leaues they cut very small, and weaue them, and so make sailes of them, for all maner of shipping, or els very fine mats. And then the first rinde of the Nut they stampe, and make thereof perfect Ockam to calke shippes, great and small: and of the hard barke thereof they make spoones and other vessels for meat, in such wise that there is no part thereof throwen away or cast to the fire. When these Mats be greene they are full of an excellent sweet water to drinke: and if a man be thirsty, with the liquour of one of the Mats he may satisfie himselfe: and as this Nut ripeneth, the liquour thereof turneth all to kernell. There goeth out of Chaul for Mallaca, for the Indies, for Macao, for Portugall, for the coasts of Melinde, for Ormus, as it were an infinite number and quantity of goods and merchandise that come out of the kingdome of Cambaia, as cloth of bumbast white, painted, printed, great quantity of Indico, Opium, Cotton, Silke of euery sort, great store of Boraso in Paste, great store of Fetida, great store of yron, corne, and other merchandise. [Sidenote: Great ordinance made in pieces, and yet seruiceable.] The Moore king Zamalluco is of great power, as one that at need may command, and hath in his camp, two hundred thousand men of warre, and hath great store of artillery, some of them made in pieces, which for their greatnesse can not bee carried to and fro: yet although they bee made in pieces, they are so commodious that they worke with them maruellous well, whose shotte is of stone, and there hath bene of that shot sent vnto the king of Portugall for the rarenes of the thing. The city where the king Zamalluco hath his being, is within the land of Chaul seuen or eight dayes iourney, which city is called Abneger. Three score and tenne miles from Chaul, towards the Indies, is the port of Dabul, an hauen of the king Zamalluco: from thence to Goa is an hundred and fifty miles.

Goa.

[Sidenote: The chiefe place the Portugals have in the Indies.] Goa is the principall city that the Portugals haue in the Indies, wherein the Viceroy with his royall Court is resident, and is in an Iland which may be in circuit fiue and twenty or thirty miles: and the city with the boroughs is reasonable bigge, and for a citie of the Indies it is reasonable faire, but the Iland is farre more fairer: for it is as it were full of goodly gardens, replenished with diuers trees and with the Palmer trees as is aforesayd. This city is of great trafique for all sorts of marchandise which they trade withall in those parts:

and the fleet which commeth euery yeere from Portugall, which are fiue or sixe great shippes that come directly for Goa, arriue there ordinarily the sixth or tenth of September, and there they remaine forty or fifty dayes, and from thence they goe to Cochin, where they lade for Portugall, and often times they lade one shippe at Goa and the other at Cochin for Portugall. Cochin is distant from Goa three hundred miles. The city of Goa is situate in the kingdome of Dialcan a king of the Moores, whose chiefe city is vp in the countrey eight dayes iourney, and is called Bisapor: the king is of great power, for when I was in Goa in the yeere of our Lord 1570, this king came to giue assault to Goa, being encamped neere vnto it by a riuer side with an army of two hundred thousand men of warre, and he lay at this siege foureteene moneths in which time there was peace concluded, and as report went amongst his people, there was great calamity and mortality which bred amongst them in the time of Winter, and also killed very many elephants. [Sidenote: A very good sale for horses.] Then in the yeere of our Lord 1567, I went from Goa to Bezeneger the chiefe city of the king dome of Narsinga eight dayes iourney from Goa, within the land, in the company of two other merchants which carried with them three hundred Arabian horses to that king: because the horses of that countrey are of a small stature, and they pay well for the Arabian horses: and is requisite that the merchants sell them well, for that they stand them in great charges to bring them out of Persia to Ormus, and from Ormus to Goa, where the ship that bringeth twenty horses and vpwards payeth no custome, neither ship nor goods whatsoeuer; whereas if they bring no horses, they pay 8 per cento of all their goods: and at the going out of Goa the horses pay custome, two and forty pagodies for euery horse, which pagody may be of sterling money sixe shillings eight pence, they be pieces of golde of that value. So that the Arabian horses are of great value in those countreys, as 300, 400, 500 duckets a horse, and to 1000 duckets a horse.

Bezeneger.

The city of Bezeneger was sacked in the yeere 1565, by foure kings of the Moores, which were of great power and might: the names of these foure kings were these following, the first was called Dialcan, the second Zamaluc, the third Cotamaluc, and the fourth Viridy: and yet these foure kings were not able to ouercome the city and the king of Bezeneger, but by treason. The king of Bezeneger was a Gentile, and had, amongst all other of his captaines, two which were notable, and they were Moores: and these two captaines had either of them in charge threescore and ten or fourescore thousand men. These two captaines being of one religion with the foure kings which were Moores, wrought meanes with them to betray their owne king into their hands. [Footnote: A most vnkind and wicked treason against their prince: this they haue for giuing credit to strangers, rather then to their owne natiue people.] The king of Bezeneger esteemed not the force of the foure kings his enemies, but went out of his city to wage battell with them in the fieldes; and when the armies were ioyned, the battell lasted but a while not the space of foure houres, because the two traitourous captaines, in the chiefest of the fight, with their companies turned their faces against their king, and made such disorder in his armie, that as astonied they set themselues to flight. Thirty yeeres was this kingdome gouerned by three brethren which were tyrants, the which keeping the rightful king in prison, it was their vse euery yeere once to shew him to the people, and they at their pleasures ruled as they listed. These brethren were three captaines belonging to the father of the king they kept in prison, which when he died, left his sonne very yong, and then they tooke the gouernment to themselues. The chiefest of these three was called Ramaragio, and sate in the royall throne, and was called the king: the second was called Temiragio, and he tooke the gouernment on him: the third was called Bengatre, and he was captaine generall of the army. These three brethren were in this battell, in the which the chiefest and the last were neuer heard of quicke nor dead. [Sidenote: The sacking of the city.] Onely Temiragio fled in the battel, hauing lost one of his eyes: when the newes came to the city of the ouerthrow in the battell, the wiues and children of these three tyrants, with their lawfull king (kept prisoner) fled away, spoiled as they were, and the foure kings of the Moores entred the city Bezeneger with great triumph, and there they remained six moneths, searching vnder houses and in all places for money and other things that were hidden, and then they departed to their owne kingdomes because they were not able to maintaine such a kingdome as that was, so farre distant from their owne countrey.

When the kings were departed from Bezeneger, this Temiragio returned to the city, and then beganne for to repopulate it, and sent word to Goa to the Merchants, if they had any horses, to bring them to him, and he would pay well for them, and for this cause the foresayd two Merchants that I went in company withall, carried those horses that they had to Bezeneger. [Sidenote: An excellent good policy to intrap men.] Also this Tyrant made an order or lawe, that if any Merchant had any of the horses that were taken in the foresayd battell or warres, although they were of his owne marke, that he would giue as much for them as they would: and besides he gaue generall safe conduct to all that should bring them. When by this meanes he saw that there were great store of horses brought thither vnto him, hee gaue the Merchants faire wordes, vntill such time as he saw they could bring no more. Then he licenced the Merchants to depart, without giuing them any thing for their horses, which when the poore men saw, they were desperate, and as it were mad with sorrow and griefe.

I rested in Bezeneger seuen moneths; although in one moneth I might haue discharged all my businesse, for it was necessary to rest there vntill the wayes were cleere of theeues, which at that time ranged vp and downe. And in the time I rested there, I saw many strange and beastly deeds done by the Gentiles. First, when there is any Noble man or woman dead, they burne their bodies: and if a married man die, his wife must burne herselfe aliue, for the loue of her husband, and with the body of her husband: so that when any man dieth, his wife will take a moneths leaue, two or three, or as shee will, to burne her selfe in, and that day being come, wherein shee ought to be burnt, that morning shee goeth out of her house very earely, either on horsebacke or on an eliphant, or else is borne by eight men on a smal stage: in one of these orders she goeth, being apparelled like to a Bride, carried round about the City, with her haire downe about her shoulders, garnished with iewels and flowers, according to the estate of the party, and they goe with as great ioy as Brides doe in Venice to their nuptials: shee carrieth in her left hand a looking glasse, and in her right hand an arrow, and singeth thorow the City as she passeth, and sayth, that she goeth to sleepe with her deere spowse and husband. [Sidenote: A discription of the burning place.] She is accompanied with her kindred and friends vntill it be one or two of the clocke in the afternoone, then they goe out of the City, and going along the riuers side called Nigondin, which runneth vnder the walles of the City, vntill they come vnto a place where they vse to make this burning of women, being widdowes, there is prepared in this place a great square caue, with a little pinnacle hard by it, foure or fiue steppes vp: the foresayd caue is full of dried wood. [Sidenote: Feasting and dancing when they should mourne.] The woman being come thither, accompanied with a great number of people which come to see the thing, then they make ready a great banquet, and she that shall be burned eateth with as great ioy and gladnesse, as though it were her wedding day: and the feast being ended, then they goe to dancing and singing a certeine time, according as she will. After this, the woman of her owne accord, commandeth them to make the fire in the square caue where the drie wood is, and when it is kindled, they come and certifie her thereof, then presently she leaueth the feast, and taketh the neerest kinseman of her husband by the hand, and they both goe together to the banke of the foresayd riuer, where shee putteth off all her iewels and all her clothes, and giueth them to her parents or kinsefolke and couering herselfe with a cloth, because she will not be seene of the people being naked, she throweth herselfe into the riuer, saying, O wretches, wash away your sinnes. Comming out of the water, she rowleth herselfe into a yellow cloth of fourteene braces long: and againe she taketh her husbands kinseman by the hand, and they go both together vp to the pinnacle of the square caue wherein the fire is made. When she is on the pinnacle, shee talketh and reasoneth with the people, recommending vnto them her children and kindred. Before the pinnacle they vse to set a mat, because they shall not see the fiercenesse of the fire, yet there are many that will haue them plucked away, shewing therein an heart not fearefull, and that they are not affrayd of that sight. When this silly woman hath reasoned with the people a good while to her content, there is another women that taketh a pot with oile, and sprinckleth it ouer her head, and with the same she anoynteth all her body, and afterwards throweth the pot into the fornace, and both the woman and the pot goe together into the fire, and presently the people that are round about the fornace throw after her into the caue great pieces of wood, so by this meanes, with the fire and with the blowes that she hath with the wood throwen after her, she is quickly dead, and after this there groweth such sorrow and such lamentation among the people, that all their mirth is turned into howling and weeping, in such wise, that a man could scarse beare the hearing of it. [Sidenote: Mourning when they should reioice.] I haue seene many burnt in this maner, because my house was neere to the gate where they goe out to the place of burning: and when there dieth any great man, his wife with all his slaues with whom hee hath had carnall copulation, burne themselues together with him. Also in this kingdome I haue seene amongst the base sort of people this vse and order, that the man being dead, he is carried to the place where they will make his sepulchre, and setting him as it were vpright, then commeth his wife before him on her knees, casting her armes about his necke, with imbracing and clasping him, vntill such time as the Masons haue made a wall round about them, and when the wall is as high as their neckes, there commeth a man behinde the women and strangleth her: then when she is dead, the workemen finish the wall ouer their heads, and so they lie buried both together. Besides these, there are an infinite number of beastly qualities amongst them, of which I haue no desire to write. [Sidenote: The cause why the women do so burne themselues.] I was desirous to know the cause why these women would so wilfully burne themselues against nature and law, and it was told mee that this law was of an antient time, to make prouision against the slaughters which women made of their husbands. For in those dayes before this law was made, the women for euery little displeasure that their husbands had done vnto them, would presently poison their husbands, and take other men, and now by reason of this law they are more faithfull vnto their husbands, and count their liues as deare as their owne, because that after his death her owne followeth presently.

In the yeere of our Lord God 1567, for the ille successe that the people of Bezeneger had, in that their City was sacked by the foure kings, the king with his Court went to dwell in a castle eight dayes iourney vp in the land from Bezenger, called Penegonde. Also six dayes iourney from Bezenger, is the place where they get Diamants: I was not there, but it was tolde me that it is a great place, compassed with a wall, and that they sell the earth within the wall, for so much a squadron, and the limits are set how deepe or how low they shall digge. Those Diamante that are of a certaine sise and bigger then that sise, are all for the king, it is many yeeres agone, since they got any there, for the troubles that haue bene in that kingdome. The first cause of this trouble was, because the sonne of this Temeragio had put to death the lawfull king which he had in prison, for which cause the Barons and Noblemen in that kingdome would not acknowledge him to be their king, and by this meanes there are many kings, and great diuision in that kingdome, and the city of Bezeneger is not altogether destroyed, yet the houses stand still, but empty, and there is dwelling in them nothing, as is reported, but Tygers and other wilde beasts. The circuit of this city is foure and twentie miles about, and within the walles are certeine mountaines. The houses stand walled with earth, and plaine, all sauing the three palaces of the three tyrant brethren, and the Pagodes which are idole houses: these are made with lime and fine marble. I haue seene many kings Courts, and yet haue I seene none in greatnesse like to this of Bezeneger, I say, for the ordes of his palace, for it hath nine gates or ports. First when you goe into the place where the king did lodge, there are fiue great ports or gates: these are kept with Captaines and souldiers: then within these there are foure lesser gates: which are kept with Porters. Without the first gate there is a little porch, where there is a Captaine with fiue and twentie souldiers, that keepeth watch and ward night and day: and within that another, with the like guard, wherethorow they come to a very faire Court, and at the end of that Court there is another porch as the first, with the like guard, and within that another Court. And in this wise are the first fiue gates guarded and kept with those Captaines: and then the lesser gates within are kept with a guard of Porters: which gates stand open the greatest part of the night, because the custome of the Gentiles is to doe their businesse, and make their feasts in the night, rather then by day. The city is very safe from theeues, for the Portugall merchants sleepe in the streets, or vnder porches, for the great heat which is there, and yet they neuer had any harme in the night. At the end of two monethes, I determined to goe for Goa in the company of two other Portugall Marchants, which were making ready to depart, with two palanchines or little litters, which are very commodious for the way, with eight Falchines which are men hired to cary the palanchines, eight for a palanchine, foure at a time: they carry them as we vse to carry barrowes. [Sidenote: Men ride on bullocks and trauell with them on the way.] And I bought me two bullocks, one of them to ride on, and the other to carry my victuals and prouision, for in that countrey they ride on bullocks with pannels, as we terme them, girts and bridles, and they haue a very good commodious pace. From Bezeneger to Goa in Summer it is eight dayes iourney, but we went in the midst of Winter, in the moneth of Iuly, and were fifteene dayes comming to Ancola on the sea coast, so in eight dayes I had lost my two bullocks: for he that carried my victuals, was weake and could not goe, the other when I came vnto a riuer where was a little bridge to passe ouer, I put my bullocke to swimming, and in the middest of the riuer there was a little Iland, vnto the which my bullocke went, and finding pasture, there he remained still, and in no wise we could come to him: and so perforce, I was forced to leaue him, and at that time there was much raine, and I was forced to go seuen dayes a foot with great paines: and by great chance I met with Falchines by the way, whom I hired to carry my clothes and victuals. We had great trouble in our iourney, for that euery day wee were taken prisoners, by reason of the great dissension in that kingdome: and euery morning at our departure we must pay rescat foure or fiue pagies a man. And another trouble wee had as bad as this, that when as wee came into a new gouernours countrey, as euery day we did, although they were al tributary to the king of Bezeneger, yet euery one of them stamped a seueral coine of Copper, so that the money that we tooke this day would not serue the next: at length, by the helpe of God, we came safe to Ancola, which is a country of the Queene of Gargopam, tributary to the king of Bezeneger. [Sidenote: The marchandise that come in and out to Bezeneger euery yere.] The marchandise that went euery yere from Goa to Bezeneger were Arabian Horses, Veluets, Damasks, and Sattens, Armesine of Portugall, and pieces of China, Saffron, and Skarlets: and from Bezeneger they had in Turky for their commodities, iewels, and Pagodies which be ducats of golde: [Sidenote: the apparell of those people.] the apparell that they vse in Bezeneger is Veluet, Satten, Damaske, Scarlet, or white Bumbast cloth, according, to the estate of the person with long hats on their heads, called Colae, made of Veluet, Satten, Damaske, or Scarlet, girding themselues in stead of girdles with some fine white bombast doth: they haue breeches after the order of the Turks: they weare on their feet plaine high things called of them Aspergh, and at their eares they haue hanging great plenty of golde.

Returning to my voyage, when we were together in Ancola, one of my companions that had nothing to lose, tooke a guide, and went to Goa, whither they goe in foure dayes, the other Portugall not being disposed to go, tarried in Ancola for that Winter. [Sidenote: Their Winter is our Summer.] The Winter in those parts of the Indies beginneth the fifteenth of May, and lasteth vnto the end of October: and as we were in Ancola, there came another Marchant of horses in a palanchine, and two Portugall souldiers which came from Zeilan, and two cariers of letters, which were Christians borne in the Indies; all these consorted to goe to Goa together, and I determined to goe with them, and caused a pallanchine to be made for me very poorely of Canes; and in one of them Canes I hid priuily all the iewels I had, and according to the order, I tooke eight Falchines to cary me:

and one day about eleuen of the clocke wee set forwards on our iourney, and about two of the clocke in the afternoone, as we passed a mountains which diuideth the territory of Ancola and Dialcan, I being a little behinde my company was assaulted by eight theeues, foure of them had swordes and targets, and the other foure had bowes and arrowes. When the Falchines that carried me vnderstood the noise of the assault, they let the pallanchine and me fall to the ground, and ranne away and left me alone, with my clothes wrapped about me: presently the theeues were on my necke and rifeling me, they stripped me starke naked, and I fained my selfe sicke, because I would not leaue the pallanchine, and I had made me a little bedde of my clothes; the theeues sought it very narrowly and subtilly, and found two pursses that I had, well bound vp together, wherein I had put my Copper money which I had changed for foure pagodies in Ancola. The theeues thinking it had beene so many duckats of golde, searched no further: then they threw all my clothes in a bush, and hied them away, and as God would haue it, at their departure there fell from them an handkercher, and when I saw it, I rose from my Pallanchine or couch, and tooke it vp, and wrapped it together within my Pallanchine. Then these my Falchines were of so good condition, that they returned to seeke mee, whereas I thought I should not haue found so much goodnesse in them: because they were payed their mony aforehand, as is the vse, I had thought to haue seene them no more. Before their comming I was determined to plucke the Cane wherein my iewels were hidden, out of my coutch, and to haue made me a walking staffe to carry in my hand to Goa, thinking that I should haue gone thither on foot, but by the faithfullness of my Falchines, I was rid of that trouble, and so in foure dayes they carried me to Goa, in which time I made hard fare, for the theeues left me neither money, golde, nor siluer, and that which I did eat was giuen me of my men for Gods sake: and after at my comming to Goa I payed them for euery thing royally that I had of them. [Sidenote: Foure small fortes of the Portugals.] From Goa I departed for Cochin, which is a voyage of three hundred miles, and betweene these two cities are many holdes of the Portugals, as Onor, Mangalor, Barzelor, and Cananor. The Holde or Fort that you shall haue from Goa to Cochin that belongeth to the Portugals is called Onor, which is in the kingdome of the queene of Battacella, which is tributary to the king of Bezeneger: there is no trade there, but onely a charge with the Captaine and company he keepeth there. And passing this place, you shall come to another small castle of the Portugals called Mangalor, and there is very small trade but onely for a little Rice: and from thence you goe to a little fort called Bazelor, there they haue good store of Rice which is carried to Goa: and from thence you shall goe to a city called Cananor, which is a harquebush shot distant from the chiefest city that the king of Cananor hath in his kingdome being a king of the Gentiles: and he and his are very naughty and malicious people, alwayes hauing delight to be in warres with the Portugales, and when they are in peace, it is for their interest to let their merchandize passe: there goeth out of this kingdom of Cananor, all the Cardamomum, great store of Pepper, Ginger, Honie, ships laden with great Nuts, great quantitie of Archa, which is a fruit of the bignesse of Nutmegs, which fruite they eate in all those partes of the Indies and beyond the Indies, with the leafe of an Herbe which they call Bettell, the which is like vnto our Iuie leafe, but a litle lesser and thinner: [Sidenote: Bettel is a very profitable herbe in that countrey.] they eate it made in plaisters with the lime made of Oistershels, and thorow the Indies they spend great quantitie of money in this composition, and it is vsed daily, which thing I would not haue beleeued, if I had not seene it. The customers get great profite by these Herbes, for that they haue custome for them. When this people eate and chawe this in their mouthes, it maketh their spittle to bee red like vnto blood, and they say, that it maketh a man to haue a very good stomacke and a sweete breath, but sure in my iudgement they eate it rather to fulfill their filthie lustes, and of a knauerie, for this Herbe is moyst and hote, and maketh a very strong expulsion. [Sidenote: Enimies to the king of Portugall.] From Cananor you go to Cranganor, which is another smal Fort of the Portugales in the land of the king of Cranganor, which is another king of the Gentiles, and a countrey of small importance, and of an hundreth and twentie miles, full of thieues, being vnder the king of Calicut, a king also of the Gentiles, and a great enemie to the Portugales, which when hee is alwayes in warres, hee and his countrey is the nest and resting for stranger theeues, and those bee called Moores of Carposa, because they weare on their heads long red hats, and these thieues part the spoyles that they take on the Sea with the king of Calicut, for hee giueth leaue vnto all that will goe a rouing, liberally to goe, in such wise, that all along that coast there is such a number of thieues, that there is no sailing in those Seas but with great ships and very well armed, or els they must go in company with the army of the Portugals from Cranganor to Cochin is 15. miles.

Cochin.

[Sidenote: Within Cochin is the kingdom of Pepper.] Cochin is, next vnto Goa, the chiefest place that the Portugales haue in the Indies, and there is great trade of Spices, drugges, and all other sortes of merchandize for the kingdome of Portugale, and there within the land is the kingdome of Pepper, which Pepper the Portugales lade in their shippes by bulke and not in sackes: [Marginal note: The Pepper that the Portugals bring, is not so good as that which goeth for Mecca, which is brought hither by the streights.] the Pepper that goeth for Portugale is not so good as that which goeth for Mecca, because that in times past the officers of the king of Portugale made a contract with the king of Cochin, in the name of the king of Portugale, for the prizes of Pepper, and by reason of that agreement betweene them at that time made, the price can neither rise nor fall, which is a very lowe and base price, and for this cause the villaines bring it to the Portugales, greene and full of filthe. The Moores of Mecca that giue a better price, haue it cleane and drie, and better conditioned. All the Spices and drugs that are brought to Mecca, are stollen from thence as Contrabanda. Cochin is two cities, one of the Portugales, and another of the king of Cochin: that of the Portugales is situate neerest vnto the Sea, and that of the king of Cochin is a mile and a halfe vp higher in the land, but they are both set on the bankes of one riuer which is very great and of a good depth of water, which riuer commeth out of the mountaines of the king of the Pepper, which is a king of the Gentiles, in whose kingdom are many Christians of saint Thomas order: the king of Cochin is also a king of the Gentiles and a great faithfull friend to the king of Portugale, and to those Portugales which are married, and are Citizens in the Citie Cochin of the Portugales. And by this name of Portugales throughout all the Indies, they call all the Christians that come out of the West, whether they bee Italians, Frenchmen, or Almaines, and all they that marrie in Cochin do get an office according to the trade he is of: [Sidenote: Great priuiledges that the citizens of Cochin haue.] this they haue by the great priuileges which the Citizens haue of that city, because there are two principal commodities that they deale withal in that place, which are these. The great store of Silke that commeth from China, and the great store of Sugar which commeth from Bengala: the married Citizens pay not any custome for these two commodities: for they pay 4. per cento custome to the king of Cochin, rating their goods at their owne pleasure. Those which are not married and strangers, pay in Cochin to the king of Portugale eight per cento of all maner of merchandise. I was in Cochin when the Viceroy of the king of Portugale wrought what hee coulde to breake the priuilege of the Citizens, and to make them to pay custome as other did: at which time the Citizens were glad to waigh their Pepper in the night that they laded the ships withall that went to Portugale and stole the custome in the night. The king of Cochin hauing vnderstanding of this, would not suffer any more Pepper to bee weighed. Then presently after this, the marchants were licensed to doe as they did before, and there was no more speach of this matter, nor any wrong done. This king of Cochin is of a small power in respect of the other kings of the Indies, for hee can make but seuentie thousand men of armes in his campe: hee hath a great number of Gentlemen which hee calleth Amochi, and some are called Nairi: these two sorts of men esteeme not their liues any thing, so that it may be for the honour of their king, they will thrust themselues forward in euery danger, although they know they shall die. These men goe naked from the girdle vpwardes, with a clothe rolled about their thighs, going barefooted, and hauing their haire very long and rolled vp together on the toppe of their heads, and alwayes they carrie their Bucklers or Targets with them and their swordes naked, these Nairi haue their wiues common amongst themselues, and when any of them goe into the house of any of these women, hee leaueth his sworde and target at the doore, and the time that hee is there, there dare not any bee so hardie as to come into that house. The kings children shall not inherite the kingdome after their father, because they hold this opinion, that perchance they were not begotten of the king their father, but of some other man, therfore they accept for their king, one of the sonnes of the kings sisters, or of some other woman of the blood roial, for that they be sure, they are of the blood roiall.

[Sidenote: A very strange thing hardly to be beleeued.] The Nairi and their wiues vse for a brauerie to make great holes in their eares, and so bigge and wide, that it is incredible, holding this opinion, that the greater the holes bee, the more noble they esteeme themselues. I had leaue of one of them to measure the circumference of one of them with a threed, and within that circumference I put my arme vp to the shoulder, clothed as it was, so that in effect they are monstrous great. Thus they doe make them when they be litle, for then they open the eare, and hang a piece of gold or lead thereat, and within the opening, in the whole they put a certaine leafe that they haue for that purpose, which maketh the hole so great. They lade ships in Cochin for Portugale and for Ormus, but they that goe for Ormus carrie no Pepper but by Contrabanda, as for Sinamome they easilie get leaue to carrie that away, for all other Spices and drugs they may liberally carie them to Ormus or Cambaia, and so all other merchandize which come from other places, but out of the kingdom of Cochin properly they cary away with them into Portugale great abundance of Pepper, great quantitie of Ginger dried and conserued, wild Sinamon, good quantity of Arecca, great store of Cordage of Cairo, made of the barke of the tree of the great Nut, and better then that of Hempe, of which they carrie great store into Portugale.

[Sidenote: Note the departing of ships from Cochin.] The shippes euery yeere depart from Cochin to goe for Portugall, on the fift day December, or the fift day of Ianuary. Nowe to follow my voyage for the Indies: from Cochin I went to Coulam, distant from Cochin seuentie and two miles, which Coulam is a small Fort of the king of Portugales, situate in the kingdom of Coulam, which is a king of the Gentiles, and of small trade: at that place they lade onely halfe a ship of Pepper, and then she goeth to Cochin to take in the rest, and from thence to Cao Comori is seuentie and two miles, and there endeth the coast of the Indies: and alongst this coast, neere to the water side, and also to Cao Comori, downe to the lowe land of Chialon, which is about two hundred miles, the people there are as it were all turned to the Christian faith: there are also Churches of the Friers of S.

Pauls order, which Friers doe very much good in those places in turning the people, and in conuerting them, and take great paines in instructing them in the law of Christ.

The fishing for Pearles.

[Sidenote: The order how they fish for pearles.] The Sea that lieth betweene the coast which descendeth from Cao Comori, to the lowe land of Chiaoal, and the Iland Zeilan, they call the fishing of Pearles, which fishing they make euery yeere, beginning in March or Aprill, and it lasteth fiftie dayes, but they doe not fishe euery yeere in one place, but one yeere in one place, and another yeere in another place of the same sea. When the time of this fishing draweth neere, then they send very good Diuers, that goe to discouer where the greatest heapes of Oisters bee vnder water, and right agaynst that place where greatest store of Oisters bee, there they make or plant a village with houses and a Bazaro, all of stone, which standeth as long as the fishing time lasteth, and it is furnished with all things necessarie, and nowe and then it is neere vnto places that are inhabited, and other times farre off, according to the place where they fishe. The Fishermen are all Christians of the countrey, and who so will may goe to fishing, paying a certaine dutie to the king of Portugall, and to the Churches of the Friers of Saint Paule, which are in that coast. All the while that they are fishing, there are three or foure Fustes armed to defend the Fishermen from Rouers. It was my chance to bee there one time in my passage, and I saw the order that they vsed in fishing, which is this. There are three or foure Barkes that make consort together, which are like to our litle Pilot boates, and a litle lesse, there goe seuen or eight men in a boate: and I haue seene in a morning a great number of them goe out, and anker in fifteene or eighteene fadome of water, which is the Ordinarie depth of all that coast. When they are at anker, they cast a rope into the Sea, and at the ende of the rope, they make fast a great stone, and then there is readie a man that hath his nose and his eares well stopped, and annointed with oyle, and a basket about his necke, or vnder his left arme, then hee goeth downe by the rope to the bottome of the Sea, and as fast as he can he filleth the basket, and when it is full, he shaketh the rope, and his fellowes that are in the Barke hale him vp with the basket: and in such wise they goe one by one vntill they haue laden their barke with oysters, and at euening they come to the village, and then euery company maketh their mountaine or heape of oysters one distant from another, in such wise that you shall see a great long rowe of mountaines or heapes of oysters, and they are not touched vntill such time as the fishing bee ended, and at the ende of the fishing euery companie sitteth round about their mountaine or heape of oysters, and fall to opening of them, which they may easilie doe because they bee dead, drie and brittle: and if euery oyster had pearles in them, it would bee a very good purchase, but there are very many that haue no pearles in them: when the fishing is ended, then they see whether it bee a great gathering or a badde: there are certaine expert in the pearles whom they call Chitini, which set and make the price of pearles [Marginal note: These pearles are prised according to the caracts which they weigh, euery caract is 4. graines, and these men that prise hem haue an instrument of copper with holes in it, which be made by degrees for to sort the perles withall.] according to their carracts, beautie, and goodnesse, making foure sortes of them. The first sort bee the round pearles, and they be called Aia of Portugale, because the Portugales doe buy them. The second sorte which are not round, are called Aia of Bengala. The third sort which are not so good as the second, they call Aia of Canara, that is to say, the kingdome of Bezeneger. The fourth and last sort, which are the least and worst sort, are called Aia of Cambaia. Thus the price being set, there are merchants of euery countrey which are readie with their money in their handes, so that in a fewe dayes all is bought vp at the prises set according to the goodnesse and caracts of the pearles.

In this Sea of the fishing of pearles is an Iland called Manar, which is inhabited by Christians of the countrey which first were Gentiles, and haue a small hold of the Portugales being situate ouer agaynst Zeilan: and betweene these two Ilands there is a chanell, but not very big, and hath but a small depth therein; by reason whereof there cannot any great shippe passe that way, but small ships, and with the increase of the water which is at the change or the full of the Moone, and yet for all this they must vnlade them and put their goods into small vessels to lighten them before they can passe that way for feare of Sholdes that lie in the chanell, and after lade them into their shippes to goe for the Indies, and this doe all small shippes that passe that way, but those shippes that goe for the Indies Eastwardes, passe by the coast of Coromandel, on the other side by the land of Chilao which is betweene the firme land and the Iland Manor: and going from the Indies to the coast of Coromandel, they loose some shippes, but they bee emptie, because that the shippes that passe that way discharge their goods at an Iland called Peripatane, and there land their goods into small flat bottomed boates which drawe litle water, and are called Tane, and can run ouer euery Shold without either danger or losse of any thing, for that they tarrie in Peripatane vntill such time as it bee faire weather. Before they depart to passe the Sholds, the small shippes and flat bottomed boates goe together in companie, and when they haue sailed sixe and thirtie miles, they arriue at the place where the Sholdes are, and at that place the windes blowe so forciblie, that they are forced to goe thorowe, not hauing any other refuge to saue themselues. The flat bottomed boates goe safe thorow, where as the small shippes if they misse the aforesayd chanell, sticke fast on the Sholdes, and by this meanes many are lost: and comming backe for the Indies, they goe not that way, but passe by the chanell of Manar as is abouesayd, whose chanell is Oazie, and if the shippes sticke fast, it is a great chance if there be any danger at all. The reason why this chanell is not more sure to goe thither, is, because the windes that raigne or blowe betweene Zeilan and Manar, make the chanell so shalow with water, that almost there is not any passage. From Coa Comori to the Iland of Zeilan is 120. miles ouerthwart.

Zeilan. [Footnote: Ceylon.]

Zeilan is an Iland, in my iudgement, a great deale bigger then Cyprus: on that side towards the Indies lying Westward is the citie called Columba, which is a hold of the Portugales, but without walles or enimies. It hath towards the Sea a free port, the awfull king of that Iland is in Colombo, and is turned Christian, and maintained by the king of Portugall, being depriued of his kingdome. The king of the Gentiles, to whom this kingdome did belong, was called Madoni, which had two sonnes, the first named Barbinas the prince; and the second Ragine. This king by the pollicie of his yoonger sonne, was depriued of his kingdome, who because hee had entised and done that which pleased the armie and souldiours, in despight of his father and brother being prince, vsurped the kingdome, and became a great warriour. First, this Iland had three kings; the King of Cotta with his conquered prisoners: the king of Candia, which is a part of that Iland, and is so called by the name of Candia, which had a reasonable power, and was a great friend to the Portugals, which sayd that hee liued secretly a Christian; the third was the king of Gianifampatan. In thirteene yeeres that this Ragine gouerned this Iland, he became a great tyrant.

In this Iland there groweth fine Sinamom, great store of Pepper, great store of Nuttes and Arochoe: there they make great store of Cairo [Footnote: Cairo is a stuffe that they make rope with, the which is the barke of a tree.] to make Cordage: it bringeth foorth great store of Christall Cats eyes, or Ochi de Gati, and they say that they finde there some Rubies, but I haue sold Rubies well there that I brought with me from Pegu. I was desirous to see how they gather the Sinamom, or take it from the tree that it groweth on, and so much the rather, because the time that I was there, was the season which they gather it in, which was in the moneth of Aprill, at which time the Portugals were in armes, and in the field, with the king of the countrey; yet I to satisfie my desire, although in great danger, tooke a guide with mee and went into a wood three miles from the Citie, in which wood was great store of Sinamome trees growing together among other wilde trees; and this Sinamome tree is a small tree, and not very high, and hath leaues like to our Baie tree. In the moneth of March or Aprill, when the sappe goeth vp to the toppe of the tree, then they take the Sinamom from that tree in this wise. [Sidenote: The cutting and gathering of Sinamom.] They cut the barke of the tree round about in length from knot to knot, or from ioint to ioint, aboue and belowe, and then easilie with their handes they take it away, laying it in the Sunne to drie, and in this wise it is gathered, and yet for all this the tree dieth not, [Sidenote: A rare thing.] but agaynst the next yeere it will haue a new barke, and that which is gathered euery yeere is the best Sinamome: for that which groweth two or three yeares is great, and not so good as the other is; and in these woods groweth much Pepper.

Negapatan.

From the Iland of Zeilan men vse to goe with small shippes to Negapatan, within the firme land, and seuentie two miles off is a very great Citie, and very populous of Portugals and Christians of the countrey, and part Gentiles: it is a countrey of small trade, neither haue they any trade there, saue a good quantitie of Rice, and cloth of Bumbast which they carie into diuers partes: it was a very plentifull countrey of victuals but now it hath a great deale lesse; and that abundance of victuals caused many Portugales to goe thither and build houses, and dwell there with small charge.

This Citie belongeth to a nobleman of the kingdome of Bezeneger being a Gentile, neuerthelesse the Portugales and other Christians are well intreated there, and haue their Churches there with a monasterie of Saint Francis order, with great deuotion and very well accommodated, with houses round about: yet for all this, they are amongst tyrants, which always at their pleasure may doe them some harme, as it happened in the yeere of our Lord God one thousand fiue hundred, sixtie and fiue: [Sidenote: A foolish feare of Portugals.] for I remember very well, how that the Nayer, that is to say, the lord of the citie, sent to the citizens to demaund of them certaine Arabian horses, and they hauing denied them vnto him, and gainesayd his demaund, it came to passe that this lord had a desire to see the Sea, which when the poore citizens vnderstood, they doubted some euill, to heare a thing which was not woont to bee, they thought that this man would come to sacke the Citie, and presently they embarked themselues the best they could with their mooueables, marchandize, iewels, money, and all that they had, and caused the shippes to put from the shore. When this was done, as their euill chance would haue it, the next night following, there came such a great storme that it put all the shippes on land perforce, and brake them to pieces, and all the goods that came on land and were saued, were taken from them by the souldiours and armie of this lord which came downe with him to see the Sea, and were attendant at the Sea side, not thinking that any such thing would haue happened.

Saint Thomas or San Tome.

[Sidenote: St. Thomas his sepulchre.] From Negapatan following my voyage towards the East an hundred and fiftie miles, I found the house of blessed

Saint Thomas, which is a Church of great deuotion, and greatly regarded of the Gentiles for the great miracles they haue heard to haue bene done by that blessed Apostle: neere vnto this Church the Portugals haue builded them a Citie in the countrey subiect to the king of Bezeneger, which Citie although it bee not very great, yet in my iudgement, it is the fairest in all that part of the Indies: and it hath very faire houses and faire gardens in vacant places very well accommodated: it hath streetes large and streight, with many Churches of great deuotion, their houses be set close one vnto another, with little doores, euery house hath his defence, so that by that meanes it is of force sufficient to defend the Portugals against the people of that countrey. The Portugals there haue no other possession but their gardens and houses that are within the citie: the customes belong to the king of Bezeneger, which are very small and easie, for that it is a countrey of great riches and great trade: there come euery yeere two or three great ships very rich, besides many other small ships: one of the two great ships goeth for Pegu, and the other for Malacca, laden with fine Bumbast [Marginal Note: A painted kind of cloth and died of diuers colours which those people delight much in, and esteeme them of great price.] cloth of euery sort, painted, which is a rare thing, because those kinde of clothes shew as they were gilded, with diuers colours, and the more they be washed, the liuelier the colours will shew. Also there is other cloth of Bumbast which is wouen with diuers colours, and is of great value: also they make in Sant Tome great store of red Yarne, which they die with a roote called Saia, and this colour will neuer waste, but the more it is washed, the more redder it will shew: they lade this yarne the greatest part of it for Pegu, because that there they worke and weaue it to make cloth according to their owne fashion, and with lesser charges. It is a maruelous thing to them which haue not seene the lading and vnlading of men and marchandize in S. Tome as they do: it is a place so dangerous, that a man cannot bee serued with small barkes, neither can they doe their businesse with the boates of the shippes, because they would be beaten in a thousand pieces, but they make certaine barkes (of purpose) high, which they call Masadie, they be made of litle boards; one board being sowed to another with small cordes, and in this order are they made. And when they are thus made, and the owners will embarke any thing in them, either men or goods, they lade them on land, and when they are laden, the Barke-men thrust the boate with her lading into the streame, and with great speed they make haste all that they are able to rowe out against the huge waues of the sea that are on that shore, vntill that they carie them to the ships: and in like maner they lade these Masadies at the shippes with merchandise and men. When they come neere the shore, the Barke-men leap out of the Barke into the Sea to keepe the Barke right that she cast not athwart the shore, and being kept right, the Suffe of the Sea setteth her lading dry on land without any hurt or danger, and sometimes there are some of them that are ouerthrowen, but there can be no great losse, because they lade but a litle at a time. All the marchandize they lade outwards, they emball it well with Oxe hides, so that if it take wet, it can haue no great harme.

[Sidenote: In the Iland of Banda they lade Nutmegs for there they grow.] In my voyage, returning in the yeere of our Lord God one thousand, fiue hundred, sixtie and sixe, I went from Goa vnto Malacca, in a shippe or Gallion of the king of Portugal, which went vnto Banda for to lade Nutmegs and Maces: from Goa to Malacca are one thousand eight hundred miles, we passed without the Iland Zeilan, and went through the chanell of Nicubar, or els through the chanell of Sombero, which is by the middle of the Iland of Sumatra, called in olde time Taprobana: [Sidenote: In the Ilands of Andemaon, they eate one another.] and from Necubar to Pegu is as it were a rowe or chaine of an infinite number of Ilands, of which many are inhabited with wilde people, and they call those Ilands the Ilands of Andemaon, and they call their people sauage or wilde, because they eate one another: also these Ilands haue warre one with another, for they haue small Barkes, and with them they take one another, and so eate one another: and if by euil chance any ship be lost on those Ilands, as many haue bene, there is not one man of those ships lost there that escapeth vneaten or vnslaine. These people haue not any acquaintance with any other people, neither haue they trade with any, but liue onely of such fruites as those Ilands yeeld: and if any ship come neere vnto that place or coast as they passe that way, as in my voyage it happened as I came from Malacca through the chanell of Sombrero, there came two of their Barkes neere vnto our ship laden with fruite, as with Mouces which wee call Adam apples, with fresh Nuts, and with a fruite called Inani, which fruite is like to our Turneps, but is very sweete and good to eate: they would not come into the shippe for any thing that wee could doe: neither would they take any money for their fruite, but they would trucke for olde shirtes or pieces of olde linnen breeches, these ragges they let downe with a rope into their Barke vnto them, and looke what they thought those things to bee woorth, so much fruite they would make fast to the rope and let vs hale it in: and it was told me that at sometimes a man shall haue for an old shirt a good piece of Amber.

Sumatra.

This Iland of Sumatra is a great Iland and deuided and gouerned by many kings, and deuided into many chanels, where through there is passage: upon the headland towards the West is the kingdom of Assi gouerned by a Moore king: this king is of great force and strength, as he that beside his great kingdom, hath many Foists and Gallies. In his kingdom groweth great store of Pepper, Ginger, Beniamin: he is an vtter enemy to the Portugals, and hath diuers times bene at Malacca to fight against it, and hath done great harme to the boroughes thereof, but the citie alway withstood him valiantly, and with their ordinance did great spoile to his campe. At length I came to the citie of Malacca.

The Citie Malacca.

Malacca is a Citie of marueilous great trade of all kind of marchandize, which come from diuers partes, because that all the shippes that saile in these seas, both great and small, are bound to touch at Malacca to paie their custome there, although they vnlade nothing at all, as we do at Elsinor: and if by night they escape away, and pay not their custome, then they fall into a greater danger after: for if they come into the Indies and haue not the seale of Malacca, they pay double custome. I haue not passed further then Malacca towards the East, but that which I wil speake of here is by good information of them that haue bene there. The sailing from Malacca towards the East is not common for all men, as to China and Iapan, and so forwards to go who will, but onely for the king of Portugall and his nobles, with leaue granted vnto them of the king to make such voiage, or to the iurisdiction of the captaine of Malacca, where he expecteth to know what voiages they make from Malacca thither, and these are the kings voiages, that euery yere there departeth from Malacca 2. gallions of the kings, one of them goeth to the Moluccos to lade Cloues, and the other goeth to Banda to lade Nutmegs and Maces. These two gallions are laden for the king, neither doe they carie any particular mans goods, sauing the portage of the Mariners and souldiers, and for this cause they are not voiages for marchants, because that going thither, they shal not haue where to lade their goods of returne; and besides this, the captaine wil not cary any marchants for either of these two places. There goe small shippes of the Moores thither, which come from the coast of Iaua, and change or guild their commodities in the kingdom of Assa, and these be the Maces, Cloues, and Nutmegs, which go for the streights of Mecca. The voiages that the king of Portugall granteth to his nobles are these, of China and Iapan, from China to Iapan, and from Iapan to China, and from China to the Indies, and the voyage of Bengala, Maluco, and Sonda, with the lading of fine cloth, and euery sort of Bumbast cloth. Sonda is an Iland of the Moores neere to the coast of Iaua, and there they lade pepper for China. [Sidenote: The ship of drugs, so termed of the Portugals.] The ship that goeth euery yeere from the Indies to China, is called the ship of Drugs, because she carieth diuers drugs of Cambaia, but the greatest part of her lading is siluer. From Malacca to China is eighteene hundred miles: and from China to Iapan goeth euery yeere a shippe of great importance laden with Silke, which for returne of their Silke bringeth barres of siluer which they trucke in China. The distance betweene China and Iapan is foure and twentie hundred miles, and in this way there are diuers Ilands not very bigge, in which the Friers of saint Paul, by the helpe of God, make many Christians there like to themselues. From these Ilands hitherwards the place is not yet discouered for the great sholdnesse of Sandes that they find. The Portugals haue made a small citie neere vnto the coast of China called Macao, whose church and houses are of wood, and it hath a bishoprike, but the customs belong to the king of China, and they goe and pay the same at a citie called Canton which is a citie of great importance and very beautifull two dayes iourney and a halfe from Macao. The people of China are Gentiles, and are so iealous and fearefull, that they would not haue a stranger to put his foote within their land: so that when the Portugals go thither to pay their custome, and to buy their merchandize, they will not consent that they shall lie or lodge within the citie, but send them foorth into the suburbes. The countrey of China [Marginal note: China is vnder the gouerment of the great Tartar.] is neere the kingdom of great Tartria, and is a very great countrey of the Gentiles and of great importance, which may be iudged by the rich and precious marchandize that come from thence, then which I beleeue there are not better nor in greater quantitie, in the whole world besides.

First, great store of golde, which they carie to the Indies, made in plates like to little shippes, and in value three and twentie caracts a peece, very great aboundance of fine silke, cloth of damaske and taffata, great quantitie of muske, great quantitie of Occam in barres, great quantitie of quicksiluer and of Cinaper, great store of Camfora, an infinite quantitie of Porcellane, made in vessels of diuerse sortes, great quantitie of painted cloth and squares, infinite store of the rootes of China: and euery yeere there commeth from China to the Indies, two or three great shippes, laden with most rich and precious merchandise. [Sidenote: A yeerely Carouan from Persia to China.] The Rubarbe commeth from thence ouer lande, by the way of Persia, because that euery yeere there goeth a great Carouan from Persia to China, which is in going thither six monethes. The Carouan arriueth at a Citie called Lanchin, the place where the king is resident with his Court. I spake with a Persian that was three yeeres in that citie of Lanchin, and he tolde me that it was a great Citie and of great importance. The voiages of Malacca which are in the iurisdiction of the Captaine of the castle, are these: Euery yeere he sendeth a small shippe to Timor to lade white Sandols, for all the best commeth from this Iland: there commeth some also from Solor, but that is not so good: also he sendeth another small ship euery yere to Cauchin China, to lade there wood of Aloes, for that all the wood of Aloes commeth from this place, which is in the firme land neere vnto China, and in that kingdome I could not knowe how that wood groweth by any meanes. [Sidenote: A market kept aboord of the ships.] For that the people of the countrey will not suffer the Portugales to come within the land, but onely for wood and water, and as for all other things that they wanted, as victuals or marchandise, the people bring that a boord the ship in small barkes, so that euery day there is a mart kept in the ship, vntill such time as she be laden: also there goeth another ship for the said Captaine of Malacca to Sion, to lade Verzino: all these voiages are for the Captaine of the castle of Malacca, and when he is not disposed to make these voiages he selleth them to another.

The citie of Sion, or Siam.

[Sidenote: A prince of marueilous strength and power.] Sion was the imperiall seat, and a great Citie, but in the yeere of our Lord God one thousand five hundred sixtie and seuen, it was taken by the king of Pegu, which king made a voyage or came by lande foure moneths iourney with an armie of men through his lande, and the number of his armie was a million and foure hundreth thousand men of warre: when hee came to the Citie, he gaue assault to it, and besieged it one and twentie monthes before he could winne it, with great losse of his people, this I know, for that I was in Pegu sixe monethes after his departure, and sawe when that his officers that were in Pegu, sent fiue hundreth thousand men of warre to furnish the places of them that were slaine and lost in that assault: yet for all this, if there had not beene treason against the citie, it had not beene lost: for on a night there was one of the gates set open, through the which with great trouble the king gate into the citie, and became gouernour of Sion: and when the Emperour sawe that he was betrayed, and that his enemie was in the citie, he poysoned himselfe: and his wiues and children, friends and noblemen, that were not slaine in the first affront of the entrance into the citie, were all caried captiues into Pegu, where I was at the comming home of the king with his triumphs and victorie, which comming home and returning from the warres was a goodly sight to behold, to see the Elephants come home in a square, laden with golde, siluer, iewels, and with Noble men and women that were taken prisoners in that citie.

Now to returne to my yoyage: I departed from Malacca in a great shippe which went for Saint Tome, being a Citie situate on the coast of Coromandel: and because the Captaine of the castles of Malacca had vnderstanding by aduise that the king of Assi [Marginal note: Or Achem.] would come with a great armie and power of men against them, therefore vpon this he would not giue licence that any shippes should depart: Wherefore in this ship wee departed from thence in the night, without making any prouision of our water: and wee were in that shippe foure hundreth and odde men: [Sidenote: The mountaines of Zerzeline.] we departed from thence with intention to goe to an Iland to take in water, but the windes were so contrary, that they would not suffer vs to fetch it, so that by this meanes wee were two and fortie dayes in the sea as it were lost, and we were driuen too and fro, so that the first lande that we discouered, was beyonde Saint Tome, more then fiue hundreth miles, which were the mountaines of Zerzerline, neere vnto the kingdome of Orisa, and so wee came to Orisa with many sicke, and more that were dead for want of water: and they that were sicke in foure dayes dyed; and I for the space of a yeere after had my throat so sore and hoarse, that I could neuer satisfie my thirst in drinking of water: I iudge the reason of my hoarsenesse to bee with soppes that I wet in vineger and oyle, wherewith I susteyned my selfe many dayes. There was not any want of bread nor of wine: but the wines of that countrey are so hot that being drunke without water they will kill a man: neither are they able to drinke them: when we beganne to want water, I sawe certaine Moores that were officers in the ship, that solde a small dish full for a duckat, after this I sawe one that would haue giuen a barre of Pepper, which is two quintalles and a halfe, for a litle measure of water, and he could not haue it. Truely I beleeue that I had died with my slaue, whom then I had to serue mee, which cost mee verie deare: but to prouide for the daunger at hand, I solde my slaue for halfe that he was worth, because that I would saue his drinke that he drunke, to serue my owne purpose, and to saue my life.

Of the kingdome of Orisa, and the riuer Ganges.

Orisa was a faire kingdome and trustie, through the which a man might haue gone with golde in his hande without any daunger at all, as long as the lawefull King reigned which was a Gentile, who continued in the citie called Catecha, which was within the lande size dayes iourney. This king loued strangers marueilous well, especially marchants which had traffique in and out of his kingdome, in such wise that hee would take no custome of them, neither any other grieuous thing. [Sidenote: The commodities that go out of Orisa.] Onely the shippe that came thither payde a small thing according to her portage, and euery yeere in the port of Orisa were laden fiue and twentie or thirtie ships great and small, with ryce and diuers sortes of fine white bumbaste cloth, oyle of Zerzeline which they make of a seed, and it is very good to eate and to fry fish withal, great store of butter, Lacca, long pepper, Ginger, Mirabolans dry and condite, great store of cloth of herbes, which is a kinde of silke which groweth amongst the woods without any labour of man, [Marginal note: This cloth we call Nettle cloth.] and when the bole thereof is growen round as bigge as an Orenge, then they take care onely to gather them. About sixteene yeeres past, this king with his kingdome were destroyed by the king of Patane, which was also king of the greatest part of Bengala, and when he had got the kingdome, he set custome there twenty pro cento, as Marchants paide in his kingdome: but this tyrant enioyed his kingdome but a small time, but was conquered by another tyrant, which was the great Mogol king of Agra, Delly, and of all

Cambaia, without any resistance. I departed from Orisa to Bengala, to the harbour Piqueno, which is distant from Orisa towardes the East a hundred and seuentie miles. [Sidenote: The riuer of Ganges.] They goe as it were rowing alongst the coast fiftie and foure miles, and then we enter into the riuer Ganges: from the mouth of this riuer, to a citie called Satagan, where the marchants gather themselues together with their trade, are a hundred miles, which they rowe in eighteene houres with the increase of the water: in which riuer it floweth and ebbeth as it doth in the Thamis, and when the ebbing water is come, they are not able to rowe against it, by reason of the swiftnesse of the water, yet their barkes be light and armed with oares, like to Foistes, yet they cannot preuaile against that streame, but for refuge must make them fast to the banke of the riuer vntill the next flowing water, and they call these barkes Bazaras and Patuas: they rowe as well as a Galliot, or as well as euer I haue seene any. A good tides rowing before you come to Satagan, you shall haue a place which is called Buttor, and from thence vpwards the ships doe not goe, because that vpwardes the riuer is very shallowe, and litle water. Euery yeere at Buttor they make and vnmake a Village, with houses and shoppes made of strawe, and with all things necessarie to their vses, and this village standeth as long as the ships ride there, and till they depart for the Indies, and when they are departed, euery man goeth to his plot of houses, and there setteth fire on them, which thing made me to maruaile. For as I passed vp to Satagan, I sawe this village standing with a great number of people, with an infinite number of ships and Bazars, and at my returne comming downe with my Captaine of the last ship, for whom I tarried, I was al amazed to see such a place so soone razed and burnt, and nothing left but the signe of the burnt houses. The small ships go to Satagan, and there they lade.

Of the citie of Satagan.

[Sidenote: The commodities that are laden in Satagan.] In the port of Satagan euery yeere lade thirtie or fiue and thirtie ships great and small, with rice, cloth of Bombast of diuerse sortes, Lacca, great abundance of sugar, Mirabolans dried and preserued, long pepper, oyle of Zerzeline, and many other sorts of marchandise. The citie of Satagan is a reasonable faire citie for a citie of the Moores, abounding with all things, and was gouerned by the king of Patane, and now is subiect to the great Mogol. I was in this kingdome foure moneths, whereas many marchants did buy or fraight boates for their benefites, and with these barkes they goe vp and downe the riuer of Ganges to faires, buying their commoditie with a great aduantage, because that euery day in the weeke they haue a faire, now in one place, and now in another, and I also hired a barke, and went vp and downe the riuer and did my businesse, and so in the night I saw many strange things. The kingdome of Bengala in times past hath bene as it were in the power of

Moores, neuerthelesse there is great store of Gentiles among them; alwayes whereas I haue spoken of Gentiles, is to be vnderstood Idolaters, and whereas I speak of Moores I meane Mahomets sect. [Sidenote: A ceremony of the gentiles when they be dead.] Those people especially that be within the land doe greatly worship the riuer of Ganges: for when any is sicke, he is brought out of the countrey to the banke of the riuer, and there they make him a small cottage of strawe, and euery day they wet him with that water, whereof there are many that die, and when they are dead, they make a heape of stickes and boughes and lay the dead bodie thereon, and putting fire thereunto, they let the bodie alone vntill it be halfe rosted, and then they take it off from the fire, and make an emptie iarre fas about his necke, and so throw him into the riuer. These things euery night as I passed vp and downe the riuer I saw for the space of two moneths, as I passed to the fayres to buy my commodities with the marchants. And this is the cause that the Portugales will not drinke of the water of the riuer Ganges, yet to the sight it is more perfect and clearer then the water of Nilus is. From the port Piqueno I went to Cochin, and from Cochin to Malacca, from whence I departed for Pegu being eight hundred miles distant. That voyage is woont to be made in fiue and tweutie or thirtie dayes, but we were foure moneths, and at the ende of three moneths our ship was without victuals. The Pilot told vs that wee were by his altitude not farre from a citie called Tanasary, in the kingdome of Pegu, and these his words were not true, but we were (as it were) in the middle of many Ilands, and many vninhabited rockes, and there were also some Portugales that affirmed that they knew the land, and knewe also where the citie of Tanasari was.

[Sidenote: Marchandise comming from Sion.] This citie of right belongeth to the kingdome of Sion, which is situate on a great riuers side, which commeth out of the kingdome of Sion: and where this riuer runneth into the sea, there is a village called Mirgim, in whose harbour euery yeere there lade some ships with Verzina, Nypa, and Beniamin, a few cloues, nutmegs and maces which come from the coast of Sion, but the greatest marchandise there is Verzin and Nypa, which is an excellent wine, which is made of the flower of a tree called Nyper. [Sidenote: Niper wine good to cure the French disease.] Whose licquour they distill, and so make an excellent drinke cleare as christall, good to the mouth, and better to the stomake, and it hath an excellent gentle vertue, that if one were rotten with the French pockes, drinking good store of this, he shall be whole againe, and I haue seene it proued, because that when I was in Cochin, there was a friend of mine, whose nose beganne to drop away with that disease, and he was counselled of the doctors of phisicke, that he should goe to Tanasary at the time of the new wines, and that he should drinke of the myper wine, night and day, as much as he could before it was distilled, which at that time is most delicate, but after that it is distilled, it is more strong, and if you drinke much of it, it will fume into the head with drunkennesse. This man went thither, and did so, and I haue seene him after with a good colour and sound. This wine is very much esteemed in the Indies, and for that it is brought so farre off, it is very deare: in Pegu ordinarily it it good cheape, because it is neerer to the place where they make it, and there is euery yeere great quantitie made thereof. And returning to my purpose, I say, being amongst these rockes, and farre from the land which is ouer against Tanasary, with great scarcitie of victuals, and that by the saying of the Pylot and two Portugales, holding then firme that wee were in front of the aforesayd harbour, we determined to goe thither with our boat and fetch victuals, and that the shippe should stay for vs in a place assigned. We were twentie and eight persons in the boat that went for victuals, and on a day about twelue of the clocke we went from the ship, assuring our selues to bee in the harbour before night in the aforesaid port, wee rowed all that day and a great part of the next night, and all the next day without finding harbour, or any signe of good landing, and this came to passe through the euill counsell of the two Portugales that were with vs.

For we had ouershot the harbour and left it behind vs, in such wise that we had lost the lande inhabited, together with the shippe, and we eight and twentie men had no maner of victuall with vs in the boate, but it was the Lords will that one of the Mariners had brought a little rice with him in the boate to barter away for some other thing, and it was not so much but that three or foure men would haue eaten it at a meale: I tooke the gouernment of this Ryce, promising that by the helpe of God that Ryce should be nourishment for vs vntil it pleased God to send vs to some place that was inhabited: [Sidenote: Great extemitie at sea.] and when I slept I put the ryce into my bosome because they should not rob it from me: we were nine daies rowing alongst the coast, without finding any thing but countreys vninhabited, and desert Ilands, where if we had found but grasse it would haue seemed sugar vnto vs, but wee could not finde any, yet we found a fewe leaues of a tree, and they were so hard that we could not chewe them, we had water and wood sufficient, and as wee rowed, we could goe but by flowing water, for when it was ebbing water, wee made fast our boat to the banke of one of those Ilandes, and in these nine dayes that we rowed, we found a caue or nest of Tortoises egges, wherein were one hundred fortie and foure egges, the which was a great helpe vnto vs: these egges are as bigge as a hennes egge, and haue no shell about them but a tender skinne, euery day we sodde a kettle full of those egges, with an handfull of rice in the broth thereof: it pleased God that at the ende of nine dayes we discouered certaine fisher men, a fishing with small barkes, and we rowed towardes them, With a good cheare, for I thinke there were neuer men more glad then we were, for wee were so sore afflicted with penurie, that we could scarce stande on our legges. Yet according to the order that we set for our ryce, when we sawe those fisher men, there was left sufficient for foure dayes. [Sidenote: Tauay vnder the king of Pegu.] The first village that we came to was in the gulfe of Tauay, vnder the king of Pegu, whereas we found great store of victuals: then for two or three dayes after our arriuall there, we would eate but litle meate any of vs, and yet for all this, we were at the point of death the most part of vs. From Tauay to Martauan, in the kingdome of Pegu, are seuentie two miles. We laded our bote with victuals which were aboundantly sufficient for sixe moneths, from whence we departed for the port and Citie of Martauan, where in short time we arriued, but we found not our ship there as we had thought we should, from whence presently we made out two barkes to goe to looke for her. And they found her in great calamitie and neede of water, being at an anker with a contrary winde, which came very ill to passe, because that she wanted her boat a moneth, which should haue made her prouision of wood and water, the shippe also by the grace of God arriued safely in the aforesaid port of Martauan.

The Citie of Martauan.

[Sidenote: Martauan a citie vnder the king of Pegu.] We found in the Citie of Martauan ninetie Portugales of Merchants and other base of men, which had fallen at difference with the Retor or gouernour of the citie, and all for this cause, that certaine vagabondes of the Portugales had slaine fiue falchines of the king of Pegu, which chaunced about a moneth after the king of Pegu was gone with a million and foure hundred thousand men to conquere the kingdome of Sion. [Sidenote: A custome that these people haue when the king is in the warres.] They haue for custome in this Countrey and kingdome, the king being wheresoeuer his pleasure is to bee out of his kingdome, that euery fifteene dayes there goeth from Pegu a Carouan of Falchines, with euery one a basket on his head full of some fruites or other delicates or refreshings, and with cleane clothes: it chaunced that this Carauan passing by Martauan, and resting themselues there a night, there happened betweene the Portugales and them wordes of despight, and from wordes to blowes, and because it was thought that the Portugales had the worse, the night following, when the Falchines were a sleepe with their companie, the Portugales went and cut off their heads. [Sidenote: A law in Pegu for killing of men.] Now there is a law in Pegu, that whosoeuer killeth a man, he shall buy the shed blood with his money, according to the estate of the person that is slaine, but these Falchines being the seruants of the king, the Retors durst hot doe any thing in the matter, without the consent of the king, because it was necessarie that the king should knowe of such a matter. When the king had knowledge thereof, he gaue commaundement that the malefactors should be kept vntill his comming home, and then be would duely minister iustice, but the Captaine of the Portugales would not deliuer those men, but rather set himselfe with all the rest in armes, and went euery day through the Citie marching with his Drumme und ensignes displayd. [Sidenote: Great pride of the Portugales.] For at that time the Citie was emptie of men, by reason they were gone all to the warres, and in businesse of the king: in the middest of this rumour wee came thither, and I thought it, a strange thing to see the Portugales vse such insolencie in another mans Citie. And I stoode in doubt of that which came to passe, and would not vnlade my goods because that they were more sure in the shippe then on the land, the greatest part of the lading was the owners of the shippe, who was in Malacca, yet there were diuerse marchants there, but their goods were of small importance, all those marchants tolde me that they would not vnlade any of their goods there, vnlesse I would vnlade first, yet after they left my counsell and followed their owne, and put their goods a lande and lost euery whit. The Retor with the customer sent for mee, and demaunded why I put not my goods a lande, and payed my custome as other men did? To whom I answered, that I was a marchant that was newly come thither, and seeing such disorder amongst the Portugales, I doubted the losse of my goods which cost me very deare, with the sweate of my face, and for this cause I was determined not to put my goods on lande, vntil such time as his honour would assure me in the name of the king, that I should haue no losse, and although there came harme to the Portugales, that neither I nor my goods should haue any hurt, because I had neither part nor any difference with them in this tumult: my reason sounded well in the Retors eares, and so presently he sent for the Bargits, which are as Counsellors of the Citie, and then they promised mee on the kings head or in the behalfe of the king, that neither I nor my goods should haue any harme, but that we should be safe and sure: of which promise there were made publike notes. And then I sent for my goods and had them on land, and payde my custome, which is in that countrey ten in the hundreth of the same goods, and for my more securitie I tooke a house right against the Retors house. The Captaine of the Portugales, and all the Portugall marchants were put out of the Citie, and I with twentie and two poore men which were officers in the shippe had my dwelling in the Citie. [Sidenote: A reuenge on the Portugales.] After this the Gentiles deuised to be reuenged of the Portugales; but they would not put it in execution, vntil such time as our small shippe had discharged all her goods, and then the next night following came from Pegu foure thousand souldiers with some Elephants of warre; and before that they made any tumult in the citie, the Retor sent, and gaue commaundement to all Portugales that were in the Citie, when they heard any rumour or noyse, that for any thing they should not goe out of their houses, as they tendered their owne health. Then foure houres within night I heard a great rumour and noyse of men of warre, with Elephants which threw downe the doores of the ware-houses of the

Portugales, and their houses of wood and strawe, in the which tumult there were some Portugales wounded, and one of them slaine; and others without making proofe of their manhoode, which the day before did so bragge, at that time put themselues to flight most shamefully, and saued themselues a boord of litle shippes, that were at an anker in the harbour, and some that were in their beds fled away naked, and that night they caried away all the Portugalles goods out of the suburbes into the Citie, and those Portugales that had their goods in the suburbes also. After this the Portugales that were fledde into the shippes to saue themselues, tooke a newe courage to themselues, and came on lande and set fire on the houses in the suburbes, which houses being made of boorde and strawe, and the winde blowing fresh, in small time were burnt and consumed, with which fire halfe the Citie had like to haue beene burnt; when the Portugales had done this, they were without all hope to recouer any part of their goods againe, which goods might amount to the summe of sixteene thousand duckats, which, if they had not set fire to the towne, they might haue had againe without any losse at all. Then the Portugales vnderstanding that this thing was not done by the consent of the king, but by his Lieutenant and the Retor of the citie were very ill content, knowing that they had made a great fault, yet the next morning following, the Portugales beganne to bende and shoot their ordinance against the Citie, which batterie of theirs continued foure dayes, but all was in vaine, for the shotte neuer hit the Citie, but lighted on the top of a small hill neere vnto it, so that the citie had no harme. When the Retor perceiued that the Portugales made battery against the Citie, be tooke one and twentie Portugales that were there in the Citie, and sent them foure miles into the Countrey, there to tarry vntill such time as the other Portugales were departed, that made the batterie, who after their departure let them goe at their owne libertie without any harme done vnto them. I my selfe was always in my house with a good guard appointed me by the Retor, that no man should doe me iniurie, nor harme me nor my goods; in such wise that hee perfourmed all that he had promised me in the name of the king, but he would not let me depart before the comming of the king, which was greatly to my hinderance, because I was twenty and one moneths sequestred, that I could not buy nor sell any kinde of marchandise. Those commodities that I brought thither, were peper, sandols, and Porcellan of China: so when the king was come home, I made my supplication vnto him, and I was licenced to depart when I would.

From Martauan I departed to goe to the chiefest Citie in the kingdome of Pegu, which is also called after the name of the kingdome, which voyage is made by sea in three or foure daies: they may goe also by lande, but it is better for him that hath marchandize to goe by sea and lesser charge. And in this voyage you shall haue a Macareo, which is one of the most marueilous things [Marginal note: A thing most marueilous, that at the comming of a tide the earth should quake.] in the world that Nature hath wrought, and I neuer saw any thing so hard to be beleeued as this, to wit, the great increasing and diminishing of the water there at one push or instant, and the horrible earthquake and great noyse that the said Macareo maketh where it commeth. We departed from Martauan in barkes, which are like to our Pylot boates, with the increase of the water, and they goe as swift as an arrowe out of a bow, so long as the tide runneth with them, and when the water is at the highest, then they drawe themselues out of the Channell towardes some banke, and there they come to anker, and when the water is diminished, then they rest on dry land: and when the barkes rest dry, they are as high from the bottome of the Chanell, as any house top is high from the ground. [Sidenote: This tide is like to the tides in our riuer of Seuerne.] They let their barkes lie so high for this respect, that if there should any shippe rest or ride in the Chanell, with such force commeth in the water, that it would ouerthrowe shippe or barke: yet for all this, that the barkes be so farre out of the Chanell, and though the water hath lost her greatest strength and furie before it come so high, yet they make fast their prowe to the streme, and oftentimes it maketh them very fearefull, and if the anker did not holde her prowe vp by strength, shee would be ouerthrowen and lost with men and goods. [Sidenote: These tides make their iust coarse as ours doe.] When the water beginneth to increase, it maketh such a noyse and so great that you would think it an earthquake, and presently at the first it maketh three waues. So that the first washeth ouer the barke, from stemme to sterne, the second is not so furious as the first, and the thirde rayseth the Anker, and then for the space of sixe houres while the water encreaseth, they rowe with such swiftnesse that you would thinke they did fly: in these tydes there must be lost no iot of time, for if you arriue not at the stagions before the tyde be spent, you must turne back from whence you came. For there is no staying at any place, but at these stagions, and there is more daunger at one of these places then at another, as they be higher and lower one then another. When as you returne from Pegu to Martauan, they goe but halfe the tide at a time, because they will lay their barkes vp aloft on the bankes, for the reason aforesayd. I could neuer gather any reason of the noyse that this water maketh in the increase of the tide, and in deminishing of the water. There is another Macareo in Cambaya, [Sidenote: The Macareo is a tide or a currant.] but that is nothing in comparison of this. By the helpe of God we came safe to Pegu, which are two cities, the olde and the newe, in the olde citie are the Marchant strangers, and marchants of the Countrey, for there are the greatest doings and the greatest trade. This citie is not very great, but it hath very great suburbes. Their houses be made with canes, and couered with leaues, or with strawe, but the marehants haue all one house or Magason, which house they call Godon which is made of brickes, and there they put all their goods of any valure, to saue them from the often mischances that there happen to houses made of such stuffe. In the newe citie is the pallace of the king, and his abiding place with all his barons and nobles, and other gentlemen; and in the time that I was there, they finished the building of the new citie: it is a great citie, very plaine and flat, and foure square, walled round about and with ditches that compasse the wals about with water, in which ditches are many crocodils, it hath no drawe bridges, yet it hath twentie gates, fiue for euery square on the walles, there are many places made for centinels to watch, made of wood and couered or guilt with gold, the streetes thereof are the fayrest that I haue seene, they are as straight as a line from one gate to another, and standing at the one gate you may discouer to the other, and they are as broad as 10 or 12 men may ride a breast in them: [Sidenote: A rich and stately palace.] and those streetes that be thwart are faire and large, these streetes, both on the one side and on the other, are planted at the doores of the houses, with nut trees of India, which make a very commodious shadowe, the houses be made of wood and couered with a kind of tiles in forme of cups, very necessary for their vse, the kings palace is in the middle of the citie, made in forme of a walled castle, with ditches full of water round about it, the lodgings within are made of wood all ouer gilded, with fine pinacles, and very costly worke, couered with plates of golde. Truely it may be a kings house: within the gate there is a faire large court, from the one side to the other, wherein there are made places for the strongest and stoutest Eliphants appointed for the seruice of the kings person, and amongst all other Eliphants, he hath foure that be white, a thing so rare that a man shall hardly finde another king that hath any such, and if this king knowe any other that hath white Eliphantes, he sendeth for them as for a gift. The time that I was there, there were two brought out of a farre Countrey, and that cost me something the sight of them, for they commaund the marchants to goe to see them, and then they must giue somewhat to the men that bring them: the brokers of the marchants giue for euery man halfe a duckat, which they call a Tansa, [Marginal note: This money called Tansa is halfe a duckat which may be three shillings and foure pence.] which amounteth to a great summe, for the number of merchants that are in that citie; and when they haue payde the aforesayde Tansa, they may chuse whether they will see them at that time or no, because that when they are in the kings stall, euery man may see them that will: but at that time they must goe and see them, for it is the kings pleasure it should be so. This king amongst all other his titles, is called the King of the white Eliphantes and it is reported that if this king knewe any other king that had any of these white Eliphantes, and woud not send them vnto him, that he would hazard his whole kingdome to conquer them, he esteemeth these white Eliphantes very deerely, and they are had in great regard, and kept with very meete seruice, euery one of them is in a house, all guilded ouer, and they haue their meate giuen them in vessels of siluer and golde, there is one blacke Eliphant the greatest that hath bene seene, and is kept according to his bignesse, he is nine cubites high, which is a marueilous thing. [Sidenote: A warlike policie.] It is reported that this king hath foure thousand Eliphantes of warre, and all haue their teeth, and they vse to put on their two vppermost teeth sharpe spikes of yron, and make them fast with rings, because these beastes fight, and make battell with their teeth; hee hath also very many yong Eliphants that haue not their teeth sprowted foorth: also this king hath a braue deuise in hunting to take these Eliphantes when hee will, two miles from the Citie. [Sidenote: An excellent deuise to hunt, and take wilde Elephants.] He hath builded a faire pallace all guilded, and within it a faire Court, and within it and rounde about there are made an infinite number of places for men to stande to see this hunting: neere vnto this Pallace is a mighty great wood, through the which the hunts-men of the king ride continually on the backs of the feminine Eliphants, teaching them in this businesse. Euery hunter carieth out with him fiue or sixe of these feminines, and they say that they anoynt the secret places with a certaine composition that they haue, that when the wilde Eliphant doeth smell thereunto, they followe the feminines and cannot leaue them: when the hunts-men haue made prouision and the Eliphant is so entangled, they guide the feminines towards the Pallace which is called Tambell, and this Pallace hath a doore which doth open and shut with engines, before which doore there is a long streight way with trees on both the sides, which couereth the way in such wise as it is like darkenesse in a corner: the wilde Eliphant when he commeth to this way, thinketh that he is in the woods. At end of this darke way there is a great field, when the hunters haue gotten this praye, when they first come to this field, they send presently to giue knowledge thereof to the Citie, and with all speed there go out fiftie or sixtie men on horsebacke, and doe beset the fielde rounde about: in the great fielde then the females which are taught in this businesse goe directly to the mouth of the darke way, and when as the wilde Eliphant is entred in there, the hunters shoute and make a great noyse, as much as is possible, to make the wilde Eliphant enter in at the gate of that Pallace, which is then open, and as soone as he is in, the gate is shut without any noyse, and so the hunters with the female Eliphants and the wilde one are all in the Court together, and then within a small time the females withdraw themselues away one by one out of the Court, leauing the wilde Eliphant alone: [Sidenote: An excellent pastime of the Eliphants.] and when he perceiueth that he is left alone, he is so madde that for two or three houres to see him, it is the greatest pleasure in the world: he weepeth, hee flingeth, hee runneth, he iustleth, hee thrusteth vnder the places where the people stand to see him, thinking to kil some of them, but the posts and timber is so strong and great, that hee cannot hurt any body, yet hee oftentimes breaketh his teeth in the grates; at length when hee is weary and hath laboured his body that hee is all wet with sweat, then hee plucketh in his truncke into his mouth, and then hee throweth out so much water out of his belly, that he sprinckleth it ouer the heades of the lookers on, to the vttermost of them, although it bee very high: and then when they see him very weary, there goe certaine officers into the Court with long sharpe canes [Marginal note: These canes are like to them in Spain which they call Ioco de tore.] in their hands, and prick him that they make him to goe into one of the houses that is made alongst the Court for the same purpose: as there are many which are made long and narrow, and when the Eliphant is in, he cannot turne himself to go backe againe. And it is requisite that these men should be very wary and swift, for although their canes be long, yet the Eliphant would kill them if they were not swift to saue themselues: at length when they haue gotten him into one of those houses, they stand ouer him in a loft and get ropes vnder his belly and about his necke, and about his legges, and binde him fast, and so let him stand foure or fiue dayes, and giue him neither meate nor drinke. At the ende of these foure or fiue dayes, they vnloose him and put one of the females vnto him, and giue him meate and drinke, and in eight dayes he is become tame. In my. iudgement there is not a beast so intellectiue as are these Eliphants, nor of more vnderstanding in al the world: for he wil do all things that his keeper saith, so that he lacketh nothing but humaine speech.

It is reported that the greatest strength that the king of Pegu hath is in these Eliphants, for when they goe to battell, they set on their backes a Castle of wood bound thereto, with bands vnder their bellies: and in euery Castle foure men very commodiously set to fight with harqubushes, with bowes and arrowes, with darts and pikes, and other launcing weapons: and they say that the skinne of this Eliphant is so hard, that an harquebusse will not pierce it, vnlesse it bee in the eye, temples, or some other tender place of his body. [Sidenote: A goodly order in a barbarous people.] And besides this, they are of great strength, and haue a very excellent order in their battel, as I haue seene at their feastes which they make in the yeere, in which feastes the king maketh triumphes, which is a rare thing and worthy memorie, that in so barbarous a people should be such goodly orders as they haue in their armies, which be distinct in squares of Eliphants, of horsemen, of harquebushers and pikemen, that truly the number of men are infinite: but their armour and weapons are very nought and weake as well the one as the other: they haue very bad pikes, their swords are worse made, like long kniues without points, his harquebushes are most excellent, and alway in his warres he hath eightie thousand harquebushes, and the number of them encreaseth dayly. Because the king will haue them shoote every day at the Plancke, and so by continuall exercise they become most excellent shot: also hee hath great ordinance made of very good mettall; to conclude there is not a King on the earth that hath more power or strength then this king of Pegu, because hee hath twentie and sixe crowned kings at his commaunde. He can make in his campe a million and a halfe of men of warre in the fielde against his enemies. The state of his kingdome and maintenance of his army, is a thing incredible to consider, and the victuals that should maintaine such a number of people in the warres: but he that knoweth the nature and quality of that people, will easily beleeue it. [Sidenote: Eating of serpents.] I haue seene with mine eyes, that those people and souldiers haue eaten of all sorts of wild beastes that are on the earth, whether it bee very filthie or otherwise all serueth for their mouthes: yea, I haue seene them eate Scorpions and Serpents, also they feed of all kinde of herbes and grasse. So that if such a great armie want not water and salt, they will maintaine themselues a long time in a bush with rootes, flowers and leaues of trees, they cary rice with them for their voyage, and that serueth them in stead of comfits; it is so daintie vnto them. This king of Pegu hath not any army or power by sea, but in the land, for people, dominions, golde and siluer, he farre exceeds the power of the great Turke in treasure and strength. [Sidenote: The riches of the king of Pegu.] This king hath diuers Magasons full of treasure, as gold, and siluer, and euery day he encreaseth it more and more, and it is neuer diminished. Also hee is Lord of the Mines of Rubies, Safires and Spinels. Neere vnto his royall pallace there is an inestimable treasure whereof hee maketh no accompt, for that it standeth in such a place that euery one may see it, and the place where this treasure is, is a great Court walled round about with walles of stone, with two gates which stand open euery day. And within this place or Court are foure gilded houses couered with lead, and in euery one of these are certaine heathenish idoles of a very great valure. In the first house there is a stature of the image of a man of gold very great, and on his head a crowne of gold beset with most rare Rubies and Safires, and round about him are 4. litle children of gold. In the second house there is the stature of a man of siluer, that is set as it were sitting on heapes of money: whose stature in height, as hee sitteth, is so high, that his highnesse exceeds the height of any one roofe of an house; I measured his feete, and found that they were as long as all my body was in height, with a crowne on his head like to the first. And in the thirde house, there is a stature of brasse of the same bignesse, with a like crowne on his head. In the 4. and last house there is a stature of a man as big as the other, which is made of Gansa, which is the metall they make their money of, and this metall is made of copper and leade mingled together. This stature also hath a crowne on his head like the first: this treasure being of such a value as it is, standeth in an open place that euery man at his pleasure may go and see it: for the keepers therof neuer forbid any man the sight thereof. I say as I haue said before, that this king euery yere in his feastes triumpheth: and because it is worthy of the noting, I thinke it meet to write therof, which is as foloweth. [Sidenote: The great pompe of the king.] The king rideth on a triumphant cart or wagon all gilded, which is drawen by 16. goodly horses: and this cart is very high with a goodly canopy ouer it, behind the cart goe 20. of his Lords and nobles, with euery one a rope in his hand made fast to the cart for to hold it vpright that it fal not. The king sitteth in the middle of the cart; and vpon the same cart about the king stande 4. of his nobles most fauored of him, and before this cart wherein the king is goeth all his army as aforesaid, and in the middle of his army goeth all his nobilitie, round about the cart, that are in his dominions, a marueilous thing it is to see so many people, such riches and such good order in a people so barbarous as they be. This king of Pegu hath one principal wife which is kept in a Seralio, he hath 300. concubines, of whom it is reported that he hath 90. children. [Sidenote: The order of Iustice.] This king sitteth euery day in person to heare the suites of his subiects, but he nor they neuer speake one to another, but by supplications made in this order. [Sidenote: No difference of persons before the King in controuersies or in iustice.] The king sitteth vp aloft, in a great hall, on a tribunall seat, and lower vnder him sit all his Barons round about, then those that demaund audience enter into a great Court before the king, and there set them downe on the ground 40. paces distant from the kings person, and amongst those people there is no difference in matters of audience before the king, but all alike, and there they sit with their supplications in their hands, which are made of long leaues of a tree, these leaues are 3. quarters of a yard long, and two fingers broad, which are written with a sharpe iron made for that purpose, and in those leaues are their supplications written, and with their supplications, they haue in their hands a present or gift, according to the waightines of their matter. Then come the secretaries downe to read these supplications, taking them and reading them before the king, and if the king think it good to do to them that fauour or iustice that they demaund, then he commandeth to take the presents out of their hands: but if he thinke their demand be not iust or according to right, he commandeth them away without taking of their gifts or presents. In the Indies there is not any marchandise that is good to bring to Pegu, vnlesse it bee at some times by chance to bring Opium of Cambaia, and if he bring money he shall lose by it. Now the commodities that come from S. Tome are the onely marchandise for that place, which is the great quantity of cloth made, which they vse in Pegu: which cloth is made of bombast wouen and painted, so that the more that kinde of cloth is washed, the more liuelie they shewe their colours, which is a rare thing, and there is made such accompt of this kinde of cloth which is so great importance, that a small bale of it will cost a thousand or two thousand duckets. Also from S. Tome they layd great store of red yarne, of bombast died with a roote which they call Saia, as aforesayd, which colour will neuer out. With which marchandise euery yeere there goeth a great shippe from S. Tome to Pegu, of great importance, and they vsually depart from S. Tome to Pegu the 11. or 12. of September, and if she stay vntill the twelfth, it is a great hap if she returne not without making of her voiage. Their vse was to depart the sixt of September, and then they made sure voyages, and now because there is a great labour about that kind of cloth to bring it to perfection, and that it be well dried, as also the greedinesse of the Captaine that would made an extraordinary gaine of his fraight, thinking to haue the wind alwayes to serue their turne, they stay so long, that at sometimes the winde turneth. For in those parts the windes blow firmely for certaine times, with the which they goe to Pegu with the winde in poope, and if they arriue not there before the winde change, and get ground to anker, perforce they must returne backe againe: for that the gales of the winde blowe there for three or foure moneths together in one place with great force. But if they get the coast and anker there, then with great labour they may saue their voyage. Also there goeth another great shippe from Bengala euery yeere, laden with fine cloth of bombast of all sorts, which arriueth in the harbour of Pegu, when the ship that commeth from S. Tome departeth. The harbour where these two ships arriue is called Cosmin. From Malaca to Martauan, which is a port in Pegu, there come many small ships, and great, laden with pepper, Sandolo, Porcellan of China, Camfora, Bruneo and other marchandise. The ships that come from Mecca enter into the port of Pegu and Cirion, and those shippes bring cloth of Wooll, Scarlets, Veluets, Opium, and Chickinos, [Sidenote: The Chikinos are pieces of gold worth sterling 7. shillings.] by the which they lose, and they bring them because they haue no other thing that is good for Pegu: but they esteeme not the losse of them, for they make such great gaine of their commodities that they cary from thence out of that kingdome. Also the king of Assi his ships come thither into the same port laden with peper; from the coast of S. Tome of Bengala, out of the Sea of Bara to Pegu are three hundreth miles, and they go it vp the riuer in foure daies, with the encreasing water, or with the flood, to a City called Cosmin, and there they discharge their ships, whither the Customers of Pegu come to take the note and markes of all the goods of euery man, and take the charge of the goods on them, and conuey them to Pegu, into the kings house, wherein they make the custome of the marchandize. When the Customers haue taken the charge of the goods and put them into barks, the Retor of the City giueth licence to the Marchants to take barke, and goe vp to Pegu with their marchandize; and so three or foure of them take a barke and goe vp to Pegu in company. [Sidenote: Great rigour for the stealing of customes.] God deliuer euery man that hee giue not a wrong note, and entrie, or thinke to steale any custome: for if they do, for the least trifle that is, he is vtterly vndone, for the king doeth take it for a most great affront to bee deceiued of his custome: and therefore they make diligent searches, three times at the lading and vnlading of the goods, and at the taking of them a land. In Pegu this search they make when they goe out of the ship for Diamonds, Pearles, and fine cloth which taketh little roome: for because that all the iewels that come into Pegu, and are not found of that countrey, pay custome, but Rubies, Safyres, and Spinels pay no custome in nor out: because they are found growing in that Countrey. I haue spoken before, how that all Marchants that meane to goe thorow the Indies, must cary al manor of houshold stuffe with them which is necessary for a house, because that there is not any lodging nor Innes nor hostes, nor chamber roome in that Countrey, but the first thing a man doth when he commeth to that City is to hier a house, either by the yeere or by the moneth, or as he meanes to stay in those parts.

In Pegu their order is to hire their houses for sixe moneths. Nowe from Cosmin to the Citie of Pegu they goe in sixe houres with the flood, and if it be ebbing water, then they make fast their boate to the riuer side, and there tary vntil the water flow againe. [Sidenote: Description of the fruitfulnesse of that soyle.] It is a very commodious and pleasant voyage, hauing on both sides of the riuers many great vilages, which they call Cities: in the which hennes, pigeons, egges, milke, rice, and other things be very goode cheape. It is all plaine, and a goodly Countrey, and in eight dayes you may make your voyage vp to Macceo, distant from Pegu twelue miles, and there they discharge their goods, and lade them in Carts or waines drawen with oxen, and the Marchants are caried in a closet which they call Deling, [Sidenote: Deling is a small litter carried with men as is aforesaid.] in the which a man shall be very well accommodated, with cushions under his head, and couered for the defence of the Sunne and raine, and there he may sleep if he haue will thereunto: and his foure Falchines cary him running away, changing two at one time and two at another. The custome of Pegu and fraight thither, may amount vnto twentie or twentie two per cento, and 23. according as he hath more or lesse stolen from him that day they custome the goods. It is requisite that a man haue his eyes watchfull, and to be carefull, and to haue many friendes, for when they custome in the great hall of the king, there come many gentlemen accompanied with a number of their slaues, and these gentlemen haue no shame that their slaues rob strangers; whether it be cloth in shewing of it or any other thing, they laugh at it. And although the Marchants helpe one another to keepe watch, and looke to their goods, they cannot looke therto so narrowly but one or other will rob something, either more or lesse, according as their marchandise is more or lesse: and yet on this day there is a worse thing then this: although you haue set so many eyes to looke there for your benefit, that you escape vnrobbed of the slaues, a man cannot choose but that he must be robbed of the officers of the custome house. For paying the custome with the same goods oftentimes they take the best that you haue, and not by rate of euery sort as they ought to do, by which meanes a man payeth more then his dutie. At length when the goods be dispatched out of the custome house in this order, the Marchant causeth them to be caried to his house, and may do with them at his pleasure.

There are in Pegu 8. brokers of the kings, which are called Tareghe, who are bound to sell all the marchandize which come to Pegu, at the common or the currant price: then if the marchants wil sell their goods at that price, they sel them away, and the brokers haue two in the hundreth of euery sort of marchandise, and they are bound to make good the debts of those goods, because they be sold by their hands or meanes, and on their wordes, and oftentimes the marchant knoweth not to whom he giueth his goods, yet he cannot lose anything thereby, for that the broker is bound in any wise to pay him, and if the marchant sel his goods without the consent of the broker, yet neuerthelesse he must pay him two per cento, and be in danger of his money: [Sidenote: A lawe for Bankrupts.] but this is very seldom seene, because the wife, children, and slaues of the debtor are bound to the creditor, and when his time is expired and paiment not made, the creditor may take the debtor and cary him home to his house, and shut him vp in a Magasin, whereby presently he hath his money, and not being able to pay the creditor, he may take the wife, children, and slaues of the debtor and sel them, for so is the lawe of that kingdome. [Sidenote: Euery man may stampe what money he wil.] The currant money that is in this city, and throughout all this kingdom is called Gansa or Ganza, which is made of Copper and leade: It is not the money of the king, but euery man may stamp it that wil, because it hath his iust partition or value: but they make many of them false, by putting ouermuch lead into them, and those will not passe, neither will any take them. With this money Ganza, you may buy golde or siluer, Rubies and Muske, and other things. For there is no other money currant amongst them. And Golde, siluer and other marchandize are at one time dearer than another, as all other things be.

This Ganza goeth by weight of Byze, and this name of Byza goeth for the accompt of the weight, and commonly a Byza of a Ganza is worth (after our accompt) halfe a ducat, litle more or lesse: and albeit that Gold and siluer is more or lesse in price, yet the Byza neuer changeth: euery Byza maketh a hundreth Ganza of weight, and so the number of the money is Byza. [Sidenote: How a man may dispose himselfe for the trade in Pegu.] He that goeth to Pegu to buy Iewels, if he wil do well, it behoueth him to be a whole yere there to do his businesse. For if so be that he would return with the ship he came in, he cannot do any thing so conueniently for the breuitie of the time, because that when they custome their goods in Pegu that come from S. Tome in their ships, it is as it were about Christmas: and when they haue customed their goods, then must they sell them for their credits sake for a moneth or two: and then at the beginning of March the ships depart. The Marchants that come from S. Tome take for the paiment of their goods, gold and siluer, which is neuer wanting there. [Sidenote: Good instructions.] And 8. or 10. daies before their departure they are all satisfied: also they may haue Rubies in paiment, but they make no accompt of them: and they that will winter there for another yere, it is needfull that they be aduertized, that in the sale of their goods, they specifie in their bargaine, the terme of two or 3. moneths paiment, and that their paiment shal be in so many Ganza, and neither golde nor siluer: because that with the Ganza they may buy and sel euery thing with great aduantage. And how needfull is it to be aduertized, when they wil recouer their paiments, in what order they shal receiue their Ganza? Because he that is not experienced may do himselfe great wrong in the weight of the Gansa, as also in the falsenesse of them: in the weight he may be greatly deceiued, because that from place to place it doth rise and fall greatly: and therefore when any wil receiue money or make paiment, he must take a publique wayer of money, a day or two before he go about his businesse, and giue him in paiment for his labour two Byzaes a moneth, and for this he is bound to make good all your money, and to maintaine it for good, for that hee receiueth it and seales the bags with his scale: and when hee hath receiued any store, then hee causeth it to bee brought into the Magason of the Marchant, that is the owner of it.

That money is very weightie, for fortie Byza is a strong Porters burden; and also where the Marchant hath any payment to be made for those goods which he buyeth, the Common wayer of money that receiueth his money must make the payment thereof. So that by this meanes, the Marchant with the charges of two Byzes a moneth, receiueth and payeth out his money without losse or trouble. [Sidenote: The marchandizes that goe out of Pegu.] The Marchandizes that goe out of Pegu are Gold, Siluer, Rubies, Saphyres, Spinelles, great store of Beniamin, long peper, Leade, Lacca, rice, wine, some sugar, yet there might be great store of sugar made in the Countrey, for that they haue aboundance of Canes, but they giue them to Eliphants to eate, and the people consume great store of them for food, and many more doe they consume in vaine things, as these following. In that kingdome they spend many of these Sugar canes in making of houses and tents which they call Varely for their idoles, which they call Pagodes, whereof there are great aboundance, great and smal, and these houses are made in forme of little hilles, like to Sugar loaues or to Bells, and some of these houses are as high as a reasonable steeple, at the foote they are very large, some of them be in circuit a quarter of a mile. The saide houses within are full of earth, and walled round about with brickes and dirt in steade of lime, and without forme, from the top to the foote they make a couering for them with Sugar canes, and plaister it with lime all ouer, for otherwise they would bee spoyled, by the great aboundance of raine that falleth in those Countreys. [Sidenote: Idol houses couered with gold.] Also they consume about these Varely or idol houses great store of leafe-gold, for that they ouerlay all the tops of the houses with gold, and some of them are couered with golde from the top to the foote: in couering whereof there is great store of gold spent, for that euery 10. yeeres they new ouerlay them with gold, from the top to the foote, so that with this vanitie they spend great aboundance of golde. For euery 10. yeres the raine doth consume the gold from these houses. And by this meanes they make golde dearer in Pegu then it would bee, if they consumed not so much in this vanitie. Also it is a thing to bee noted in the buying of iewels in Pegu, that he that hath no knowledge shall haue as good iewels, and as good cheap, as he that hath bene practized there a long time, which is a good order, and it is in this wise. There are in Pegu foure men of good reputation, which are called Tareghe, or brokers of Iewels. These foure men haue all the Iewels or Rubies in their handes, and the Marchant that wil buy commeth to one of these Tareghe and telleth him, that he hath so much money to imploy in Rubies. [Sidenote: Rubies exceeding cheape in Pegu.] For through the hands of these foure men passe all the Rubies: for they haue such quantitie, that they knowe not what to doe with them, but sell them at most vile and base prices. When the Marchant hath broken his mind to one of these brokers or Tareghe, they cary him home to one of their Shops, although he hath no knowledge in Iewels: and when the Iewellers perceiue that hee will employ a good round summe, they will make a bargaine, and if not, they let him alone. The vse generally of this Citie is this: that when any Marchant hath bought any great quantitie of Rubies, and hath agreed for them, hee carieth them home to his house, let them be of what value they will, he shall haue space to looke on them and peruse them two or three dayes: and if he hath no knowledge in them, he shall alwayes haue many Marchants in that Citie that haue very good knowledge in Iewels; with whom he may alwayes conferre and take counsell, and may shew them vnto whom he will; and if he finde that hee hath not employed his money well, hee may returne his Iewels backe to them whom hee had them of, without any losse at all. Which thing is such a shame to the Tareghe to haue his Iewels returned, that he had rather beare a blow on the face then that it should be thought that he solde them so deere to haue them returned. [Sidenote: An honest care of heathen people.] For these men haue alwayes great care that they afford good peniworths, especially to those that haue no knowledge. This they doe, because they woulde not loose their credite: and when those Marchants that haue knowledge in Iewels buy any, if they buy them deere, it is their own faults and not the brokers: yet it is good to haue knowledge in Iewels, by reason that it may somewhat ease the price. [Sidenote: Bargaines made with the nipping of fingers vnder a cloth.] There is also a very good order which they haue in buying of Iewels, which is this; There are many Marchants that stand by at the making of the bargaine, and because they shall not vnderstand howe the Iewels be solde, the Broker and the Marchants haue their hands vnder a cloth, and by touching of fingers and nipping the ioynts they know what is done, what is bidden, and what is asked. So that the standers by knowe not what is demaunded for them, although it be for a thousand or 10. thousand duckets. For euery ioynt and euery finger hath his signification. For if the Marchants that stande by should vnderstand the bargaine, it would breede great controuersie amongst them. And at my being in Pegu in the moneth of August, in Anno 1569, hauing gotten well by my endeuour, I was desirous to see mine owne Countrey, and I thought it good to goe by the way of S. Tome, but then I should tary vntil March.

In which iourney I was counsailed, yea, and fully resolued to go by the way of Bengala, with a shippe there ready to depart for that voyage. And then wee departed from Pegu to Chatigan a great harbour or port, from whence there goe smal ships to Cochin, before the fleete depart for Portugall, in which ships I was fully determined to goe to Lisbon, and so to Venice. [Sidenote: This Touffon is an extraordinary storme at Sea.] When I had thus resolued my selfe, I went a boord of the shippe of Bengala, at which time it was the yeere of Touffon: concerning which Touffon ye are to vnderstand, that in the East Indies often times, there are not stormes as in other countreys; but euery 10. or 12. yeeres there are such tempests and stormes, that it is a thing incredible, but to those that haue seene it, neither do they know certainly what yeere they wil come.

[Sidenote: The Touffon commeth but euery 10. or 12. yeeres.] Vnfortunate are they that are at sea in that yere and time of the Touffon, because few there are that escape that danger. In this yere it was our chance to be at sea with the like storme, but it happened well vnto vs, for that our ship was newly ouer-planked, and had not any thing in her saue victuall and balasts, Siluer and golde, which from Pegu they cary to Bengala, and no other kinde of Marchandise. This Touffon or cruel storme endured three dayes and three nights: in which time it caried away our sailes, yards, and rudder; and because the shippe laboured in the Sea, wee cut our mast ouer boord: which when we had done she laboured a great deale more then before, in such wise, that she was almost full with water that came ouer the highest part of her and so went downe: and for the space of three dayes and three nights sixtie men did nothing but hale water out of her in this wise, twentie men in one place, and twentie men in another place, and twentie in a thirde place: and for all this storme, the shippe was so good, that shee tooke not one iot of water below through her sides, but all ran downe through the hatches, so that those sixtie men did nothing but cast the Sea into the Sea.

And thus driuing too and fro as the winde and Sea would, we were in a darke night about foure of the clocke cast on a sholde: yet when it was day, we could neither see land on one side nor other, and knew not where we were: And as it pleased the diuine power, there came a great waue of the Sea, which draue vs beyonde the should. [Sidenote: A manifest token of the ebbing and flowing in those Countries.] And when wee felt the shippe aflote, we rose vp as men reuiued, because the Sea was calme and smooth water, and then sounding we found twelue fadome water, and within a while after wee had but sixe fadome, and then presently we came to anker with a small anker that was left vs at the sterne, for all our other were lost in the storme: and by and by the shippe stroke a ground, and then we did prop her that she should not ouerthrow.

When it was day the shippe was all dry, and wee found her a good mile from the Sea on drie land. [Sidenote: This Island is called Sondiua.] This Touffon being ended, we discouered an Island not farre from vs, and we went from the shippe on the sands to see what Island it was: and wee found it a place inhabited, and, to my iudgement, the fertilest Island in all the world, the which is diuided into two parts by a chanell which passeth betweene it, and with great trouble we brought our ship into the same chanel, which parteth the Island at flowing water, and there we determined to stay 40. dayes to refresh vs. And when the people of the Island saw the ship, and that we were comming a land: presently they made a place of bazar or a market, with shops right ouer against the ship with all maner of prouision of victuals to eate, which they brought downe in great abundance, and sold it so good cheape, that we were amazed at the cheapenesse thereof. I bought many salted kine there, for the prouision of the ship, for halfe a Larine a piece, which Larine may be 12. shillings sixe pence, being very good and fat; and 4. wilde hogges ready dressed for a Larine, great fat hennes for a Bizze a piece, which is at the most a pennie: and the people told vs that we were deceiued the halfe of our money, because we bought things so deare. Also a sacke of fine rice for a thing of nothing, and consequently all other things for humaine sustenance were there in such aboundance, that it is a thing incredible but to them that haue seene it. [Sidenote: Sondiua is the fruitfullest Countrey in al the world.] This Island is called Sondiua belonging to the kingdome of Bengala, distant 120. miles from Chatigan, to which place wee were bound. The people are Moores, and the king a very good man of a Moore king, for if he had bin a tyrant as others be, he might haue robbed vs of all, because the Portugall captaine of Chatigan was in armes against the Retor of that place, and euery day there were some slaine, at which newes we rested there with no smal feare, keeping good watch and ward aboord euery night as the vse is, but the gouernour of the towne did comfort vs, and bad vs that we should feare nothing, but that we should repose our selues securely without any danger, although the Portugales of Chatigan had slaine the gouernour of that City, and said that we were not culpable in that fact: and moreouer he did vs euery day what pleasure he could, which was a thing contrary to our expectations considering that they and the people of Chatigan were both subiects to one king. [Sidenote: Chatigan is a port in Bengala, whither the Portugales go with their ships.] We departed from Sondiua, and came to Chatigan the great port of Bengala, at the same time when the Portugales had made peace and taken a truce with the gouernours of the towne, with this condition that the chiefe Captaine of the Portugales with his ship should depart without any lading: for there were then at that time 18. ships of Portugales great and small. This Captaine being a Gentleman and of good courage, was notwithstanding contented to depart to his greatest hinderance, rather than hee would seeke to hinder so many of his friends as were there, as also because the time of the yeere was spent to go to the Indies. The night before he departed, euery ship that had any lading therein, put it aboord of the Captaine to helpe to ease his charge and to recompense his courtesies. [Sidenote: The King of Rachim, or Aracam, neighbour to Bengala.] In this time there came a messenger from the king of Rachim to this Portugal Captaine, who saide in the behalfe of his king, that hee had heard of the courage and valure of him, desiring him gently that he would vouchsafe to come with the ship into his port, and comming thither he should be very wel intreated. This Portugal went thither and was very well satisfied of this King.

This King of Rachim hath his seate in the middle coast betweene Bengala and Pegu, and the greatest enemie he hath is the king of Pegu: which king of Pegu deuiseth night and day how to make this king of Rachim his subiect, but by no meanes hee is able to doe it: because the king of Pegu hath no power nor armie by Sea. And this king of Rachim [Marginal note: Or, Aracam.] may arme two hundreth Galleyes or Fusts by Sea, and by land he hath certaine sluses with the which when the king of Pegu pretendeth any harme towards him, hee may at his pleasure drowne a great part of the Countrey. So that by this meanes hee cutteth off the way whereby the king of Pegu should come with his power to hurt him.

[Sidenote: The commodities that goe from Chatigan to the Indies.] From the great port of Chatigan they cary for the Indies great store of rice, very great quantitie of Bombast cloth of euery sort, Suger, corne, and money, with other marchandize. And by reason of the warres in Chatigan, the Portugall ships taried there so long, that they arriued not at Cochin so soone as they were wont to doe other yeeres. For which cause the fleete that was at Cochin [Marginal note: The Portugal ships depart toward Portugall out of the harbor of Cochin.] was departed for Portugal before they arriued there, and I being in one of the small shippes before the fleete, in discouering of Cochin, we also discouered the last shippe of the Fleete that went from Cochin to Portugall, where shee made saile, for which I was marueilously discomforted, because that all the yeere following, there was no going for Portugale, and when we arriued at Cochin I was fully determined to goe for Venice by the way of Ormus, [Sidenote: Goa was besieged.] and at that time the Citie of Goa was besieged by the people of Dialcan, but the Citizens forced not this assault, because they supposed that it would not continue long. For all this I embarked my selfe in a Galley that went for Goa, meaning there to shippe my selfe for Ormus: but when we came to Goa, the Viceroy would not suffer any Portugal to depart, by reason of the warres. And being in Goa but a small time, I fell sicke of an infirmitie that helde mee foure moneths: which with phisicke and diet cost me eight hundreth duckets, and there I was constrained to sell a smal quantitie of Rubies to sustaine my neede: and I solde that for fiue hundreth duckets, that was worth a thousand. And when I beganne to waxe well of my disease, I had but little of that money left, euery thing was so scarse: For euery chicken (and yet not good) cost mee seuen or eight Liuers, which is sixe shillings, or sixe shillings eight pence. Beside this great charges, the Apothecaries with their medicines were no small charge to me. At the ende of sixe moneths they raised the siege, and then I beganne to worke, for Iewels were risen in their prices: for whereas before I sold a few of refused Rubies, I determined then to sell the rest of all my Iewels that I had there, and to make an other voyage to Pegu. [Sidenote: Opium a good commoditie in Pegu.] And for because that at my departure from Pegu, Opium was in great request, I went then to Cambaya to imploy a good round summe of money in Opium, and there I bought 60. percels of Opium, which cost me two thousand and a hundreth duckets, euery ducket at foure shillings two pence. Moreouer I bought three bales of Bombast cloth, which cost me eight hundred duckats, which was a good commoditie for Pegu: when I had bought these things, the Viceroy commanded that the custome of the Opium should be paide in Goa, and paying custome there I might cary it whither I would. I shipped my 3. bales of cloth at Chaul in a shippe that went for Cochin, and I went to Goa to pay the aforesaid custome for my Opium, and from Goa I departed to Cochin in a ship that was for the voyage of Pegu, and went to winter then at S. Tome. When I come to Cochin, I vnderstood that the ship that had my three bales of cloth was cast away and lost, so that I lost my 800. Serafins or duckats: and departing from Cochin to goe for S. Tome, in casting about for the Island of Zeilan the Pilote was deceiued, for that the Cape of the Island of Zeilan lieth farre out into the sea, and the Pilot thinking that he might haue passed hard aboord the Cape, and paying roomer in the night; when it was morning we were farre within the Cape, and past all remedy to go out, by reason the winds blew so fiercely against vs. So that by this meanes we lost our voyage for that yere, and we went to Manar with the ship to winter there, the ship hauing lost her mastes, and with great dilligence we hardly saued her, with great losses to the Captaine of the ship, because he was forced to fraight another ship in S. Tome for Pegu with great losses and interest, and I with my friends agreed together in Manar to take a bark to cary vs to S. Tome; which thing we did with al the rest of the marchants; and arriuing at S. Tome I had news through or by the way of Bengala, that in Pegu Opium was very deare, and I knew that in S. Tome there was no Opium but mine to go for Pegu that yere, so that I was holden of al the marchants there to be very rich: and so it would haue proued, if my aduerse fortune had not bin contrary to my hope, which was this. At that time there went a great ship from Cambaya, to the king of Assi, with great quantitie of Opium, and there to lade peper: in which voyage there came such a storme, that the ship was forced with wether to goe roomer 800. miles, and by this meanes came to Pegu, whereas they arriued a day before mee; so that Opium which was before very deare, was now at a base price: so that which was sold for fiftie Bizze before, was solde for 2. Bizze and an halfe, there was such quantitie came in that ship; so that I was glad to stay two yeres in Pegu vnlesse I would haue giuen away my commoditie: and at the end of two yeres of my 2100. duckets which I bestowed in Cambaya, I made but a thousand duckets. Then I departed againe from Pegu to goe for the Indies for Chaul, and from Chaul to Cochin, and from Cochin to Pegu. Once more I lost occasion to make me riche, for whereas I might haue brought good store of Opium againe, I brought but a little, being fearefull of my other voyage before. In this small quantitie I made good profite. And now againe I determined to go for my Countrey, and departing from Pegu, I tarried and wintered in Cochin, and then I left the Indies and came for Ormus.

I thinke it very necessary before I ende my voyage, to reason somewhat, and to shewe what fruits the Indies do yeeld and bring forth. First, In the Indies and other East parts of India there is Peper and ginger, which groweth in all parts of India. And in some parts of the Indies, the greatest quantitie of peper groweth amongst wilde bushes, without any maner of labour: sauing, that when it is ripe they goe and gather it. The tree that the peper groweth on is like to our Iuie, which runneth vp to the tops of trees wheresoeuer it groweth: and if it should not take holde of some tree, it would lie flat and rot on the ground. This peper tree hath his floure and berry like in all parts to our Iuie berry, and those berries be graines of peper: so that when they gather them they be greene, and then they lay them in the Sunne, and they become blacke.

The Ginger groweth in this wise: the land is tilled and sowen, and the herbe is like to Panizzo, and the roote is the ginger. These two spices grow in diuers places.

The Cloues come all from the Moluccas, which Moluccas are two Islands, not very great, and the tree that they grow on is like to our Lawrell tree.

The Nutmegs and Maces, which grow both together, are brought from the Island of Banda, whose tree is like to our walnut tree, but not so big.

All the good white Sandol is brought from the Island of Timor. Canfora being compound commeth all from China, and all that which groweth in canes commeth from Borneo, and I thinke that this Canfora commeth not into these parts: for that in India they consume great store, and that is very deare. The good Lignum Aloes commeth from Cauchinchina.

The Beniamin commeth from the kingdome of Assi and Sion.

Long pepper groweth in Bengala, Pegu, and Iaua.

Muske [Marginal note: This Muske the Iewes doe counterfeit and take out halfe the good muske and beat the flesh of an asse and put in the roome of it.] commeth from Tartaria, which they make in this order, as by good information I haue bene told. There is a certaine beast in Tartaria, which is wilde and as big as a wolfe, which beast they take aliue, and beat him to death with small staues that his blood may be spread through his whole body, then they cut it in pieces and take out all the bones, and beat the flesh with the blood in a morter very smal, and dry it, and make purses to put it in of the skin, and these be the cods of muske.

Truely I know not whereof the Amber is made, and there are diuers opinions of it, but this is most certaine, it is cast out of the Sea, and throwne on land, and found vpon the sea bankes.

The Rubies, Saphyres, and the Spinels be gotten in the kingdome of Pegu. The Diamants come from diuers places; and I know but three sorts of them. That sort of Diamants that is called Chiappe, commeth from Bezeneger. Those that be pointed naturally come from the land of Delly, and from Iaua, but the Diamants of Iaua are more waightie then the other. I could neuer vnderstand from whence they that are called Balassi come. [Sidenote: The Balassi grow in Zeilan.]

Pearles they fish in diuers places, as before in this booke is showne.

From Cambaza commeth the Spodiom which congeleth in certaine canes, whereof I found many in Pegu, when I made my house there, because that (as I haue sayd before) they make their houses there of wouen canes like to mats. From Chaul they trade alongst the coast of Melinde in Ethiopia,

[Marginal note: On the coast of Melynde in Ethiopia, in the land of Cafraria, the great trade that the Portugals haue.] within the land of Cafraria: on that coast are many good harbors kept by the Moores. Thither the Portugals bring a kinde of Bombast cloth of a low price, and great store of Paternosters or beads made of paltrie glasse, which they make in Chaul according to the vse of the Countrey: and from thence they cary Elephants teeth for India, slaues called Cafari, and some Amber and Gold. On this coast the king of Portugall hath his castle called Mozambique, which is of as great importance as any castle that hee hath in all his Indies vnder his protection, and the Captaine of this castle hath certaine voyages to this Cafraria, to which places no Marchants may goe, but by the Agent of this Captaine: [Sidenote: Buying and selling without words one to another.] and they vse to goe in small shippes, and trade with the Cafars, and their trade in buying and selling is without any speach one to the other. In this wise the Portugals bring their goods by litle and litle alongst the Sea coast, and lay them downe: and so depart, and the Cafar Marchants come and see the goods, and there they put downe as much gold as they thinke the goods are worth, and so goe their way and leaue their golde and the goods together, then commeth the Portugal, and finding the golde to his content, hee taketh it and goeth his way into his ship, and then commeth the Cafar, and taketh the goods and carieth them away: and if he finde the golde there still, it is a signe that the Portugals are not contented, and if the Cafar thinke he hath put too little, he addeth more, as he thinketh the thing is worth: and the Portugales must not stand with them too strickt; for if they doe, then they will haue no more trade with them: For they disdaine to be refused, when they thinke that they haue offered ynough, for they bee a peeuish people, and haue dealt so of a long time: [Sidenote: Golden trades that the Portugals haue.] and by this trade the Portugals change their commodities into gold, and cary it to the Castle of Mozambique, which is an Island not farre distant from the firme land of Cafraria on the coast of Ethiopia, and is distant from India 2800. miles. Nowe to returne to my voyage, when I came to Ormus, I found there Master Francis Berettin of Venice, and we fraighted a bark together to goe for Basora for 70. duckets, and with vs there went other Marchants, which did ease our fraight, and very commodiously wee came to Basora and there we stayed 40. dayes for prouiding a Carouan of barks to go to Babylon, because they vse not to goe two or 3. barkes at once, but 25. or 30. because in the night they cannot go, but must make them fast to the banks of the riuer, and then we must make a very good and strong guard, and be wel prouided of armor, for respect and safegard of our goods, because the number of theeues is great that come to spoile and rob the marchants. And when we depart for Babylon we goe a litle with our saile, and the voyage is 38. or 40. dayes long, but we were 50. dayes on it. When we came to Babylon we stayed there 4.

moneths, vntill the Carouan was ready to go ouer the wildernes, or desert for Alepo; in this city we were 6. Marchants that accompanied together, fiue Venetians and a Portugal: whose names were as followeth, Messer Florinasa with one of his kinsmen, Messer Andrea de Pola, the Portugal and M. Francis Berettin and I, and so wee furnished our selues with victuals and beanes for our horses for 40. dayes; [Marginal note: An order how to prouide to goe ouer the Desert from Babylon to Alepo.] and wee bought horses and mules, for that they bee very good cheape there, I my selfe bought a horse there for 11. akens, and solde him after in Alepo for 30. duckets. Also we bought a Tent which did vs very great pleasure: we had also amongst vs 32. Camels laden with marchandise: for the which we paid 2. duckets for euery camels lading, and for euery 10. camels they made 11, for so is their vse and custome. We take also with vs 3. men to serue vs in the voyage, which are vsed to goe in those voyages for fiue D d. a man, and are bound to serue vs to Alepo: so that we passed very well without any trouble: when the camels cried out to rest, our pauilion was the first that was erected. The Carouan maketh but small iourneis about 20. miles a day, and they set forwards euery morning before day two houres, and about two in the afternoone they sit downe. We had great good hap in our voyage, for that it rained: For which cause we neuer wanted water, but euery day found good water, so that we could not take any hurt for want of water. Yet we caried a camel laden alwayes with water for euery good respect that might chance in the desert, so that wee had no want neither of one thing, nor other that was to bee had in the countrey. For wee came very well furnished of euery thing, and euery day we eat fresh mutton, because there came many shepheards with vs with their flocks, who kept those sheepe that we bought in Babylon, and euery marchant marked his sheepe with his owne marke, and we gaue the shepheards a Medin, which is two pence of our money for the keeping and feeding our sheep on the way and for killing of them. And beside the Medin they haue the heads, the skinnes, and the intrals of euery sheepe they kil. We sixe bought 20. sheepe, and when we came to Alepo we had 7. aliue of them. And in the Carouan they vse this order, that the marchants doe lende flesh one to another, because they will not cary raw flesh with them, but pleasure one another by lending one one day and another another day.

[Sidenote: 36. Dayes iourney ouer the wildernes.] From Babylon to Alepo is 40. dayes iourney, of the which they make 36. dayes ouer the wildernes, in which 36. dayes they neither see house, trees nor people that inhabite it, but onely a plaine, and no signe of any way in the world. The Pilots goe before, and the Carouan followeth after. And when they sit downe all the Carouan vnladeth and sitteth downe, for they know the stations where the wells are. I say, in 36. dayes we pass ouer the wildernesse. For when wee depart from Babylon two dayes we passe by villages inhabited vntil we haue passed the riuer Euphrates. And then within two dayes of Alepo we haue villages inhabited. [Sidenote: An order how to prouide for the going to Ierusalem.] In this Carouan there goeth alway a Captaine that doth Iustice vnto all men: and euery night they keepe watch about the Carouan, and comming to Alepo we went to Tripoli, whereas Master Florin, and Master Andrea Polo, and I with a Frier, went and hired a barke to goe with vs to Ierusalem. Departing from Tripolie, we arriued at Iaffa: from which place in a day and a halfe we went to Ierusalem, and we gaue order to our barke to tary for vs vntill our returne. [Sidenote: The author returned to Venice 1581.] Wee stayed in Ierusalem 14. dayes, to visite those holy places: from whence we returned to Iaffa, and from Iaffa to Tripolie, and there wee shipped our selues in a ship of Venice called the Bagazzana: And by the helpe of the deuine power, we arriued safely in Venice the fift of Nouember 1581. If there be any that hath any desire to goe into those partes of India, let him not be astonied at the troubles that I haue passed: because I was intangled in many things: for that I went very poore from Venice with 1200. duckets imployed in marchandize, and when I came to Tripolie, I fell sicke in the house of Master Regaly Oratio, and this man sent away my goods with a small Carouan that went from Tripolie to Alepo, and the Carouan was robd, and all my goods lost sauing foure chests of glasses which cost me 200. duckets, of which glasses I found many broken: because the theeues thinking it had bene other marchandize, brake them vp, and seeing they were glasses they let them all alone. And with this onely stocke I aduentured to goe into the Indies: And thus with change and rechange, and by diligence in my voyage, God did blesse and helpe mee, so that I got a good stocke. I will not be vnmindfull to put them in remembrance, that haue a desire to goe into those parts, how they shall keepe their goods, and giue them to their heires at the time of their death, [Marginal note: A very good order that they haue in those Countreys for the recouering of the goods of the dead.] and howe this may be done very securely. In all the cities that the Portugales haue in the Indies, there is a house called the schoole of Sancta misericordia comissaria: the gouernours whereof, if you giue them for their paines, will take a coppy of your will and Testament, which you must alwayes cary about you; and chiefly when you go into the Indies. In the countrey of the Moores and Gentiles, in those voyages alwayes there goeth a Captaine to administer Iustice to all Christians of the Portugales. Also this captaine hath authoritie to recouer the goods of those Marchants that by chance die in those voyages, and they that haue not made their Wills and registred them in the aforesayde schooles, the Captaines wil consume their goods in such wise, that litle or nothing will be left for their heires and friends. Also there goeth in these same voyages some marchants that are commissaries of the schoole of Sancta misericordia, that if any Marchant die and haue his Will made, and hath giuen order that the schoole of Misericordia shall haue his goods and sell them, then they sende the money by exchange to the schoole of Misericordia in Lisbone, with that copie of his Testament, then from Lisbon they giue intelligence thereof, into what part of Christendome soeuer it be, and the heires of such a one comming thither, with testimoniall that they be heires, they shall receiue there the value of his goods: in such wise that they shall not loose any thing. But they that die in the kingdome of Pegu loose the thirde part of their goods by antient custome of the Countrey, that if any Christian dieth in the kingdome of Pegu, the king and his officers rest heires of a thirde of his goods, and there hath neuer bene any deceit or fraude vsed in this matter. I haue knowen many rich men that haue dwelled in Pegu, and in their age they haue desired to go into their owne Countrey to die there, and haue departed with al their goods and substance without let or troubles.

[Sidenote: Order of apparel in Pegu.] In Pegu the fashion of their apparel is all one, as well the noble man as the simple: the onely difference is in the finenes of the cloth, which is cloth of Bombast one finer then another, and they weare their apparell in this wise: First a white Bombast cloth which serueth for a shirt, then they gird another painted bombast cloth of foureteene brases, which they binde vp betwixt their legges, and on their heads they weare a small tock of three braces, made in guize of a myter, and some goe without tocks, and cary (as it were) a hiue on their heades, which doeth not passe the lower part of his eare, when it is lifted vp: they goe all bare footed, but the Noble men neuer goe on foote, but are caried by men in a seate with great reputation, with a hat made of the leaues of a tree to keepe him from the raine and Sunne, or otherwise they ride on horsebacke with their feete bare in the stirops. [Sidenote: The order of the womens apparel in Pegu.] All sorts of women whatsoeuer they be, weare a smocke downe to the girdle, and from the girdle downewards to the foote they weare a cloth of three brases, open before; so straite that they cannot goe, but they must shewe their secret as it were aloft, and in their going they faine to hide it with their hand, but they cannot by reason of the straitnes of their cloth. They say that this vse was inuented by a Queene to be an occasion that the sight thereof might remoue from men the vices against nature, which they are greatly giuen vnto; which sight should cause them to regard women the more. Also the women goe bare footed, their armes laden with hoopes of golde and Iewels: And their fingers full of precious rings, with their haire rolled vp about their heads. Many of them weare a cloth about their shoulders instead of a cloake.

Now to finish that which I haue begunne to write, I say, that those parts of the Indies are very good, because that a man that hath litle, shall make a great deale thereof; alwayes they must gouerne themselues that they be taken for honest men. For why? to such there shal neuer want helpe to doe wel, but he that is vicious, let him tary at home and not go thither, because he shall alwayes be a beggar, and die a poore man.

* * * * *

The money and measures of Babylon, Balsara, and the Indies, with the customes, &c. written from Aleppo in Syria, An. 1584. by M. Will. Barret.

BABYLON:

The weight, measure, and money currant there, and the customes of marchandize.

A Mana of Babylon is of Aleppo 1 roue 5 ounces and a halfe: and 68 manas and three seuenth parts, make a quintall of Aleppo, which is 494 li. 8 ounces of London: and 100 manas is a quintall of Babylon, which maketh in Aleppo 146 roues, and of London 722 li. and so much is the sayd quintall: but the marchants accord is by so much the mana, and in the sayd place they bate the tare in all sorts of commodities, according to the order of Aleppo touching the tare.

The measure of Babylon is greater then that of Aleppo 21 in the 100. For bringing 100 pikes of any measurable ware from Aleppo thither, there is found but 82 pikes in Babylon, so that the 100 pikes of Babylon is of Aleppo 121 pikes, very litle lesse.

The currant mony of Babylon are Saies, which Say is 5 medines, as in Aleppo, and 40 medines being 8 Saies make a duckat currant, and 47 medines passe in value as the duckat of gold of Venice, and the dollars of the best sort are worth 33 medines. The roials of plate are sold by the 100 drams at prise, according as they be in request: but amongst the marchants they bargaine by the 100 metrals, which are 150 drams of Aleppo, which 150 drams are 135 single roials of plate: but in the mint or castle, they take them by the 100 drams, which is 90 roials of plate, and those of the mint giue 5 medines lesse in each 100 drams then they are woorth to be sold among the marchants, and make paiment at the terme of 40 dayes in Sayes.

The custome in Babylon, as wel inward as outward, is in this maner: Small wares at 6 per 100, Coral and amber at 5 and a halfe per 100, Venice cloth, English cloth, Kersies, Mockairs, Chamblets, Silks, Veluets, Damasks, Sattins and such like at 5 per 100: and they rate the goods without reason as they lust themselues. The Toafo, Boabo, and other exactions 6 medines per bale, all which they pay presently in ready mony, according to the custome and vse of the emperor.

To the Ermin of the mint the ordinarie vse is to giue 30 Saies in curtesie, otherwise he would by authoritie of his office come aboord, and for despight make such search in the barke, that he would turne all things topsie teruie.

BALSARA:

The weight, measure, and money in the citie of Balsara.

A Mana of Balsara answereth 5 roues 2 ounces and a halfe of Aleppo weight, and 19 manas and one 4 part of Balsara, answereth the quintall of Aleppo, which is 494 roues, 8 ounces English, and 20 manas is the quintall of Balsara, which is 104 Alepine, and of London 514 li. 8. ounces, and so much is the sayd quintall, but the marchants bargaine at so much the mana or wolsene (which is all one) and they abate the tare in euery mana, as the sort of spice is, and the order taken therefore in that place.

The measure of Balsara is called a pike, which is iust as the measure of Babylon, to say, 100 pikes of Balsara make of Aleppo 121 pikes, vt supra in the rate of Babylon.

The currant mony of Balsara is as foloweth. There is a sort of flusses of copper called Estiui, whereof 12 make a mamedine, which is the value of one medine Aleppine, the said mamedine is of siluer, hauing the Moresco stampe on both sides, and two of these make a danine, which is 2 medines Aleppine.

The said danine is of siluer, hauing the Turkesco stampe on both sides, and 2 and a halfe of these make a Saie, which is in value as the Saie of Aleppo.

The said Saie is of the similitude and stampe of Aleppo, being (as appeares) 60 estiues. Also one Say and 20 estiues make a larine, which is of Aleppo money 6 medines and a halfe.

The sayd larine is a strange piece of money, not being round as all other currant money in Christianitie, but is a small rod of siluer of the greatnesse of the pen of a goose feather, wherewith we vse to write, and in length about one eight part thereof, which is wrested, so that the two ends meet at the iust halfe part, and in the head thereof is a stampe Turkesco, and these be the best currant money in all the Indias, and 6 of these larines make a duckat, which is 40 medines or eight Saies of Aleppo.

The duckat of gold is woorth there 7 larines, and one danine, which is of Aleppo money 48 medines and a halfe.

The Venetian money is worth larines 88 per hundred meticals which is 150 drams of Aleppo, vt supra.

The roials of plate are worth 88 larines by the 100 meticals, and albeit among the marchants they sel by the 100 meticals, yet in the mint or castle, they sel by the 100 drams, hauing there lesse then the worth 5 medines in each hundred drams, and haue their paiment in 40 dayes made them in Saies or larines.

The custome of the said places, aswell inward as outward, are alike of all sorts of goods, to say 6 by the 100, and Toafo, Boabo, and scriuan medines 6 by the bale inward and outward, to say, 3 inward, and as much outward: but whoso leaueth his goods in the custome house paieth nothing, where otherwise at the taking thereof away, he should pay 3 med. by the bale, and of the said goods there is no other duty to pay, and this commeth to passe when the customers esteeme the goods too high. For in such a case they may be driuen to take so much commoditie as the custome amounteth to, and not to pay them in money, for such is the order from the Grand Signior.

Hauing paid the custome, it behoueth to haue a quittance or cocket sealed and firmed with the customers hand, in confirmation of the dispatch and clearing, and before departure thence, to cause the sayd customer to cause search to be made, to the end that at the voiages returne there be no cauilation made, as it oftentimes happeneth.

Note that 100 meticals of Balsara weigh 17 ounces and a halfe sottile Venetian, and of Aleppo drams 150, vt supra.

The fraight of the barkes from Ormuz to Balsara, I would say from Balsara to Ormuz, they pay according to the greatnesse thereof. To say, for cariage of 10 cares 180 larines, those of 15 cares 270 larines, those of 20 cares 360 larines, those of 30 cares 540 larines. Note that a cara is 4 quintals of Balsara. They pay also to the pilot of the bark for his owne cariage one care, and to all the rest of the mariners amongst them 3. cares fraight, which is in the whole 4 cares, and paying the abouesayd prises and fraights, they are at no charges of victuals with them, but it is requisite that the same be declared in the charter partie, with the condition that they lade not aboord one rotilo more then the fraight, vnder paines that finding more in Ormuz, it is forfeit, and besides that to pay the fraight of that which they haue laden.

And in this accord it behoueth to deale warilie, and in the presence of the Ermin or some other honest man (whereof there are but few) for they are the worst people in all Arabia. And this diligence must be put in execution, to the end the barks may not be ouerladen, because they are to passe many sands betwixt Balsara and Ormuz.

ORMVZ:

The weight, measure, and money currant in the kingdom of Ormuz:

Spices and drugs they weigh by the bar, and of euery sort of goods the weight is different. To say, of some drugs 3 quintals, and 3 erubi or roues, and other some 4 quintals 25 rotiloes, and yet both is called a barre, which barre, as well as great as litle, is 20 frasoli, and euery frasoll is 10 manas, and euery mana 23 chiansi, and euery chianso 10 meticals and a halfe. [Sidenote: What a rotilo is.] Note that euery quintall maketh 4 erubi or roues, and euery roue 32 rotiloes, and euery rotilo 16 ounces, and euery ounce 7 meticals, so that the quintall commeth to be 128 rotiloes, which is Aleppine 26 rotiloes and one third part, which is 132 li. English weight. And contrarywise the quintal of Aleppo (which is 494 rotiloes 8 ounces English) maketh 477 rotiloes and a halfe of Ormuz, which is 3 quintals 2 roues, 29 rotiloes and a halfe.

Note that there are bars of diuers weights, vt supra, of which they bargaine simply, according to the sort of commoditie, but if they bargaine of the great barre, the same is 7 quintals and 24 rotiloes, which is 958 li. 9 ounces of London weight, and of Aleppo 193 rotiloes and a halfe.

Touching the money of Ormuz, they bargaine in marchandize at so many leches by the barre, which lech is 100 Asaries, and maketh larines 100 and a halfe, which maketh pardaos 38, and larines one halfe, at larines 5 by the pardao. One asarie is sadines 10, and euery sadine is 100. danarie.

The larine is worth 5 sadines and one fourth part, so that the sadine is worth of Aleppo mony 1 medine and 1 fourth part, and the larine as in Balsara worth of Aleppo mony 6 medines and a half.

The pardao is 5 larines of Balsara.

There is also stamped in Ormuz a seraphine of gold, which is litle and round, and is worth 24 sadines, which maketh 30 medines of Aleppo.

The Venetian mony is worth in Ormuz larines 88 per 100 meticals, and the roials are worth larines 86 lesse one sadine, which is euery thousand meticals, 382 asures: but those that will not sel them, vse to melt them, and make them so many larines in the king of Ormuz his mint, whereby they cleare 2 per 100, and somewhat more: and this they doe because neither Venetian money nor roials run as currant in Ormuz, per aduise.

The measure of Ormuz is of two sorts, the one called codo which increaseth vpon the measure of Aleppo 3 per 100, for bringing 100 pikes of any measurable wares from Aleppo to Ormuz, it is found in Ormuz to be 103 codes. Also these measures of Ormuz increase vpon those of Balsara and Babylon 25 and two third parts per 100: for bringing 100 pikes of any measurable wares from Balsara or Babylon, there is found in Ormuz 125 codes and two third parts.

The other measure is called a vare, which was sent from the king of Portugall to the India, by which they sell things of small value, which measure is of 5 palmes or spans, and is one code and two third parts, so that buying 100 codes of any measurable wares, and returning to measure it by the sayd vare, there are found but 60 vares, contrarywise 100 vares make 166 codes and two third parts.

Note that al such ships as lade horses in Ormuz for Goa or any other place of India, lading 10 horses or vpwards, in what places soeuer the said horses be taken a shore in the India, the marchandize which is to be discharged out of that ship wherein the said horses come, are bound to pay no custome at all, but if they lade one horse lesse then ten, then the goods are bound to pay the whole custome. And this law was made by Don Emanuel king of Portugall, but it is to be diligently foreseene, whither all those horses laden be bound to pay the king his custome: for many times by the king of Portugall his commandement, there is fauour shewed to the king of Cochin his brother in armes, so that his horses that come in the same ship, are not to answere custome. As for example: If there were 4 horses laden in one ship, all which were to pay custome to the king, and one other of the king of Cochins which were not to pay any custome, the same causeth all the marchandize of that ship to be subiect to pay custome, per aduise. But if they lade ten horses vpon purpose to pay the king his custome in Goa, and in the voyage any of them should die in that case, if they bring the taile of the dead horse to the custome in Goa, then the marchandize is free from all custome, because they were laden in Ormuz to pay custome in Goa. Moreouer, if the horses should die before the midst of the voyage, they pay no custome at all, and if they die in the midst of the voyage, then they pay halfe custome, but if any horse die after the mid voiage, they pay custome no lesse than if they arriue safe. Notwithstanding, the marchandize (whether the said horses die before or in the mid voyage or after the mid voiage) are free from all custome.

The custome of Ormuz is eleuen in the 100, to say, 10 for the king, and 1 for the arming of the foists: but for small wares as glasses, and looking glasses of all sorts, and such like, made for apparell, pay no custome. But cloth of Wooll, Karsies, Mockaires, Chamlets, and all sortes of Silke, Saffron, and such like, pay custome, being esteemed reasonably.

There is also another custome, which they call caida, which is, that one bringing his goods into Ormuz, with purpose to send the same further into India, the same are bound to pay 3 by the 100, but none other are bound to pay this custome, except the Armenians, Moores, and Iewes: for the Portugals and Venetians pay nothing thereof.

Note that in Ormuz they abate tare of all sorts of commodities, by an order obserued of custome.

The fraight from Ormuz to Chaul, Goa, and Cochin, is as followeth: Mokaires, larines 6 per table of 60 pikes. Aquariosa 8 larines by ordinarie chist, raisins 10 by chist, which is a quintall of roues 128. Ruuia of Chalangi larines 10 per quintall, glasses larines 8 per chist, of 4 foote and a halfe, glasses in great chists 14 and 15 larines by chist. Small wares larines 12 by chist of fiue foot. Tamari for Maschat sadines 2 and a half, and 3 by the fardle. Tamarie for Diu and Chaul 4 sadines, and 4 and a halfe by bale. Other drugs and things which come from Persia pay according to the greatnesse of the bales.

The fraight mentioned, they pay as appeareth, when they ship the sayd goods in ships where horses goe: otherwise not hauing horses, they pay somewhat lesse, because of the custom which they are to pay.

The vse of the India ships is, that the patrones thereof are not at any charge neither with any passenger, not yet with any mariner in the ship, but that euery one at the beginning of the voyage doe furnish to maintaine his owne table (if he will eate) and for drinke they haue a great iarre of water, which is garded with great custodie.

GOA.

The weight, measure, and mony currant in Goa.

The quintall of Goa is 5 manas, and 8 larines, and the mana is 24 rotilos, so that the quintall of Goa is 128 rot. and euery rot. is 16 ounces, which is of Venice weight 1 li. and a halfe, so that the quintall of Goa is 192 li. sotile Venice, which is 26 rotiloes 8 ounces Aleppine, and of London weight 132 li. English, as the weight of Ormuz.

All the marchandize, spices and drugs, are sold by this quintal, except some drugs, as lignum de China, Galanga, and others, whereof they bargaine at so much per candill, aduertising that there be two sorts of candill, one of 16 manas, the other of 20 manas, that of 16 manas commeth to be iust 3 quintals, and that of 26 manas, 3 quintals, 3 roues. Note that 4 roues make a quintall, and the roue is 32 rotiloes, as in Ormuz.

There is also another weight which they call Marco, which is eight ounces or halfe a rotilo of Goa, and 9 ounces of Venice sotile: with this they weigh amber, corall, muske, ambracan, ciuet, and other fine wares.

There is also another sort of weight called Mangiallino, which is 5 graines of Venice weight and therewith they weigh diamants and other iewels.

[Sidenote: Muske of Tartarie by the way of China.] Note that in Goa they vse not to abate any tare of any goods, except of sacks or wraps, and therefore it requireth great aduisement in buying of the goods, especially in the muske of Tartaria which commeth by way of China in bladders, and so weigh it without any tare rebating.

The measure of Goa is called a tode, which encreaseth vpon the measure of Babylon and Balsara after the rate of 17 and one eight part by the 100, so that bringing 100 pikes of any measurable ware from thence to Goa, it is found 117 pikes 7 eight parts, and bringing 100 codes from Ormuz to Goa, there is found but 93 codes and one fourth part.

There is also the vare in Goa, which is iust as the vare of Ormuz, and therewith they measure onely things that are of small value.

For the mony of Goa, there is a kind of mony made of lead and tin mingled, being thicke and round, and stamped on the one side with a spheare or globe of the world, and on the other side two arrowes and 5 rounds: and this kind of mony is called Basaruchi, and 15 of these make a vinton of naughty mony, and 5 vintons make a tanga, and 4 vintenas make a tanga of base money: so that the tanga of base mony is 60 basaruchies, and the tanga of good mony 75. basaruchies, and 5 tangas make a seraphine of gold, which in merchandize is worth 5 tangas good money: but if one would change them into basaruchies, he may haue 5 tangas, and 16 basaruchies, which ouerplus they cal cerafagio, and when they bargain of the pardaw of gold, each pardaw is ment to be 6 tangas good mony, but in merchandise they vse not to demaund pardawes of gold in Goa, except it be for iewels and horses, for all the rest they take of seraphines of siluer, per aduiso.

The roials of plate, I say, the roial of 8 are worth per custome and commandement of the king of Portugall 400 reies, and euery rey is one basaruchie and one fourth part, which maketh tangas 6, and 53 basaruchies as their iust value, but for that the said roials are excellent siluer and currant in diuers places of the India, and chiefly in Malacca, when the ships are to depart at their due times (called Monsons) euery one to haue the said roials pay more then they are worth, and the ouerplus, as is abouesaid they call serafagio. And first they giue the iust value of the 100 roials of 8, at 5 tangas 50 basaruchies a piece, which done, they giue seraphins 5, 6, 7, 8, 9, 10, 12, 15, vntill 22 by the 100, according as they are in request.

The ducket of gold is worth 9 tangas and a halfe good money, and yet not stable in price, for that when the ships depart from Goa to Cochin, they pay them at 9 tangas and 3 fourth partes, and 10 tangas, and that is the most that they are woorth.

The larines are woorth by iust value basaruchies 93 and 3 fourth parts, and 4 larines make a seraphine of siluer, which is 5 tangas of good money, and these also haue serafagion of 6, 7, 8, 10, vntill 16, by the hundred, for when the ships depart for the North, to say, for Chaul, Diu, Cambaia, or Bassaim, all cary of the same, because it is money more currant then any other.

There is also a sort of seraphins of gold of the stampe of Ormuz, whereof there are but fewe in Goa, but being there, they are woorth fiue larines and somewhat more, according as they are in request.

There is also another litle sort of mony, round, hauing on the one side a crosse, and on the other side a crowne, which is woorth one halfe a tanga of good money, and another of the same stampe lesse than that which they call Imitiuo de buona moneda, which is worth 18 basaruches 3 fourth parts a piece.

Note that if a man bargaine in marchandize, it behooueth to demaund tangas of good money: for by nominating tangas onely, is vnderstood to be base money of 60 basaruches, which wanteth of the good money vt supra.

The custome of Goa is 8 in the 100 inwards, and as much outward, and the goods are esteemed iustly rather to the marchants aduantage then the kings. The custome they pay in this order. Comming with a ship from Ormuz to Goa without horses, they pay 8 in the 100 whether they sell part or all, but if they would carie of the sayd marchandise to any other place, they pay none other custome, except others buy it and carie it foorth of the countrey, and then they pay it 8 in the 100. And if one hauing paied the custome should sell to another with composition to passe it forth as for his proper accounts to saue the custome, this may not be, because the seller is put to his oth, whether he send the goods for his owne account, or for the account of any others that haue bought the same, and being found to the contrary they pay custome as abouesaid. And in this order the marchants pay of all the goods which come from any part of the Indies. But if they come from Ormuz to Goa with horses, they are not subiect to pay any custome inward, notwithstanding if they send all or any part thereof for any other place, or returne it to Ormuz, they pay the custome outward, although they could not sell.

They vse also in Goa amongst the common sort to bargaine for coales, wood, lime, and such like, at so many braganines, accounting 24 basaruches for one braganine, albeit there is no such mony stamped. The custome of the Portugals is, that any Moore or Gentile, of what condition or state soeuer he be, may not depart from Goa to go within the land, without licence of certaine deputies deputed for that office, who (if they be Moores or Gentiles) doe set a seale vpon the arme, hauing thereon the armes of Portugal, to be knowen of the porters of the citie, whether they haue the said licence or no.

COCHIN.

The weight, measure, and money, currant in Cochin.

All the marchandise which they sell or buy within the sayd citie, they bargaine for at so many serafines per quintal, which is 128. rotilos of iust weight, with the quintal and rotilo of Goa and Ormuz: aduertising that there are diuers sorts of bars according to the sorts of commodities, and in traffiquing, they reason at so much the bar. Note that there are bars of 3 quintals and 3 quintals and halfe, and 4 quintals. They abate a vsed tare of all marchandize, according to the sort of goods, and order taken for the same.

The measure of Goa and Cochin are all one.

The money of Cochin are all the same sorts which are currant in Goa, but the duckat of gold in value is 10 tangas of good money.

The custome of Cochin as wel inward as outward for all strangers is eight in the hundred, but those that haue bene married foure yeere in the countrey pay but foure in the hundred, per aduiso.

MALACCA.

The weight, measure, and money of Malacca.

For the marchandise bought and sold in the citie they reckon at so much the barre, which barre is of diuers sorts, great and small, according to the ancient custome of the said citie, and diuersitie of the goods. But for the cloues they bargaine at so much the barre, which barre is 3 quintals, 2 roues and 10 rotilos. As I haue abouesaid, all kind of drugs haue their sorts of barres limited. Note that euery quintal is 4 roues, and euery roue 32 rotilos, which is 128 rotilos the quintall, the which answereth to Aleppo 95 rotilos, and to London 472 li. per quintal.

The measures of Malacca are as the measures of Goa. In Malacca they abate tare according to their distinction and agreement, for that there is no iust tare limited.

For the money of Malacca, the least money currant is of tinne stamped with the armes of Portugall, and 12 of these make a Chazza.

The Chazza is also of tinne with the said armes, and 2. of these make a challaine.

The Challaine is of tinne with the said armes, and 40 of these make a tanga of Goa good money, but not stamped in Malacca.

There is also a sort of siluer money which they call Patachines, and is worth 6 tangas of good money, which is 360 reyes, and is stamped with two letters, S. T. which is S. Thomas on the one side, and the armes of Portugall on the other side.

There is also a kind of mony called Cruzados stamped with the atmes of Portugall, and is worth 6 tangas good mony, the larines are euery 9 of them worth 2 cruzados, which is 12 tangas good mony, and these larines be of those which are stamped in Balsara and Ormuz.

The roials of 8 they call Pardaos de Reales, and are worth 7 tangas of good money.

The custome of Malacca is 10 in the 100 as wel inward as outward, and those which pay the custome inwards, if in case they send the same goods for any other place within terme of a yeere and a day, pay no custome for the same.

A note of charges from Aleppo to Goa, as foloweth.

For camels from Aleppo to Birrha. Medines 60 per somme.[A]
For mules from Aleppo to Birrha, med. 45. per somme.
For custome at Birrha, med. 10. per somme.
For Auania of the Cady at Birrha, med. 200.
For 4 dishes raisins, and 20 pounds sope, med. 35.
For a present to the Ermine the summe of med. 400.
For a barke of 30 or 35 sommes. Duc. 60 is med. 2400. per barke.
For meat for the men the summe of med. 200.
For custome at Racca the summe of med. 5. per somme.
For 3 platters of raisins, and 15 pounds of sope, med. 25.
For custome to king Aborissei, Duc. 20 is med. 800
For custome at Dea the summe of med. 230. per barke
For 4 dishes raisins, and 20 pounds of sope, med. 35.
For custom at Bosara, the summe of med. 10. per barke.
For 2 dishes raisins, and 10 pound of sope, med. 17.
For custome in Anna, in 10 per summe, med. 10. per somme.
For 4 dishes of raisins and 20 pound of sope, med. 35.
For custome in Adite, medines 10 per barke, med. 10. per barke.
For 2 dishes raisins, and 10 pound of sope, med. 17.
For custome at Gweke, med. 10. per barke.
For 2 dishes raisins, and 20 pound of sope, med. 17.
For custome at Ist, med. 10. per somme.
For 4 platters raisins, and 20 pound of sope, med. 35.
Charges of presents at Felugia, med. 30.
For camels from Felugia to Babylon, med. 30. per somme.
For custome in Babylon, as in the booke appeareth.
For a barke from Babylon to Balsara, med. 900.
For custome of small wares, at Corno med. 20. per somme.
For custome of clothes at Corno, the summe of med. per somme.
For 3 dishes raisins, and 20 pound of sope, med. 26.

For fraight from Balsara to Ormus, according to the greatnesse, as in this booke appeareth.
For custome in Ormus, as is abouesaid in this booke.
For fraight from Ormus to Goa, as is in this booke shewed.
For custome in Goa, as is abouesaid.

[A: Or, by the Camels burden.]

A declaration of the places from whence the goods subscribed doe come.

Cloues, from Maluco, Tarenate, Amboina, by way of Iaua.
Nutmegs, from Banda.
Maces from Banda, Iaua, and Malacca.
Pepper Gawrie, from Cochin.
Pepper common from Malabar.
Sinnamon, from Seilan.
Tinne, from Malacca.
Sandals wilde, from Cochin.
Sandales domestick, from Malacca.
Verzini, from S. Thomas, and from China.
Spicknard from Zindi, and Lahor.
Quicksiluer, from China.
Galls, from Cambaia, Bengala, Istria and Syria.
Ginger Dabulin, from Dabul.
Ginger Belledin, from the Countrie within Cambaia.
Gmger Sorattin, from Sorat within Cambaia.
Ginger Mordassi, from Mordas within Cambaia.
Ginger Meckin, from Mecca.
Mirabolans of all sorts, from Cambaia.
White sucket, from Zindia, Cambaia, and China.
Corcunia, from diuers places of India.
Corall of Leuant, from Malabar.
Chomin, from Balsara.
Requitria, from Arabia Felix.
Garble of Nutmegs from Banda.
Sal Armoniacke, from Zindi and Cambaia.
Zedoari, from diuers places of India.
Cubeb, from China.
Amomum, from China.
Camphora, from Brimeo neere to China.
Myrrha, from Arabia Felix.
Costo dulce, from Zinde, and Cambaia.
Borazo, from Cambaia, and Lahor.
Asa fetida, from Lahor.
Waxe, from Bengala.

Seragni, from Persia.
Cassia, from Cambaia, and from Gran Cayro.
Storax calamita, from Rhodes, to say, from Aneda, and Canemarie within Caramania.
Storax liquida, from Rhodes.
Tutia, from Persia.
Cagiers, from Malabar, and Maldiua.
Ruuia to die withall, from Chalangi.
Alumme di Rocca, from China, and Constantinople.
Chopra, from Cochin and Malabar.
Oppopanax, from Persia.
Lignum Aloes, from Cochin, China, and Malacca.
Demnar, from Siacca and Blinton.
Galangæ, from China, Chaul, Goa, and Cochin.
Laccha, from Pegu, and Balaguate.
Carabbe, from Almanie.
Coloquintida, from Cyprus.
Agaricum, from Alemania.
Scamonea, from Syria, and Persia.
Bdellium, from Arabia felix, and Mecca.
Cardamomum small, from Barcelona.
Cardamomum great, from Bengala.
Tamarinda, from Balsara.
Aloe Secutrina, from Secutra.
Aloe Epatica, from Pat.
Safran, from Balsara, and Persia.
Lignum de China, from China.
Rhaponticum, from Persia, and Pugia.
Thus, from Secutra.
Turpith, from Diu, and Cambaia.
Nuts of India, from Goa, and other places of India.
Nux vomica, from Malabar.
Sanguis Draconis, from Secutra.
Armoniago, from Persia.
Spodio di Cana, from Cochin.
Margaratina, from Balaguate.
Muske from Tartarie, by way of China.
Ambracban, from Melinde, and Mosombique.
Indico, from Zindi and Cambaia.
Silkes fine, from China.
Long pepper, from Bengala and Malacca.
Latton, from China.
Momia, from the great Cayro.

Belzuinum Mandolalo, from Sian, and Baros.
Belzuinum burned, from Bonnia.
Castorium, from Almania.
Corallina, from the red sea.
Masticke, from Sio.
Mella, from Romania.
Oppium, from Pogia, and Cambaia.
Calamus Aromaticus, from Constantinople.
Capari, from Alexandria and other places.
Dates, from Arabia felix and Alexandria.
Dictamnum album, from Lombardia.
Draganti, from Morea.
Euphorbium, from Barbaria.
Epithymum, from Candia.
Sena, from Mecca.
Gumme Arabike, from Zaffo.
Grana, from Coronto.
Ladanum, from Cyprus and Candia.
Lapis lazzudis, from Persia.
Lapis Zudassi, from Zaffetto.
Lapis Spongij is found in sponges.
Lapis Hæmatites, from Almanie.
Manna, from Persia.
Auripigmentum, from manie places of Turkie.
Pilatro, from Barbaria.
Pistaches, from Doria.
Worme-seede, from Persia.
Sumack, from Cyprus.
Sebesten, from Cyprus.
Galbanum from Persia.
Dente d'Abolio, from Melinde, and Mosambique.
Folium Indicum, from Goa, and Cochin.
Diasprum viride, from Cambaia.
Petra Bezzuar, from Tartaria.
Sarcacolla, from Persia.
Melleghete, from the West parts.
Sugo di Requillicie, from Arabia felix.
Chochenillo, from the West India.
Rubarbe, from Persia, and China.

The times or seasonable windes called Monsons, wherein the ships depart from place to place in the East Indies.

Note that the Citie of Goa is the principall place of all the Orientall India, and the winter there beginneth the 15 of May with very great raine, and so continueth till the first of August, so that during that space, no shippe can passe ouer the barre of Goa, because through the continuall shoures of raine all the sandes ioyne together neere vnto a mountaine called Oghane, and all these sandes being ioyned together, runne into the shoales of the barre and port of Goa, and can haue no other issue, but to remaine in that port, and therefore it is shut vp vntill the first of August, but at the 10 of August it openeth by reason of the raine which ceaseth, and the sea doeth then scoure the sands away againe.

The monson from Goa to the Northward, to say, for Chaul, Diu, Cambaia, Daman, Basaim, and other places.

The ships depart from betwixt the tenth and 24 of August, for the Northward places abouesayde, and to these places they may saile all times of the yeere, except in the winter, which beginneth and endeth at the times abouesaid.

The monson from the North parts, for Goa.

The ships depart from Chaul, Diu, Cambaia, and other places Northwards for
Goa, betwixt the 8 and 15 of Ianuarie, and come to Goa about the end of Februarie.

The first monson from Diu for the straight of Mecca.

The ships depart from Diu about the 15 of Ianuarie, and returne from the straights to Diu in the moneth of August.

The second monson from Diu for the straight of Mecca.

The ships depart betwixt the 25 and first of September, and returne from the straights to Diu, the first and 15 of May.

The monson from Secutra for Ormus.

The ships depart about the tenth of August for Ormus: albeit Secutra is an Iland and hath but few ships, which depart as abouesaid.

The monson wherein the Moores of the firme land come to Goa.

About the fifteenth of September the Moores of the firme lande beginne to come to Goa, and they come from all parts, as well from Balaguate, Bezenegar, as also from Sudalacan, and other places.

The monson wherein the Moores of the firme land depart from Goa.

They depart from Goa betwixt the 10 and 15 day of Nouember. Note that by going for the North is ment the departing from Goa, for Chaul, Diu, Cambaia, Daman, Basaim, Ghassain, and other places vnto Zindi: and by the South is vnderstood, departing from Goa, for Cochin, and all that coast vnto Cape Comori.

The first monson from Goa for Ormus.

The shippes depart in the moneth of October from Goa, for Ormus, passing with Easterly windes along the coast of Persia.

The second monson from Goa to Ormus.

The ships depart about the 20 of Ianuarie passing by the like nauigation and windes as in the first monson, and this is called of the Portugals and Indians Entremonson.

The third monson from Goa to Ormus.

The ships depart betwixt the 25 of March, and 6 of Aprill, hauing Easterly windes, till they passe Secutra, and then they find Westerly windes, and therefore they set their course ouer for the coast of Arabia, till they come to Cape Rasalgate and the Straight of Ormus, and this monson is most troublesome of all: for they make two nauigations in the heigth of Seylan, which is 6 degrees and somewhat lower.

The first monson from Ormus for Chaul, and Goa.

The ships depart from Ormus for Chaul, and Goa in the moneth of September, with North and Northeast windes.

The second monson from Ormus for Chaul and Goa.

The second monson is betwixt the fiue and twentie and last of December, with like winds as the former monson.

The third monson from Ormus for Chaul and Goa.

The third monson the ships depart from Ormus, for Chaul and Goa, betwixt the first and 15. of April, and they saile with Southeast windes, East and Northeast windes, coasting vpon the Arabia side from Cape Mosandon vnto Cape Rasalgate, and hauing lost the sight of Cape Rasalgate, they haue Westerly windes, and so come for Chaul and Goa, and if the said ships depart not before the 25 of April, they are not then to depart that monson, but to winter in Ormus because of the winter.

The first monson from Ormus for Zindi.

The ships depart from Ormus betwixt the 15 and 26 of Aprill.

The second monson from Ormus for Zindi.

The ships depart betwixt the 10 and 20 of October for Zindi from Ormus.

The monson from Ormus for the red sea.

The ships depart from Ormus betwixt the first and last of Ianuarie.

Hitherto I haue noted the monsons of the ships departing from Goa to the Northward: Now follow the monsons wherein the ships depart from Goa, to the Southward.

The Monson from Goa for Calicut, Cochin, Seilan, and all that coast.

The ships depart from those places betwixt the 1 and 15 of August, and there they find it nauigable all the yeere except in the winter, which continueth as is aforesayd, from the 15 of May till the 10 of August. [Sidenote: Note.] In like maner the ships come from these places for Goa at euery time in the yeere except in the winter, but of all other the best time is to come in Nouember, December and Ianuary.

The first monson from Goa, for Pegu.

The ships depart from Goa, betwixt the 15 and 20 of April, and winter at S. Thomas, and after the 5 of August, they depart from S. Thomas for Pegu.

The second monson from Goa, for Pegu.

The ships depart from Goa betwixt the 8 and 24 of August, going straight for Pegu, and if they passe the 24 of August, they cannot passe that monson, neither is there any more monsons till April as is aforesaid. [Sidenote: Marchandize good for Pegu.] Note that the chiefest trade is to take money of S. Thomas rials, and patechoni, and to goe to S. Thomas, and there to buy Tellami, which is fine cloth of India, whereof there is great quantitie made in Coromandel, and brought thither, and other marchandise are not good for that place except some dozen of very faire Emeraulds orientall. For of golde, siluer, and Rubies, there is sufficient store in Pegu.

The monson from Pegu for the Indies.

The ships depart from Pegu betwixt the 15 and 25 of Ianuarie, and come to Goa about the 25 of March, or in the beginning of April. Note, that if it passe the 10 of May before the sayde ships be arriued in Goa, they cannot come thither that monson, and if they haue not then fet the coast of India, they shall with great perill fetch S. Thomas.

The first monson from Goa for Malacca.

The ships depart betwixt the 15 and last of September, and arriue in Malacca about the end of October.

The second monson from Goa to Malacca.

The ships depart about the 5 of May from Goa, and arriue in Malacca about the 15 of Iune.

The first monson from Malacca to Goa.

The ships depart about the 10 of September, and come to Goa about the end of October.

The second monson from Malacca to Goa.

The ships depart from Malacca about the 10 of February, and come to Goa about the end of March. But if the said ships should stay till the 10 of May they cannot enter into Goa, and if at that time also they should not be arriued at Cochin, they are forced to returne to Malacca, because the winter and contrary windes then come vpon them.

The monson from Goa for China.

The ships depart from Goa in the moneth of April.

The monson from China for Goa.

The ships depart to be the 10 of May in Goa, and being not then arriued, they turne backe to Cochin, and if they cannot fetch Cochin, they returne to Malacca.

The monson from Goa to the Moluccaes.

The ships depart about 10 or 15 of May, which time being past, the shippes can not passe ouer the barre of Goa for the cause abouesaid.

The monson of the ships of the Moluccaes arriuall in Goa.

The ships which come from the Moluccaes arriue vpon the bar of Goa about the 15. of April.

The monsons of the Portingall ships for the Indies.

[Sidenote: Note.] The ships which come from Portugall depart thence ordinarily betwixt the tenth and fifteenth of March, comming the straight way during the moneth of Iuly to the coast of Melinde, and Mosambique, and from thence goe straight for Goa, and if in the moneth Iuly they should not be at the coast of Melinde, they can in no wise that yeere fetch Melinde, but returne to the Isle of Saint Helena, and so are not able, that time being past, to fetch the coast of India, and to come straight for Goa. Therefore (as is abouesaid) they returne to the Island of Saint Helena, and if they cannot make the said Island, then they runne as lost vpon the Coast of Guinea: but if the said ships be arriued in time vpon the coast of Melinde, they set forwardes for Goa, and if by the fifteenth of September they cannot fetch Goa, they then goe for Cochin, but if they see they cannot fetch Cochin, they returne to Mosambique to winter there vpon the sayd coast. [Sidenote: Note.] Albeit in the yeere of our Lord 1580 there arriued the ship called San Lorenzo, being wonderfull sore sea-beaten, the eight of October, which was accounted as a myracle for that the like had not beene seene before.

The monson from India for Portugall.

The shippes depart from Cochin betweene the fifteenth and last of Ianuary, going on till they haue sight of Capo de buona speranza, and the Isle of Saint Helena, which Islande is about the midway, being in sixteene degrees to the South. And it is a litle Island being fruitfull of all things which a man can imagine, with great store of fruit: and this Island is a great succour to the shipping which returne for Portugall. And not long since the said Island was found by the Portugales, and was discouered by a shippe that came from the Indies in a great storme, in which they found such abundance of wilde beastes, and boares, and all sort of fruite, that by meanes thereof that poore ship which had been foure moneths at sea, refreshed themselues both with water and meate very well, and this Island they called S. Helena, because it was discouered vpon S. Helens day. And vndoubtedly this Island is a great succour, and so great an ayde to the ships of Portugall, that many would surely perish if that helpe wanted. And therefore the king of Portugall caused a Church to be made there for deuotion of S. Helena: where there are onely resident Eremits, and all other are forbidden to inhabite there by the kings commaundement, to the ende that the ships may be the more sufficiently furnished with victuals, because the ships which come from India come but slenderly victualled, [Sidenote: Note.] because there groweth no corne there, neither make they any wine: but the ships which come from Portugall to the Indies touch not in the sayd Island, because they set out being sufficiently furnished with bread and water from Portugall for eight moneths voyage. Any other people then the two Eremites abouesaid, cannot inhabite this Island, except some sicke man that may be set there a shore to remaine in the Eremites companie, for his helpe and recouery.

The monson from Goa to Mosambique.

The ships depart betwixt the 10 and 15 of Ianuarie.

The monson from Mosambique to Goa.

The ships depart betweene the 8 and last of August, and arriue in Chaul or Goa in the moneth of October, till the 15 of Nouember.

The monson from Ormus to Bengala.

The ships depart betwixt the 15 and 20 of Iune, and goe to winter at Teue and depart thence about the 15 of August for Bengala.

* * * * *

A briefe extract specifying the certaine dayly paiments, answered quarterly in time of peace, by the Grand Signior, out of his Treasurie, to the Officers of his Seraglio or Court, successiuely in degrees: collected in a yeerely totall summe, as followeth.

For his owne diet euery day, one thousand and one aspers, according to a former custome receiued from his auncestors: notwithstanding that otherwise his diurnall expence is very much, and not certainly knowen, which summe maketh sterling mony by the yere, two thousand, one hundred, 92. pounds, three shillings, eightpence.

The fiue and fourtie thousand Ianizaries dispersed in sundry places of his dominions, at sixe aspers the day, amounteth by the yeere to fiue hundreth, fourescore and eleuen thousand, and three hundreth pounds.

The Azamoglans, tribute children, farre surmount that number, for that they are collected from among the Christians, from whom betweene the yeeres of sixe and twelue, they are pulled away yeerely perforce: whereof I suppose those in seruice may be equall in number with the Ianizaries abouesayd, at three aspers a day, one with another, which is two hundred fourescore and fifteene thousand, sixe hundred and fiftie pounds.

The fiue Bassas, whereof the Viceroy is supreme, at one thousand aspers the day, besides their yerely reuenues, amounteth sterling by the yeere to ten thousand, nine hundred and fiftie pounds.

The fiue Beglerbegs, chiefe presidents of Greece, Hungary, and Sclauonia, being in Europe, in Natolia, and Caramania of Asia, at one thousande aspers the day: as also to eighteene other gouernours of Prouinces, at fiue hundred aspers the day, amounteth by the yeere, to thirtie thousand sixe hundred, and threescore pounds.

The Bassa, Admirall of the Sea, one thousand aspers the day, two thousand, one hundred foure score and ten pounds.

The Aga of the Ianizaries, generall of the footemen, fiue hundred aspers the day, and maketh by the yeere in sterling money, one thousand, foure score and fifteene pounds.

The Imbrahur Bassa, Master of his horse, one hundred and fiftie aspers the day, is sterling money, three hundred and eight and twenty pounds.

The chiefe Esquire vnder him, one hundred and fiftie aspers, is three hundred and eight and twenty pounds.

The Agas of the Spahi, Captaines of the horsemen, sixe, at one hundred and fiftie aspers to either of them, maketh sterling, one thousand, nine hundred, three score and eleuen pounds.

The Capagi Bassas head porters foure, one hundred and fiftie aspers to ech, and maketh out in sterling money by the yeere, one thousand, three hundred, and fourteene pounds.

The Sisinghir Bassa, Controller of the housholde, one hundred and twentie aspers the day, and maketh out in sterling money by the yeere, two hundred, threescore and two pounds, sixteene shillings.

The Chaus Bassa, Captaine of the Pensioners, one hundred and twentie aspers the day, and amounteth to by the yeere in sterling money, two hundred, threescore and two pounds, sixteene shillings.

The Capigilar Caiasi Captaine of his Barge, one hundreth and twentie aspers the day, and maketh out by the yeere in sterling money, two hundred, threescore and two poundes, sixteene shillings.

The Solach Bassi, Captaine of his guard, one hundred and twentie aspers, two hundred, three score and two pounds, sixteene shillings.

The Giebrigi Bassi, master of the armoury, one hundred and twentie aspers, two hundred, three score and two pounds, sixteene shillings.

The Topagi Bassi, Master of the artillerie, one hundred and twentie aspers, two hundred, three score and two pounds, sixteene shillings.

The Echim Bassi, Phisition to his person, one hundred and twentie aspers, two hundred, three score and two pounds, sixteene shillings.

To fourtie Phisitions vnder him, to ech fourtie aspers, is three thousand, eight hundred, three score and sixe pounds, sixteene shillings.

The Mustafaracas spearemen, attending on his person, in number fiue hundred, to either three score aspers, and maketh sterling, threescore and fiue thousand, and seuen hundred pounds.

The Cisingeri gentlemen, attending vpon his diet, fourtie, at fourtie aspers ech of them, and amounteth to sterling by the yeere, three thousand, fiue hundred and foure pounds.

The Chausi Pensioners, foure hundred and fourtie, at thirtie aspers, twenty eight thousand, nine hundred and eight pounds.

The Capagi porters of the Court and City, foure hundred, at eight aspers, and maketh sterling money by the yeere, seuen thousand, and eight pounds.

The Solachi, archers of his guard, three hundred and twenty, at nine aspers, and commeth vnto in English money, the summe of sixe thousand, three hundred and sixe pounds.

The Spahi, men of Armes of the Court and the City, ten thousand, at twenty fiue asters, and maketh of English money, fiue hundred, forty and seuen thousand, and fiue hundred pounds.

The Ianizaires sixteene thousand, at six aspers, is two hundred and ten thousand, and two hundred and forty pounds.

The Giebegi furbushers of armor, one thousand, fiue hundred, at sixe aspers, and amounteth to sterling money, nineteene thousand, seuen hundred, and fourescore pounds.

The Seiesir, seruitors in his Equier or stable, fiue hundred, at two aspers, and maketh sterling money, two thousand, one hundred, fourescore and ten pounds.

The Saesi, Sadlers and bit makers, five hundred, at seuen aspers, seuen thousand, six hundred, threescore and fiue pounds.

The Catergi, Carriers vpon Mules, two hundred, at fiue aspers, two thousand, one hundred, fourescore and ten pounds.

The Cinegi, Carriers vpon Camels, one thousand, fiue hundred, at eight aspers, and amounteth in sterling money, to twenty sixe thousand, two hundred, and fourescore pounds.

The Reiz, or Captaines of the Gallies, three hundred, at ten aspers, and amounteth in English money by the yeere, the summe of sixe thousand, fiue hundred, threescore and ten pounds.

The Alechingi, Masters of the said Gallies, three hundred, at seven aspers, foure thousand, fiue hundred, fourescore and nineteene pounds.

The Getti, Boateswaines thereof, three hundred, at sixe aspers, is three thousande, nine hundred, fourty and two pounds.

The Oda Bassi, Pursers, three hundred, at fiue aspers, maketh three thousand two hundred, and fourescore pounds.

The Azappi souldiers two thousand sixe hundred at foure Aspers, whereof the six hundred do continually keepe the gallies, two and twentie thousand, seuen hundred fourescore and six pounds.

The Mariers Bassi masters over the shipwrights and kalkers of the navie, nine, at 20. Aspers the piece, amounteth to three thousand fourescore and foure pound, foure shillings.

The Master Dassi shipwrights and kalkers, one thousand at fourteene aspers, which amounteth by the yeere, to thirtie thousand, sixe hundred threescore pound.

Summa totalis of dayly paiments amounteth by the yeere sterling, one million, nine hundred threescore eight thousand, seuen hundred thirty fiue pounds, nineteene shillings eight pence, answered quarterly without default, with the summe of foure hundred fourescore twelue thousand, one hundred fourescore and foure pounds foure shillings eleven pence, and is for every day fiue thousand three hundred, fourescore and thirteene pounds, fifteene shillings ten pence.

Annuities of lands neuer improued, fiue times more in value then their summes mentioned, giuen by the saide Grand Signior, as followeth.

To the Viceroy for his Timar or annuitie 60. thousand golde ducats.
To the second Bassa for his annuitie 50. thousand ducats.
To the third Bassa for his annuitie 40. thousand ducats.
To the fourth Bassa for his annuitie 30. thousand ducats.
To the fifth Bassa for his annuitie 20. thousand ducats.
To the Captaine of the Ianizaries 20. thousand ducats.
To the Ieu Merhorbassi master of his horse 15. thousand ducats.
To the Captaine of the pensioners 10. thousand ducats.
To the Captaine of his guard 5. thousand ducats.

Summa totalls 90. thousand li. sterling.

Beside these aboue specified, be sundry other annuities giuen to diuers others of his aforesaid officers, as also to certaine called Sahims, diminishing from three thousand to two hundred ducats, esteemed treble to surmount the annuitie abouesaid.

The Turkes chiefe officers.

The Viceroy is high Treasurer, notwithstanding that vnder him be three subtreasurers called Teftadars, which bee accomptable to him of the receipts out of Europe, Asia and Africa, saue their yeerely annuitie of lands.

The Lord Chancellor is called Nissangi Bassa, who sealeth with a certaine proper character such licences, safe conducts, passeports, especiall graunts, &c. as proceed from the Grand Signior: notwithstanding all letters to forreine princes so firmed be after inclosed in a bagge, and sealed by the Grand Signior, with a signet which he ordinarily weareth about his necke, credited of them to haue bene of ancient appertayning to king Salomon the wise.

The Admirall giueth his voyce in the election of all Begs, Captaines of the Islandes, to whom hee giueth their charge, as also appointeth the

Subbasses, Bayliffes or Constables ouer Cities and Townes vpon the Sea coastes about Constantinople, and in the Archipelago, whereof hee reapeth great profit.

The Subbassi of Pera payeth him yeerely fifteene thousande ducats, and so likewise either of the others according as they are placed.

The Ressistop serueth in office to the Viceroy and Chancellor, as Secretary, and so likewise doeth the Cogie Master of the Rolls, before which two, passe all writings presented to, or granted by the said Viceroy and Chancellor, offices of especiall credite and like profile, moreouer rewarded with annuities of lands.

There are also two chiefe Iudges named Cadi Lesker, the one ouer Europe, and the other ouer Asia and Africa, which in Court doe sit on the Bench at the left hand of the Bassas. These sell all offices to the vnder Iudges of the land called Cadies, whereof is one in euery Citie or towne, before whom all matters in controuersie are by iudgement decided, as also penalties and corrections for crimes ordained to be executed vpon the offenders by the Subbassi.

The number of Souldiers continually attending vpon the Beglerbegs the gouernours of Prouinces and Saniacks, and their petie Captaines mainteined of these Prouinces.

The Beglerbegs of

Græcia, fourtie thousand persons.
Buda, fifteene thousand persons.
Sclauonia, fifteene thousand persons.
Natolia, fifteene thousand persons.
Caramania, fifteene thousand persons.
Armenia, eighteene thousand persons.
Persia, twentie thousand persons.
Vsdrum, fifteene thousand persons.
Chirusta, fifteene thousand persons.
Caraemiti, thirtie thousand persons.
Gierusal, two and thirtie thousand persons.

The Beglerbegs of

Bagdat, fiue and twentie thousand persons.
Balsara, two and twenty thousand persons.
Lassaija, seuenteene thousand persons.
Alepo, fiue and twentie thousand persons.
Damasco, seuenteene thousand persons.
Cayro, twelue thousand persons.

Abes, twelue thousand persons.
Mecca, eight thousand persons.
Cyprus, eighteene thousand persons.
Tunis in Barbary, eight thousand persons.
Tripolis in Syria, eight thousand persons.
Alger, fourtie thousand persons.

Whose Sangiacks and petie Captaines be three hundred sixtie eight, euery of which retaining continually in pay from fiue hundreth to two hundreth Souldiers, may be one with another at the least, three hundreth thousand persons.

Chiefe officers in his Seraglio about his person. Be these—

Capiaga, High Porter.
Alnader Bassi, Treasurer.
Oda Bassi, Chamberlaine.
Killergi Bassi, Steward.
Saraiaga, Comptroller.
Peskerolen, Groome of the chamber.
Edostoglan, Gentleman of the Ewer.
Sehetaraga, Armour bearer.
Choataraga, he that carieth his riding cloake.
Ebietaraga, Groome of the stoole.

There be many other maner Officers, which I esteeme superfluous to write.

The Turkes yeerely reuenue.

The Grand Signiors annual reuenue is said to be fourteene Millions and an halfe of golden ducats, which is sterling fiue millions, eight score thousand pounds.

The tribute payd by the Christians his Subiects is one gold ducat yeerely for the redemption of euery head, which may amount vnto not so litle as one Million of golden ducats, which is sterling three hundred threescore thousand pounds.

Moreouer, in time of warre, he exacteth manifolde summes for maintenance of his Armie and Nauie of the said Christians.

The Emperour payeth him yeerely tribute for Hungary, threescore thousand dollers, which is sterling thirteene thousand pound, besides presents to the Viceroy and Bassas, which are said to amount to twentie thousand dollers.

Ambassadors Allowances.

The Ambassadour of the Emperour is allowed one thousand Aspers the day.

The Ambassadour of the French king heretofore enioyed the like: but of late yeeres by meanes of displeasure conceiued by Mahumet then Viceroy, it was reduced to sixe crownes the day, beside the prouision of his Esquire of his stable.

The Ambassadours of Poland, and for the state of Venice are not Ligiers as these two abouesaid. The said Polack is allowed 12. Frenche crownes the day during his abode, which may be for a moneth. Very seldome do the state of Venice send any Ambassador otherwise, then enforced of vrgent necessity: but in stead thereof keepe their Agent, president ouer other Marchants of them termed a bailife, who hath none allowance of the Grand Signior, although his port and state is in maner as magnifical as the other aforesaid Ambassadors. The Spanish Ambassador was equall with other in Ianizaries: but for so much as he would not according to custome folow the list of other Ambassadors in making presents to the Grand Signior, he had none alowance. His abode there was 3. yeres, at the end whereof, hauing concluded a truce for six yeres, taking place from his first comming in Nouember last past 1580. he was not admitted to the presence of the Grand Signior.

* * * * *

To the Worshipfull and his very loving Vncle M. Rowland Hewish, Esquier, at
  Sand in Devonshire.

Sir, considering the goodnesse of your Nature which is woont kindely to accept from a friend, euen of meane things being giuen with a good heart, I haue presumed to trouble you with the reading of this rude discourse of my trauels into Turkie, and of the deliuerie of the present with such other occurrents as there happened woorthie the obseruation: of all which proceedings I was an eie-witnesse, it pleasing the Ambassadour to take mee in with him to the Grand Signior. If for lacke of time to put it in order I haue not performed it so well as it ought, I craue pardon, assuring you that to my knowledge I haue not missed in the trueth of any thing. If you aske me what in my trauels I haue learned, I answere as a noble man of France did to the like demaund, Hoc vnum didici, mundi contemptum: and so concluding with the wise man in the booke of the Preacher, that all is vanitie, and one thing onely is necessarie, I take my leaue and commit you to the Almightie. From London the 16. March 1597.

Your louing Nephew
Richard Wrag.

A description of a Voiage to Constantinople and Syria, begun the 21. of March 1593. and ended the 9. of August, 1595. wherein is shewed the order
of deliuering the second Present by Master Edward Barton her maiesties Ambassador, which was sent from her Maiestie to Sultan Murad Can, Emperour of Turkie.

We set saile in the Ascension of London, a new shippe very well appointed, of two hundred and three score tunnes (whereof was master one William Broadbanke, a prouident and skilfull man in his facultie) from Grauesend the one and twentie of March 1593. And vpon the eight of Aprill folowing wee passed the streights of Gibraltar, and with a small Westerne gale, the 24. of the same, we arriued at Zante an Iland vnder the Venetians. The fourth of May wee departed, and the one and twentie wee arriued at Alexandretta in Cilicia in the very bottome of the Mediterrane sea, a roade some 25. miles distance from Antioch, where our marchants land their goods to bee sent for Aleppo. From thence wee set saile the fift of Iune, and by contrary windes were driuen vpon the coast of Caramania into a road neere a litle Iland where a castle standeth, called Castle Rosso, some thirtie leagues to the Eastwards of the Rhodes, where after long search for fresh water, we could finde none, vntil certaine poore Greekes of the Iland brought vs to a well where we had 5 or 6 tuns. That part of the country next the sea is very barren and full of mountains, yet found we there an olde tombe of marble, with an epitaph of an ancient Greeke caracter, by antiquity neere worne out and past reading; which to the beholders seemed a monument of the greatnesse of the Grecian monarchy. [Sidenote: Candie.] From thence we went to the Rhodes, and by contrary windes were driuen into a port of Candy, called Sittia: this Iland is vnder the Venetians, who haue there 600 souldiers, besides certaine Greeks, continually in pay. Here with contrary winds we stayed six weeks, and in the end, hauing the winde prosperous, we sailed by Nicaria, Pharos, Delos, and Andros, with sight of many other Ilands in the Archipelago, and arriued at the two castles in Hellespont the 24 of August. Within few dayes after we came to Galipoli some thirty miles from this place, where foure of vs tooke a Parma or boat of that place, with two watermen, which rowed us along the Thracian shore to Constantinople, which sometime sailing and sometime rowing, in foure dayes they performed. The first of September we arriued at the famous port of the Grand Signior, where we were not a little welcome to M. Edward Barton vntil then her Maiesties Agent, who (with many other great persons) had for many dayes expected the present. [Sidenote: The Ascension arriued at the 7 towers.] Fiue or six dayes after the shippe arriued neere the Seuen towers, which is a very strong hold, and so called of so many turrets, which it hath, standing neere the sea side, being the first part of the city that we came vnto. [Sidenote: The ship saluteth the grand Signior.] Heere the Agent appointed the master of the Ascension to stay with the shippe vntill a fitte winde and opportunity serued to bring her about the Seraglio to Salute the Grand Signior in his moskyta or church: for you shall vnderstand that he hath built one neere the wall of his Seraglio or pallace adioyning to the Sea side; whereunto twise or thrise a weeke he resorteth to performe such religious rites as their law requireth: where hee being within few dayes after, our shippe set out in their best maner with flagges, streamers and pendants of diuers coloured silke, with all the mariners, together with most of the Ambassadours men, hauing the winde faire, and came within two cables length of this his moskita, where (hee to his great content beholding the shippe in such brauery) they discharged first two volies of small shot, and then all the great ordinance twise ouer, there being seuen and twentie or eight and twentie pieces in the ship. Which performed, he appointed the Bustangi-Bassa or captaine of the great and spacious garden or parke, to giue our men thankes, with request that some other day they would shew him the like sporte when hee would have the Sultana or Empresse a beholder thereof, which few dayes after at the shippes going to the Custome-house they performed.

The grand Signiors salutation thus ended, the master brought the ship to an anker at Rapamat neere the ambassadors house, where hee likewise saluted him with all his great ordinance once ouer, and where he landed the Present, the deliuerie whereof for a time was staied: the cause of which staie it shall neither be dishonorable for our nation, or that woorthie man the ambassador to shew you. [Sidenote: The cause of staying the present.] At the departure of Sinan Bassa the chiefe Vizir, and our ambassadors great friend toward the warres of Hungarie there was another Bassa appointed in his place, a churlish and harsh natured man, who vpon occasion of certaine Genouezes, escaping out of the castles standing toward the Euxine Sea, nowe called the black Sea, there imprisoned, apprehended and threatened to execute one of our Englishmen called Iohn Field, for that hee was taken thereabouts, and knowen not many dayes before to haue brought a letter to one of them: vpon the soliciting of whose libertie there fell a iarre betweene the Bassa (being now chiefe Vizir) and our ambassador, and in choler he gaue her maiesties ambassador such words, as without sustaining some great indignitie hee could not put vp. [Sidenote: An Arz to the grand Signior] Whereupon after the arriual of the Present, he made an Arz, that is, a bill of Complaint to the grand Signior against him, the manner in exhibiting whereof is thus performed.

The plaintifes expect the grand Signiors going abroad from his pallace, either to Santa Sophia or to his church by the sea side, whither, with a Perma (that is one of their vsuall whirries) they approch within some two or three score yards, where the plaintife standeth vp, and holdeth his petition ouer his forehead in sight of the grand Signior (for his church is open to the Sea side) the rest sitting still in the boat, who appointeth one of his Dwarfes to receiue them, and to bring them to him. A Dwarfe, one of the Ambassadors fauorites, so soone as he was discerned, beckned him to the shore side, tooke his Arz, and with speed caried it to the grand Signior. Now the effect of it was this; that except his highnesse would redresse this so great an indignitie, which the Vizir his slaue had offered him and her maiestie in his person, he was purposed to detaine the Present vntill such time as he might by letters ouer-land from her maiestie bee certified, whither she would put vp so great an iniurie as it was. [Sidenote: The great hall of Iustice.] Whereupon he presently returned answere, requesting the ambassador within an houre after to goe to the Douan of the Vizir, vnto whom himselfe of his charge would send a gowne of cloth of gold, and commaund him publikely to put it vpon him, and with kind entertainment to imbrace him in signe of reconciliation. [Sidenote: Reconceliation with the Vizir made.] Whereupon our ambassador returning home, tooke his horse, accompanied with his men, and came to the Vizirs court, where, according to the grand Signiors command, he with all shew of kindnesse embraced the ambassador, and with curteous speeches reconciled himselfe, and with his own hands put the gowne of cloth of gold vpon his backe. Which done, hee with his attendants returned home, to the no small admiration of all Christians, that heard of it, especially of the French and Venetian ambassadors, who neuer in the like case against the second person of the Turkish Empire durst haue attempted so bold an enterprise with hope of so friendly audience, and with so speedie redresse. This reconciliation with the great Vizir thus made, the ambassador prepared himselfe for the deliuerie of the Present, which vpon the 7 of October 1593. in this maner he performed.

[Sidenote: The ambassador goeth to the court with the present.] The Ascension with her flags and streamers, as aforesaid, repaired nigh vnto the place where the ambassador should land to go vp to the Seraglio: for you must vnderstand that all Christian ambassadors haue their dwelling in Pera where most Christians abide, from which place, except you would go 4 or 5 miles about, you cannot go by land to Constantinople, whereas by Sea it is litle broder then the Thames. Our Ambassador likewise apparelled in a sute of cloth of siluer, with an vpper gowne of cloth of gold, accompanied with 7 gentlemen in costly sutes of Sattin, with 40 other of his men very well apparelled, and all in one liuerie of sad French russet cloth gownes, at his house tooke boate: at whose landing the ship discharged all her ordinance, where likewise attended 2 Bassas, with 40 or 50 Chauses to accompany the ambassador to the court, and also horses for the ambassador and his gentlemen, very richly furnished, with Turkish seruants attendant to take the horses when they should light. [Sidenote: The Ambass. came to the

Seraglio.] The ambassador thus honorably accompanied, the Chauses foremost, next his men on foote all going by two and two, himselfe last with his Chause and Drugaman or Interpreter, and 4 Ianissaries, which he doeth vsually entertaine in his house to accompany him continually abroad, came to the Seraglio about an Engush mile from the water side, where first hee passed a great gate into a large court (much like the space before Whitehall gate) where he with his gentlemen alighted and left their horses. From hence they passed into an other stately court, being about 6 score in bredth, and some 10 score yards long, with many trees in it: where all the court was with great pompe set in order to entertaine our ambassador. [Sidenote: All these are captaines of hundreds and of fifties.] Vpon the right hand all the length of the court was a gallerie arched ouer, and borne vp with stone pillars, much like the Roiall Exchange, where stood most of his guard in rankes from the one end to the other in costly aray, with round head pieces on their heads of mettall and gilt ouer, with a great plume of fethers somewhat like a long brush standing vp before. On the left hand stood the Cappagies or porters, and the Chauses. All these courtiers being about the number of 2000. (as I might well gesse) most of them apparelled in cloth of gold, siluer, veluet, sattin and scarlet, did together with bowing their bodies, laying their hands vpon their brests in curteous maner of salutation, entertain the Ambassador: who likewise passing between them, and turning himself sometime to the right hand and sometime to the left, answered them with the like. [Sidenote: The ambassador receiued by the Vizir with all kindnesse.] As he thus passed along, certaine Chauses conducted him to the Douan, which is the seat of Iustice, where certaine dayes of the weeke the grand Vizir, with the other Vizirs, the Cadi-lesker or lord chiefe Iustice, and the Mufti or high priest do sit to determine vpon such causes as be brought before them, which place is vpon the left side of this great court, whither the ambassador with his gentlemen came, where hee found the Vizir thus accompanied as aforesayd, who with great shew of kindnes receiued him: and after receit of her maiesties letters, and conference had of the Present, of her maiesties health, of the state of England, and such other matters as concerned our peaceable traffique in those parts: [Sidenote: Diner brought in.] dinner being prepared was by many of the Courtiers brought into another inner roome next adioining, which consisted of an hundred dishes or therabouts, most boiled and rosted, where the ambassador accompanied with the Vizirs went to dinner, his gentlemen likewise with the rest of his men hauing a dinner with the like varietie prepared vpon the same side of the court, by themselues sate downe to their meat, 40 or 50 Chauses standing at the vpper end attending vpon the gentlemen to see them serued in good order; their drinke was water mingled with rose water and sugar brought in a Luthro (that is a goates skinne) which a man carieth at his backe, and vnder his arme letteth it run out at a spout into cups as men will call for it. [Sidenote: Diner taken away] The dinner thus with good order brought in, and for halfe an houre with great sobrietie and silence performed, was not so orderly taken vp; for certaine Moglans officers of the kitchin (like her maiesties black guard) came in disordered maner and tooke away the dishes, and he whose hungry eie one dish could not satisfie, turned two or three one into the other, and thus of a sudden was a cleane riddance made of all. The ambassador after dinner with his gentlemen, by certaine officers were placed at the vpper ende vpon the left side of the court, nere vnto a great gate which gaue entrance to a third court being but litle, paued with stone. [Sidenote: Gownes of cloth of gold for the ambassador and his gentlemen.] In the midst whereof was a litle house built of marble, as I take it, within which sate the grand Signor, according to whose commandement giuen there were gownes of cloth of gold brought out of the wardrope, and put vpon the ambassador and 7 of his gentlemen, the ambassador himselfe hauing 2, one of gold and the other of crimosin veluet, all the rest one a piece. [Sidenote: The Present.] Then certaine Cappagies had the Present, which was in trunks there ready, deliuered them by the ambassadors men, it being 12 goodly pieces of gilt plate, 36 garments of fine English cloth of al colors, 20 garments of cloth of gold, 10 garments of sattin, 6 pieces of fine Holland, and certaine other things of good value; al which were caried round about the court, each man taking a piece, being in number very neere 100 parcels, and so 2 and 2 going round that all might see it, to the greater glory of the present, and of him to whom it was giuen: [Sidenote: The Present viewed.] they went into the innermost court passing by the window of that roome, where the grand Signior sate, who, as it went by to be laid vp in certaine roomes adioining, tooke view of all. Presently after the present followed the ambassador with his gentlemen; at the gate of which court stoode 20 or 30 Agaus which be eunuchs. Within the court yard were the Turkes Dwarfes and Dumbe men, being most of them youths. At the doore of his roome stood the Bustangi-bassa, with another Bassa to lead the ambassador and his folowers to the grand Signior who sate in a chaire of estate, apparelled in a gowne of cloth of siluer. The floore vnder his feete, which part was a foote higher then the rest, was couered with a carpet of green sattin embrodered most richly with siluer, orient perles and great Turkesses; the other part of the house was couered with a carpet of Cornation sattin imbrodered with gold, none were in the roome with him, but a Bassa who stood next the wall ouer against him banging down his head, and looking submissely vpon the ground as all his subjects doe in his presence. [Sidenote: The ambassador kisseth the grand Signiors hand.] The ambassador thus betwixt two which stood at the doore being led in, either of them taking an arme, kissed his hand, and so backward with his face to the Turke they brought him nigh the dore againe, where he stood vntill they had likewise done so with all the rest of his gentlemen. [Sidenote: The ambassadors demands granted.] Which ended, the ambassador, according as it is the custome when any present is deliuered, made his three demaunds, such as he thought most expedient for her maiesties honor, and the peaceable traffique of our nation into his dominions: whereunto he answered in one word, Nolo, which is in Turkish as much as, it shal be done: for it is not the maner of the Turkish emperor familiarly to confer with any Christian ambassador, but he appointeth his Vizir in his person to graunt their demaunds if they be to his liking: as to our ambassador he granted all his demands, and gaue order that his daily allowance for his house of mony, flesh, wood, and haie, should be augmented with halfe as much more as it had bene before. Hereupon the ambassador taking his leaue, departed with his gentlemen the same way he came, the whole court saluting him as they did at his comming in: and comming to the second court to take our horses, after we were mounted, we staied halfe an houre, vntil the captain of the guard with 2000 horsemen at the least passed before, after whom folowed 40 or 50 Chauses next before the ambassador to accompany him to his house. And as before at his landing, so now at his taking boat, the ship discharged all her great ordinance, where arriuing, he likewise had a great banquet prepared to entertaine those which came to bring him home. [Sidenote: The Sultanas present.] The pompe and solemnitie of the Present, with the day thus ended, he shortly after presented the Sultana or empresse who (by reason that she is mother to him which was heire to the crown Imperial) is had in far greater reuerence then any of his other Queens or concubines. The Present sent her in her maiesties name was a iewel of her maiesties picture, set with some rubies and diamants, 3 great pieces of gilt plate, 10 garments of cloth of gold, a very fine case, of glass bottles siluer and gift, with 2 pieces of fine Holland, which so gratefully she accepted, as that she sent to know of the ambassador what present he thought she might return that would most delight her maiestie: who sent word that a sute of princely attire being after the Turkish fashion would for the rarenesse thereof be acceptable in England. [The Sultanas present to the Queene. Letters sent for England.] Whereopon she sent an vpper gowne of cloth of gold very rich, an vnder gowne of cloth of siluer, and a girdle of Turkie worke, rich and faire, with a letter of gratification, which for the rarenesse of the stile, because you may be acquainted with it, I haue at the ende of this discourse hereunto annexed, which letter and present, with one from the grand Signor, was sent by M. Edward Bushell, and M. William Aldridge ouer-land the 20 of March, who passed through Valachia and Moldauia, and so through Poland, where Michael prince of Valachia, and Aron Voiuoda prince of Moldauia receiuing letters from the ambassador, entertained them with al curtesie, through whose meanes by the great fauour which his lordship had with the grand Signior, they had not long before both of them bene aduanced to their princely dignities. [Sidenote: The other Vizirs presented.] Hee likewise presented Sigala the Admirall of the Seas, with Abrim Bassa, who maried the great Turkes daughter, and all the other Vizirs with diuers pieces of plate, fine English cloth and other costly things: the particulars whereof, to auoid tediousnesse, I omit. [Sidenote: The Ascension departeth.] All the presents thus ended, the ship shooting ten pieces of ordinance at the Seraglio point, as a last farewell, departed on her iourney for England the first of Nouember, my selfe continuing in Constantinople vntill the last of Iuly after. This yere in the spring there was great preparation for the Hungarian wars: and the great Turke threatned to goe himselfe in person: but like Heliogabalus, his affections being more seruiceable to Venus then to Mars, he stayed at home. Yet a great army was dispatched this yere; who, as they came out of Asia to goe for Hungary, did so pester the streets of Constantinople for the space of two moneths in the spring time, as scarse either Christian or Iew could without danger of losing his money passe vp and downe the city. What insolencies, murders and robberies were committed not onely vpon Christians but also vpon Turks I omit to write, and I pray God in England the like may neuer be seene: and yet I could wish, that such amongst vs as haue inioyed the Gospel with such great and admirable peace and prosperity vnder her Maiesties gouerment this forty yeeres, and haue not all this time brought forth better fruits of obedience to God, and thankfulnesse to her Maiesty, were there but a short time to beholde the miserable condition both of Christians and others liuing vnder such an infidell prince, who not onely are wrapped in most palpable and grosse ignorance of minde, but are cleane without the meanes of the true knowledge of God: I doubt not but the sight hereof (if they be not cleane void of grace) would stirre them vp to more thankefulnesse to God, that euer they were borne in so happy a time, and vnder so wise and godly a prince professing the true religion of Christ.

The number of souldiours which went to the warres of Hungary this yeere were 470000, as by the particulars giuen by the Admirall to the Ambassadour hereunder doe appeare. Although all these were appointed and supposed to goe, yet the victories which the Christians in the spring had against the Turks strooke such a terrour in many of the Turkish souldiours, as by report diuers vpon the way thither left their Captaines and stole away.

The number of Turkish souldiours which were appointed to goe into Hungary
  against the Christian Emperour. May 1594.

Sinan Bassa generall, with the Saniacke masould, that is, out of office,
  with the other Saniacks in office or of degree, 40000.

Achmigi, that is, Aduenturers, 50000.
The Agha or Captaine with his Ianisaries, and his Giebegies, 20000.
The Beglerbeg of Græcia, with all his Saniacks, 40000.
The company of Spaheis or horsemen, 10000.
The company of Silitari, 6000.
The company of Sagbulue and of Solbulue both together, 8000.
The Bassa of Belgrad. }
The Bassa of Temiswar. }
The Bassa of Bosna. } 80000.
The Bassa of Buda. }
The Siniack of Gersech. }

Out of Asia.

The Bassa of Caramania. }
The Bassa of Laras. }
The Bassa of Damasco. }
The Bassa of Suas. } 120000
The Bassa of Van or Nan. }
The Bassa of Vsdrum. }
Of Tartars there be about 100000. }

Thus you may see that the great Turke maketh warre with no small numbers. And in anno 1597, when Sultan Mahomet himselfe went in person into Hungary, if a man may beleeue reports, he had an army of 600000.

For the city of Constantinople you shall vnderstand that it is matchable with any city in Europe, as well in bignesse as for the pleasant situation thereof, and commodious traffike and bringing of all maner of necessary prouision of victuals, and whatsoeuer els mans life for the sustentation thereof shall require, being seated vpon a promontory, looking toward Pontus Euxinus vpon the Northeast, and to Propontis on the Southwest, by which two seas by shipping is brought great store of all maner of victuals. The city it selfe in forme representeth a triangular figure, the sea washing the walles vpon two sides thereof, the other side faceth the continent of Thracia; the grand Signiors seraglio standeth vpon that point which looketh into the sea, being cut off from the city by a wall; so that the wall of his pallace conteineth in circuit about two English miles: the seuen towers spoken of before stand at another corner, and Constantines olde pallace to the North at the third corner. The city hath a threefolde wall about it; the innermost very high, the next lower then that, and the third a countermure and is in circuit about ten English miles: it hath foure and twentie gates: and when the empire was remooued out of the West into the East, it was inriched with many spoiles of olde Rome by Vespasian and other emperours, hauing many monuments and pillars in it worthy the obseruation; amongst the rest in the midst of Constantinople standeth one of white marble called Vespasians pillar, of 38 or 40 yards high, which hath from the base to the top proportions of men in armour fighting on horsebacke: it is likewise adorned with diuers goodly buildings and stately Mesquitas, whereof the biggest is Sultan Solimans a great warriour, which liued in the time of Charles the fifth; but the fairest is Santa Sophia, which in the time of the Christian emperours was the chiefe cathedrall church, and is still in greatest account with the great Turke: it is built round like other Greekish churches, the pavements and walles be all of marble, it hath beneath 44 pillars of diuers coloured marble of admirable height and bignesse, which stand vpon great round feet of brasse, much greater then the pillars, and of a great height, some ten yards distant from the wall: from which vnto these pillars is a great gallery built, which goeth round about the church; and vpon the outside of the gallery stand 66 marble pillars which beare vp the round roofe being the top of the church: it hath three pulpits or preaching places, and about 2000 lampes brought in by the Turke. Likewise vpon one side in the top is the picture of Christ with the 12 Apostles, but their faces are defaced, with two or three ancient tombs of Christians: to the West sticketh an arrow in the toppe of the Church, which, as the Turks report, Sultan Mahomet shot when he first tooke the city. Neere adioyning be two chapels of marble, where lie buried most of the emperours with their children and sultanas. The 16 of Iuly, accompanied with some other of our nation we went by water to the Blacke sea, being 16 miles distant from Constantinople, the sea al the way thither being little broader then the Thames; both sides of the shore are beautified with faire and goodly buildings. At the mouth of this Bosphorus lieth a rocke some fourescore yards from the maine land, wherevpon standeth a white marble pillar called Pompeys pillar, the shadow whereof was 23 foote long at nine of the clocke in the forenoone: over against it is a turret of stone upon the maine land 120 steps high, hauing a great glass-lanthorne in the toppe foure yards in diamiter and three in height, with a great copper pan in the midst to holde oile, with twenty lights in it, and it serueth to giue passage into this straight in the night to such ships as come from all parts of those seas to Constantinople: it is continually kept by a Turke, who to that end hath pay of the grand Signior. And thus hauing spent eleuen moneths in Constantinople, accompanied with a chause, and carying certaine mandates from the grand Signior to the Bassa of Aleppo for the kinde vsage of our nation in those parts, the 30 of Iuly I tooke passage in a Turkish carmosale or shippe bound for Sidon; and passing thorow Propontis, hauing Salimbria with Heraclia most pleasantly situated on the right hand, and Proconesus now called Marmora on the left, we came to Gallipoly, and so by Hellespont, betweene the two castles before named called Sestos and

Abydos, famous for the passages made there both by Xerxes and great Alexander, the one into Thracia, the other into Asia, and so by the Sigean Promontory, now called Cape Ianitzary, at the mouth of Hellespont vpon Asia side, where Troy stood, where are yet ruines of olde walles to be seene, with two hils rising in a piramidall forme, not vnlikely to be the tombs of Achilles and Ajax. From thence we sailed along, hauing Tenedos and Lemnos on the right hand, and the Troian fields on the left: at length we came to Mitylen and Sio long time inhabited by the Genoueses, but now vnder the Turke. The Iland is beautified with goodly buildings and pleasant gardens, and aboundeth with fruits, wine, and the gum masticke. From thence sailing alongst the gulfe of Ephesus with Nicaria on the right hand, Samos and Smirna on the left, we came to Patmos, where S. Iohn wrote the Revelation. The Iland is but small, not aboue five miles in compasse: the chiefe thing it yeeldeth is corn: it hath a port for shipping, and in it is a monastery of Greekish Caloieros. From thence by Cos (now called Lango) where Hipocrates was borne: and passing many other Ilands and rocks, we arriued at Rhodes, one of the strongest and fairest cities of the East: here we stayed three or foure dayes; and by reason of a By which went in the ship to Paphos in Cyprus, who vsed me with all kindnesse, I went about the city, and tooke the view of all: which city is still with all the houses and walles thereof maintained in the same order as they tooke it from the Rhodian knights. Ouer the doores of many of the houses, which be strongly built of stone, do remaine vndefaced, the armes of England, France, Spaine, and many other Christian knights, as though the Turkes in the view thereof gloried in the taking of all Christendome, whose armes they beholde. From thence we sailed to Paphos an olde ruinous towne standing vpon the Westerne part of Cyprus, where S. Paul in the Acts conuerted the gouernor. Departing hence, we came to Sidon, by the Turkes called Saytosa, within tenne or twelue miles of the place where Tirus stood, which now being eaten in by the sea, is, as Ezekiel prophesied, a place for the spreading out of a net. Sidon is situated in a small bay at the foot of mount Libanus, vpon the side of an hill looking to the North: it is walled about, with a castle nigh to the sea, and one toward the land which is ruinated, but the walle thereof standeth. Some halfe mile vp toward the mountaine be certaine ruines of buildings, with marble pillars, remaining: heere for three dayes we were kindly entertained of the Captaine of the castle: and in a small barke we sailed from hence along the shore to Tripoli, and so to Alexandretta, where the 24 of August we arriued. From thence with a Venetian carauan we went by land to Aleppo, passing by Antioch, which is seated vpon the side of an hill, whose walles still stand with 360 turrets upon them, and neere a very great plaine which beareth the name of the city, thorow which runneth the riuer Orontes, in Scripture called Farfar. In Aleppo I stayed vntill February following; in this city, as at a mart, meete many nations out of Asia with the people of Europe, hauing continuall traffike and interchangeable course of marchandise one with another: the state and trade of which place, because it is so well knowen to most of our nation I omitte to write of. The 27 of February I departed from Aleppo, and the fifth of March imbarked my selfe at Alexandretta in a great ship of Venice called the Nana Ferra, to come to England. The 14 we put into Salino in Cyprus, where the ship staying many dayes to lade cotton wool, and other commodities, in the meane time accompanied with M. William Barret my countrey man, the master of the ship a Greeke, and others wee tooke occasion to see Nicosia, the chiefe city of this Iland, which was some twenty miles from this place, which is situated at the foot of an hill: to the East is a great plaine, extending it selfe in a great length from the North to the South: it is walled about, but of no such strength as Famagusta (another city in this Iland neere the Sea side) whose walles are cut out of the maine rocke. In this city be many sumptuous and goodly buildings of stone, but vninhabited; the cause whereof doth giue me iust occasion to shew you of a rare iudgement of God vpon the owners sometime of these houses, as I was credibly informed by a Cipriot, a marcham of, great wealth in this city. [Sidenote: A great iudgement of God vpon the noble men of Cyprus.] Before it came in subiection to the Turks, while it was vnder the Venetians, there were many barons and noble men of the Cipriots, who partly by vsurping more superiority ouer the common people then they ought, and partly through their great reuenues which yeerly came in by their cotton wooll and wines, grew so insolent and proud, and withall so impiously wicked, as that they would at their pleasure command both the wiues and children of their poore tenants to serue their vncleane lusts, and holding them in such slauery as though they had beene no better then dogges, would wage them against a grayhound or spaniell, and he who woon the wager should euer after holde them as his proper goods and chattels, to doe with them as he listed, being Christians as well as themselues, if they may deserue so good a name. As they behaued themselues most vnchristianly toward their brethren, so and much more vngodly (which I should haue put in the first place) did they towards God: for as though they were too great, standing on foot or kneeling to serue God, they would come riding on horsebacke into the church to heare their masse: which church now is made a publicke basistane or market place for the Turkes to sell commodities in: but beholde the iudgement of the righteous God, who payeth the sinner measure for measure. The Turkes the yeere before the ouerthrowe giuen them at Lepanto by Don Iohn tooke Cyprus. These mighty Nimrods fled some in holes and some into mountaines to hide themselues; whereupon the Turkes made generall proclamation, that if they would all come in and yeeld themselues, they would restore them to their former reuenues and dignities: who not mistrusting the mischieuous pretense of the Turkes, assembled together to make themselues knowen; whom after the Turkes had in possession, they (as the Lords executioners) put them with their wiues and children all to the sword, pretending thereby to cut of all future rebellion, so that at this day is not one of the noble race knowen aliue in the Iland, onely two or three remaine in Venice but of litle wealth, which in the time of the warres escaped. After we had stayed in this Iland some thirty dayes, we set saile in the foresayd shippe being about the burthen of 900 tunnes, hauing in her passengers of diuers nations, as Tartars, Persians, Iewes, and sundry Christians. Amongst all which I had often conference with a Iew, who by reason of his many yeeres education at Safet a place in Iudea neere Ierusalem, where they study the Rabbines with some other arts as they thinke good, as also: for his trauels into Persia and Ormus, he seemed to be of good experience in matters abroad, who related vnto me such conference as he had with a Baniane at Ormus, being one of the Indians inhabiting the countrey of Cambaia. [Sidenote: Indians skilful in Astronomy.] This Baniane being a Gentile had skill in Astronomie, as many of that nation haue, who by his books written in his owne tongue and Characters, could tell the time of Eclipses both of Sunne and Moone, with the Change and Full, and by iudgement in Astrologie gaue answere to any question demanded. Being asked concerning his opinion in religion, what he thought of God? He made answere that they held no other god but the sun, (to which planet they pray both at the rising and setting) as I haue seene sundry doe in Aleppo: his reason was drawen from the effects which it worketh in giuing light to the moone and other starres, and causing all things to grow and encrease vpon the earth: answere was made, that it did moue with the rest as the wheeles of a clocke, and therefore of force must haue a moouer. Likewise in the Eclipse being darkened it is manifestly prooued that it is not god, for God is altogether goodnesse and brightnesse, which can neither be darkened nor receiue detriment or hurt: but the Sunne receiueth both in the Eclipse, as is aparant: to which hee could not answere; but so they had receiued from their ancestors, that it was without beginning or ende, as in any Orbicular or round body neither beginning or end could be found. He likewise sayd, that there were other Gentiles in the Indies which worship the moone as chiefe, and their reason is. The moone when she riseth goeth with thousands of starres accompanied like a king, and therefore is chiefe: but the Sunne goeth alone, and therefore not so great. Against whom the Banianes reason, that it is not true; because the Moone and starres receiue their light from the Sunne, neither doth the Sunne vouchsafe them his company but when he list, and therefore like a mighty prince goeth alone, yet they acknowledge the Moone as Queene or Viceroy. Law they hold hone, but only seuen precepts which they say were giuen them from their father Noe, not knowing Abraham or any other. [Sidenote: The seven precepts of Banianes.] First, to honor father and mother;

secondly, not to steale; thirdly not to commit adultery; fourthly not to kill any thing liuing; fiftly, not to eat any thing liuing; sixtly not to cut their haire; seuenthly to go barefoot in their churches. These they hold most strictly, and by no means will breake them: but he that breaketh one is punished with twenty stripes; but for the greatest fault they will kill none, neither by a short death nor a long, onely he is kept some time in prison with very little meat, and hath at the most not aboue twenty or fiue and twenty stripes. In the yeere they haue 16 feasts, and then they go to their church, where is pictured in a broad table the Sun, as we vse to paint it, the face of a man with beames round about, not hauing any thing els in it. At their feast they spot their faces in diuers parts with saffron all yellow, and so walke vp and downe the streets; and this they doe as a custome. They hold, there shalbe a resurrection, and all shall come to iudgement, but the account shalbe most streight, insomuch that but one of 10000 shalbe receiued to fauor, and those shall liue againe in this world in great happinesse: the rest shalbe tormented. And because they will escape this iudgdment, when any man dieth, he and his wife be both burnt together euen to ashes, and then they are thrown into a river, and so dispersed as though they had neuer bene. If the wife will not burne with her dead husband, she is holden euer after as a whore. And by this meanes they hope to escape the iudgement to come. As for the soule, that goeth to the place from whence it came, but where the place is they know not. That the body should not be made againe they reason with the philosophers, saying, that of nothing nothing can be made (not knowing that God made the whole world and their god the Sun of nothing) but beholding the course of nature, that nothing is made but by a meanes, as by the seed of a man is made another, and by corne cast into the ground there commeth vp new corne: so, say they, man cannot be made except some part of him be left, and therefore they burne the whole: for if he were buried in the earth, they say there is a small bone in the necke which would neuer be consumed: or if he were eaten by a beast, that bone would not consume, but of that bone would come another man; and then the soule being restored againe, he should come into iudgement, whereas now the body being destroyed, the soule shall not be iudged: for their opinion is, that both body and soule must be vnited together, as they haue sinned together, to receiue iudgement; and therefore the soule alone cannot. Their seuen precepts which they keepe so strictly are not for any hope of reward they haue after this life, but onely that they may be blessed in this world, for they thinke that he which breaketh them shall haue ill successe in all his businesse.

They say, the three chiefe religions in the world be of the Christians, Iewes, and Turks, and yet but one of them true: but being in doubt which is the truest of the three, they will be of none: for they hold that all these three shall be iudged, and but few of them which be of the true shall be saued, the examination shall be so straight; and therefore, as I haue sayd before, to preuent this iudgement, they burne their bodies to ashes. They say, these three religions haue too many precepts to keepe them all wel, and therefore wonderfull hard it wil be to make account, because so few doe obserue all their religion aright. And thus passing the time for the space of three moneths in this sea voyage, we arriued at Venice the tenth of Iune: and after I had seene Padua, with other English men, I came the ordinary way ouer the Alpes, by Augusta, Noremberg and so for England; where to the praise of God I safely arriued the ninth of August 1595.